DREAMS ACROSS THE DIVIDE

STORIES OF THE MONTANA PIONEERS

Linda Wostrel, Editor

FOREWORD BY STEPHEN AMBROSE

ILLUSTRATIONS BY R. F. MORGAN

SONS and DAUGHTERS of MONTANA PIONEERS

DREAMS ACROSS THE DIVIDE

STORIES OF THE MONTANA PIONEERS

Linda Wostrel, Editor

FOREWORD BY STEPHEN AMBROSE

ILLUSTRATIONS BY R. F. MORGAN

Copyright 2001 by The Sons & Daughters of Montana Pioneers

Library of Congress Control Number 2001091333

ISBN 1-931291-13-6 (hardcover edition)
ISBN 1-931291-12-8 (softcover edition)

Published in The United States of America

ALL RIGHTS RESERVED
No part of this publication may be reproduced, stored in a retrieval system, or transmitted in any form or by any means without the prior written permission of the copyright owner or the publisher.

STONEYDALE PRESS PUBLISHING COMPANY
523 Main Street • P.O. Box 188
Stevensville, Montana 59870
Phone: 406-777-2729
E-mail: stoneydale@montana.com

Table of Contents

Inside Front Cover: W. W. DeLacy 1865 Map (1899 Pioneer Society Book)
Letter, Montana Governor Judy Martz 4
Foreword, Stephen Ambrose 5
Preface 6
Introduction, Editor Linda Wostrel 7
Montana Is..., Mike Logan 9
The Society of Montana Pioneers...1884 to Today 13
    Society of Montana Pioneers
    Sons and Daughters of Montana Pioneers
    Montana Pioneer Pin
    Assistance to Elderly Pioneers and the Leggat Fund
    Historical Landmarks
    Montana Pioneer Convention Photos
    Descendants of Montana Pioneers
    Veterans and Pioneers Memorial Building
    Society of Montana Pioneers Dissolved
    Today's Society
    Shirley Groff Letter
To Montana Pioneers, Sam E. McDowell 33
Montana Pioneer Courts, Hon. W. Y. Pemberton 36
Montana Pioneer Day, Miss Cartwright 41
Pioneer Histories 45
    Note: Alphabetical Listing by Name in Index
Photo Section 392
Appendix 407
Index 408
Montana Pioneer List – 2001 411
Sons and Daughters of Montana Pioneers Past Presidents
    and Secretaries 444
Sons and Daughters of Montana Pioneers Convention Sites ... 447
Inside Back Cover: Rand McNally & Co. 1885 History of Montana

Judy H. Martz
Governor
State of Montana

OFFICE OF THE GOVERNOR

STATE OF MONTANA

JUDY H. MARTZ
GOVERNOR

STATE CAPITOL
PO BOX 200801
HELENA, MONTANA 59620-0801

March 21, 2001

The Montana Pioneer Heritage book is a collection of stories about the men and women who braved the perils of the unknown and blazed a trail into what was to become the Great State of Montana. Their stories provide insight into the lives of people who sought the promise of fortune, or perhaps just the adventure of a new life.

Montana pioneers were representative of European, Asian, and African-American ancestry. These pioneers came as fur traders, gold miners, farmers, ranchers, and businessmen and were the foundation of this state. They strived to develop a country in which to raise their families and eventually become an integral part of the nation. The natural resources Montana had to offer the world, such as copper from the Butte/Anaconda mines, were instrumental in making Montana a viable part of the industrial world in the east.

Montana has gone from a sparsely settled territory to a player in the high-tech industry. The inventive, hardworking, and honest character of the Montana pioneers is still apparent in the Montanans of today.

This book will help all of us honor the sacrifices these pioneers made in order build Montana into the state that we proudly call home.

Sincerely,

JUDY MARTZ
Governor

Foreword

Montanans have long been known as a special breed. The land here makes great demands on those determined to wrest a living from it. Montanans still contend with cold winters, hot summers, drought, hail, floods, grasshoppers, and of course high winds. Even at the dawn of the 21st Century, making a life here is still more difficult than in other parts of our country. But an even starker picture emerges if you look at life in the Montana territory during the 19th Century – especially prior to the coming of the Great Northern Railroad. Even at its best, scratching a living from the land was a crap shoot. At its worst, life in the territory could be brutal and unforgiving.

People knew all of this, but they came anyway. Reasons varied – more economic opportunity, more personal and political freedom. The very human sentiment of wishing for a change of scenery, or a change of trade. For whatever reasons, many came, most survived, and some even prospered. Most found that the independence, vastness, and beauty that Montana offered outweighed the perils mentioned above.

Dreams Across The Divide tells the story of these hopes and fears. It is a treasure to all of those who are curious about the day-to-day concerns of the pioneer. This is not just a story of the "great men" such as Fergus, Stuart, and Kohrs, but also of those whose ambitions were more modest. People who simply wanted a better life than they had left behind, for themselves and their progeny. This wonderful compilation chronicles the struggles of the great and the small, and we are all richer for knowing the epic that was the life of the 19th Century pioneer.

Stephen Ambrose
Author and Historian
Helena, Montana
June, 2001

Preface

Linda Wostrel learned the value of hard work, enterprise and honesty as a child growing up on a farm in Northeastern Nebraska. The values that she learned as child in rural Nebraska are evident in the tiny seed of an idea, to write a book using personal stories and records of our ancestors, that she first planted with Shirley Herrin, Secretary-Treasurer of The Sons and Daughters of the Montana Pioneers, in 1996. She then presented the idea at The Son and Daughters of Montana Pioneers Convention in Virginia City, Montana in 1997, where it was voted on overwhelmingly to proceed with the anthology. Linda sowed the seed, cultivated it, nurtured it, and now with the support of many members and friends it has become a reality.

Linda recognized the value of recording those soon to be forgotten adventures of our ancestors when she came to Montana from her home in Nebraska in the early 1980's to research her great grandfather, William J. Doney, a bullwhacker who arrived in Bannack, Montana Territory, on October 3, 1867. Finding his story stimulated the idea to do an anthology of such stories because many details are lost by the passing of generations. Such stories and personal accounts are the foundation of our nation and its growth. History books record the results of a concerted effort but not the details of real living souls with their emotions, life styles, and hardships. Linda says that even though she lives and works in Nebraska, her heart belongs to Montana.

An enormous amount of work has gone into the planning and execution of this book and most of the credit goes to Linda Wostrel and Shirley Herrin. Linda and Shirley both have deep roots in Montana and are interested in the preservation of the stories and legacies of our Montana Pioneer ancestors.

Linda then spent numerous hours collecting, compiling, editing, and preparing these accounts along with other material for publication with the help and support of Shirley Herrin, who spent numerous hours in providing photographs and researching and typing lists of the pioneers and the past presidents. Shirley Groff did some footwork, the kind that took personal attention and miles to accomplish.

This book would not have been possible without the efforts of the members of The Sons and Daughters of Montana Pioneers and their contributions from individual family records and collections. The Sons and Daughters owe gratitude to all those who contributed this book's success.

Introduction

"The men who made this great enterprise a possibility, who paved the way for to-day's event were the Pioneers, who left the luxuries and pleasures of the East and braved danger in a thousand forms to come here and make these mountains habitable." – **General U.S. Grant, at the completion of the Northern Pacific Railroad at Gold Creek, Deer Lodge County, September 8, 1883.**

The "boys of 1864" knew when they came to Montana they were making history. They intuitively understood their actions were helping to lay the foundation for the Montana Territory that later became the state of Montana.

In the 1884 call for a Pioneers' Association, John Russell Wilson penned the words, "The events of our early pioneer history are rapidly fading from the memory of Montanians…and the actors themselves…are as rapidly passing away". The Pioneers banded together to collect and publish their stories and chartered the Sons and Daughters of Montana Pioneers to keep the stories and memories alive.

These early Pioneers included men who became very well known in Montana – Granville Stuart, Conrad Kohrs, Walter W. DeLacy, James Fergus, Sidney C. Edgerton, William A. Clark and others. But the Pioneers also included people you may not have heard of – ordinary people who risked all to help settle Montana. These dedicated and courageous men and women have helped give us our heritage.

Not since the *Society of Montana Pioneers, Vol. I,* published in 1899, has a collection of remembrances been published and made available to the public about this proud, independent group known affectionately as the "Montana Pioneers". In this book we have focused on eighty-nine of their stories – all who arrived in Montana before December 31, 1868. These histories, and the majority of accompanying photographs, were generously provided by direct descendants of the Montana Pioneers who carry on the Montana Pioneers Society directives – now through The Sons and Daughters of Montana Pioneers Society.

This book is dedicated to our Montana Pioneer ancestors. It is fitting that we remember – and honor – their great contribution to the settlement of Montana. As quoted in the minutes from the first meeting of the Sons and Daughters in 1892, we need to… "perpetuate the sacrifices and heroic virtues of our parents who blazed the trail into this country". That is our mission. That is the reason for this book. All net proceeds will be made available to promote awareness and to educate our youth on Montana's Pioneer history.

Many friends, descendants of Montana Pioneers, Sons and Daughters of Montana Pioneers Board members and others have contributed to the preparation of this book – the list is too numerous to mention. I owe a debt of gratitude for your help. Thank you.

I am also grateful to Governor Judy Martz and Stephen Ambrose for their endorsement and foreword, Robert Morgan for generously providing the illustrations as well as the painting for the cover, Mike Logan for allowing us to include his poem *Montana Is...*, to Dale Burk of Stoneydale Press for his help on the project and his passion for Montana history, and The Montana Historical Society in Helena for providing the opportunity to research their early Montana Pioneer documents. I am personally grateful to my Great Grandparents, William J. and Susan (Hitchens) Doney, whose visionary decision to come to Montana allows me to belong to this Society and to claim Montana as home.

In reading this book, I hope you obtain a better understanding and appreciation for our Montana Pioneers.

Linda Wostrel
Editor
May, 2001

Montana Is . . .

A poem by Mike Logan

Montana Is . . .

    A fish hawk's nest
    A whitetail fawn
    And silver fog when comes the dawn.
    It's brandin' calves
    A harvest moon
    And bugles in the afternoon.

    It's bighorn rams
    And mounded stacks
    A weasel on the railroad tracks.
    A paintbrush red
    A big necked buck
    And rifles in an old blue truck.

    It's hangin' spurs
    A wagon's rest
    A sunset painted on the west.
    A shake roofed barn
    A hitch of blacks
    The makin's in Bull Durham sacks.

    It's great horned owls
    A heron's catch
    And blue grouse eggs about to hatch.
    It's loggin' rigs
    A gentle rain
    A sunlit field of ripened grain.

It's shootin' stars
A snowswept ridge
A river crossed without a bridge.
It's well worn chaps
And mule deer's eyes
A champion steer that takes the prize.

It's crumblin' kilns
A red school house
And, struttin' proud, an old sage grouse.
It's bison herds
And dreams long gone
A portrait of a whistlin' swan.

It's wilderness
Abandoned mines
A winter sun that barely shines.
It's frost flocked trees
A sundown team
The answer to a hunter's dream.

It's cottonwoods
And goldeneye
And snow geese back to fill the sky.
It's heelin' dogs
And loadin' chutes
And Charlie Russell's high square buttes.

It's antelope
And huge snow plows
And cuttin' out the heavy cows.
An eagle's watch
Fawns sittin' tight
The lonesome sound of geese at night.

It's rainbow's end
And threshing bees
And quick red squirrels that lunch in trees.
It's shining lakes
And cold duck blinds
And bullet holes in frosted signs.

It's silhouettes
And tracks in snow
An evening on a high plateau.
It's closin' gates
A wooly flock
A mantled ground squirrel on a rock.

It's ridin' fence
A packer's string
And flowers so bright they seem to sing.
It's mountain goats
And hay new mowed
A pickup on a dusty road.

It's workin' hands
A river's course
And irrigatin' on a horse.
It's fishermen
And hook jawed trout
And prairie dogs just peekin' out.

It's tumbleweeds
A capitol dome
A momma osprey comin' home.
It's ptarmigan
A hay sled full
And snowfall on a blizzard bull.

It's marmot kings
And final turns
A fireset when the forest burns.
It's pickup men
A cactus flower
And, on a hill, an old firetower.

It's bitterroot
A country church
A chipmunk on a sagebrush perch.
It's winter elk
A cattle pen
And beargrass in a shaded glen.

It's grizzly bears
And snow capped peaks
And avocets with upturned beaks.
It's rodeos
And national parks
And wild free songs of meadowlarks.

It's aspen leaves
And early rides
And stackin' hay with beaverslides.
It's old homesteads
And aging mills
And monuments in greening hills.

            Montana Is . . .

The Society of Montana Pioneers
...1884 to Today

Society of Montana Pioneers

On July 26, 1884, a "Call For A Pioneers Association" was published by John Russell Wilson, Dillon Montana. It called for a meeting that would lead to the organization of a Pioneers Association:

All pioneer citizens of Montana who were residents within its limits at the date of the creation of the Territory – May 26, 1864 – are cordially invited to attend a meeting to be held at the Court House, in the city of Helena, the capital of the Territory, on Wednesday, September 10, 1884 at 10 o'clock A. M. (the day being during Fair Week), for the purpose of organizing a Pioneers' Association or Society of Pioneers...

On September 10, 1884, a hundred of the "boys of 64" met at the courthouse in Helena to take preliminary steps for the permanent organization of the "Society of Montana Pioneers". Many who attended the 1884 meeting had not seen each other since the exciting days of '63 and '64 at Alder Gulch. Samuel T. Hauser presided over the meeting and Colonel Wilbur F. Sanders explained the purpose of the proposed organization – to band the pioneers together into a mutual association to collect and put in shape the early history of Montana. A constitution and by-laws were adopted and the following officers were elected: **President** – James Fergus, **Vice Presidents** – Walter W. DeLacy, Granville Stuart, Joseph A. Browne, James M. Arnoux, Thomas H. Irvine, John X. Beidler, John Potter, Henry H. Mood, Conrad Kohrs, Perry W. McAdow, Enoch H. Wilson, Caleb E. Irvine, and Christopher P. Higgins. **Corresponding Secretary** – Wilbur F. Sanders, **Recording Secretary** – George W. Irvin II, **Treasurer** – Samuel T. Hauser. Each Vice President was the chairman of a county organization of Pioneers.

The following day, about two hundred sixty men and women signed the constitution and these pioneers became charter members. In 1909, the qualification for membership was changed to those who were residents prior to December 31, 1868. This rule remains in force today.

Sons and Daughters of Montana Pioneers

Just eight years after the Society of Montana Pioneers was organized, The Sons and Daughters of Montana Pioneers was established by the Pioneers Society on August 18, 1892 while the Pioneers were holding their meeting. Colonel Charles D. Curtis was the father of the movement to have the Sons and Daughters of Montana Pioneers established. The first president was Albert Y. Loeb, with Harvey English as Treasurer. The account in the *Helena Herald* read as follows:

About 40 young people of both sexes met in the district courtroom, department two, in pursuance of a published call for the purpose of forming a society of the sons and daughters of Montana pioneers. These gentlemen and ladies represent, in measure, the flower of the state's youth, talent and beauty. Thirty-nine names were enrolled at this, their first meeting. It was decided that the society shall hereafter meet with the pioneers each year.

A quote taken from the minutes of the first meeting read as follows: *That it is the object of this meeting that, to perpetuate the sacrifices and heroic virtues of our parents who blazed the trail into this country, we do here and now organize a Society to be called the Society of the Sons and Daughters of Montana Pioneers.*

An immediate, major project of the Sons and Daughters of Montana Pioneers Society was to secure the names of all persons eligible for membership under the constitution and to collect such bits of information as the date and place of birth, route traveled to Montana, day and place of arrival, occupation and address. In 1899 the information listing over 1,800 pioneers was published in *Society of Montana Pioneers, Vol. I.* This book also includes maps, photos and lists of officers.

In 1914, the Secretary realized there should be a place where the Pioneers could rest, smoke and "swap yarns" as they called it. So with the consent of the Executive Board, a tent, two dozen chairs and a couch was taken to the fair grounds during fair week. A tent was used for four years, even for serving coffee and wafers.

In 1917, a 20' x 40' log cabin was put together with pegs under the supervision of the Society President Mr. Fred Scheuer of Butte. The cabin was built on the State Fairgrounds (Lewis & Clark County) as a meeting place for the Montana Pioneers to rest and visit with one another during the fair. It was a great gathering place of the Pioneers until it was destroyed by fire caused from a bolt of lightning in July, 1922. W. A. Clark Jr. donated $500 for its replacement and the new log cabin contained relics, furniture, photos, horses, deer heads, books and other memorabilia to help the Pioneers feel at home. It stood until the 1960s when it was dismantled.

Montana Pioneer Pin

As a means of honoring the Pioneer, a pin was developed soon after the Pioneer Society was formed. The origin of the pin has not been confirmed, but it is believed that Granville Stewart designed it and pins were given to original Montana Pioneers. The pin, made of solid gold, is a gold pan – a little smaller than a dime – with gold nuggets in the bottom of the pan. On the inside lip of the pan are the words "Montana Pioneers". An Indian is looking into the setting sun and sees the pioneers coming in their wagons. Most likely it was meant to signify the end of the Indian's reign and the beginning of the white man's.

At the eighth annual meeting of the Sons and Daughters of Montana Pioneers, held September 8, 1900, a motion was made to the effect and the design of the gold pan with the pick and shovel crossed upon it and appropriately lettered was adopted as the official emblem of the Society.

In 1901, the Committee that was appointed at the 1900 meeting to carry out the design of the Society pin reported and displayed a number of pins at $3.00, $5.00 and $9.00. The $3.00 pin was the size of a dime and enameled to represent the color of a gold pan, the $4.00 pin about the size of a five cent piece enameled in dark blue and the $9.00 pin was made of solid gold throughout with enameled lettering.

Many of the Montana Pioneers were buried wearing their original Montana Pioneers pin and therefore few have survived. However, some of the original Pioneer pins have been handed down to present-day Society members who proudly wear them in honor of their Pioneer heritage.

Assistance to Elderly Pioneers and the Leggat Fund

As the original Pioneers aged, it was of great concern to the membership that the state provide a home for invalid and indigent pioneers. At the 1912 meeting of the Sons and Daughters of Montana Pioneers meeting a motion was made by Mr. John M. Evans of Missoula for the establishment of a home for the needy Pioneers. Mr. Evens declared that "relief for them is just as commendable as homage to the memory of those who pass beyond". The following motion was adopted as a Resolution and read as follows:

That the Sons and Daughters of Montana Pioneers in annual session assembled ask the state of Montana to establish, equip and maintain a home for the needy Pioneers of this State and that a copy of this resolution be furnished to the Governor and each member of the Legislature at the next session thereof.

While the members of the Society worked towards having the state support a home for invalid and indigent pioneers, no home was ever built. Therefore, the Pioneers established the Leggat Fund within the Society to help the Pioneers. It was named after Rod D. Leggat of Butte an early pioneer who helped start the fund in 1914. Mr. Legget wrote to Norman B. Holter, Charles Power and Clinton H. Moore, members of the Society:

It sometimes happens that some of the old timers of Montana become in need of assistance in the later years of their lives on account of physical weakness or financial adversity, and a little assistance at such time will be very welcome to them and it will be gratifying to me to have my money spent in giving such assistance.

Many in the Society contributed to the fund and in 1924, the balance in the Leggat trust fund totaled $10,000. Applications for aid were available to all Pioneers in need and all monies collected were used to assist Pioneers that were ill or found themselves in financial need. Money from this fund was also used to provide the needy Pioneer a proper funeral as well as to mark graves.

Historical Landmarks

Other projects developed included placing monuments to mark historic places in the state – such as the Mullan Road markers, where gold was discovered on Gold Creek and in Alder Gulch. The Society today is still active in marking historical landmarks.

Montana Pioneers of 1862. Back row, left to right: Granville Stuart, Conrad Kohrs, Joseph Browne and Matthew Carroll. Front row, left to right: Charles Rumley, James Fergus, W. W. DeLacy, Homer Hewins and S. T. Hauser. (Courtesy Montana Historical Society, Helena)

First meeting of the Society of Montana Pioneers — Helena, September 11, 1884. (Courtesy Montana Historical Society, Helena)

Society of Montana Pioneers – Helena, 1891. (Courtesy Montana Historical Society, Helena)

First meeting of the Sons and Daughters of Montana Pioneers — Helena, August 18, 1892. (Courtesy Montana Historical Society, Helena)

Society of Montana Pioneers – Virginia City, 1899. (Courtesy Sons and Daughters of Montana Pioneers, Helena)

Society of Montana Pioneers – Missoula, 1901. (Courtesy Montana Historical Society, Helena)

Society of Montana Pioneers – Great Falls, 1903. (Courtesy Sons and Daughters of Montana Pioneers, Helena)

Society of Montana Pioneers – Anaconda, 1906. (Courtesy Montana Historical Society, Helena)

Society of Montana Pioneers – Bozeman, 1912. (Courtesy Carma Jean Gilligan)

Society of Montana Pioneers — Butte, 1919. (Courtesy Sons and Daughters of Montana Pioneers, Helena)

Society of Montana Pioneers – Deer Lodge, 1936. (Courtesy Montana Historical Society, Helena)

Descendants of Montana Pioneers

After receiving approval from the Montana Pioneers, a motion was made at the Society September 5-8, 1917, meeting to amend the Constitution and eliminate the age limit for Sons and Daughters as well as add that all grandchildren and direct descendants to be entitled to join the Society.

Veterans and Pioneers Memorial Building

The State of Montana incorporated the Society in 1935 and this status allowed them to hold property and inherit legacies. Subsequently, the Society acquired 63 lots in Helena adjacent to the Capitol building in 1941 and made a gift of that land to the State of Montana with the assurance that the Society was insured for future generations a place where historic documents and records, artifacts and relics and art of historic import could be preserved and maintained. The Society was also provided a permanent location to house its records and those of the parent organization, the Society of Montana Pioneers. The Veteran's and Pioneers Memorial building and the Sam W. Mitchell Building were constructed on a portion of these lots. On August 24, 1951, the dedication of the new Veterans and Pioneers Memorial building was held. Byron O. Wickham, President of the Society of Montana Pioneers, and Byron Kantner, President of the Sons and Daughters of Montana Pioneers, were included in the list of dignitaries providing remarks at the dedication.

In accordance with Section 22-3-302, MCA, the Montana Pioneers utilize a vault and third floor office for the purpose of housing its books, records, documents and other property and an office for its state headquarters. The Sons and Daughters of Montana Pioneers continue to have an office in the Veteran's and Pioneers Memorial building that also houses the Montana Historical Society at 225 No. Roberts Street, Helena, Montana 59620.

Society of Montana Pioneers Dissolved

During the 1962 annual conventions of The Society of Montana Pioneers (their 78th) and the Sons and Daughters of Montana Pioneers that was held in Butte on August 24-25, the remaining eight original members of the Montana Pioneers elected to dissolve the parent organization. Only one of the eight surviving members, Lumen W. Allen, 94 President, was present and agreed that "the current meeting here (Butte) should be the last for the Pioneers". Mr. Lumen W. Allen was the last of the surviving

Pioneers and passed away on February 19, 1970, in Butte at the age of 102.

Today's Society

The Society of the Sons and Daughters of Montana Pioneers holds their annual convention in August at various locations throughout the state. The agenda for the meeting includes conducting the business of the Society, electing new members, honoring deceased members, learning about Montana past history through guest speakers and touring historical points. The Society's purpose still remains the "perpetuation of the History, Principles, Heritage of those Pioneers who dreamed of and worked to create what is now known as the State of Montana" and remains active in this endeavor.

The meetings of the Sons and Daughters have been annual except for the years when conventions were vacated due to depression or war. Membership is open to those persons who are direct lineal descendants of Pioneers who arrived by December 31, 1868. Persons interested in obtaining more information on membership should contact the Secretary of The Sons and Daughters of Montana Pioneers at 225 North Roberts Street, Helena, Montana 59620.

SONS and DAUGHTERS of MONTANA PIONEERS

Montana Pioneer Heritage Book
By Shirley A. Groff, Past President

The Montana Heritage book is a chronological anthology of stories of individual Montana Pioneers who struggled through the many developmental stages that make Montana and its people unique. It was because of the adversities and efforts of those rugged individuals that Montana evolved into what it is today. Their stories can be likened to a very thick and rich tapestry, interwoven with and strengthened by a raw justice code laced with intrigue, which brings life to those colorful individuals, their adventures, and efforts to bring law and order to an untamed land. Their integrity, ingenuity, persistence, hard work, and finally their success all laid a solid foundation for modern Montana.

The Montana Pioneers are a part of the Great Westward movement. They came from all nationalities and all walks of life, bringing with them their knowledge, skills, customs, and traditions. They came for many reasons, fleeing the effects of the civil wars or oppression in their homelands, to find new identities and opportunities, or perhaps just looking for adventure.

The Montana Heritage Book makes these unique stories fit into a cohesive story. One might ask, "What part did my ancestor play in the whole picture?

Its beginning started with the Lewis and Clark Expedition, 1804-1806. Lewis and Clark paved the way for the fur traders, the military, the miners, the farmers and ranchers, timber industry, later the railroad and statehood – each group bringing its own unique sets of troubles and circumstances. The Lewis and Clark Expedition was one of the best-organized and executed military expeditions ever. It stretched the first long, strong, colorful strands in the warp, woof, and web of the grand tapestry of Montana.

The fur traders followed on the heels of Lewis and Clark, adding their adventures with the wild untamed areas, their encounters with the Indians, animals, and elements, and adding more strong and colorful strands to an ever-growing picture.

A military presence was need to keep routes safe and add a degree of law and order for those who would open the west. The military had its own unique adventures, mistakes, and defeats, adding still another dimension to the richness of Montana's historical beginnings.

It was not long until gold was discovered in Montana, and the lawlessness of the era took over. Montana was so vast that it was impossible for the legal system to work effectively. The military had too much territory to police. Enter the vigilantes, miners' courts, and eventually the establishment of law and order, once more adding to the strands of our tapestry. More and more people came as other rich mineral deposits were found.

The agricultural industry was born out of the necessity to feed the ever-growing population. With it came problems with the Indians, the elements, range wars, and learning how to live on the land, adding still more colorful strands to the every-growing tapestry.

Montana was on the move and needed better transportation, so in the 1880s the railroads replaced the steamboats on the Missouri River, bringing faster communication and more people, adding still more richness to the tapestry.

Statehood was looming on the horizon and with it still more struggles to set up a new state government, enhancing and building still another dimension to the tapestry.

Montana was then and still is on the move. Montanans have gone from slates to satellite communication, from animal power to jet airplanes, all in a matter of 100 years. Wide distances have been breeched by computer technologies, bringing Montanans from the vast outreaches closer together and they are finding that no matter how far they are spread in miles, they are still a cohesive unit. The basic principles of integrity, ingenuity, persistence, and genuine hard work are still holding strong in the tapestry of Montana today.

To Montana Pioneers

By Sam E. McDowell

Montana is an empire, in these old United States –

A host of sturdy pioneers have entered through her gates;

And today her towns and cities are ranked among the best

That can be found in any state throughout the Great Northwest.

In homes of sweet contentment, these dear old people live,

Who feel that Mother Nature gave all she had to give

When she gave to them Montana, in which to live and die,

With her beauties and her wonders, perched up here just 'neath the sky.

A grander, better people, never yet have graced this earth;

We of a younger generation can't realize their worth.

They stayed, through want or plenty; they stuck through drought or rain,

They suffered untold hardships, but never would complain.

They tell us of the changes old Father Time has wrought

Since the time when they first came here, and about the fights they fought;

How one time they "ketched" a horse thief, and hung him to a tree –

And saw some sights they're surely glad their children didn't see.

Within their great dominion, are mountains capped with snow,

There are prairies, hills and valleys, where once grazed the buffalo.

Where of old the Indian ponies played out on the open plain.

Now are homes, and schools, and churches, and waving fields of grain,

Their work and perseverance brought about this mighty change,

And now instead of bison, sheep and cattle roam the range;

Where the prairies once were waving with luxuriant native grass,

Now you hear the shriek and rattle of freight trains as they pass.

Ah, those pioneers of the west! We point to them with pride,

At their homes you found a welcome – the latchstring hung outside;

And no matter what the task was, a helping hand they'd lend –

It never got too hot or cold, for them to help a "friend."

They love the lofty mountains, with their ever-changing moods,

Love to listen to the silence of their lonely solitudes;

They love the warm chinook winds, that melt the winter snow

And bring back to them the memories of summers long ago.

Where once stood the Indian tepee, now the white man's "tepee" stands,

The Indians, like the buffalo, are on allotted lands –

Or else they've crossed the Great Divide, where no "Pale Face's" gun resounds.

And are riding unmolested on their happy hunting grounds.

The pioneers will soon vanish o'er the trail the Indian trod,

Their sturdy pioneer spirit will be left alone with God,

If I could keep on writing, for a hundred million years,

I couldn't pay full tribute to Montana's Pioneers.

Source: *Taken from the Society of Montana Pioneers, Historian's Annual Report, Forty-Fourth Annual Convention, Missoula, Montana, August 4, 5, and 6, 1927*

Montana Pioneer Courts

Prepared and presented by the President of the Society of Montana Pioneers, Honorable W. Y. Pemberton on Wednesday, August 16, 1911, during the annual meeting of the Society of Montana Pioneers.

It may be of interest to the people of this day and generation to know something of courts and the practice therein of the early pioneers in the section of country embraced within the boundaries of Montana. The pioneers came to this country before Montana was organized into a territory – even before the name Montana had been spoken or heard among these mountains.

No statutes had been enacted. No courts had been created by law. Notwithstanding, we were a part of Idaho. No official court or statute of that territory was to be found, seen or heard of in this part of the world. The people preceded the law and its machinery. But they brought with them their knowledge of natural and constitutional law and justice bred and born in the American people and to which they are loyally devoted, everywhere and under all circumstances.

The pioneers were principally gold hunters. Where they discovered diggings they found themselves in possession of property – vast and rich frequently, which as American citizens they knew they had the natural and constitutional right to protect and enjoy. Notwithstanding they had no statutes and no legally organized courts – they speedily found a way to have both.

As soon as a discovery was made, the miners organized a mining district. They met in mass meetings and passed laws for the government of the district. They elected a recorder, a sheriff and a "miners' judge". They passed laws fixing the fees and defining the powers of these officers. The miners' judge had jurisdiction of all matters civil and criminal – regardless of the amount involved or the character of the offense charged. Appeals were allowed from the decisions and judgements of miners' court to the people in mass meeting assembled. But appeals were seldom taken.

The decisions of the miners' court were generally just and the trials fair. Their orders and judgement were as strictly obeyed and respected as the decrees of any court. The judge was generally some prominent man well versed in mining law and respected for his intelligence, character and integrity. These courts had the moral support of the people by whom they were elected and from whom they derived their powers. Politics seldom entered into their election. In their administration of the law, charges of corruption and scandals were unknown. A desire to do justice was the cardinal and controlling rule and law governing these primitive courts. The principal business before these courts involved mining titles and matters incident thereto. But they were courts of general jurisdiction. In fact, they were the only courts in the country and murder cases were as much within their jurisdiction as cases involving the title to mining claims.

The first great murder trial before a miners' court in this country was the George Ives trial. And truly it was a great trial. Don L. Byam was the judge. The main street of the town of Nevada in Alder Gulch was the courtroom. George Ives was the noted defendant. Colonel W. F. Sanders and Major Charles S. Bagg prosecuted in behalf of the people. Alexander Davis, J. M. Thurmond and H.P.A. Smith defended. The charge was murder. The jury consisted of 24 sturdy miners. The trial was public. Ives was not tried by the Vigilance Committee as many erroneously suppose. He was tried and executed before the Vigilance Committee was organized. W. H. Patton and I were selected to write down the testimony of the witnesses.

The judge sat in a half-circle around a big log fire for it was cold – it was about the 20th of December 1863. George Ives (the prisoner), Mr. Patton and myself were within the half circle. Hundreds of determined men stood around the court and the jury during the entire trial, which lasted two or three days.

I said it was a great trial. It was. It was a grand court. There were no paraphernalia or insignia of office to impress and awe the beholder there. But surrounded by the snow-covered mountains, sitting in that open street in midwinter, no court ever had more vital questions presented to it than the one presided over by that grand old gray-bearded man Don L. Byam.

Crime was rampant. Robbery and murder had become crimes committed by men whose duty it was to protect the lives and property of the people. A great crisis had arisen in the history of the people struggling for life and fortune in their newfound home. The lawless cutthroats had tendered the issue as to whether the people should live and enjoy the fruits of their discovery and labor. Here in this great trial and before this grand court, the people had accepted the issue thus tendered.

It was a battle royal. The result was by no means certain. It was a debatable question whether the lawless or law-abiding were in the ascendancy. This was to be determined in the wonderful trial. Both elements were there in force. Both determined, both armed. But as the battle waged, the friends of law and order gathered strength and competed to come extend the organization of their forces. You could look into the eyes and faces of the honest people as they stood guard around that court and jury, sitting out in the street under the cold, blue heavens and read the thoughts that filled their souls. You could discover their determination to see justice done though the heavens should fall. This resolution and determination having been taken, the battle was won. Lawlessness, assassination, murder, crime – however well organized – could not withstand these resolute and invincible men who were fighting for their lives and homes.

At the conclusion of the able and eloquent arguments of counsel, the jury retired. Mr. Patton and myself were carried along by the jury so that, in the event of any dispute as to the testimony, we could refer to our notes. We were placed in a corner of the large jury room of a log cabin and the jury proceeded to ballot.

There was but one ballot – "guilty of murder as charged". It was unanimous. It was right. It was just. By another ballot, the jury fixed the death penalty – by the law and practice of those courts the jury named the penalty.

There were but three penalties in vogue – banishment, whipping and death by hanging.

Two hours after the verdict was returned, Ives was hanged. Law and order had achieved a great and lasting victory. For the first time, life and property were rendered safe and secure in these mountains.

I have purposely avoided giving the facts and circumstances of the homicide of which Ives was convicted. These are all matters of history. The object I have in view in writing this paper is to point out the origin, necessity, jurisdiction and usefulness of the miners' courts in the early days of the country's history. They were demanded by the necessities of the times. The people in the exercise of their inherent rights of protection to life and property created them. They served a necessary and noble purpose. When the conditions and circumstances were changed and there was no longer a necessity for their existence, they passed away – leaving behind them a record which entitles them to the everlasting gratitude of the people.

The execution of Ives did not at once absolutely demoralize and disorganize the lawless element – they were inclined to resent and avenge his death. I can never forget how things looked and I recall many incidents that occurred in the little town of Nevada that night after Ives was executed. It was after dark when he was hanged. The people were standing out in the street and in the cold talking about the tragic event. They were nearly alarmed. The situation looked gloomy. Hard things were said. Threats were made. It looked as if a spark might create an explosion.

The incident that occurs to me deserves mention, I think, in the history of that day. I was standing on the street talking to someone when I heard a man who was standing in the middle of the street say with a hideous oath, "Let's take him back of the house and kill him." This, of course, attracted my attention and excited my curiosity to know who was meant to be the victim of this man's wrath. There were three men in the knot when came the dreadful threat. Immediately one of the three said, "Yonder he stands now." One of them said, "I will call him," and at once he called Colonel Sanders.

In going to the men, Colonel Sanders had to pass near where I stood. I at once went to meet him. I told him what I had heard and advised him not to go behind the houses with the men. He said, "I guess they won't kill me." He insisted upon going with them and I then asked him if he was armed. He said he was. I then said, "If you will go, I shall go too." He then walked to the three men. One of them said, " We want to see you back here." They crossed the street, one man leading the way. Colonel Sanders followed him, the other two following him, and I followed them between the log houses, which were built a little apart.

The front men and Colonel Sanders had gotten out of the passageway into the rear of the house and the rest of us were following when bang went a gun!

The two men in front of me jumped out from behind the houses and I rushed out as fast as I could – expecting to find the Colonel killed. When I got out, however, I saw that all three of the men were running away and Colonel Sanders was standing there with his overcoat on fire. I asked him if he was hurt. He said "No."

The truth of it was that about the time the killing was to have commenced, Colonel Sanders' pistol was discharged in his overcoat pocket as he was in the act of drawing the weapon. This stampeded the assassins and saved the Colonel's life – and perhaps mine. Colonel Saunders had taken, as is shown, a fearless and active part in the prosecution of Ives. It was beyond doubt the purpose of these men was to murder him as a matter of revenge.

It is a great pity, an irreparable loss amounting to a calamity that no copy of the great speech of Colonel Sanders in the Ives trial was ever taken or preserved. Colonel Sanders was a great orator and thousands of our people have heard and enjoyed his splendid speeches in the courts and on the platform. But those who did not hear his speech in the Ives trial never heard the best effort in the lifetime of this gifted man. During its delivery on that cold winter day there stood these hundreds of sturdy miners in the street of Nevada – motionless and spellbound by the marvelous appeal on that marvelous occasion by this wonderful man to the jury and the people, calling upon and urging them to do their duty in the struggle for the protection of their homes, property and lives in their new mountain land. And never did a great speech go home without more directness and force to the hearts of honest and determined men. This great speech – if we had it in the archives and history of the state – would constitute a monument to these peerless pioneers that would stand in glory's sky haloed with the golden sunlight, when the bronze statue being erected now by a grateful people to his memory shall have crumbled into dust.

On the day George Ives was hung, a real democracy was established in these mountains. Its formation was laid upon the bones of the desperado and outlaw. And Sanders is entitled to be called its Pericles.

A generation has passed away since those dreadful days with their exciting events. But the influence of the miners' courts, and especially of the Ives trial upon the people of Montana, has not passed away and will not for generations to come. These courts and the result of this trial taught the people that life and property were worth defending at all hazards and that the enforcement of the law was the only hope of human safety and liberty.

Since Montana has had a history, the people have never forgotten the lessons they learned in those early crucial days. The devotion of the people to the law, the estimate they early learned to place upon life, liberty and property have made our state a palladium of safety to the peaceable, law-abiding citizen and a place to be avoided by the assassin and desperado.

So long as our people keep in mind these lessons and teach them to their children will Montana be worthy of the patriotic devotion and pride of her sons and daughters.

Editor's Note:

Mr. W. Y. Pemberton played a direct role in the George Ives trial. It should be noted that his recounting of the trial differs slightly from that of N. P. Langford in *Vigilante Days and Ways* and *Dimsdale's Vigilantes of Montana* by Al Noyes whose information was gathered from persons at the trial – neither Langford or Dimsdale were present at the proceedings. The editor has transcribed W. Y. Pemberton's speech directly from the proceedings of the Twenty-eighth Annual Meeting notes of the Society of Montana Pioneers held in Butte, Montana August 16-17, 1911.

William Young Pemberton came to Virginia City, Montana Territory in 1863 (he graduated from Cumberland Law School in Lebanon, Tennessee in 1861). He worked in various capacities becoming the second chief justice of the Montana Supreme Court in 1893. He served for a term of six years and later became Librarian of the Montana State Historical Society. He was respected throughout Montana for his dedicated service to the state.

Montana Pioneer Day

Presented at the 1903 Society of Montana Pioneer meeting in Great Falls, Montana, by Miss Cartwright, an Eighth Grade Student of Helena High School.

Pioneer Days of Montana

An endless subject and one upon which volumes might be written with but little effort is the "Pioneer Days of Montana". One never tires of speaking of the events concerning these noble types of manhood, who braved the perils of famine, hunger and disease to carve a home for themselves and their children out of this western wilderness. They deserve praise and eulogy, yes and even reverence, for without them what might this western wilderness be today?

As each day passes, however, we hear of one here, one there, passing over the great divide which knows no return. In a few more years, those who crossed the country in the early sixties will be no more and will only be held in fond remembrances.

Let us look back for half a decade and see what the conditions were then and what a beautiful home has been carved out – and seemed to easterners as distant as England and even Australia. But few men had come in this direction, for gold had not been discovered here yet. The first great rush west was in 1849 when gold was discovered in Sutter's Mill in California. In those days Chicago seemed far west and Minnesota was even a wilderness.

The discovery of gold spread like wildfire – penetrating even to far off China and soon it seemed as if half the world was on the move to the land of the golden west. These were the good old Pioneer Days and those who came west during those stirring times were what we now term the Pioneers. Thousands upon thousands of persons left their farms, shops, professions and callings of every description and started west – the gold fever coursing wildly through their veins. They came overland and many bones of human beings blazed the trails for those behind. Three months or more of traveling behind ox teams, beneath the blazing sun and sometimes with little water could not be endured by all who braved the attempt, but those who succeeded well deserved their reward. Fathers, brothers, nephews and uncles all joined in the onward rush – all in the hope of bettering their fortunes. Many returned and brought joy and happiness to their loved ones – others never returned. After wearily waiting year after year, those at home gave them up for lost and they were probably never heard from anymore. These were the ones who were not successful. Sickness and misfortune may have overtaken them.

After a few years in California, parties of emigrants began to explore other territory. No longer did all pioneers go to California – many went to Oregon and finally early in the 1860's Montana commenced to receive a quota of the vast mass of humanity that crossed the plains. Some farmed, some mined and others brought stocks of goods and kept stores. The majority of those that came west, however, were in search of the golden metal.

Gold would be discovered in a little camp one day and the next would be deserted. New discoveries spread like wildfire and no sooner would a new camp be reached than the entire population of the latter would be on the move. Thus was Montana, the Treasure State, finally settled.

As the years went by, the population began to increase and soon farms and ranches were taken up and tilled. Many of these old Pioneers can still be found. Some have lived on their ranches upwards of thirty years.

These are the real pioneers who carved homes for themselves out of the valleys and forests.

In the 1860's and early 1870's, luxuries were high in price, and almost unobtainable. Farmers lived on what they raised and earned their living by the sweat of their brow. Food and clothing were brought in at enormous expense and consequently commanded high prices. It was not uncommon to get $10 for a 'boiled shirt' or a $100 for a suit of clothes. A dinner cost from $2.00 to $2.50 and a sack of flour, in many instances, cost $100. Beans were $5.00 per pound and a pound of butter brought $10.00. Bacon and ham were high and many times could not be obtained. With clothing and provisions at those high prices, it was no small wonder that the miner was almost forced to be successful.

Here fish and game were plentiful. Deer, buffalo and other animals abounded and fresh meet could be obtained by just going after it.

Educational and social advantages in those days were practically none. The Pioneer read newspapers that strayed into his path and was happy if the paper was no more than a month to six weeks old when received. Travel was slow and mail was irregular. Many times friends and relatives were unable to locate their dear ones and events sometimes occurred a year before they were made known. There were practically no schools or chances to obtain an education until later. There was no time for these things and what little education the children received during those early periods was obtained at the fireside.

The perils of these early days must also be taken into consideration. This country abounded with Indians and it was unsafe to travel. While crossing the plains many times large wagon trains composed of 100 wagons and up to 250 men were attacked by Indians with many men, women and children dying along the trail.

As can be seen by the brief outline which I have given, our fathers must have borne and suffered much in carving civilization out of this western wilderness. What praises they deserve! What reverence they should be paid on account of it!

Gradually, however, as the years passed and the onward rush of civilization increased, everything changed. The railroad pushed westward and soon small towns were established along the line. A school was established in a lonely mining camp and soon a church was built. The railroad brought thousands of new inhabitants and soon where there were only small settlements flourishing cities could be found. Telegraph service came with the railroad and even before the hardy pioneer realized it, the east had moved west.

Where forty years ago the bear and buffalo held undisturbed possession and where the Indian had his freedom unmolested, civilization has been established through our pioneers.

But the pioneer days are over and we may well say to our pioneer fathers to whom we owe so much:

"Here's to you and your families. May you all live long and prosper".

Editor's Note:

In 1902 at the annual Society of Montana Pioneers meeting, interest was taken by the pioneers to work through the Legislative Assembly of the State of Montana to pass a law providing for Pioneer Day. The law designated the last Friday in May as Pioneer Day and provided for its observance in the public schools and for an award of a Pioneer Medal for the best essay on Pioneer history.

The date of Pioneer Day was no doubt intended to mark as near as possible the anniversary of the organization of the Territory on May 26, 1864. The Pioneer observation day was later changed to November 1.

The purpose of the essay was to hand down to passing generations the exact historic facts connected and associated with the Pioneers of the State of Montana. The Montana Board of Education reviewed the submitted essays and chose a winning paper. The winner receiving a medal presented by a high-ranking official of the State of Montana.

The Honorable James Donovan, the Attorney General of the State of Montana, introduced the winner of the 1903 Pioneer Days award. Miss Cartwright was presented with a medal and then read her essay to the attendees of the fall meeting of the Society of Montana Pioneers in Great Falls, Montana.

Pioneer Histories

George Washington Allen

Submitted by William Attix Allen, Grandson

George Washington Allen was born June 1, 1828, in Wake County, North Carolina, the eldest son of Moses Harrison Allen and Lucy Williams (Rhodes) Allen. His parents were slave owners.

According to his own account, George Washington Allen left home as a boy because his parents would not send him to school and had forced him to work with the slaves. His brother was reputed to have been a lawyer, but this information has proved to be incorrect. There is no record that George Washington Allen ever wrote to, or received letters from, North Carolina.

He appeared on the 1855 tax list in St. Mark's District, Wake County, North Carolina, without land or slaves. In 1855 he was married in White County, Arkansas, to Cinthy Anne Adkins. In the 1860 U. S. Census for White County, Arkansas, he appeared with a wife and three young daughters.

He enlisted in March 1862 as a private in ADAM's Regiment, Arkansas Infantry, which was later absorbed into the 23rd Arkansas Infantry Regiment. He was slightly wounded in the battle of Corinth in October 1862 and was captured. His name was on the list of prisoners aboard the *Dacotah* in transit from Columbus, Kentucky, to Vicksburg, Mississippi. It is believed he was suffering from typhoid during the trip and cured himself by drinking milk that he stole from the galley. He was exchanged in November 1862.

The name *George Allen* continued to appear on his company muster roll with the notation "absent on parole…" until April 1863. He did not return to the 23rd Arkansas, but was assigned as first sergeant in the 15th Arkansas Infantry Regiment. On July 9, 1863, he was captured at Port Hudson, Louisiana, and released on parole July 12 of the same year. Ulysses S. Grant implied it in his memoirs that virtually all of the paroled Confederates in this area deserted at this time. Passage through the Union lines to the territories was generously granted to the Confederates in order to expedite desertions.

On December 19, 1864, he preempted 80 acres on the east bank of the South Platte River in Arapahoe County, Colorado Territory. In his land entry file is a loyalty oath to the Government of the United States and a preemption affidavit both with his signature. A witness swore that George Allen was in Colorado from August 27, 1863, to December 19, 1864. In

February 1865 he sold his 80 acres for $1,000.

In December 1865 the *Virginia City Montana Post* advertised that G. W. Allen had an unclaimed letter at the post office in Virginia City, Madison County, Montana Territory. Several other notifications continued to appear throughout 1866, with the last such notification appearing on March 9, 1867. The Virginia City deed records in 1866 show G. W. Allen participating with several partners in buying and selling mining claims.

On September 13, 1867, George filed a ranch claim for 160 acres on the east bank of the Madison River in Gallatin County, Montana Territory. He appeared in this area in the 1870 Census for Gallatin County, Montana Territory.

Mary Catherine (Rea) Allen – age 17.

On January 4, 1872, the *Bozeman Advant Weekly Courier* reported the marriage of G. W. Allen and Mary Catherine Rea as taking place on December 28, 1871. Mary Catherine Rea had arrived in Virginia City with her parents, William Franklin Rea and Sarah Ann (Hudson) Rea, on September 4, 1864, but had moved to Gallatin City where they also appeared in the 1870 census. Mary Catherine Rea was a woman of exceptional beauty in her youth and once shared the title of "Belle of Montana" with another young woman. George did not mention to his prospective bride that he had an earlier marriage in Arkansas although his daughter, Marion Elizabeth (Allen) Shearon, was living in 1880 when she sent a photograph of herself from Little Rock, Arkansas, to her uncle Romulus and Aunt Tilitha Allen in North Carolina. (Romulus was the brother of George Washington Allen.)

George and Mary had four children: William Amonet Allen born September 20, 1872; Sallie R. Allen born August 30, 1874; Katherine Rea Allen born December 13, 1877; and Georgia Belle Allen born October 31, 1882. All of the descendants, except one grandson, Charles Leon Anceney the son of Katherine Rea (Allen) Anceney, have either died or moved away from Gallatin County.

George died July 31, 1882, as the result of an eye infection. His widow remarried William M. James December 23, 1885. The James family had three children: Harry, Edward, and Leslie. Edward and Leslie had no children. Harry James moved to Lewistown, Montana, and had a large family, most of whom are still living.

George's personality must be inferred from the public record. He was highly regarded in Gallatin County and was considered affluent for the times. His dying words were "My only regret is that I have not been able to break Kate's spirit." Kate added her own comment to posterity when informed of her father's death. "Good!" she exclaimed, "Now he can't whip me anymore."

Zadock Montgomery Allen

Submitted by William M. McCall, Great-Grandson

Zadock Montgomery Allen was the son of James and Frances (Jones) Allen of Kentucky, and grandson of Benjamin and Margaret (----) Allen of Virginia. Benjamin Allen aided the cause of the American Revolution in public service in Botetourt, Virginia. His great-grandparents were Robert Allen and Robert's second wife, widow Sara Givens. Robert Allen was born in Armagh County, Ireland, of a Scotch Presbyterian family.

Zadock Allen was born February 7, 1824, at Bowling Green, Kentucky. Tired of plantation life, Zadock left for Newton, Iowa, where he was a blacksmith and a mason. On October 28, 1845, he married Alice Rachel Mann. Alice was born on November 28, 1828, and died in Newton on August 4, 1854. Zadock then married Almira Osborn on September 21, 1858. Almira was born in Columbus, Ohio, and was the sister of Major General Thomas Osborn of the Union Army.

Zadock Allen made 11 trips across the plains before bringing his family to Montana. He had traveled to Denver, Colorado, and the Montana towns of Bannack, Virginia City, Alder, Butte, and Helena. He was a surveyor, blacksmith, lay leader, and Bible reader.

His wife Almira said, "so impressed was he with the possibilities of Montana that he convinced me that we should leave the settled state of Iowa and take part in the up-building of this territory as it was then."

The Allen family came to Montana in 1866 by ox-team over the old Yellowstone trail. The trip lasted five months. There were 144 wagons and 100 milk cows.

Zadock Montgomery Allen

Arriving at Omaha from Iowa, they joined the government troops coming through on the Yellowstone Trail to Fort Laramie. The wagon train was corralled twice by the Indians to fight, but there were too many men in the train so the old chief made a sign and came forward to make peace. The Indians that corralled the train were Crows. The Crow Indians were afraid of Sioux Indians, so they traveled with the wagon train for several weeks for its protection. During this trip, Indians killed one scout, and another man was pulled into the river by his whip that was made of heavy leather. There were times when they did cross paths with friendly Indians and the children would cry to get out of the wagon and play with the papooses.

The wagon train went north to the Big Horn River in June. They found the river swollen by the rains and the crossing very dangerous. The roads were bad and they slowed travel. Crossing streams and rivers was hazardous. Finally they came to Bozeman, but decided it was not safe there because of the possibility of attacks from Indians. They went on to Helena with some miners whom Z. M. Allen knew from his earlier visits. They moved to Willow Creek, now known as Harrison, and established the Allen ranch. Ulysses S. Grant signed their homestead papers.

The day after they arrived in Montana, in October 1866, the Allen's daughter, Helen, was born. This was one of the first wagon trains penetrating the vast unpopulated Rocky Mountain region. The two other Montana families on the wagon train were the Selways of Dillon, Montana, and the Pauls of Great Falls, Montana.

Almira (Osborn) Allen

Allen had a blacksmith shop in Alder and made the first sledge hammer used in placer mining at Silver Bow. He made most of his tools and nails. He helped build the first house in Butte and Pony where his family operated a hotel (sometimes up to 60 men lodged there). He also had a blacksmith shop and livery stable. He was a Justice of the Peace for the towns of Harrison and Pony. He had been a wagon boss, Vigilante, and Mason. He was known as "Dad" Allen. The Allen homestead survived seven years of grasshopper plagues and a devastatingly cold winter, which had frozen most of the cattle to death.

In 1873 his daughter Inez, then married to Jack McClatchey, and her half-sister Sarah, and friends, made a two-month trip through Yellowstone Park. They may have been some of the first white women to visit the park. Later in 1877 the Indians in Yellowstone were hostile and the Nez Percé with Yellow Wolf attacked the Radersberg party.

Several of the Allen children lived to be 90 or more. Luman Allen, born in 1868, lived to the age of 102 passing away in Butte, MT, in 1970. Shortly before he died Luman stated, "It's like writing the last page of a history book – there is no more." He made this comment to a Butte reporter when he became the last surviving member of the Society of Montana Pioneers. He was the only living original member to attend the Society's final meeting on August 25, 1962.

Zadock Allen's children from his first marriage to Alice (Mann) Allen were William, Sarah, James, and John. From his second marriage to Almira (Osborn) Allen his children were Inez, Julia Mae, Fannie, Helen, Luman, Charles, Maggie, Thomas, Almira and Loretta.

Sarah, Z. M. Allen's oldest daughter, was the first teacher in Jefferson City and Fannie was the first teacher in Livingston. Inez married Jack McClatchey in Pony on September 2, 1878, and moved with him in 1882 to Benson's Landing east of the present Livingston. There they operated the stage station and Jack drove the stage that carried the daily mail to Bozeman. Mrs. McClatchy was the first to open a dress making shop in Livingston. After her husband's death, Inez married Frank Robson and later moved to Coeur d'Alene, Idaho.

Zadock Allen died August 4, 1888, at Harrison, Montana, and Almira lived to be 89 years old. She died April 8, 1922. Both are buried in Harrison, Montana.

Warren Strickland Baxter

Submitted by Grandson Lyle Baxter
and Great-Grandson Bruce Baxter

Warren Strickland Baxter (1844-1905) departed Illinois for Montana at age 19. On March 24, 1864, he left the family farm near Shelbyville, Illinois, and joined his boyhood friend, Albert Ward, bound for the Alder Gulch gold strike. One of them had a horse and the other a cow. They got a wagon and joined Captain Townsend's wagon train. As they took turns walking beside the wagon, they could only travel a few miles a day. They sometimes encountered Indians. One day two men with the wagon train were killed as they herded horses a short distance from camp. The trip took over four months and they arrived in Virginia City, Montana, on August 20, 1864.

Mr. Baxter found employment hauling lumber. In the spring of 1865 he traveled north to Helena to go logging, and later freighting. He also ran a stagecoach station between Craig and Augusta (somewhere near present Bowman's Corner). In 1870 he purchased a hay ranch in the Prickly

Pear valley (north of Helena).

In 1870 Warren went "back to the states" to Illinois, where he became engaged. He gave his fiancée a ring made of pure Last Chance Gulch gold that he had mined. (He later regretted not adding alloy to the gold as the ring wore thin.) He returned to Montana allowing a five-year engagement. For a time, he worked for Wells Fargo hauling freight and supplies to the Mormon colony. In conversations with Brigham Young, Warren told Brigham that he was going to marry a girl named Young. Brigham promptly presented a set of silver flatware as a wedding gift.

Warren returned to Illinois, and in 1875 was married to Sarah Elizabeth Young (1847-1928), a niece of Davy Crockett. (Sarah was a daughter of Ruth Crockett whose father was William Crockett, Davy's brother. Ruth Crockett married Thomas Young.)

Warren S. and Sarah E. (Young) Baxter

The newlyweds traveled by train to the railhead at Ogden, Utah, where Warren had left his team and wagon in care of a "herd boy." When the Baxters arrived in Ogden, they found the horses had wandered away and were lost. Warren left Sarah with a kind Mormon family. After searching for two weeks, he found the team wandering back toward home. The 500-mile wagon trip from Ogden to Helena, many times over mountainous terrain, took several weeks.

In 1877 Warren Baxter sold his Prickly Pear ranch (now under Lake Helena) for a good profit. He bought another ranch nearer to Ten Mile Creek (where Montana Avenue now crosses Munger Lane) north of Helena. He sold this property in 1889 and bought 1,230 acres, called the Sentinel Rock Ranch, near Wolf Creek.

In politics, Warren Baxter gave his allegiance to the Democratic Party. The church affiliation of both Warren and Sarah Baxter was to the Christian Church. They were early day members of the present congregation at 311 Power Street, Helena, Montana.

Warren and Sarah Baxter raised five children: Mary, George, Ross, Jessie and Delbert. Mary Baxter died young. Mr. Baxter himself was stricken with consumption (tuberculosis). He sold the Wolf Creek property and in 1903 bought a house at 827-12th Avenue in Helena. In 1904 their son Delbert drowned in a reservoir on the Floweree ranch near Wolf Creek where he had been working. Delbert was 18 at the time of his death.

Warren and Sarah both died at the house in Helena, and it remained the home of their children, George and Jessie, until Jessie's death in 1963. Neither George nor Jessie ever married. The Society of Montana Pioneers were pallbearers at Warren's funeral. The immediate family lies in the Benton Avenue Pioneers Cemetery in Helena.

Warren and Sarah's son, Ross (1879-1956), was born at the Ten Mile Creek ranch. In 1911 Ross married Mabel Ellen Kinney (1890-1983). Mabel is a descendent of the Beach pioneer family. Ross and Mabel ranched near Coeur D'Alene, Idaho; Logan, Montana, and Helena Valley, Montana. During the depression and World War II, they operated a boarding house in Helena and later at the former Canyon Ferry Dam, now under present Canyon Ferry Lake. Ross worked there as an oiler. Ross and Mabel had a daughter, Louise, and a son, Lyle. Lyle and his namesake descendants reside in western Montana and near Helena. Louise died in 1987. A daughter in Seattle survives her.

Among the relatives of the Baxters was Robert M. Craven. Mr. Craven was the great-uncle of Mrs. Ross (Mabel Kinney) Baxter. Robert

Baxter home in Helena, Montana.

Craven was the first Methodist preacher licensed in Montana (1872). Mr. Craven was the first preacher to marry in Montana, to Miss Mary Frazier. The Craven's children, Warren and Ida, are believed to be the first native-born Montanans to graduate from a Montana high school, at Bozeman in 1892. Reverend Craven performed the marriage ceremony for Ross and Mabel Baxter at the Kinney family home in Helena Valley.

In 1870 the *Helena Herald* records that Robert M. Craven and Miss Mary E. Frazier were married at the home of Calvin Beach, in the Prickly Pear valley, by the Reverend S.J. Lathrop, on Sunday, June 5, 1870. The same minister married two other couples on this same date.

The *Herald* reported that:

> "two of the parties who were joined in the holy bonds of wedlock Sunday were the recipients of a shivaree. Their peaceful slumbers and happy dreams were disturbed by the discordant sounds of gongs, tin pans, bass drums, bagpipes, horns and other instruments which made the night hideous with their unearthly noises."

The editor must have had his sleep disturbed, as he continued on with the description of the shivaree.

> "A mock serenade of this character when it disturbs no one but the happy couple is bad enough, but when sick babies and tired

mothers and the whole neighborhood are annoyed, we say that such a proceeding is barbarous and should not be countenanced in any civilized community."

A footnote on the Beach family is a reminder of the times in which they lived:

Mabel Baxter's grandparents, Calvin and Margaret (Frazier) Beach had ten children. A diphtheria epidemic hit the Helena valley in 1885, and within four months, five of the ten Beach children died from the disease. A sixth child died of pneumonia in 1889. One of the rows of headstones in Forestvale Cemetery reads:

"Beneath this stone in soft repose is laid a mother's dearest pride."

George Beatty

Submitted by Wes Beatty, Great-Grandson

George Beatty was born in County Tyrone, Cork, Ireland, on May 11, 1837. In June 1847 his parents John and Mary Beatty and their family of eight children (four girls and four boys) left Ireland at the time of the potato famine. After landing in New York, the parents resided in New York City until their deaths.

George worked in a piano factory, but while in his teens was told by physicians that he had a heart ailment and should seek outdoor employment. So on April 1, 1856, he enlisted in the 2nd U.S. Dragoons, Company F and was first sent to Fort Riley, Kansas. He spent the next five years working out of Fort Laramie, Wyoming, fighting Indians and trailing outlaws. Dragoons was a European name for mounted cavalry.

On March 4, 1861 (on Lincoln's inauguration day), returning from mounted patrol, Corporal George Beatty was one of seven detailed to trail a band of horse thieves when two white men ran off with the government's entire herd of forty horses and mules at Fort Laramie.

The seven men searched the Black Hills, traveled south along the North Platte River in Wyoming with six Dragoons and one driving a six-mule team pulling a supply wagon. At Box Elder, Wyoming, they picked up the trail and found the horses with one of the thieves five miles below Sweet Water Bridge. The thief was soon captured. Corporal Beatty's orders were to shoot or hang all the captured thieves. Fifteen minutes later the men had the thief on a barrel with a rope around his neck.

On their return, Corporal George Beatty caught sight of the other thief, "Lame Charley," with two men. He started after him. Charley hid. They searched high and low but finally had to give up the chase.

Sometime later near Scottsbluff, Nebraska, J. A. Slade, Station Agent, captured Charley, brought him to Fort Laramie and hung him. But just before being hung "Lame Charley" related that in the earlier chase, he had hid behind a big snowdrift with his mule and expressed regret that he had not killed George then. He said he could easily have done so, but since his double-barreled rifle could have killed only two men, the third man would have gotten him. Charley said if they had found him, George Beatty would have been his first shot.

On April 1, 1861, he received his discharge from the army at Fort Laramie. That fall George volunteered and went to Oregon with the First Oregon Volunteers organized for the protection of immigrants. For two months he shoed horses, set railroad ties, and other such jobs.

He passed the winter in Walla Walla, Washington, and in the spring of 1862 went to Florence, Idaho, prospecting along the Salmon River. In 1862, George and his two partners, James McGuire and C. A. Falen, arrived in Bannack, Montana.

Hearing of a big strike, George and five others started for what is now Three Forks, Montana. On their way they met a band of Crow Indians who forced them to go to their camp. The Indians released them the next morning after some dickering, but followed and surrounded them and drove off their horses. Three of the party followed the Indians and after an exchange of shots, the horses were recaptured.

While at Three Forks, he loaned his horse and revolver to Billy Porter so Billy could stake a claim at Alder Gulch. Billy split the claim between himself, George and seven others. George's share (one-sixteenth) was directly opposite Wallace Street in Virginia City. Every evening while working the claim, George would go to Bissell's Butcher Shop for steak while the partner would burn off the quick silver from the riffles in the two sluice boxes they were using. Upon his return there would be $20.00 of gold in the pan to split. This went on for several weeks. One evening, a stranger came and offered George $150 for his interest in the claim – George accepted on the spot. After returning from the butcher shop earlier than usual that night, George found $40 of gold in the pan instead of $20 – George told his partner what he thought of him!

George took the $150, borrowed $80 more to buy a wagon and yoke of oxen, and began cutting and hauling logs needed for the construction of Virginia City.

In May 1864 George got together five yoke of oxen with wagons and began freighting from steamboats at Fort Benton back to Virginia City.

The scariest incident of George's life happened while at Fort Benton. The Fort cook asked George to help drive in a herd of cattle grazing by the Milk River near the fort. George volunteered but asked for a horse and rifle. The cook gave him his own Smith and Wesson carbine and Jim Forbes gave him an old wind-blown plug. After riding out to where the cattle were, the cook pointed to the cattle and said he would take one bunch and George should take the other.

George Beatty – age 57.

Just after they separated, George happened to look up and saw a bunch of Sioux Indians coming directly for them. The cook could not hear George yelling at him. As George told it, " I was thinking, you will see them soon enough. Oh say, but wasn't I scared! All my life passed in review before me. Things I'd learned in Sunday school as well as the preaching at prayer meetings flashed before me and I thought I'd be in hell in less than fifteen minutes. I looked up at the beautiful July sky with not a cloud in sight. I prayed, Oh Lord deliver me from these Indians and I will be a better boy."

The fear all left me I thought, "I have seven shots, I must get them before they get me. The Indians had only bows and arrows, as the trading posts were forbidden to sell them ammunition. They rode past me. Four went after the cook. I tried to make a dash for the Indians but my horse would not move. To save my life, I could not get my horse to move. Finally after sitting still for a few minutes, the horse went off at a slow walk. The Indians then came out of the timber. I thought I must make these Indians think I am after their scalps, so I turned my horse and made for them as fast as he would go. They turned back. I stopped and shouted as loud as I could. The Indians left. The next morning we found the body of

George Beatty Homestead – circa 1865.

George Beatty home – circa 1895.

the cook pierced by six or seven arrows. It was the scare of my life."

For a year in his many trips freighting and prospecting, George kept his eyes out for a good place to settle. In 1865 George homesteaded on Beaver Creek near Winston, Montana. He always believed that his was the first homestead taken up in Montana. It was reported that in 1865 George raised a crop of potatoes, which he sold for ten cents a pound to G. M. Filson to feed the passengers on the Diamond City stage. He sold his hay as high as $110 a ton.

The homesteaders (called squatters) had to survey their own land, build fences and put up rough cabins in which to live. Having settled down and become a farmer, George returned east to take a wife, marrying Mary Leticia Waddell on January 1, 1869. Mary, a native of Brooklyn, had been corresponding with George. On the return trip he obtained a mule team at Council Bluffs, Iowa, loaded his freight on wagons, and began the five-month tedious trip to the Montana Territory. The wagon trail was soft from spring rains and he soon had to trade his small-footed mules for yokes of oxen to complete the trip over the Bozeman Trail. When the official survey was made in 1867, it was discovered that Mr. Beatty had built his cabin and barns on land actually belonging to George and Sarah Filson. The Filsons sold George the land the buildings were on.

Mary was a gracious and refined lady. Her beautiful clothes were the envy of every pioneer woman who she met. For a young woman who had never been out of New York City before, the rugged life in a one-room, dirt roofed shack with Indians peering in the windows must have been too hard on her.

Mary Beatty died eight years later on October 29, 1876, at the age of 28. She left behind three children: Mary Belle, age 7; Alice Leticia, age 6; and Hamilton Wesley, age 5.

One of George Beatty's main sources of income was raising vegetables and hauling them to the mining camps at Diamond City, White City, and other camps in both the Big Belt and Elkhorn Mountains of Montana with his teams and wagons. Often he was gone all day and sometimes even overnight, leaving the three small children to care for themselves. When they saw Indians they would hide in a large oat box in the kitchen until the Indians had left.

A friend of Beatty, Alex Watson, convinced George to correspond with an acquaintance from Pennsylvania, a maiden schoolteacher whose name was also Beatty. After about a year of correspondence with Maggie, George Beatty told relatives that his "heart" was giving him trouble. In

1879 he leased out the ranch, took the children and went by steamboat and then railroad to Pennsylvania. Margaret (Maggie) Melissa Beatty and George Beatty were married July 27, 1879.

When the lease on his ranch was up, they came back to Montana, this time all the way by railroad since a line had now been extended from Ogden, Utah, to Dillon, Montana. Maggie Beatty proved herself to be very capable as a mother and wife, able to handle the austere frontier life. By 1895 they had saved enough to build themselves a fine new two-story house on Beaver Creek, near Winston, Montana, where they lived until their deaths. Maggie Beatty passed away in 1908. George Beatty was alert and active right up until the time of his death on April 30, 1934.

Because of his doctor's prognosis of a short life, George purchased a gray metal tombstone early in life. His grandchildren never forgot that tombstone sitting eerily in the Beatty's attic. Today it marks his grave in the Masonic part of Benton Cemetery in Helena.

George Beatty was well known throughout Montana, having been a charter member of the Masonic Lodge #1, Virginia City – the first Masonic Lodge and Eastern Star. On his 94th birthday, he was declared the oldest living Mason in the state – both in age and length of membership – having been made a master Mason in Virginia City in 1865. He was the last living charter member of Morning Star Lodge #5 A. F. and A. M. of Helena organized in 1866.

His interest in the political and governmental processes never waned. He had many friends some of who were W. A. Clark, James Ferrous, Hugh F. Galen and C. A. Broadwater.

George was a school trustee and clerk for many years. For two years, 1903 and 1904, he was vice-president of the Montana Pioneer Society for Broadwater County and in 1899 was president of the Broadwater County Pioneer Society. He was a member of the Society of Montana Pioneers beginning in 1884.

After George's spiritual conversion due to surviving the Indians, he made good his promise to God "to be a better boy" by helping to establish both Townsend and Winston Methodist Episcopal Churches. He served as an active member and trustee and steward of his church. He was prominent in temperance work and his home was always open to traveling circuit rider evangelists including Brother Van. He attributed his prosperity and long life to having always observed the Sabbath, never "doing a lick of work on Sunday."

The Beatty children all stayed in Montana. Mary Belle (1869-1946) never married and helped take care of her father in his later years. Alice Leticia (1870-1942) married Will Fisher, settled at the foot of Whites Gulch in Broadwater County and had three daughters, Annie, Mildred and Alice Luella. Hamilton Wesley Beatty (1872-1918) married Johanna C. Hollman in 1902 and settled near his father's ranch. They had four children – two boys and two girls.

Thedore Bedard

Submitted by Robert L. Deschamps, Jr., Great-Grandson

Thedore Bedard, one of the prominent early settlers of Frenchtown, and one of the proprietors of the Western Hotel, was born at St. Mary's, Canada, on August 22, 1843. Thedore was of French extraction and his ancestors were among the early settlers of Canada. His father was Flavian Bedard.

Thedore Bedard was reared to manhood in his native country where he learned the trade of blacksmith. In 1864 he crossed the plains from St. Louis, Missouri, to Alder Gulch, Montana, with ox teams, consuming five months on the journey.

After arriving at Alder Gulch, Mr. Bedard was engaged in making tools for the miners until 1869. He ran a blacksmith shop in this city for a year and a half, and then, in company with Edmond Hamel, embarked in the stock business in Grass Valley. The firm became prominent breeders of horses and cattle, and owned 3,000 acres of valuable land. They were proprietors of the hotel and flouring mill. The hotel was built in 1870, and since 1882 was owned by Messrs. Bedard and Hamel. They were the leading hotel men of Frenchtown, and were obliging and liberal in all their dealings and were deserving of the prosperity they enjoyed.

On July 10, 1869, Mr. Bedard was united in marriage with Miss Maggie Fauthaume. Maggie was a native of Pennsylvania and her ancestors were from Paris. They had eight children: Theodore, Maggie, Henry, Addie, Alma, Florence, Joseph, and Freddie.

Mr. Bedard was formerly a Democrat, but became identified with the People's party. He served for many years as one of the trustees of the school district, and took an active interest in all educational work. The family belonged to the Catholic Church and aided liberally in the construction of the beautiful church edifice in Frenchtown.

Thedore and Maggie both passed away at the St. Patrick's Hospital in Missoula, Montana, and are buried in the old St. Mary's Cemetery there.

Mr. Bedard was a charter member of the Society of Montana Pioneers and all through his life was active in the civic affairs of the community.

Oliver Louis Bernier

Submitted by Ethel B. LaRock, Granddaughter

Oliver Louis Bernier was born in Kankakee, Illinois, July 1, 1846, the son of Frank and Margaret LaVeau Bernier. His family had moved to Illinois from Quebec, Canada, some years before his birth. His first language was French and he spoke English with a thick accent all his life.

Oliver was apprenticed to a broom maker when he was in his early teens. This was not to his liking, so at the age of 13, he resolved to go west and follow the lure of gold in California.

"Before going west, he visited relatives in Canada and from there went to New York City where he took a boat for Panama. He crossed the isthmus and took another boat to the gold diggings in San Francisco. Although the town was young, it was busy and exciting. Some had struck it rich but many more like Oliver, barely made a living. Oliver returned home, more experienced but none the richer. He found Illinois much too small and longed for the unsettled west. He found work as a bull whacker for an outfit coming to Montana." (Vertical File, Montana Historical Library, Helena, MT, 1930)

"He arrived in Virginia City, Montana, in July 1865 via the Bozeman Trail Cut-off. The wagon train had traveled from St. Joseph, Missouri. The trip lasted three months and although many mishaps were encountered Indians never attacked them. It happened to be the time of high water and as the Indian tribes were divided by swollen streams they were kinder to white men who often took them across the rivers with their wagons and oxen." (Vertical File, Montana Historical Library, Helen, MT, 1930)

"Once, Mr. Bernier was forced to swim the rushing waters of the North Platte River. He had tried to help an ox that was caught in quicksand on the edge of the island and just as he loosened the ox, the current rushed in, carrying him and the beast down stream. Both floated with the current until they reached the shore." (*Great Falls Tribune*, 3 May 1933, pg. 4)

"Bernier's job as a bull whacker was hard, he walked most of the way. At night a corral was made of a circle of wagons and in the enclosure, the stock were loosened while some men slept, and others watched for Indians." (*Great Falls Tribune,* 3 May 1933, pg. 4)

"When these pioneers reached Virginia City, some went prospecting for gold immediately. Young Bernier obtained work from John Creighton to build the first telegraph line from Virginia City, Montana, to Salt Lake City, Utah. This was completed on November 2, 1866, the day the first message was sent form Virginia City.

When the workmen reached Salt Lake City, Mr. Bernier was surprised to find such an up-to-date city so far west. He had lived for a time in Brooklyn, New York, and was familiar with the large cities of that period and was astonished to find a theater in Salt Lake City that compared favorable with those of the larger cities of the eastern section of the United States. Mr. Creighton treated the men to tickets for the Hot Springs and the theater. The tired and dusty men spent the afternoon at the Hot Springs where the baths refreshed them for the entertainment in the evening at the theater. This was the largest theater west of Chicago at that time. It cost $250,000 and seated 1800 people." (Vertical File on Oliver Bernier, Montana Historical Library, 1930.)

"After the completion of the telegraph line, Bernier remained in Utah and for some time, buying up dried fruits of all kinds for Creighton, who shipped it to the mining camps of Montana." (Vertical File on Oliver Bernier, Montana Historical Library, 1930.)

Young Bernier drifted to Bozeman and worked for Bud McAdoo for six years, earning enough to purchase a small ranch adjoining the Nelson Story property near Bozeman.

"He did teaming at this time for soldiers at Fort Ellis. It was on one of his trips for the Fort that he passed over the Custer Battlefield, where still laid unburied some of Custer's 250 slaughtered soldiers, who were killed by 10,000 of Sitting Bull's warriors. These, he helped to bury." (Great Falls Tribune, 29 November 1935, pg. 11. See appendix on Fort Ellis.)

"The next summer a number of Bozeman settlers discovered

all of their horses gone. They tracked them and found them driven at a breakneck speed by eight Indians. Bernier and his companions opened fire on the Indians and terrified them so that they forgot to drive the stolen horses across the Yellowstone River, but instead plunged into the river themselves. Only two reached the opposite shore. The bodies of the other six were later washed ashore. They were riddled by bullets." (*Great Falls Tribune,* 29 November 1935, pg. 11.)

Bernier had many tales of early encounters of pioneers and Indians. Usually the Indians were more interested in horses than in doing harm to freighters. On one of his trips into "Yellowstone Country," he found that nearly all of an Indian village had died during the winter from smallpox. Their bodies had been wrapped and placed in trees as a form of burial. Many had been Bernier's friends.

"The rich farm land about Bozeman soon attracted new settlers, Oliver being one of them. The settlers raised grain. For part of the year, Oliver freighted for the military post of Fort Ellis. Here he used horses instead of oxen and it was not long until horse trading and riding became the favorite diversion next to gambling. After gold was discovered in Helena, Mr. Bernier became a freighter to Utah, hauling fresh and dried fruits to Helena.

Often late frosts made it necessary to build a smudge of fire around the wagons to save the fresh fruit and again Indians had to be persuaded with a gun to assure safe delivery of the fruit to Helena." (*Great Falls Tribune*, 3 May 1933, pg. 4.)

Fort Benton on the Missouri was the main port for traffic from the East to the gold camps of Montana, and Helena in particular. In 1878 Bernier began freighting supplies from Fort Benton to Helena. Indians were active and caused a lot of trouble to freighters who banded together and traveled in long trains.

"It was on one of these trips, while camped at Sun River, that all the mules and horses of the outfit were stolen. This time they tracked the mules to Canada to Sitting Bull's camp near Wood Mountain. They had an interpreter with them and also a number of Canadian Mounted Police. When they made known their mission to Sitting Bull through the interpreter, the chief let out a loud yell and started gesturing to his braves. In a few hours, horses and mules and braves came in a larger number than these white men had ever seen and Sitting Bull allowed them to pick out their stolen mules.

The trip to Canada had, however, held up the freight for four months and when they finally reached Helena, there was much rejoicing, especially by a girl who would not get married until her trunk arrived from Fort Benton." (*Great Falls Tribune,* 3 May 1933, pg. 4.)

Bernier was in Fort Benton the night General Thomas Meagher was drowned in 1867. Bernier remembered seeing "the governor" on the street of Fort Benton. (Vertical File, Montana Historical Library, 1930, pg. 2.)

"Passing up and down the Benton Road so often, helped Mr. Bernier to locate a good place for a sawmill later. In 1884 he had a sawmill near Lyon Creek, up from present day Wolf Creek (then called Carterville). Some of early day hotels and other business houses obtained a great deal of their lumber from his mill and county bridges were built of timber he furnished. Lumber was hauled a long distance then, some of it was used to erect the old Christian Church in Augusta in the day of Rev. Job Little." (*Great Falls Tribune*, 3 May 1933, pg. 4.)

"Oliver was forced to give up freighting in 1882 when he dislocated his left shoulder in a runaway. The injury was a handicap to him all of his life, for the doctor who treated him, thinking his shoulder was broken, bandaged it for that instead of springing the arm back into place." (*Great Falls Tribune*, 3 May 1933, pg. 4.)

He managed his sawmill for many years moving it to the middle and south fork of the Dearborn River as timber became scarcer in the area. He disposed of the mill in 1900, selling it to the Bean Brothers and Fred Urion.

Bernier also took up a homestead on Flat Creek about the same time as he began the sawmill. He increased his holdings by buying a few small ranches and began raising cattle. Until 1919 Bernier was one of the leading cattlemen of the country.

In 1887, he married Mary Ellen Mahoney, a second-generation Irish lady. She was born in New York and came to Montana by riverboat from Bismark, North Dakota, to Fort Benton with her mother, sisters, and a brother. They joined an older brother, Dan Mahoney, who was already established in Helena. Bernier met Mary in Helena.

Following their marriage, the Berniers made their home on the Flat Creek homestead. They had five children: Walter, Olive, Frances (Frankie), Dick, and Dan. Life on a homestead was a challenge. They raised cattle and fields of hay. Mary and Oliver were stubborn gardeners and tried to grow many types of things, some successfully and some not. The cold winters and hot dry summers limited the type of trees and crops, which thrived.

Early in his homesteading phase, Bernier planted some one thousand saplings as part of a "tree claim." Of all the trees planted, the only successful stand was a patch of large willows on the home place. In later years, his son Walter and wife Louise owned the homestead and the willows were used as the motif for the interior of their new home built in the 1930's.

Oliver and Mary Ellen (Mahoney) Bernier – circa 1900-05.

Flat Creek is about 60 miles from Helena, Montana, and about 15 miles from Augusta. Each fall the Berniers stocked up with food and supplies for the long winter. This involved traveling to Helena by wagon and took several days. Both Mary and Oliver were outgoing individuals and had many friends along the way. When they reached Helena, they were guests at Mary's mother's home on Lawrence Street.

These visits were a treat for Mary as she could buy a new hat and also visit with her sisters, Cathrin Butler, Johanna LaReau, and Nellie Mooso (Mauseau), and her brothers, Dan and John Mahoney. Cathrin was married to William Butler and Johanna (Jo) was married to William LaReau. Nellie was married to Finley Mooso (Mauseau). LaReau and Butler were Montana pioneers. The Butler home on Benton Avenue is a historical site called "the May Butler home," and the structure is described in "Historical Homes of Helena." For Bernier the trip to Helena was a time to talk of trade, beef prices and politics with his cronies.

This shopping trip involved buying all that was needed by the family until spring. These staples included: flour, salt, sugar, potatoes, rice, canned goods of a limited variety, apples, soup, dried apricots, peaches, and raisins. A "hog" of whiskey or brandy was a must as Bernier always had a drink each night before supper. (Note: The author's mother, Olive Bernier LaRock, always used the term "hog" and she used her hands indicating a small keg holding about two gallons of liquor. However, the Webster's Dictionary lists a "hog" as about 63 gallons capacity so the term may be inaccurate.) A grand treat for the family was oysters. Yard goods were purchased as Mary sewed all of the clothing for the family.

On the ranch, vegetables and staples were stored in a root cellar that protected items from both cold and heat. The springhouse provided summer cooling for cream, milk, and butter. They raised chickens and butchered cattle for beef. Pigs were bought from a neighbor and smoked for ham and bacon. Mary was said to be "a prime cook and set a fine table."

The Berniers were a tidy lot and Mary was an organizer. Each of the children had specific chores. Frankie helped with the cooking and Olive helped with the sewing. Olive also had the job of overseeing the Saturday night baths of the two little boys, Dick and Dan. One evening when Olive was bathing the two little fellows in a wash tub, company arrived and, to her everlasting embarrassment, they escaped her supervision and came dancing out to greet the guests in the state in which they were born.

Both Bernier girls helped with the ironing. Flat irons were heated on the wood stove and great care was needed to keep the irons both hot and clean. Nearly all the shirts and dresses were made of cotton, requiring both starch and ironing. The same was true of the petticoats worn by Mary and the girls. A "scorch" was taken quite seriously.

Mary scrubbed the floors on her hands and knees, every Saturday. Bernier was in the habit of going to Augusta for the day as he was banished from the house. He would bring back from Augusta one pint of beer for Mary, her reward and treat for the week.

As a daily ritual, Mary followed the example set by her mother, that a lady had "her work" done by one o'clock. The afternoon was set-aside for rest and visiting. At four, of course, the evening preparations began. Getting dinner for the family, milking the cows, separation of the milk, feeding the stock, et cetera, was all part of the evening chores.

Each spring the house was re-papered on the inside. Old newspapers were used and then whitewashed. Occasionally real wallpaper was available. The outside "privy" got the same treatment.

Olive and Frankie (Frances) told this story about their father. Their mother normally braided their hair each morning. When she became ill, Bernier prepared the girls for the morning including the hair braiding. He dutifully fixed each little girl's hair into one six-plait braid at the top of her head; much in the manner he plaited the tails and manes of the horses. Olive and Frankie said they couldn't blink until noon, as their braids were so tight.

Christmas was celebrated with visits and parties among the neighbors. Presents were not exchanged, nor was a tree put up as part of their Christmas tradition. It was however a joyful time and Christmas dinner included a small roasted pig served with an apple in its mouth. Mary prepared mincemeat pies, and just before baking, Bernier would carefully ladle a tablespoon of brandy into each pie with great ceremony. Oranges at Christmas were the ultimate treat.

Elementary school was offered nearby, summer and fall mostly. The schoolteacher usually boarded with a local family. One of the teachers was a man who stayed with the Berniers. All the Bernier children were in school and Mary provided a daily lunch box for all of them including the teacher. Much to the amazement and envy of some fellow students, this included a whole pie (six pieces). In the evening, this teacher read aloud from either an outdated newspaper or from his own treasured books.

After finishing the eighth grade, the children were sent away to attend high school. The girls (Olive and Frankie) were sent to stay with their Aunt "Kate" Butler in Helena. The boys were sent to stay with the

Story family in Bozeman.

Nelson Story was a friend of Bernier and a strong supporter of education, owning a Presbyterian Academy. He donated 40 acres of land and buildings for the campus of the now Montana State University of 1893. The citizens of Bozeman gave another 160 acres to the University. Mr. Story had bought out Bernier's land years before. This land became part and parcel of the University then called the College of Agriculture and Mechanics, which began regular classes on September 15, 1893. (Newton C. Abbott, *Montana in the Making*, Billings Gazette Pub. Co., Billings, MT, 1959. Pg. 417.)

Girls were eligible to attend "Normal" school at the age of sixteen to prepare to become teachers. Olive attended the "Normal" school in Dillon, Montana, for two years and Frankie also attended for some time.

Walt and Dick stayed home working the ranch or for other ranchers. The youngest son, Dan, went to Bozeman to attend school but later died unexpectedly in 1913. According to family lore, he died because he "grew too fast." He was well over six feet tall at this young age.

Mary Bernier became ill the same fall of Dan's death, and the local doctors were unable to help her. Bernier took her to the clinic in Rochester, Minnesota, for diagnosis. She had untreatable stomach cancer and died on the train trip returning home. She had lived to see her first grandchild born, however, Olive's first son, Richard LaRock.

Gilman, Montana, three months old.

Following Mary's death, Bernier continued ranching at Flat Creek, acquiring more land and speculating in various ventures. One of his ventures was the "Gilman State Bank," Gilman, Montana. Gilman was a town founded when the Great Northern Railway bypassed Augusta three

First train, Gilman, Montana.

miles away. Gilman became a small but booming town. The townsite company gave them a building site on the "best corner" in town on which to build the bank. The bank building was, and is, a solid brick building. Bernier was also an officer at the Bank.

Bernier, like many in the area, believed in the future of Gilman as he passed his homestead to his son, Walter, and he bought three houses in Gilman and put his life's savings into the bank (1901-1912).

"The Gilman State Bank closed on 28 November 1923, following a pattern experienced by many of the 214 banks in Montana that failed during the early years of the 1920's. (Jeffrey Cunniff, "The Gilman State Bank : Case Study of a Montana Bank Failure (1910-1923)," Master Thesis, University of Montana, 1971, pg. 31.)

The years following 1917 had been bad ones for Montana and particularly Montana ranchers. Beef prices were low and the drought was severe during this period. Bernier sold many of his holdings and cattle to satisfy the debts owed by the bank. He ended up with 320 acres of land and enough to live on. Another venture of his, which also went under as a result of the bank failure, was "The Great Northern Meat Packing Plant." This plant is located on the outskirts of East Helena, Montana. He had quite a lot of money invested in this plant. However, it stood derelict from 1921 to 1993 when the land on which the brick foundation stood was purchased by Lee and Patti Scott for their business "EH Rental." They planned to tear out this foundation only to discover that it was still structurally sound and so it is currently part of their building.

Following the bank failure, the Great Northern Railroad moved their lines into Augusta in 1923. May Benjamin Freisan (Bernier's granddaughter) remembers the bewilderment that she and her siblings felt as "Gilman" was moved "down the road" to Augusta. The business and residents of Gilman deserted the area leaving only the bank building on the main street.

"Bernier was undaunted, however, and he lived at his Gilman home, a pleasant place with cottonwood trees, a garden and a small pasture. In 1935 Bernier died in his own home at the age of eighty-five, by his own reckoning. His family later said he was probably older, but we still go by his own figures. He was a courageous old Frenchman, with a very sharp mind and wit. He was a great influence on his grandchildren. He told us always to go on with courage and to believe in yourself in spite of odds against you. He was a generous and loving grandfather who loved us and seldom criticized us." (Mary B. Freisen, *In the Shadow of the Rockies,* 1978, pg. 105-106.)

His daughter, Frankie Benjamin Risley, had lived near him during his last years and he enjoyed her and her family and the attention they gave him through his later years. He was buried in the Augusta cemetery next to Mary and their son Daniel. Also buried there is his son-in-law, George Benjamin, and a granddaughter, Baby Elizabeth Benjamin.

Oliver was a member of the "Society of Montana Pioneers." He was survived by his daughter, Frances and her children, William, Daniel, Louise, Ruth, Richard, and May Benjamin, and Eileen, Clyde, and Ann Risley; daughter Olive Bernier LaRock and her children, Richard, William, Frederick John, Louis, James, Claire, Elinor, Frances, and Ethel; his son, Walter and his children Frederick and William (Laddie); and son Richard and his children Arthur and Auriel Bernier. Two of his grandsons were killed in World War II. They were William (Laddie) Bernier and Richard LaRock.

Colonel Charles P.H. Bielenberg

Submitted by James P. Kovatch, Great-Great-Grandson

Charles Peter Henry Bielenberg was born in Wevelsfleth, a fishing village in the province of Holstein – at that time a possession of Denmark, now Germany, on May 1, 1846.

His mother, Gesche Krause Kohrs Bielenberg was widowed in 1835. Her husband at that time was Carston Kohrs, a distiller and brewer. He also owned a vinegar and oatmeal factory. Several children were born of this union including their youngest child, Carston Conrad Kohrs who was to become associated with his half brothers later in Montana Territory in the land and cattle business.

Gesche married Claus Bielenberg in 1844. Three more children were born of this union: twin brothers –John and Charles and Nicholas.

In July 1854, the Bielenberg family immigrated to the United States and settled in Davenport, Iowa. Gesche's older son, Henry, daughter Kate and her husband owned a store and sausage factory in Davenport. As a result, the three younger boys eventually worked in either the packing plant or store and learned the business.

On May 7, 1864, at the age of 18 Charles enlisted in the 44th Regt.

Infantry Iowa Volunteers. He was mustered into the U.S. Army at Davenport Iowa. At the end of his enlistment, September 15, 1864, he returned to Iowa. On January 21, 1865, he reenlisted. This time in the 8th Regt. Infantry Iowa Volunteers. He was deafened and taken ill during the bombardment of Mobile and the siege of Spanish Fort. In August 1865 he was hospitalized at Montgomery, Alabama from August-October and was sent back to Davenport to recuperate. He was honorably discharged on December 18, 1865.

Having recuperated from his war injuries enough to travel, he journeyed by riverboat to Montana Territory to join his brothers John and Nicholas and his half brother Conrad Kohrs who were already established in the cattle and ranching business. He had no money so had to walk from Fort Benton to Helena – arriving on June 10, 1866. He went on to Virginia

"Charlie" P.H. Bielenberg, born C.P.H. Bielenberg. Courtesy Montana Historical Society, Helena.

C.P.H. Bielenberg, G.A.R. State Patriotic Chairman. Courtesy Montana Historical Society, Helena.

City and then Deer Lodge, arriving in the fall of 1866 where he made his home.

He went into the butchering and meat cutting business and operated the City Market in Deer Lodge for 30 years. Nicholas and Conrad Kohrs were both partners in the market in the beginning. It is said that Charles furnished many free cowhides for floor coverings in miners shacks and cabins.

He was also in the cattle business with his twin brother John until John's death in 1922. The ranch was known as the Bielenberg and Brother.

Charles returned to Davenport for a visit in 1869. There he met and married Mary Wilhelmi of Herman, Missouri, in October 1869. They returned to Deer Lodge in December 1869 where they lived the rest of their lives. They had three children: Clara (Mrs. Warren Evans), Katherine (Mrs. Charles Childs) and son Charles Oscar Bielenberg. Mary died on February 11, 1887. Charles never remarried.

Clara, my great-grandmother, married Warren G. Evans (son of pioneers Luman F. Evans and Agnes Jeffery Evans – arriving in Helena in 1864). Warren G. Evans was the first County Clerk and Recorder for Powell County having been appointed in 1901, then elected in 1903 and served until 1914. Clara was her husband's deputy until 1914. She was then elected Public Administrator in 1916 and was owner and operator of Powell County Abstract Company until her death in 1950. They had four children: Agnes Mary, Charles Luke, Hugh Kirkendall (Booie) and Conrad Kohrs.

Hugh Kirkendall Evans (Booie) married Ethel E. Thompson in Deer Lodge on October 19, 1923. Hugh was elected to Powell County Clerk of the District Court in 1940. He died in office March 27, 1941. His wife Ethel was appointed to the office upon his death and was elected and reelected for six terms and served until 1966. They had three children Lois Elaine, Meryl Agnes (my mother) and Charles Warren.

Meryl Agnes Evans married Merle Steve Kovatch on June 26, 1949, and had two children, Thomas Steve and James Paul.

Charles Bielenberg was a very active member of the Grand Army of the Republic. He was known as "Colonel" Bielenberg and was appointed as G.A.R. "Patriotic Instructor" for the state of Montana. His position as patriotic instructor was a beloved duty for him. Having the financial means, he considered himself better able to bear the expenses of spreading the patriotic doctrine around the state than the Grand Army. He was well known throughout the state as an advocate of patriotic instruction to the public schools and presented hundreds of flags to schools and students along with instructions and importance of loyalty.

He led as many parades as possible on his horse Badger carrying the flag. Badger was trained to bow three times on the command "salute" when the flag passed. He also proudly walked in parades wearing his G.A.R. uniform and carrying the stars and stripes.

A room was set aside as the Patriotic Room in the Powell County Courthouse in his honor and the G.A.R. He furnished a grand piano (square Steinway) in the room for public use. The piano remained there until 1964 when the room was need for other purposes. His patriotism also was evident when he enlisted in Captain Stewart's Company No. 12, August 12-24, 1877, for the Nez Perce Indian uprising.

In an application for a Civil War pension he listed as distinguishing marks and scars as: scar on left fore arm from a bite by a pet bear.

Charles "Charlie" P.H. Bielenberg died on October 31, 1924.

Nicholas John (N.J.) Bielenberg

Submitted by Betty Newlon Hoffmann, Granddaughter

Nicholas John (N. J.) Bielenberg, born in Schleswig-Holstein, Germany on June 7, 1847, immigrated to the United States in 1854 with his brothers and parents, Claus and Margaret Bielenberg. They settled in Davenport, Iowa, where they engaged in farming.

Nick attended public schools, but his interest in practical things led him to learn the butchering trade in Davenport. When he was 16 years old, he went to Chicago where he served an apprenticeship through the winter of 1864. For his first month's work he was paid three dollars and given his board. He returned to Davenport and made plans to follow his brothers to Montana.

He arrived in Fort Benton, Montana, in the spring of 1865. He traveled up the Missouri River, which became a most memorable trip. From Davenport, Iowa, he took a riverboat to St. Louis, Missouri, and then took passage on the Bertrand up the Missouri, en route to Fort Benton. About 30 miles above Omaha, Nebraska, the boat sank, and although no lives were lost, they had to camp for 20 days on the riverbank while waiting for another boat of the same line. As they continued their trip, they were interrupted by a herd of buffalo crossing the river. This delayed them for an additional 18 hours.

Their next mishap occurred when they reached a point below the

Dry Fork of the Missouri. They struck a sand bar, and in the process of freeing the boat, broke a spar (a wooden or steel pole that may have been used in mooring a boat or in handling cargo). This delay was the most serious because they were attacked by Indians. When Nick saw the Indians approaching, he made certain his butchering tools were out of sight. The Indians killed one man, wounded another, and carried away two "whose lives were disposed in the most horrible manner." They were tied to a stake and burned alive in sight of the passengers on the boat.

They finally arrived in Fort Benton on June 18, 1865. While on the river trip to Montana, they heard of the close of the war when they passed one of the river forts.

Nicholas J. Bielenberg

Nick wanted to get to Helena, but when he landed, he had exactly 35 cents left – not enough to pay for the transport of his supply of butcher tools. The captain of the boat had grown fond of young Nick and when he heard of the dilemma, gave Nick clearance for his tools and directed the steward to supply him with the necessary provisions for the trip to Helena. A grateful Nick loaded his provisions on a mule wagon, walked along side, and arrived in Helena on July 1.

In Helena he learned of a butchering business for sale in Blackfoot City. Henry Edger, the discoverer of Alder Gulch, owned the business. Nick persuaded his two brothers Conrad Kohrs, who had settled in Deer Lodge in 1862, and John Bielenberg, who settled in 1864, to loan him the money. Nick's other brother Charles P.H. Bielenberg was to arrive later that fall in 1866.

Nick stayed at Blackfoot City until 1870. He then went to Deer Lodge where he was engaged in raising stock and buying cattle. He drove large numbers through to Cheyenne, Wyoming. The cattle were then shipped to the Chicago market.

His marriage on March 15, 1872, to Annie M. Bogk, daughter of Augustav and Margaret Bogk, proprietors of the McBurney House, a Deer Lodge landmark, is a story Nick told many times. He was working for Conrad Kohrs, his half brother, when he heard of a wedding to be held in Deer Lodge. His partner had worn the "company" party clothes and Nick had nothing but his work clothes. Not to be denied a party, he showed up with the festivities in full swing.

Annie M. (Bogk) Bielenberg

He saw a very pretty young girl and wanted to be introduced to her, but not in his work clothes. Nick found his partner, Harvey McKinstry, and after much pleading, convinced him to trade clothes just long enough to be introduced to this beautiful girl and try to get a dance with her. He was successful, and after their dance persuaded her to have supper with him. While Nick was having such a grand time, McKinstry was fuming in the background and trying to catch Nick's eye — but with no luck.

Finally, McKinstry sent a note to Nick saying, "You damn horse thief, if you don't come out here with my clothes, I'll help Con Kohrs hang you!" Nick loved to tell that story, and always ended with, "I ran the risk of getting hung to get my wife."

By 1877 Nick established a large meat business in Butte, erecting a cold storage plant. With an extensive wholesale trade, it became one of the foremost businesses of its kind in the Northwest. It later became the Butte Butchering Company.

In 1884 he joined Conrad and they engaged in an extensive cattle business. Nick had herds in the Deer Lodge Valley, and also the Big Hole Valley, in southwestern Montana. The Great Falls Tribune, March 14, 1965, recounts "Nick Bielenberg was the first white man to bring livestock into the valley for fattening, on Christmas Day 1883. Not long after Bielenberg's cattle proved the nutritional wealth of the Big Hole Valley grasses, other men began moving in stock."

Later Nick, with Joseph Toomey, became interested in an enterprise of immense proportions, especially for the time. They handled more than 130,000 head of sheep in one year. Nick was the first shipper to discover the value of "screening" in the feeding of sheep in transit. (Screening was a process used to remove unwanted material from the feed.) This proved to be very valuable when shipping the animals to the eastern markets. He and his associates were considered the fathers of the sheep industry in northern Montana.

McBurney Hotel, Deer Lodge, Montana – circa 1904. Seated in buggy at left: Arthur Menard and Fred Wildman. Standing left to right: Lee Davis, Peter Peyter, Abe Hoss, Col. McTague, Dr. F. B. Hall, Bud Brown, Henry Tramont, Unknown, Unknown, Henry Hertz, Nels Dumischel, William Courtois, boy unknown, Earl Stuart, Henry Wildman (white coat). Seated left to right: William Furay and David Upton. Seated in buggy at right: Mr. and Mrs. Aylesworth, proprietors of the hotel.

Mining was yet another of his many interests. He was president of the Champion Mining Company, vice president of the Deer Lodge Mining and Reduction Company (his brothers Conrad Kohrs, and John Bielenberg were presidents of the same company), director of the Potomac Copper Company, and vice president and director of the Tuolumme Mining Company. One of his principal interests was the Bear Gulch Mining Corporation, which operated a gold mine 14 miles from Twin Bridges, Montana. Nick's son-in-law, W. I. Higgins, was a partner, and the mine was known as the B and H mine. They built a 12-mile, 50,000-volt transmission line to the mine, making it one of the first mines in the country to be electrically operated.

Nick took an active part in the development of the city of Deer Lodge. He was one of the founders of the Citizens Water Company in January 1900. He had water rights on Cottonwood Creek dating back to September 1865. He contributed funds for the completion of the Deer Lodge Chapter House of the American Womens' League, which became the Deer Lodge Woman's Club, as a memorial to his daughter Augusta Kohrs Bielenberg. She had passed away in 1901 at 21 years of age. Augusta and her sister, Anne were attending a finishing school in Boston, Massachusetts, when she became ill with typhoid fever.

Nick's commitment to the development of the area was not just

Nicholas J. Bielenberg with horse and car at Deer Lodge Fairgrounds – circa 1920.

through his business, mining, and ranching ventures. He was also involved in the building of the Deer Lodge Hotel, which was incorporated in 1911, and a three-story brick, stone, and cast iron structure in Butte known as the Henderson and Bielenberg building. He built two lovely homes in Deer Lodge, and a summer home — one of the first at Rock Creek Lake — where he had a patented mining claim.

Among the prominent citizens of Montana who visited the Bielenberg home were Granville Stuart, Reverend William Wesley Van Orsdel, known as "Brother Van," artist Edgar S. Paxson, Jeannette Rankin, Charlie Russell's wife Nancy, and Gary Cooper.

An active Republican, Nick was a delegate in 1892 to the National Convention in Minneapolis, and in August of 1912, was a delegate to the National Progressive Convention in Chicago. The latter was the convention that nominated Theodore Roosevelt for president on the Bull Moose Party. Nick was a friend and confidant of Roosevelt's.

In the famous "Smoke Case" (Fred J. Bliss vs. The Washoe Copper Company and the Anaconda Copper Mining Company – May 5, 1905, to April 26, 1909) concerning the stack at the Anaconda smelter, Nick was the leader in the fight of the farmers and ranchers in the Deer Lodge valley. This was against the powerful interests of the famous Copper Kings.

Nick belonged to a number of organizations: Society of Montana Pioneers, Montana Stockgrowers Association, the Butte Silver Bow Club, the Elks Lodge, Deer Lodge No. 14, A.F.& A.M., Valley Chapter No. 4, Royal Arch Masons, Charter member of Ivanhoe Commandery No. 16, Knights Templar and Ancient Order of the Mystic Shrine.

Nick and Annie Bielenberg were the parents of five children, all of whom were born in Deer Lodge: Alma Margaret, 1874-1962; Howard Zenor, 1876-1953; Augusta Kohrs, 1880-1901; Anne Marie, 1883-1960; and Claude, 1888-1955. Nick's wife Annie died in 1918 while visiting in California, and Nick died at his home in Deer Lodge in 1927, at 80 years of age.

It is very evident that Nick's interests and activities were varied and extensive. He lived not only to see Montana take her place among the great western states, but he helped in great measure to contribute to that transformation.

His motto was: "Do right by all and fear no one."

Moritz Bien Family

Submitted by Mary M. McKain, Great-Granddaughter, and Dorothy Taylor, Great-Granddaughter

Moritz Emanuel Bien was born on December 24, 1830, at Naumberg, Hessen, Germany, which was then Prussia, and attended school until 14 years of age. He was trained in the harness making, saddlery, and upholstery business at Cigenhaug. After working three and one half years, he traveled as a journeyman for five years throughout Germany.

Moritz and two of his brothers came to the United States in 1852. They had followed their older brother Julius, who became a famous lithographer in New York, printing most of the early maps of the United States. Moritz worked at his trade in New York for three years and then left for San Francisco where his sister, Hanchen Hamburger, lived. He opened a furniture store with a Mr. Goldberg in San Francisco (from 1852-1855). It was during this time that he met his future wife, Johanna von Boehl, who had come to work as a governess for his sister and her husband, Asher and Hanchen Hamburger. Asher Hamburger had started the popular "People's Store" in San Francisco, but Moritz wasn't interested in that. He sold out his interest in the furniture store he had with Mr. Goldberg and went to Virginia City, Nevada, where brother Herman was attempting to start a German newspaper. He worked as a furniture factory foreman there for another until 1864.

Johanna Maria von Boehl was born in Marne, Germany, and immigrated to the United States at the age of 11 with her parents who settled in Davenport, Iowa. She was trained to be an assayer, but had not found work in her trade so she went to visit her sister Margretha Fischer in the San Francisco area in 1860. It was in San Francisco that she found work as a governess working for the Hamburger family and met her future husband, Moritz Bien, brother of Mrs. Hamburger.

After Moritz and Johanna were married in Virginia City on December 30, 1864, their next destination was Alder Gulch where they stayed for four months before going to Helena, Ophir, and Blackfoot City. Johanna baked pies for the miners and sold them for $1.00 a pie. She was well liked by the miners and by Sheriff Plummer. Although she was only 4'11," weighting about 75 pounds with a size two shoe, the miners brought her their gold for safekeeping. Sheriff Plummer protected and respected her, and she was never robbed.

In Blackfoot City, their first child, Frank, was born in 1867. In

1869 another son, Julius, was born in Blackfoot. Moritz started a restaurant in Blackfoot City and after a short time, sold it. He had discovered some time before that selling businesses was often more profitable than operating them. Washington Gulch was the next move, where he started another restaurant until fall, sold it and went to Helena. In Helena he opened a harness shop, kept it for a few months, sold it, and went back to Blackfoot where son Albert was born in 1870. He had a brewery, sold it, and moved to Deer Lodge, Montana.

Moritz Bien

In Deer Lodge, Moritz went into the brewery business again with a Mr. Whaley. He operated that for about a year before it burned. Leopold F. Schmidt, a German carpenter who helped build the Zosel Ranch house in Deer Lodge, learned the brewing business with Bien and Whaley. Schmidt later founded the Capital Brewing Company in Tumwater. He was a member of the state's committee to plan a capital building and had gone to Washington State to look at the capitol's architecture. He found an interesting artesian spring on the bank of the Deschutes River. He later called it the Olympia Brewery. Bien rebuilt the Deer Lodge brewery and operated it for another year before he opened a furniture store and mortuary.

Moritz and Johanna's daughter, Anna, was born in Deer Lodge in 1872. Clara joined the family in 1876. Now the father of five children, Moritz decided it had better be his last move. He stayed with these businesses until he retired due to illness.

Moritz was present at the driving of the Golden Spike in Garrison. Souvenirs of that event, a tiny silver figure and a little brown jug, are still in the possession of a family member.

Souvenirs given to Moritz Bien at driving of the spike for the Northern Pacific on September 8, 1883, at the mouth of Independence Gulch near Gold Creek, Montana, linking the first transcontinental railroad through Montana.

Moritz' son, Albert, became a partner with his father in the businesses. Johanna and Moritz were hard working and contributed to any community they lived in. Moritz joined the I.O.O.F. Lodge and became active in it and other business and civic organizations. He and Johanna were original members of the Society of Montana Pioneers. Moritz died on September 3, 1909. Funeral services were held at the family residence under the auspices of the I.O.O.F. Lodge, conducted by a Presbyterian minister, although by nationality Moritz was Jewish. He didn't follow the religion in spite of having a rabbi father. Johanna was Lutheran and raised the children in the Christian faith.

After Moritz' death, Johanna downsized the furniture store in Deer Lodge into a dry goods store, selling candy and household wares. The many people who came to purchase items from her store affectionately knew her as "Grandma Bien." Next she opened the Franklin 5 & 10 Cent store (May Applegate of Deer Lodge still has a plate from "Grandma's" store). Johanna died on November 13, 1923, after a gall bladder operation.

Both Moritz and Johanna were insistent that the children be educated. Frank was educated at Deer Lodge but studied higher education in Davenport, Iowa. On return to Montana, he was a bookkeeper and then postmaster at Gibbonsville, Idaho. He became ill and returned to Deer Lodge and worked with his father and brother until his death in 1901.

Julius worked at the prison for a while and then followed the call of the gold rush, dying mysteriously on the Salmon River while mining. His body was never found.

Albert studied at Trask Hall at the college in Deer Lodge. He stayed in the area, helping his father with the businesses. He married Clara Wilson of Deer Lodge, was county coroner twice, then county treasurer, Justice of the Peace, county commissioner and held office in the Grand I.O.O.F. Lodge. He also was plagued by fire, which often happened from the various fuels, open flame and combustion that were used in the business. At 6:00 p.m. on December 18, 1924, the mortuary burned. Bodies were taken to the lower floor of the courthouse. A prisoner housed in the jail and assigned to clean the courthouse, was unaware of what was housed there and entered the coroner's office. One of the bodies that had been placed there, after exposure to heat and then cold, had contracted assuming a near sitting position. The prisoner terrified fled the building and the county. He was never found again. The story appeared in the December 18 issue of the *Silver State Post*.

Johanna Maria (von Boehl) Bien

Anna studied music at Trask Hall in the college of Deer Lodge and then went to Bozeman when the college moved there. She graduated with a degree in natural science and botany. She wanted to be a mining engineer,

Bien Brewery – 1871.

but for ladies of that day, it was out of the question. She was allowed to take classes at the college in Butte but had to forget engineering. She married Denis O'Halloran from Bozeman, moved to Garrison, and then to Spokane.

Clara studied at Montana State College and became a teacher. Her first school was at Avon. She married Ben Jordan and taught in Spokane, later moving to Santa Barbara, California.

Moritz, Johanna, Frank, Albert and Albert's wife Clara, Albert's daughter Elinor and her husband, Neil McKain, are buried in Hillcrest Cemetery in Deer Lodge, Montana. More information regarding the Bien Family can be found in the *History of Montana 1739-1885* printed in 1885 by Warner & Beers Co. and many articles throughout the years printed in the *Silver State* newspaper in Deer Lodge.

George Alexander Bruffey

Submitted by Alberta G. Titus, Great-Granddaughter

George Alexander Bruffey arrived in Alder Gulch in 1863, at the age of 21. He was born September 24, 1842, in Pocahontas County, Virginia (now West Virginia), the sixth child (there were later ten children in the family) of John and Elizabeth (Call) Bruffey. When he was two years old, the family moved by wagon to Missouri where his father worked as a wagon maker. Three years later they moved to Knoxville, Iowa, where they farmed and ran a wayside house (a stop on a stage line for resting, watering and feeding the horses). George attended school in Knoxville, helped with the farm, and saw many wagon trains heading west.

He headed west himself when he was 18, spent a couple of years working in western Iowa, and then in 1862 drove some work oxen to Omaha where he remained until 1863. He again headed west to Denver and remained there making bricks until September 3, 1863, when he again joined a train of about 50 wagons headed for the Salmon River country along the Oregon Trail. Because the Civil War was in progress, when travelers reached Wyoming they were required to sign an oath of allegiance to the Union (United States), as George's group was required to do. They met some men from Alder Creek and Bannack, and decided to take another train that led to Nevada, a new town about a mile below Virginia City. They arrived there on November 12, 1863.

Bruffey witnessed the hanging of George Ives, and five other men, soon after he arrived. He mined several claims in the area, found some gold, but no great amounts.

George A. Bruffey

In August 1864 he and another man left for the Yellowstone country after hearing tales of gold and spouting volcanoes of water. After leaving Gardiner on their way to Yellowstone Lake, Bruffey and his partner met a mountain trapper who described the "water volcanoes" and other dangers of the country. Due to the uncertainties of the route and fearful of being led into an ambush by the trapper, Bruffey's party returned North through the Yellowstone River's Paradise Valley.

After more discouraging prospecting, George relocated in the

Jefferson Valley in 1866. He farmed for about a year and then went into partnership making cheese. He was quite successful in selling cheese, butter, and other goods.

He returned to Iowa in December 1870 to visit his family, whom he had not seen since heading west. It took nine days to travel from Fish Creek to Corinne, Utah, where the Union Pacific Railroad connected with the freight road from Montana. While in Iowa, he renewed his acquaintance with Matilda Jane Ridlen. He knew Matilda from his childhood. They were married in Attica, Iowa, on February 12, 1871.

Matilda Jane (Ridlen) Bruffey

In April they returned to Fish Creek taking the Union Pacific train to Corinne. Bruffey and his new wife traveled from Corinne to Fish Creek by horse drawn wagon with a ". . . supply of household goods and bedding, a fair supply of clothing and a cook stove." The trip took fourteen days and they encountered severe storms along the way. After settling in a cabin and plowing land for a garden, George took to the road again selling supplies. When fall came, he was building fences in Fish Creek, and November 24, 1871, their first child, Margera, was born. That day started an extremely bad winter, but they had banked (insulated) their cottonwood log home, daubed it with mud (closing up the chinks between the logs with a combination of mud and grass or straw), and lined it with muslin purchased in Deer Lodge. They had enough food on hand to survive the vicious winter.

George's business did well the next few years. He enlarged the store, the Fish Creek Post Office moved in, and he became the postmaster. His business became known as the Gilman and Salsbury Stage Station. He was appointed sergeant-at-arms in the legislature in 1873 In 1875 he was station keeper for the Jefferson Line at Fish Creek. The stage drivers had to make trips of 100 miles in 24 hours. They carried all the news, local and national, to the sellers along their routes. When asked how they knew something they said "dope telegraph", referring to the news they exchanged among themselves as they greased or "doped" their wagon axles at the stage stations.

In 1876 new bridges had been built as well as schools in Jefferson and Silver Star. The population was growing. On July 4th they had a big celebration with fiddling and dancing to observe the 100th birthday of the nation. In the following years, although the stage business was gone with the coming of the railroad, George's farming and stock raising were good, and he built another new home. He attended the driving of the spike on the Northern Pacific Railroad in 1883, and in 1884 was invited to the first Pioneer meeting in Helena, where they organized the Pioneer Society with

George A. Bruffey family – circa 1900. Back row: Memorus, Lora Beckman, Primus, Almeda Skillman, Emma Singleton. Middle row: Fatima Skillman, Margera Cady, Sylvia Gravelly, George A., Matilda J. Front row: George Minot, Elzinia Gravelly, Ruth.

James Fergus as president.

The fall of 1886 was dry and the winter was extremely hard. Much of the stock died. The next couple of years were dry also, prices were down, and Bruffey lost money on the sale of his horses. He had to sell his merchandise at a loss and was essentially broke. He bought a ranch on the West Boulder in 1888, and built a ranch house. He sold the West Boulder ranch in December 1890, and moved to Mission Creek in Park County. His daughter Margera, age 18; son Primus, age 16; and a younger daughter Sylvia, herded about 100 head of cattle from Fish Creek to Mission Creek. They spent the night at Fort Ellis. Margera, Primus, and Sylvia kept house for their father at the Mission Creek ranch while their mother and the rest of the family remained in Fish Creek.

By December 1891 they had cleared the land of brush, built a house, and his wife and remaining children joined them from Fish Creek. They had a dairy herd of twenty cows, cut and hauled wood to town, and were able to raise enough food to have a good living. The youngest daughter, Ruth, was born in 1893.

In the following years, they bought and operated a sawmill, built a good 10-room house, painted and plastered, built several cabins, put in an irrigation system, and planted an orchard. He was elected as a representative to the State Legislature in 1896. Ruth, the youngest daughter, was killed by

Fish Creek Post Office and Stage Station, Madison County, near Jefferson Bridge. Residence of G. A. Bruffey 1868-1890. Photo taken 1880.

a bull at age 12, and was buried across the creek from the house on land which later became a family cemetery. Their farming and stock raising did well. But after Mrs. Bruffey died on March 2, 1911, George and two of his daughters tried unsuccessfully to remain on the ranch. The daughters married and he lived with different members of the family. He remained alert and well in his later years, and in 1926 wrote *Eighty-one Years in the West*, which is the story of his life in Montana. George Bruffey died in Livingston on October 27, 1928, after a fall.

There were eleven children in the family: Margera, 1871; Almeda, 1873; Primus, 1874; Sylvia, 1876; Fatima, 1878; Memorus, 1880; Emma, 1882; Lora, 1884; George Minot, 1886; Elzinia, 1888; and Ruth, 1893.

Mr. Bruffey took "63" – ☽ – as a brand for his cattle and the ranch later became a part of the 63 Dude or Guest Ranch. It was named in the National Register of Historic Places. The old ranch house burned and was replaced, but for many years, some of the old apple trees were still there and the big old lilac bushes Mrs. Bruffey planted still blossomed.

He attended many of the Pioneer Society and Sons and Daughters of Montana Pioneers meetings. He was a vice president from Madison County in 1886, and from Park County in 1896, 1897, and 1898. I attended the meetings with him and my grandmother, Margera (Bruffey) Cady in Missoula in 1927.

He was a true pioneer who contributed much to the settling of Montana, as was his wife. In his book he refers to her as, "the companion of over forty years. . .and our guidon light."

Alexander F. Burns

Submitted by Jerry K. Burns

Alexander F. Burns was born in Clay County, Missouri, December 7, 1832. His Scottish Irish ancestors came to this country and settled in Virginia previous to the revolutionary war. His grandfather was a soldier in that war. Alexander F. Burns was the fifth born in his father's family and was reared to manhood in Missouri. In 1850, he crossed the plains to California and for two years was engaged in mining in Calaveras County. He was somewhat successful. Following his mining experience, he spent one year in agricultural pursuits in California, after which he returned to Missouri through what is now the Panama Canal.

For three years he was employed as a clerk in the store of Conrad and Clark in Missouri. This was later to become the well-known merchants of the Helena members of the firm of Clark, Conrad and Curten. A. F. Burns' next venture was in Nodaway County, Missouri, where he opened a store on his own account and which he conducted until the outbreak of the Civil War.

Alexander F. Burns

In August, 1861, he enlisted in Company H, First Missouri, Volunteer Calvary, for the Confederate service. With his command, he was on duty through Missouri, Arkansas, Mississippi, Alabama, Georgia, and Tennessee, and remained in the service until the close of the war. He participated in the battles of Lexington, Pea Ridge, Corinth, Vicksburg, and in all the campaign against Sherman through Georgia. On November 30, 1864, he was captured at Franklin, Tennessee, and spent the remainder of the war as a prisoner on Johnson Island. On several occasions he was slightly wounded, and at the battle of Atlanta was shot in the foot. From the rank of private he was promoted from time to time, and became a captain of his company. Like so many others he returned home to find his store and house destroyed.

In 1866, he crossed the plains with his family to Montana on the Bozeman Trail. He made the journey by ox team and in the company of a small group of immigrants. At Fort Reno on the Powder River, Indians attacked them. They lost two of their party and some livestock. The next year the Bozeman trail was closed because of the Indian wars.

The family's first winter in Montana was at Gallatin City, and in

1868 they filed a homestead in the Prickly Pear Valley, which was located near what is now the Warren School. Alexander then sold the land and settled on a farm that is near East Helena, before East Helena was even there. The family home still stands and is presently occupied.

William Kinnison Burns, President of Society of Montana Pioneers – 1947.

Alexander was elected to and served as a member of the first Montana State Constitutional Convention that helped in making Montana a state. He was also elected a member of the first Legislative Assembly. He was married October 1, 1857, to Miss Ann E. Kinnison, a native of Virginia and the daughter of David Kinnison, a doctor. This union produced eight children. The oldest son, Edward B. Burns, was an early member of the Montana Pioneers. The other children were Cora Burns, Jeremiah Burns, William K. Burns, Albert A. Burns, Carrie E. Burns, Annie V. Burns, and Medora Burns.

Alexander F. Burns died in East Helena on the 27th day of May, 1908. He and his wife, Ann, are both buried in the Forestvale Cemetery in Helena, Montana.

William Kinnison Burns, a son of A. F. Burns, was born in the Prickly Valley November 7, 1868. He was raised in the area and engaged in mining and ranching. When Rainbow Dam was being built he was employed as a blacksmith, a trade he learned in East Helena. In 1914 William Kinnison Burns married Marie Mestdagh. To this union was born Alexander K. Burns and William L. Burns. William K. Burns joined the

Society of Montana Pioneers in 1943, and was elected president in 1947. He lived at Rainbow Dam, Montana, for 50 years, retired in 1949, and passed away in 1955.

Jonas and Louanna Butts

Submitted by Terry Aileen (Tuttle) Maple, Great-Great-Granddaughter

Jonas and Louanna (Gist) Butts were married at the Gist home near Kansas City, Missouri in 1847. Children born to Jonas and Louanna in Missouri were Sara Ann (1851), Arminda Ellen (1858) and Derinda born January 18, 1855. Jonas and Louanna also had a son that died at birth and was buried at Independence, Missouri.

The family crossed the plains in a wagon train from Independence, Missouri, to Denver, Colorado, in 1863. "Roughing it," meant there were no roads most of the time. Only a few miles were traveled each day, rivers were often flooded, there was an every present danger of Indian attacks and routes had to be found through mountain ranges. However, the children considered this trip more or less of a lark as they did not have any luxuries and accepted things as they were. They played and had a good time whenever they could. It took a great deal of courage and determination to even start such a trip.

The Butts family arrived in Denver in late fall of 1863, remaining there over the winter and then traveled on to Virginia City, Montana, in the spring of 1864. They managed to find cabins to stay in both Denver and Virginia City, but many of the cabins had been hastily built and would be regarded as uninhabitable by today's standards. During rainy days there were many leaks and drops of water fell on the hot stove – sizzling and hissing. The rain also fell on the bed that had to be covered with canvas. The childrens' beds were built low so they could be shoved under the big beds during the day. Sometimes it was difficult to find a place for their table and chairs at mealtime as buckets, pans and tubs were set everywhere to catch the leaks.

Rumors of gold in Helena drew them into that camp. Jonas's brother Wilson Butts had moved to Helena the year before and had a one-room, dirt-floor cabin. The two men expanded the cabin and added another room and porch as well as a wood floor. The new room, known as the front room, had a full-size window instead of a half-size window that was common at the time. The girls were very proud of their big window as no one else in Last Chance Gulch had such a window. Later the porch was enclosed and used as an entrance to the house. This house is known today as the Pioneer Cabin and sets near the Federal Building on Last Chance Gulch in Helena, Montana.

After a year or two, a "Hurdy Gurdy" house was built across the gulch. The music and voices raised in song or in fighting were plainly heard. The coming and going of rough and drunk men and 'painted' women was a common sight. Jonas and Louanna felt that this was no place to raise their girls, so they sold their house to the Gilpatricks and moved to Dry Gulch near Unionville. Their luck in gold mining was not sufficient to hold them in Unionville, so they traded their mining property for farm property on Fish Creek. Jonas and Wilson farmed until Jonas died June 15, 1873, of 'consumption'. Louanna died February 3, 1884 – both Jonas and Louanna were buried at Fish Creek.

During the period before Jonas died, the Butts family milked cows and made and sold butter and cottage cheese. They evidently made quite a quantity of butter as they traveled to Helena by horse and wagon or with oxen to sell their product. At one time, their butter sold for $2.20 a pound. They kept the butter sweet by storing it in big stone crocks covering them with salt and keeping them in cool cellars. Derinda, then in her teens, loved to make the 3 to 4 day trip to Helena with her father or uncle. The trip, 75 miles over 2 mountain ranges, gave her the opportunity to visit with friends and a change from everyday monotony. The last night of the trip to Helena, they would camp at Montana City. There Derinda worked the butter and molded it into one and two pound molds so it would be easy to handle and sell. When the weather was warm, the cool mountain stream furnished water for rinsing and a cool temperature for the butter to set into shape. They would resume their journey into Helena in the wee hours of the morning so the butter could be delivered before it got too warm.

The Butts girls, like others, learned to do everything on the farm – hitch up and drive a team, saddle a horse and ride side saddle, milk the cows and tend the garden. Of course, their first chores were housekeeping and sewing. Rough board floors were scrubbed clean, often using homemade lye. Dresses were sewn by hand as it was a long time before they had a treadle sewing machine. At the time, an average woman's wardrobe consisted of one good dress, a second dress as well as one or two calico house dresses known at the time as 'wrappers'. Included in the wardrobe were two or three aprons and underwear.

Aprons were very important, as washing and ironing was a big job. Water had to be carried and heated in a boiler and the clothes were rubbed on washboards in a tub. Ironing was done with the old "sad irons". There were no dry goods stores so material was mail ordered from Denver or San Francisco. Sometimes it took months for an order to arrive. Occasionally a peddler would come by with dry goods and 'notions'. If there was any extra money (which was seldom), a little extra 'pretty' like beads or ribbons might be purchased.

Daily baths were not common nor were shampoos frequent. Two or three months went by in winter between shampoos but the girls combed and brushed their hair vigorously every day. The combs were especially fine to bring out any lint or dust. Corn meal and salt were rubbed on the scalp and combed through the hair. Derinda had beautiful, straight, heavy long hair that came to her knees.

Girls, greatly outnumbered by men, were wooed and won at an early age. Derinda had her share of beaus but at 17 she had one steady boyfriend, Harve Tuttle. After going with him for several months, she met his younger brother, Sherman, who she thought was a rather amusing fellow at first. However, he persevered and their friendship grew rapidly. Sherman and Derinda were married at Fish Creek March 16, 1873. It was a double wedding that included Celesta Jordan, a niece of Sherman, and Wes McCall. The two girls made their wedding dresses alike from gray silk sent for from San Francisco.

The congregation at church the Sunday of the wedding was prepared to see Celesta and Wes march down the aisle after the regular service, but were very surprised to see the two couples in a double wedding. Sherman and Derinda were delighted they had been able to keep their marriage a secret.

Derinda took pride in her cooking and learned early to serve delicious meals out of the plainest of materials. The old knotty boards on her floor were scrubbed so white that Brother Van Orsdale, circuit minister, once told her that he would rather eat off her floor than on some of the tables where he ate.

Sherman and Derinda's cabin was on the main road and a logical stopping place for travelers. They began to keep travelers for the noon meal as it was about halfway between Virginia City and Old Whitehall and even had some stay overnight although the accommodations were not much to brag about. Most travelers were so tired they didn't object to bedding down in the hayloft – a common practice at the time. On one occasion, Derinda got up 9 days after giving birth to prepare a meal for 14 men. She made pies, puddings, sauces and prepared vegetables from her garden. Her custard pies were delicious and well know to the regular visitors.

Sherman and Derinda had 11 children – seven sons, three daughters and one baby that died at 9 months (sex unknown). Following Sherman's death, Derinda remained in the family home for a while taking in teachers for board. This soon became too much work so the home was sold and she divided her time between the daughters Lulu and Ada. She also journeyed to California to visit her other daughter Cora and sons Sherman and Errett.

At 80, having traveled by horse and wagon, car and train, Derinda wished she could take an airplane trip as she still had her spirit of adventure – but she did not realize this final wish. She died August 26, 1936, and is buried in the Fish Creek Cemetery alongside her husband, Sherman. Her two children who died, the baby and a 13-year-old son, are also buried there with many other family members.

Derinda related much of her history to grandson, Ferson Earl Tuttle, who related it to Roy Millegan of Whitehall, Montana, as he had considerable contact with the grandparents before their deaths. I am indebted to Mr. Millegan for compiling this history and for his gracious permission to share it in this pioneer tribute.

John Byrd

Submitted by Colleen Claire Porter

As new lands opened in the West, John Byrd, like many younger sons of prominent eastern and southeastern families, moved to Smithville, Platte County, Missouri. John Byrd was born January 27, 1826, in the Shenandoah County of Virginia, the son of William and Mary (Polly) Shafer (Schaeffer) Byrd.

John Byrd married Emeline Owens, daughter of John and Lydia (Norris) Owens on May 30, 1848. John became a prosperous farmer and the father of seven children: William (1853-1854), Alfred (1854-1855), Henry (1849-1923), Rose (1856-1878), Clara (Light) (1860-1884), Alexander Marshall Robinson (Uncle Robin) (1858-1933) and John Byrd, Jr. (1862-1929).

At the outbreak of the Civil War, John joined General Sterling Price and fought for the Confederacy as a Major. The family legend has it that at the end of the war the soldiers, realizing they were fighting for a lost cause, began returning to their homes. John returned to his home after his last battle to find that the crops were gone, the slaves had disappeared, and everything was in disarray. Fearful that he would be found and either hung as a deserter, or shot as a Southern sympathizer (depending upon who discovered him) Emeline hid him in the cornfields until she could smuggle a horse to him, so he could retrieve the family savings buried in the cornfields and leave. He then fled heading for Denver, Colorado, where he was to meet Oscar A. Robertson who had been a Sergeant and his aide during their Army days. From there they planned to make their way to Pike's Peak, Colorado, in hopes of striking it rich in the goldfields.

John Byrd as a young man.

As prearranged, John met Oscar Robertson and they wintered in the area hunting buffalo. About the time they were to leave, gold had been discovered in California so the two of them left for the goldfields, taking a team of oxen with them. They crossed the Mississippi River near St. Joseph, Missouri, on May 10 and arrived in Houghton, California, on September 26, 1863, where John went into the freighting business and carried ore and supplies from Sonora to nearby mining towns. He also bought cattle in Mexico and sold them in San Francisco. In the spring of 1864, John and Robertson headed north for the goldfields in Alder Gulch when gold was discovered there. They mined awhile before going to New York Gulch (later shortened to "York"). While at Alder Gulch, he wrote to Emeline and instructed her to sell their possessions, hire a driver, join a wagon train, and meet him at New York Gulch.

Emeline sold everything in Missouri and joined John at New York Gulch in 1866. The trip was uneventful and very few Indians were seen.

Emeline acted as their interpreter for what few Indians they did encounter, using skills gained after spending much time among the Indians while in her youth as her father was an Indian Agent. The two older boys, Henry and Robin, rode along the wagons in the tree lines as guards and scouts. Both were expert riflemen and practiced that profession when riding with Deputy Marshall Steele and others during later years. Indians constantly watched the train. At one point, anyone venturing from the wagon train even to get water was shot at by Indians directing arrows at them from an island in the middle of the river across from the camp. Emeline had several head of cattle with her when joining the train. After milking the cows in the morning, the churn was placed on the back of the wagon and the sway of the wagon churned butter for them as they traveled during the day. They were one of the few families with a supply of fresh milk and butter. They spent their first winter in 1866-67 on a ranch in the Canton Valley. The following spring, they moved to Jimtown and then to New York Gulch where they resided on Soup Creek. After the arrival of Emeline at New York Gulch, two more children were born, Joseph E. (1866-1892) and Mary Magdeline ("Aunt Molly" 1870-1963).

New York Gulch was a thriving little town, but once the mines began to give out and miners began to move on, it settled down into a little community of ranchers and a few trappers and miners that refused to give up.

The chief entertainment for the citizens of the community was dances held in the schoolhouse. Everyone came from miles around bringing contributions to the potluck that would be served in the latter part of the evening. John Cotter brought out his fiddle and the families would dance the night away, only taking time out for the potluck dinner and sharing of the news of the Valley.

Gold was as evasive for John in New York Gulch as it had been elsewhere. Water was necessary to work the claims. The miners constructed a flue that would carry water from the mouth of the Missouri to the claims below. As miners working on the flue came to their own claims, they would drop out of the construction process and begin working their claims. Many miners had dropped off and the number of men working on erection of the flue declined. Out of exasperation, a miner working next to John announced that, at the rate they were dropping off, he would never reach his own claim and that he would sell it for $100.00 to anyone who would give him the money. John Byrd did just that and acquired his claim.

John's oldest sons, Robin and Henry, were trappers, miners, and ranchers whose cattle grazed the up and down the entire York Valley. Both were well known for their expertise with a rifle. Robin was such a good shot that he was banned from shooting more than one turkey at the annual St. Joseph Orphanage Turkey Shoot.

Emeline's had a brother, by the name of Sanford Owens, who was an official on one of the first railroad lines that came into Montana. He came from the East to visit the family in his private car and tried to convince Emeline to take the children and return home for a visit. She refused, saying that she would not go home until she could go back with money in her pocket and nice clothes, in other words, in the same status she as when she left. He left her a lifetime railroad pass so that she could return home, and she never went.

Neither Henry nor Robin married. They continued trapping,

John Byrd at York, Montana, in later years.

mining and raising cattle and established herds for their nieces and helped the family whenever they could. Henry died of natural causes on March 18, 1923, in one of the worst winters they had ever experienced in Millegan, Montana, and is buried about halfway up the hill behind the schoolhouse. No marker is on his grave. Robin died on June 1, 1933, from burns he received when he fell into a campfire while trapping near Three Forks, Montana. He was hospitalized in Bozeman, Montana, and is buried there as well.

Rose Byrd married Oscar A. Robertson in 1872, and the couple had two sons, Oscar Duncan Robertson (1872-1964) who married Maude Braddock, and had John Duncan, Leslie David, Robert Theodore, Winifred Louise, Sidney Woodrow, and twins Geneva Miltie and Gene Marion; and John (Uncle Byrd) Robertson (1874-1963), who married Bessie Millegan, and they had Donald Joseph, Oscar Reuben, John Byrd, Madeline Rose, Bessie Marie, Mary B., Helen G., and Cora M., all well-known in the Helena area.

Clara (Light) Byrd (1860-1884), who gained the nickname "Light" as a child because she was very petite and moved so quickly, married James L. Bompart and lived on Duck Creek, near Canton, Montana. Their daughter, Clara (1884-1953), was born here. She married Fred R. Brewer in Helena in 1903 and they had Doris Evelyn, Kenneth L., Fred Richard, Jr., and Lawrence Mayo.

John Byrd, Jr. (1862-1929) married Ina Kincaid in 1890 and had seven children: Hazel Rose, Lyle, Emeline Louise, Nellie Grace, Violet, John Henry, and William Jewel. All the children were born in York, Helena, or Stockett, Montana. John and Ina's marriage ended in divorce. John died in Great Falls, Montana, in 1929 and is buried there.

Mary Magdeline Byrd (1870-1963) married Charles Cochran in Helena at the Cosmopolitan Hotel in August of 1889. They had ten children: Ethel May who married Isaac Moses Crowe, Frances Viola, Harold Byrd who married Regina Jesivine, Raymond Herbert who married Louise Pitt, Ina Evelyn who married George Gatt, Elmer Eugene who married Edin Blevin and then Miriam Rahders, Muriel Rose who married Eugene D. Martin, Joseph E. who married Selma Walker, Mabelle Clara who married Wyman William Duncan, and Genevieve Corine who married Albert L. Olson. Many of their children were ranchers or well-known faces in the Helena area.

John Byrd died on March 18, 1905, and Emeline (Owens) Byrd died on May 17, 1894. Both are buried at Canyon Ferry Cemetery in what

Charles Cochran, wife Mary Magdeline (Byrd) Cochran and family.

today is Cemetery Island. Their daughters Clara "Light" Byrd Bompart, Rose Byrd Robertson, and son, Joseph E. Byrd (1866–1890), are buried beside their parents. When Canyon Ferry Dam was erected, the waters backed up the sides of the mountain and created Cemetery Island, which is only accessible by boat today. Before the flooding, hearses would frequently break away, careening down the mountain. The route was so treacherously steep that early burials were often delayed while mourners awaited the retrieval of the deceased's remains from the bottom of the hill.

Mary Magdeline Byrd Cochran (or Aunt Molly as she was commonly known) was often seen by Helena residents when riding in an honorary position as a Montana Pioneer in the annual Vigilante Parade. Many descendants of the Byrd family remain in the area today.

Patrick Carney

Submitted by Dorothy F. Winchell and Irene E. Johnson, Granddaughters

Patrick Carney was born March 11, 1851, in Athlone County of Westmeath Ireland. His mother died when he was very young leaving two small boys who were raised by an aunt. After Patrick's mother died, her husband John Carney came to America.

In 1862 at the age of 11, Patrick along with his older brother Mike left Ireland for a new life in America. The two young boys joined their father in Boston, Massachusetts, where they remained for several years. In 1868 at age 17, Patrick crossed the plains by wagon train and arrived in Virginia City, Montana, where he worked in and around Alder Gulch. Alder Gulch was a very rich, gold-producing area a few miles from Virginia City. He remained in Alder Gulch and achieved considerable success in a diversity of pursuits until 1873 when he went to Butte, Montana, where he continued engaging in mining and learning the trade of a mason.

On March 12, 1876, he was united in marriage to Arminda Ellen Butts at Fish Creek, near Waterloo in a double wedding ceremony. They settled in Butte and Pat began to practice his bricklaying trade. He was the

Patrick Carney, First Family. Left to Right: Thomas, Patrick, John, Ella, Lily, Arminda and Rose – circa 1888.

first bricklayer in the city of Butte and built the first brick house in 1879 at the corner of Montana Street and Granite for Henry Jacobs, Butte's first mayor.

In 1879 he acquired, by purchase and the government homestead act, a large farm in Waterloo, Montana, where he resided the remainder of his life. Waterloo is about 45 miles southwest of Virginia City. Their first home was quite small but in later years he built a nice large home which remains in the family and is occupied by a granddaughter, Molly Parent.

On December 9, 1879, he filed a declaration of intention to become a citizen of the United States of America with the Clerk of the District Court of the 3rd Judicial District of the Territory of Montana.

After settling down in Waterloo he began a new life of farming and raising stock on a homestead that became well known in Madison County as The Carney Ranch. This is where Pat Carney grew the famous big potatoes that were widely advertised on all the dining cars of the Northern Pacific Railroad as "The Great Big Baked Potato." Pat Carney became known as "The Potato King" and that title remained with him for the rest of his life.

Nine children were born to Pat and Arminda but four died while

Patrick Carney Family, 1919. Back Row: Rose Taylor, John Carney, Lily Brook, Thomas Carney, Ella Dodds. Front Row: Charles (Charley), Patrick, Ida Pauline, Ida, Alice (Patty) and Ruth.

still infants. The others were named Lily May (Brook), Rose Anna (Taylor), Thomas Edwin, John Wilson, and Ella Elizabeth (Dodds).

A great sadness came to Pat on June 21, 1895, when he lost his beloved wife. Her death was attributed to pulmonary disease. She was buried in the Fish Creek Cemetery.

On October 23, 1900, he married Ida Jeffries of Mexico, Missouri, and five children were born to them: Mayme Arminda, Alice Martha (better known as Patty Wellman), Ida Pauline (Trostle-Wall), Charles Selwin and Ruth Frances (Rollins).

Patrick and Ida (Jeffries) Carney

As a leading and influential Democrat he served as a representative from Madison County in the First and Second Legislature of the State of Montana. He also served as chairman on the Board of Commissioners, president of the Society of Montana Pioneers in 1927-28 – now known as the Sons and Daughters of Montana Pioneers, and was a trustee of the State Historical Society. He also was one of the founders and trustee of the State Orphans Home in Twin Bridges from the time of its establishment to his death some 32 years later. He also served on the local school board and was instrumental in having the Northern Pacific Railway build a branch from Whitehall to Alder.

He voluntarily laid the bricks for the first Waterloo Public School.

He was honored as the first registered guest at Butte's "Old Finlen" Hotel, and was also the last guest before it was torn down. Then again was the first guest at the "New Finlan" Hotel on February 9, 1924 (one of Montana's outstanding hotels).

Pat was very involved in the Madison County Fair at Twin Bridges and the Montana State Fair held in Helena. He took a big part in both fairs and had many agricultural exhibits on display. He took great pride on his exhibits and won numerous prizes. Some of his many trophies are on display in the museum at Virginia City.

Pat Carney, the first Mason in Madison County, later became a Master Mason. He was very active in business and political life in the Waterloo community as well as the State of Montana.

An interesting item was Pat Carney's seat at the little Waterloo Community Church. There was one certain seat that was considered Pat's chair and no one else ever considered sitting in it. Even on Sundays when he was not present the chair remained empty. It has been told that in later years he was caught dozing during church.

Another special thing to the people of Waterloo was the mile long lane of Cottonwood trees Pat planted. How beautiful they grew and they remained that way until many years after his death. Disease took some trees, and then they were further damaged when a big tornado hit Waterloo in June, 1980.

For many years Pat Carney celebrated his birthday on March 11 by having a family reunion. It was a special occasion to have all his family come home. The Brook family of six came from Jefferson Island, the Taylor family of five from Manhattan, John Carney's family of four from Dillon, the Waterloo Dodds family of eight and bachelor Tom Carney – all members from his first family. Also present were his second family of five including Mayme, Patty, Pauline, Charley, and Ruth. It was a joyous time of good food cooked by his wife Ida and conversation – catching up on all the family happenings.

After a cold winter (with spring on the way) the robins would make their appearance, the weather would warm up, and many grandchildren would have a big time. To his grandchildren this day was more exciting than Christmas.

Again more sadness entered Pat's life. In May 1919, his second daughter, Rose Taylor, suffered a heart attack and died suddenly leaving three small children. In January 1922 Mayme, his oldest daughter from his second family, died. This was too much for Pat. Since his birthday followed so soon after Mayme's death, it was decided to end this great celebration, but memories of the wonderful times will always be with the family.

Pat lived to see Montana emerge from the crude conditions of a territory to a splendid state. He was a very active man who did much for others, when possible. He kept busy with his projects of growing all sorts of vegetables and had a large apple orchard with many varieties of apples. His death in June 1928 was mourned by a loving family and many wonderful and loyal friends. Montana lost a great friend with his passing.

Milton Chaffin Family

Submitted by Ethel Chaffin (Clark), Great-Granddaughter

Milton Chaffin and his four brothers, Thomas, Elijah, Amos and Anthony, together with their families, left Fort Scott, Kansas, in 1863 as part of a train of 85 covered wagons bound for Oregon. Oxen powered the wagons with cattle and horses trailing behind. They endured mud and dust, hordes of insects, upset wagons and even an Indian attack. One cousin was killed when he fell after climbing up Chimney Rock in Nebraska. They "reconnoitered" at Bannack, but went on their laborious way over the Big Hole and Ross' Hole mountains, down the steep canyon of Trail Creek, and into the Bitterroot Valley, reaching the present site of Corvallis on September 26, 1864.

Milton Chaffin

Winter loomed in the near future. They hurried to build shelters and prepare for bad weather and called the first settlement of "white" families in the area "Chaffinville." The Indians were friendly. Many of the Chaffins were farmers, teachers, and preachers, and were instrumental in building schools and churches in Western Montana.

Milton Chaffin and his wife had four boys, John S., James, Thomas, and Samuel. The four boys grew up and married. John S. married Sabina Sanders. She died in childbirth in the Bitterroot Valley leaving three little boys: Thomas, Samuel (my father), and Edward. Relatives cared for them until they were old enough to go live with their father John S. when he married again. When Samuel was older he drove a four-horse team, hauling freight from Salmon, Idaho. Samuel married Ada Bell McClain.

John S., his second wife, and Samuel and Ada (my parents), started putting up hay for farmers around Grant and Dillon. They traveled from

*John S. and
Sabina (Sanders) Chaffin*

place to place in covered wagons. My father, brothers, and grandfather, John S., also sheared sheep for people. Milton Chaffin and his family stayed in Corvallis in a lovely, big, white house. Later when my parents, Samuel and Ada, had three girls, May, Ethel (myself), and Gladys, and a son, Virgil, we started toward Canada with his father, John S., and his stepmother. Dad got to the border and turned back. John S. went on and bought a farm in Canada. Our family turned back and my father rented a farm north of Corvallis. Many Sundays we had dinner with Milton Chaffin until they moved to California because of their health. In the Bitterroot Valley there were many uncles, aunts, and cousins as farmers.

John S. and some of my cousins fought in the Battle of the Big Hole in August, 1877. Some cousins were killed and their graves are at the battlefield. John S. was lucky and came home as a young man.

After five years my grandmother's family, the Sanders, wanted my family to move to the Flathead Valley and get land. The government was selling land because the Indians weren't farming it – they were just living on it. While we were in the Bitterroot, my sister and I went to a little country school – we had to walk three miles. My sister Clara was born there.

In 1916 we moved to Arlee, Montana, in a covered wagon. The drought came and farming was very poor unless you had lots of water. Then World War I came along. These were bad years. Everyone went broke. My father (Samuel Reese) was lucky. He got on as Deputy Sheriff at Arlee and remained there until he passed away in 1946. At Arlee my mother had two more babies, Addie Helen and Allen Reese. Addie passed away as a small baby. Allen is now living in Seeley Lake. Ada passed away in the 1950's. My father Samuel and mother Ada are buried in Missoula, Montana.

Arlee was a small town so the school was small. It only had two grades for high school, so we had to go to Missoula. After I got out of school I went into nurses training in the Deaconess in Billings and graduated in 1930. I went to college in Bozeman. From there I met my husband from Fort Shaw, a beekeeper. In 1935 we married. My husband passed away in 1982. Later my brother Virgil, and sister Gladys, passed away. My four children all have joined the Sons and Daughters of Montana Pioneers: Frances Parriera, California; Phyllis McNett, Great Falls; Dale A. Clark, Great Falls, and Ellen Hodde, Colville, Washington.

Charles Chouquette

Submitted by Frances McDonald

Charles Chouquette was born February 9, 1823, in St. Charles, Missouri, a French settlement outside St. Louis. He was one of three known children born to Henry and Rosalie (Piquette) Chouquette.

Charles (Charlie) received his early education in French speaking Catholic schools operated by the nuns. After learning the blacksmith trade, he went to Montana in 1844 working as a voyageur on a keelboat coming up the Missouri River hauling trade goods from St. Louis to Fort Union. It took 72 days for the 2,000-mile trip. Charlie was employed by Pierre Choteau's American Fur Company and is mentioned in the Fort Sarpy, Fort Union, and Fort Benton Journals.

He was married to Rosa Lee, a member of the Blackfeet Nation who was born a Piegan/Blood Indian, by Father De Smet, S.J. (Society of Jesus) in 1854 at Fort Benton. Her surname is listed as Crowfoot in Government records.

Charlie and Rosa were the parents of eleven natural children and raised two more. All of their children received an education. When their two youngest daughters, Rose and Josephine, were enrolled in 1885 with nine other Blackfeet Indian girls at the St. Peter's Mission (southwest of present day Great Falls) under Mother Amadeus, their two daughters were the only Blackfeet children able to read and write.

While living near Fort Union, Charlie was a guide for Jim Bridger and his party. One night at camp, the Crows stole their horses. The party went after the horses and were involved in a heavy battle but got their horses back plus a few belongings of the Crows. While traveling from Ft. Union to Ft. Sarpy on the Yellowstone, Charlie and James H. Chambers had their horses stolen by Crows. Making their way to the Fort on foot, they had to cross the Big Muddy River, finding it very high June 4, 1856. After shooting a deer and using the hide to make a bullboat to hold their clothes, guns and blankets, the men stripped down for the crossing. As it turned out, Chambers, who stated himself an expert swimmer, suffered cramps and after going down twice on coming up overturned the pack, which sunk to the bottom. Both men made the crossing and Charlie went back diving for his shoes, pants and a shirt, but was so displeased with the other man that he left him to keep up, some 47 miles, naked, to the Fort. Fortunately for the other man, after Charlie arrived at the Fort, a party went out to rescue Chambers.

Chouquette operated a freighting business at the mouth of Little Canyon Road near present day Canyon Creek at the same time that Malcolm Clark (massacred by Indians in 1869) had a ranch on the Wolf Creek side. Charlie built the first house in Choteau County at Fort Benton. It was there that a free trapper was trying to sell a small Indian girl in a saloon. Charlie walked in, took the frightened girl by the hand and said "This is my daughter," turned around and walked out with her. No one tried to stop them. He later was an early settler in Choteau, Montana, where his wife Rosa died and was buried there in 1886.

Charles Chouquette

Charlie Chouquette, working as an interpreter, signed the first treaty with the Blackfeet Nation. The Council was held October 16, 1855, on the North bank of the Missouri at Judith, Montana. During his life he established several ranches and freighting businesses in different locations, always moving with his Indian family northerly per government taking of the reservation and as starving Indians were forced to treaty away their shrinking reservation land. After leaving the Sun River Valley, he settled at Family near present day, Browning, Montana, where he died at the Josephine Chouquette Grant's Ranch on Willow Creek June 1, 1911, and was buried at the Holy Family Mission, Family, Montana.

On another note, Charlie's uncle, Francis Labiche, was with the Lewis and Clark Corps of Discovery. Labiche spoke several native tongues. He was attached to the permanent party as a private in the U.S. Army.

Much has been written and handed down about Charlie Chouquette. Robert Vaughn in his book, *Then and Now or Thirty-six years in the Rockies 1864-1900*, misquoted Chouquette and after that book was printed, Charlie refused to give any other interviews. A.B. Guthrie, Jr., the noted Montana author from Choteau, after researching no present day Chouquettes, used the Chouquette name for an unsavory person in his historic fictional book *Big Sky*. He later apologized to relatives that bought his book.

All his daughters married and had large families. The three sons married late in life, with one grandson being born to one of his sons, but who did not stay in Montana.

Christenot Family

Submitted by Nick Shrauger, Great-Great-Grandson of Charles and Martha Christenot

Charles Christenot had reason to be happy in January of 1869. The Supreme Court of Montana Territory upheld the judgement of the Madison County District Court in favor of Charles who had filed a mechanic's lien against the Montana Gold and Silver Mining Company. Charles, a carpenter by trade, had worked 110 days at $5.00 per day making sleds, tubs for mines, desks and ore frames and repairing buildings. This work was at Union City, the community highest up Alder Gulch and south of Virginia City. The Montana Gold and Silver Mining Company, incorporated in Pennsylvania, had acquired most of its holdings from Charles' brother Benjamin F. "Frank" Christenot. Thus comes another story of Montana pioneers.

Charles Fredrick Christenot, of Swiss descent, was born in Wellsboro, Tioga County, Pennsylvania, on July 12, 1834. His father, Fredrick, was a tanner. Not much is known about young Charles. He married Keziah Strang on February 10, 1856. They had three children: Henry (August 5, 1860), Emma (October 28, 1861) and Matty (February 19, 1864). In December of 1863 he enlisted as a private in Company C of the 12th Wisconsin Infantry Volunteers at Janesville, Wisconsin. The year 1864 was not good for Charles. He suffered a severe case of heat stroke on July 22, 1864, during the Battle for Atlanta, and then his wife Keziah died in October 1864. He was reported absent without leave during November and December, presumably to go home to settle his wife's affairs and tend to his children. Charles was discharged in July 1865 at Louisville, Kentucky.

He was 32 and listed as having dark hair, blue eyes, and fair complexion. He was five feet, seven inches tall. Charles was about to make a major change in his life.

The Battle for Atlanta claimed another casualty on that same day that Charles had heat stroke. Henry Wilton of Company K, 30th Regiment of Illinois Infantry Volunteers, was killed. Henry left his widow, the former Martha Craig, and a daughter, Alice. Somehow Charles Christenot and Martha met. They were married on May 9, 1866, in Carlyle, Clinton County, Illinois. Thus an interesting question emerges. Did Charles and Henry know each other in the war (they were in different units)? Or was

Charles F. Christenot. Arrived Alder Gulch, Montana Territory – October 12, 1866.

Martha a friend of the Strang family, or even someone hired to take care of Charles's children while he was at war? They were married by Justice of the Peace H. W. Strang. Was he Keziah's father or brother? We may never know how Martha and Charles met, but their marriage started them toward a new life in what is now Montana.

Shortly after Martha and Charles were married, they joined an ox train at Nebraska City, Nebraska, under the direction of Thomas A. Creigh. This train of 52 wagons and 235 yoke of cattle departed for Union City, Montana Territory, on June 20, 1866, with 81 tons of freight including gold crushing machinery for the mill and the mining company founded by

Charles' brother Benjamin F. Christenot, or "Frank" as he was known in Montana. Traveling with Charles and Martha were Frank, Martha's daughter Alice, Charles' father Fredrick, and Fredrick's second wife Margaret (nothing is known about Fredrick's first wife). Two other Christenot women were present. They are thought to be Amelia Christenot, a 12-year-old niece, and Azuba Smith, a 27-year-old widow of a cousin of Charles'. They arrived in Virginia City on October 12, 1866, having traveled the Bozeman Trail as one of the last immigrant trains ever to do so. Martha became pregnant while on their journey, and she gave birth to their first child, Hattie, on March 28, 1867, in Union City.

Martha (Craig) Wilton Christenot. Arrived Alder Gulch, Montana Territory – October 12, 1866.

Their journey was interesting due to the amount of heavy machinery they were transporting. Several times machinery wagons tipped over. Seven head of cattle were lost crossing the Yellowstone River. Along the way they encountered some Indian interference, but avoided serious trouble due to the size of their train. They encountered the usual difficulties of quicksand, mosquitoes, heat and cold. Several fresh graves of those killed by Indians were passed on the journey.

Their destination was not one of chance. Charles' older brother Frank (Benjamin F.) Christenot lived at Union City and was returning from Philadelphia where he had been conducting business. Frank had been in Alder Gulch as early as 1863, and had success in mining, and in buying and selling property. He no doubt told his family of riches that were waiting in the Montana territory, and they were probably anxious to make a new start in life.

Frank had been busy while living in the mining camps of Alder Gulch. One of his earliest transactions was the May 1864 purchase of a hotel and bar in Summit City. William Clark and George Burtschy were the sellers. (This was when the area was still Idaho Territory.) He didn't keep the bar and hotel for very long and continued locating and buying mining claims. It must have been an interesting time as properties changed hands at a rapid pace. In December of 1864 he bought (at a Sheriff's sale held in front of Rockafellow and Dennee's store in Virginia City) a ranch from the estate of Joseph A. Slade, who had been recently hung by Vigilantes.

Frank managed to acquire more than 87 mining properties as well as some gold. His friend Nelson Story said that, "Frank filled a small handgrip with gold ore and took it to Philadelphia." Not an easy trick during road agent days, but he got through and was able to sell his claims in Alder Gulch to the recently incorporated Montana Gold and Sliver Mining Company. Incidentally, one of the best producing lodes was the Oro Cache. He owned some claims in partnership with Nelson Story. Nelson apparently took his money to Texas and gained fame by bringing the first Longhorn cattle into Montana Territory while defying both the Indians and the Army along the Bozeman Trail. (His drive was in 1866 just shortly after the family traveled the trail.) Rich for a time, Frank lost it all in his continuing mining efforts.

The Christenot family lived and worked in Union City. Life there revolved around the operation of the Christenot Mill. Brother Frank originally crushed Oro Cache ore with an arrastra. Not content with the small returns from the arrastra, he started the mill that he sold to the Montana Gold and Silver Mining Company during his stay in Philadelphia. Ore from the Oro Cache (which lies on the ridge between Summit and Union City), as well as the General U.S. Grant lode, was processed there. The mill, one of many during those years, was unique in several aspects. It was the highest in elevation (7,500 feet), it used chilian rollers instead of stamps for crushing, and it had amalgamation barrels. The mill was operated using overhead belts and pulleys driven by a steam engine. Carpenters, boiler makers, and machinists were needed. The pay was good, if you could collect as Charles demonstrated with his mechanic's lien. By the way, Charles filed his mechanic's lien for $673.40. He ended up receiving $398.30.

The mill was actively operating in 1867 and 1868. The Montana

Post reported several instances of gold bricks being displayed at the Nolan and Weary Bank in Virginia City. But riches were to elude Charles and Martha, and at some point, they moved to Puller Hot Springs on the Ruby River.

Charles served as a constable at Puller Springs and worked in construction and as a farmer. During 1875-1878 he thought he was in partnership with Curtis Newberry, the husband of Martha's daughter Alice. He brought suit against Curtis in 1878 seeking partnership assets, but this time he lost his case. He and Martha continued adding to their family with the births of Anna (November 18, 1869), Mary (August 15, 1872), Charles (September 13, 1874), Clemmie (October 1, 1875), Amelia (June 28, 1876), George (August 3, 1878), Frank (November 2, 1880), and Fred (July 28, 1883).

Benjamin F. "Frank" Christenot, Union City – 1863.

The heat stroke suffered by Charles was exacting its toll in the form of epileptic fits. Adriel B. Davis (the Vigilante who tied the knot for the hanging of George Ives) claimed in an affidavit, that he had known Charles since 1866 and had seen many of his fits. These grew worse in length and frequency with age and Charles was sent to the sanitarium at Warm Springs on March 18, 1886. He died there on May 23, 1886.

The death of Charles left Martha with a large family and little money. She married Charles' brother Frank for a short time (as his third wife), but he soon disappeared. She obtained a divorce and was then able to get a small army pension from the Civil War service of Charles.

Martha lived with her children at various locations for the remainder of her life. Her youngest son George (as well as her daughter, Hattie and husband, John Kyle) homesteaded along the Musselshell River near Weede in 1909. Martha had a cabin there for a few years. She died June 29, 1923, leaving, besides her own children, 52 grandchildren, 46 great-grandchildren, and three great great-grandchildren. She was living in Whitehall with her daughter Hattie (Mrs. John Kyle) at the time of her death, and is buried in the South Boulder Cemetery near Whitehall.

Charles and Martha witnessed the Civil War and the development of what we know as Montana. They are pioneers who experienced the trek west in ox wagons along the Bozeman Trail, and they participated in early mining and farming. They left a legacy of family still living in, and contributing to, Montana.

Charles W. Cook

Submitted by George D. Mueller

Charles W. Cook was born at Unity, Maine, on February 24, 1839. He was the son of Daniel and Elizabeth T. (Hussey) Cook, natives of Maine. The original ancestors came from England and both families were represented in the War of 1812.

Reading of the gold strikes in Montana Territory, Cook went west at the age of 25 in 1864. From St. Joseph, Missouri, he took a steamer to Omaha, Nebraska, and there purchased a team and wagon, which he drove to Denver, Colorado. In Denver, he was hired as a drover to help herd 125 head of cattle to the new mining town of Virginia City traveling through Fort Bridger, Wyoming, and Soda Springs, Idaho. Sioux and Cheyenne Indians near Green River, Wyoming, captured his party. The group secured their release by giving the Indians a steer. The remaining cattle were delivered at Virginia City on September 22, 1864.

Finding Alder Gulch crowded, and opportunities to advance himself rather scarce, Cook moved to Last Chance Gulch and the following March (1865) he pushed on to Diamond City where he settled in Confederate Gulch and became the superintendent of the Boulder Ditch Company which supplied water to the placer mines. It was here that he developed an intense interest in the Yellowstone region and undertook to explore it. This was accomplished with his lifetime friend, David E. Folsom, and William

Peterson, both of whom were employed by the Boulder Ditch Company. They left Diamond City on September 6, 1869, and approached the Yellowstone region by way of the Trail Creek-Yellowstone River Route. They visited Tower Fall, Lamar Valley, several thermal areas on the Mirror Plateau, and spent several days at the Falls and Grand Canyon of the Yellowstone. They measured the height of both falls. Traveling up the Yellowstone, they visited the thermal areas at the Crater Hills and Mud Volcano, the outlet of Yellowstone Lake, and Midway Geyser basins, and Lower Geyser basin. They returned to Diamond City after an absence of thirty-six days.

Charles W. Cook – circa 1869.

In 1871 Cook brought a flock of sheep from Oregon to Montana and wintered them at Gallatin City. The following spring (1872) he drove them into the Smith River Valley and developed a large sheep ranch called "Unity," ten miles southwest of White Sulphur Springs. He was one of the first three men to engage in the sheep industry in Montana.

Charles Cook married Abbie W. Kennicott on June 26, 1880. They were the parents of three children.

After an absence of 53 years, Cook returned to Yellowstone Park for the fiftieth anniversary celebration and was honored as the last survivor of the original explorers of the Yellowstone Park region. He was also honored later in 1922 when Horace, M. Albright, Park Superintendent of Yellowstone Park, had the second highest peak in the park (elevation 9,742 feet) renamed Cook Peak.

Cook served as president of the Society of Montana Pioneers from 1921-1922.

In later years, Cook sold his ranch and moved to White Sulphur Springs, Montana, where he lived until his death on January 30, 1927. He is buried in the Mayn Cemetery at White Sulphur Springs.

Horace M. Albright, Superintendent Yellowstone National Park; Charles W. Cook, only survivor of the first exploring expedition in the Park, and Anna Anzer, of New York, representing the National Editorial Association. All three took part in the ceremonies celebrating the fiftieth (Golden) anniversary of the establishment of the Park. They are shown beside the memorial tablet erected at the campsite of the Washburn Expedition, whose members brought about the creation of the Park. The celebration was held on July 14, 1922, at the junction of the Gibbon and Firehole Rivers (Madison Junction). – Photo by J. E. Haynes, Yellowstone National Park official photographer.

Thomas Jeremiah Cooney

Submitted by Robert F. Cooney, Grandson

Thomas Jeremiah Cooney was born (in the vale of Avoca) in County Tyronne, North Ireland, in 1835. In 1851, at the age of 16, he came from Ireland to the East Coast of America with his parents – nothing is known of them. In 1854 he want west to Chicago, and from there to Iowa. In 1862 in Fort Atkinson, Iowa, he married Agnes Maria Cahill. Agnes was born in 1845 in Killarney, County Cork, South Ireland. As an infant her parents brought her to Iowa. Nothing is known of Agnes' mother and very little of her father, Thomas Cahill, except that he was with Thomas Cooney and his family in Montana. It is assumed that Thomas Cahill passed away about 1903 on the Cooney Ranch at Canyon Ferry.

Thomas Cooney decided to try his luck at gold mining. It's been told that he and two companions loaded their possessions into a wheelbarrow and hiked from Iowa to Colorado. In 1863 he moved north to the Montana Territory. His wife Agnes, their son Edward, and her father, Tom Cahill, crossed the plains in a wagon train and joined Thomas in Virginia City, Montana, on June 28, 1865.

Agnes Maria Cooney commented on the happy days in 1865 on the trail from Iowa to the Montana Territory.

> "We crossed the plains to Denver, and then joined 13 families headed for the gold strike in Montana. We had two yoke of fine oxen. The days were long. Twenty miles was considered a good daily distance. Sometimes the train went up mountains as steep as Mt. Helena. When we went downhill the women and children would get out and walk. There was no way to hold the oxen if they decided to run. Sometimes we walked uphill too. A scout rode ahead to find a camp spot with water and wood. Indians never gave us trouble. Sometimes squaws with papooses on their backs would come and beg for bread or biscuits. We did see graves with markers giving names of victims killed by Indians."

In Virginia City, Mr. Cooney built a little cabin about ten feet square with three tiny windows and a dirt floor. When fall came, he bought two large ox hides and pegged them across the floor. They made fine carpets. A cradle for Edward was made out of a sluice box. While living in Virginia City, Thomas and Agnes welcomed another son, George, born on April 7, 1866.

While in Virginia City, Thomas worked with the Vigilantes. He helped to capture and hang several outlaws. One, Clubfoot George, called out just before his demise, "Goodbye Cooney, I'll see you in hell."

From Virginia City, the Cooney family and Mr. Cahill went to Last Chance Gulch, Diamond City, White City (Whites Gulch), and York (some called it New York) before settling on land located on the banks of the Missouri River at the mouth of Avalanche Gulch, northeast of Helena in 1873. This land became the family ranch.

Thomas J. Cooney's cabin, Canyon Ferry Lake – circa 1900.

Mr. Cahill liked to garden, and at various gold camps he apparently raised vegetables, some of which he sold to the miners. He had a garden in Avalanche Gulch near a spring.

In 1882 the family lived at White Sulphur Springs. While here, the children trapped gophers on their "gopher ranch." They made wire branding irons and branded the gophers.

While living at Diamond City one hard winter, a neighbor asked Mr. Cooney if he could borrow a gold pan of flour for a fourth of the interest in his claims, which were just above and below Cooney's claim. Having a wife, children, and a father-in-law to feed, Cooney was running low on flour. He knew the freight wagons wouldn't get to Diamond City from town for some weeks, so he had to refuse. The next summer the neighbor struck a rich ore vein and took out over $4,000,000 in gold.

Thomas J. Cooney was County Commissioner of Meagher County for 18 years. Mr. Cooney played a very dramatic role in the elections that changed the state capital from Virginia City to Helena. The election returns sent from White Sulphur plainly showed that the city of Helena had been the choice of the Meagher County voters by a majority of 532 votes. Chairman Cooney, of the board, and Mr. Collins, board clerk, certified the results. When the certificate got to Virginia City it was found the names of the cities had been transposed and it appeared that Helena had lost Meagher County by 532 votes. A scandal brewed. Mr. Cooney hastened to Virginia City to demand the proper return be recorded and thus gave Helena the Capital. This was typical of Mr. Cooney — straightforward and vigorous, always standing formally for the truth and what he deemed to be right.

The wild hay grew abundantly on the Cooney ranch along the Missouri River in the 1880's. In 1898 the first Montana Power Company dam was built at Canyon Ferry. This dam flooded the valley located east of Canyon Ferry and formed Lake Sewell.

The Cooneys had to leave the rich river bottomland in 1899 and move up to the drier bench land at the mouth of Avalanche Creek. Here they established the home ranch once more, and lived there until 1954 when the government built the present Canyon Ferry Dam. This dam created a

Thomas J. Cooney, Sr. Family. Back Row: Thomas J. Jr., Jim Supple, George, Alfred, Edward and Frederick William. Middle Row: Emma (Hill) Cooney, Ellen (Cooney) Supple and Agnes Cooney, Georgianna (Day) Cooney. Front Row: Dr. Sidney A. Cooney, Agnes Maria (Cahill) Cooney; Ed's son, Thomas J. Cooney; Ed's daughter, Winifred (Cooney) Brown — circa 1902.

much larger lake, again flooding the better part of the Cooney Ranch.

Typical of the Irish, the family stayed at the original log home and had a party. The party continued until the water was at the doorstep. Then they hauled part of the house to higher ground. This was the nucleus for the new house – the living room and one bedroom. Two bedrooms, a kitchen, pantry and dining room were added. Much later a small, screened porch and an enclosed front porch were added. There was never running water in the house. The old well was about 25 feet from the kitchen door. Much of the bathing and clothes washing were done in the lake.

In back of the house, there were out buildings – a shed, an outhouse, and an icehouse. Below the hill by the icehouse was a fairly large root cellar. The corrals, a little tack shed, a large straw-roofed cattle shed, and a log bunkhouse were across Avalanche Creek – reached by an old wooden plank bridge.

A small one-room log cabin was also moved form the river ranch and was known as grandpa's cabin. It was right on the lakeshore about 100 yards from the main house. In the late 30's it was redone – a large window, a fireplace, and a screened porch on the east side of the house were added. It was then used as a guest cabin studio and as an art studio (for Fanny Y. Cory, Robert F. Cooney's mother). A big old willow tree provided shade.

In 1954 the little cabin, old log bunkhouse, a shed, and the windmill were moved up to the high bench. There were about 400 acres of bench land that weren't flooded. This land and buildings were sold to a neighbor, Jake Burkhart, in about 1958 – ending the era of the Cooney family ranch.

The six sons of Thomas and Agnes had diverse careers. Edward was a writer and a newsman. At the time of his death in 1929, he was editor and half-owner of the Great Falls Leader. He is buried in Great Falls, Montana.

George owned or had interest in several nightclubs, restaurants, and the Mint Bar in Helena. George always loved horses. As a very young man he was an excellent rider. He would go up the valley and race against the Indians. Usually he returned home with a sizable string of Indian ponies. He later had a racing stable. He had special dirt brought to Helena from Kentucky to build the racetrack at the Helena Fairgrounds. At that time it was probably the best track in Montana. He raced many years in Montana, on the West Coast, and in Mexico.

Thomas Jr. was a rancher and miner. At one time he had a big dredge on lower Magpie Gulch near Canyon Ferry. For many years he was a Lewis and Clark County Commissioner.

Fred was a cattle rancher. He also rounded up wild horses in the Big

Belt Mountains. For several years George Cooney had turned out quite a few of his retired racehorses into the mountains around Canyon Ferry. There, these mountain horses were a far better stock than the regular run of wild horses. These horses were branded, halter broken, and ridden at least once before being sold to the U.S. Cavalry.

For many years, Alfred was Deputy Clerk and Recorder of Lewis and Clark County.

Sidney A. was an excellent athlete. He played college football, but baseball was his favorite sport. At one time, he had to decide between professional baseball, or having a career in medicine. He chose to be a physician and surgeon and practiced for over 60 years in Helena.

Thomas and Agnes Maria also had three daughters. Ellen (Cooney) Supple was born in 1870 at Canyon Ferry, Montana and died in 1949. Agnes Cooney was born in 1879 in Canyon Ferry, Montana, and died in 1948. Winifred (Cooney) Brown was born in 1887 in Canyon Ferry, Montana and died in 1977.

Thomas died in Helena, Montana, in 1914 at the age of 79. His wife Agnes, four of his six sons, and three daughters are also buried there.

Con Coughlin

Submitted by Margaret Coughlin Sowa, Granddaughter

Con Coughlin, son of David Coughlin and Catherine Maher Coughlin, was born in Covington, Nebraska, May 13, 1859. His mother, Catherine Maher, was born in County Clare, Ireland, in the town of Carrigaholt. She came to America with neighbors at the age of 15 or 16. After a shipwreck in route, she landed in Quebec and lived in Cincinnati, Chicago, and St. Louis.

On July 14, 1856, she and David Coughlin of County Cork, Ireland, were married in St. Patrick's Church in St. Louis, Missouri. Their first son, Maurice, was born in Covington, Nebraska. My grandfather, Con, and their daughter Mary Ann, were also born in Covington. The 1860 census shows they ran a boarding house there. In 1862 the family crossed the Plains by covered wagon to the mining fields of Colorado. They were expecting their fourth son when David was killed in a mining accident. The baby was born in June of 1863. Catherine left the baby David with relatives, Mr. and Mrs. Thomas Coleman, who had just lost a child and would be able to nurse and care for him. [*Mr. and Mrs. Coleman raised David, and in*

1869 they too came to Montana by wagon train pulled by oxen where they mined in Washington Gulch. They then moved to the Nevada Creek Valley and purchased property adjoining the ranch of Mr. and Mrs. Laherty, David's mother and stepfather. Con and David later bought property together in Ovando.]

Catherine and her three small children left by wagon train for Montana where she hoped to open a boarding house for miners to support her children. They arrived at Alder Gulch, Montana, in September of that same year. She met and married William Laherty from County Tipperary in 1864. He was a loving stepfather to Con, Maurice, and Mary Ann, and later to his children Katherine, Jim, Will, and Ed. They lived in Alder Gulch for two years and then moved to the thriving mining camp of Blackfoot City. Since there was no opportunity of schools for the children, they went to the Bitterroot Valley for the school year.

Cornelius (Con) Coughlin

Their next move was to the mining town of Lincoln, where they ran a boarding house. The stage carrying passengers and mail stopped there overnight to rest and eat. One evening Catherine served dinner, as usual, to the large group. The next morning after serving breakfast, she brought out a baby son who had been born in the night – truly a hardy pioneer woman. The family lived in Lincoln for two years and then moved to Marysville. They milked cows and sold butter to the miners. As the boys became older, they helped with the milking. Con often told of his trips with Mr. Laherty in a wagon to deliver butter to the mining camps. At night, they slept in the open under the wagon. The trip back and forth often took several days. In

1881 the family purchased a ranch located three miles east of Helmville, and continued in the dairy business.

Con homesteaded near Ovando, and owned several ranches in the Helmville area, and in Deer Park. He raised and sold horses and cattle and branded them with the brand CC. He met and married Delia Mullen in July 1889. Delia was born in County Westmeath, Ireland, on April 4, 1872, and came to Helmville with Mrs. Bridget Mullen McCormick, her maternal aunt. Bridget had raised Delia after her mother's death following Delia's birth. Several of Mrs. McCormick's children settled in Helmville.

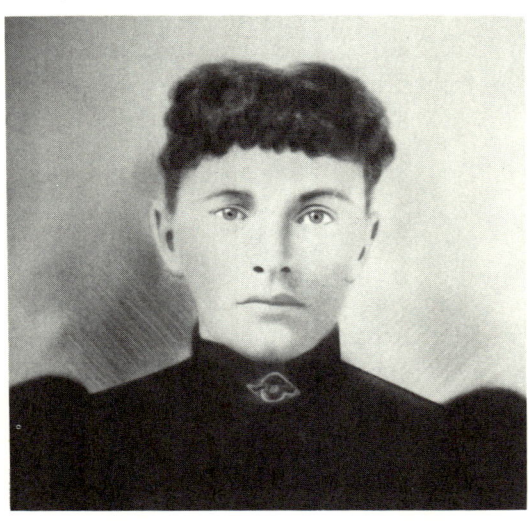

Delia (Mullen) Coughlin

Con and Delia had five children: David, William, Edward, Walter, and Ruperta. Delia died ten days after Ruperta's birth. Con's sister, Mary Ann McCormick, took Ruperta (Ruby) and raised her with her own family. Con raised the four boys who ranged in age from two to nine years. They all became outstanding citizens and family men. Con's oldest son, David, married Lucy Bignell. Emmett and his sons operated the family ranch in Helmville and is still owned by them.

William, Con's second oldest son, married Hazel Meade of Butte, and together they ran the Helmville post office and grocery store until their deaths. Their children are Jim, Arlyne Coughlin Paisley, and Wilma Coughlin Greaney.

Edward married Pauline King of Petaluma, California. They had no children.

Walter married Marie Wales, daughter of Hugh and Maggie Geary Wales. They had four children: Marilyn Coughlin Hansen, Gerald

Coughlin, Margaret Coughlin Sowa, and Myrna Coughlin. Their ranch was located seven miles north of Helmville.

Ruperta, Con's only daughter, married Earl Wales and lived on the Wales Ranch in Helmville until Earl's death, and then moved to Missoula. They had eight children. Hugh, who died at a young age, Ed, Anna Marie Wales Cooper, Jean Wales Larson, Delia Wales Cook, Joan Wales Pope, Bernadete Wales Senecal, and Shirley.

Con spent his later years between his home in Helmville and living with Walter and Marie at their ranch home. He never remarried and treasured the picture and other momentos he kept of Delia. At times he would take them out of the case that he kept them in, and tell us grandchildren about her with tears in his eyes. He enjoyed playing cards with his friends at McCormick's Bar and Candy Store. His pockets were always full of tokens (hickey's) that he won there and gave to his grandchildren. They were good for the candy, gum, and pop that McCormick's sold.

On April 22, 1935, Con died of pneumonia. All his family were around him, except Ed, who arrived from San Francisco later that evening. His wake was at the home of his son, Walter, and he was laid to rest at the side of his beloved Delia in the cemetery in Helmville.

Moses Doggett

Submitted by Robert F. Morgan, Great-Grandson

Moses Doggett was born in 1829 near Louis, Kentucky, and moved to Indiana when he was 11. When he was 18 he moved to Iowa. In 1859 until 1862 he mined in Colorado. Returning to Iowa for his family, he moved to Montana in 1863 arriving at Horse Prairie Creek by wagon train. He mined on Grasshopper Creek and Alder Gulch and built the first finished house on Idaho Street in Virginia City.

From January until October, Doggett took out $14,000 from Alder Gulch, sold his claims and moved his family to Last Chance Gulch in Helena. He purchased two claims in Dry Gulch and in a matter of days took out $1,500.

In the fall of 1865, Doggett located at Canton in Meagher County, today in Broadwater County. He took a squatter's right and engaged in the stock dairy business with Diamond City as his market. He constructed the

Moses Doggett. Arrived in Montana Territory, Horse Prairie Creek, Aug. 2, 1863.

first irrigation ditch from the Missouri in 1865 and raised a crop. In 1885 the ranch consisted of 900 acres. Moses remained here until his death in 1894.

The Canton post office was established in 1872 with William Tierney as the first postmaster. It continued until 1935. When the Canyon Ferry Dam was built and the lake filled, the Canton Valley was under water – including two islands that were owned by Doggett.

Moses Doggett was married twice, first in 1849 and again in 1859. By his first marriage he had two children, Duane and Lafayette. By his second wife, Susan Rose, he had seven. They were Charles B., Jefferson, James, Loren, Ida Montana, Benjamin Franklin (known as Robert or Bob) and Lily Mabel.

William J. "Major Bill" Doney

Submitted by Great-Granddaughter Linda F. Wostrel

William J. Doney was born at Egypt, Randolph County, Illinois, on October 22, 1842, to William Henri Doney (Dannis) (Dannie) and Marie Olivia Buatte. His French family can be traced back to approximately 1600 in Rouen, France, to Martin Dannis dit Tourangeau – my 8th Great Grandfather.

Honre and his family, Martin's son, came down the St. Lawrence to populate "New France" in Canada and settled in present day Montreal. Honre was the victim of an Indian massacre at Lachine in 1689. Honre's son Charles Danie was a voyageur and worked his way down river to Kaskaskia – an Indian village on the eastern bank of the Mississippi River about 60 miles below the present day St. Louis, Missouri. This Territory was still considered a part of French Canada at the time. The first preserved land grant by the French government was given to Charles on May 10, 1722.

The territory passed into English hands in 1763 then in 1778 Col. George Rogers Clark acting under instructions from Patrick Henry, Governor of Virginia, took back the area – enlisting some local volunteers that included some of the Danie family.

Known as part of the Northwest Territory, in 1784 the Kaskaskia area was ceded back to the United States by Virginia. On November 28, 1803, the Lewis and Clark Corps of Discovery arrived at then Fort Kaskaskia where they enlisted some volunteers for the expedition.

Left to Right: Back Row (standing): George Timmerman, Susan (Hitchens) Doney in portrait. Front Row: Myrtle (Doney) Timmerman, Pearl (Timmerman) Wostrel and William J. Doney. – painting by Nancy J. Wostrel.

The Danie family stayed in the Kaskaskia area for five generations. When William (Bill) was a boy, the family moved to Mineral Point, Wisconsin where they were engaged in mining. In 1865, Bill first heard "The Call of the West". He responded and got a job as a bullwhacker on the old Kansas Trail – following his plodding oxen between the Missouri and Denver. He spent the summer in Colorado country, but as autumn approached he was homesick for the Wisconsin forests. He took his old job and tramped back with the oxen to Wisconsin.

In the spring of 1867, he became a bullwhacker again on the western trail. The tide of emigration that season had set out toward the rich diggings of western Montana and Doney headed out again, swinging a whip over the backs of the ox team. For the third time he crossed the plains and for the first time crossed the Rocky Mountains. This was no pleasure trip. There were skirmishes with the Indians almost from the time the outfit left the Missouri River behind. It was a bad year as the plains Indians were irritable and hostile. On the western border of Nebraska, almost into Wyoming at a little settlement known as Castle Pool.

The outfit was held back for ten days by the fighting ahead in which government troops were engaged. After the Indians surrendered, the outfit was allowed to proceed. Some of the drivers had deserted early in the trip; others refused to proceed from Castle Pool. The number of bullwhackers was reduced by half but Doney stayed with the job arriving in east Bannack on October 3, 1867 – then a thriving mining camp of four to five hundred. Hearing of more luck in the placer diggings in Alder Gulch, he arrived to find that all the good diggings were taken and the only opening was for day wages, so he moved on.

After staying in Bozeman in the Gallatin Valley and finding little work, Bill rode horseback westward to Missoula arriving on Christmas Day, 1867. "It wasn't very much of a place when I came to it that Christmas Day," he said, there were two stores and a hotel besides the Missoula Mills and a few houses of folks who had started the town. There was more in Missoula in the way of winter employment than there had been anywhere else that I had visited and I stayed all that winter. It was good to me, Missoula was, and I have always liked it ever since then."

The spring of 1868 led Bill to the Pioneer district, which later became his permanent home. While the search for gold was his main focus, he also worked on the construction of the Union Pacific, which was then nearing its completion. All through the winter of 1868 he worked on the railway building in present day Utah. He quit the job in May 1869 just a week before the golden spike was driven and went into Promontory, Utah, with the big crowd to witness the official completion of the first transcontinental line of the Union Pacific and Central Pacific Railroads.

"That was the toughest, wildest crowd I ever saw," said Bill in helping the Oakes Ames folks to get their big job finished. "Two big gangs had been working, one eastward and the other westward, and there were 30,000 graders turned loose all at once when the two lines met. All of these men had been paid off. The golden spike driving had been well advertised and every crook and sure-thing man west of the Mississippi had moved to Promontory to have a share in picking the rich profits that were supposed to be there. No mining camp that I ever saw could compare in toughness with Promontory when we graders got there. It was crude, shack town – but it was wide open night and day. There was every form of gambling that could be thought of; there was one continuous round of noise and hurrah. The sure-thing games were not fast enough for some of the thugs and they robbed the paid-off men whenever they got them in singles, killing them if they couldn't get the money any other way. This was the only town I was ever in where the 'had a man for breakfast every morning.' I had heard of such places but this was the only one I ever saw. And one was enough.

William J. Doney. Parade in Deer Lodge, Montana.

A Montana Pioneer and Prospector and his home. Major William Doney of Pikes Peak, Montana.

When the spike was driven, the crowd vanished. Promontory had had its day."

Bill and two companions, who had stuck together during all the excitement, began to think again of Montana and found themselves back in Bannack in the fall of 1869. In 1870, Bill went to Deer Lodge City where he lived for a year. His principal source of income during the year was catching fish from Warm Springs Creek, above where Anaconda now stands, and as far as Silver Lake. It was good fishing and his trout were one of the things that made the Scott House famous in Deer Lodge and among passengers on the old stagecoach trail. During the summer he also found employment with Black and Morgan, the firm that had the contract for the construction of the federal prison that later became the state penitentiary in Deer Lodge.

In the fall of 1870, he went down towards Hell Gate as far as where Clinton now stands. There he remained until March 1871, when he went to Yamhill on Gold Creek – his home for the rest of his life. Aside for visits in the summer of 1885 on the Flathead Lake and the summer of 1891 when he was in the vicinity of Ovando, he was at Yamhill – placer mining and freighting – satisfied that he had found the place he sought in all his wanderings.

When he located at Yamhill, that camp and Pike's Peak its rival were flourishing placer camps. Pioneer, located below Yamhill, had a population of about 1,500 and was prosperous and lively.

On July 21, 1880, Bill married Miss Susan Hitchens of Mineral Point, Wisconsin, who arrived from that state on the day of her marriage. The Rev. J. L. Henning married them in the Presbyterian Church in Deer Lodge, Montana. On May 25, 1881, in Pioneer, Montana, the first of their three children was born Jessie May (Trafford) followed by Myrtle Beulah (Timmerman) on November 9, 1884, and Louise Pearl (Logan) on August 17, 1887. On September 26, 1896, Susan Hitchens Doney died and was buried in a meadow on the ranch of Jules Clairmont (now F. L. Bacon Ranch) north of present day Wisdom, Montana, in the Big Hole Valley. The three children were then sent to Plainview, Nebraska, to live with Susan's brother and sister, Mike and Elizabeth Hitchens, where the girls grew up, married and raised their families.

On September 8, 1883, Bill participated in the driving of another golden spike. He was one of the throng that gathered at Gold Creek station to witness the completion of The Northern Pacific – another trail of steel across the country. The driving of that spike made possible the movement of steam-driven trains along the trail that Bill had so often traveled on foot or on horseback.

In 1889 William Doney drove the first stage from Drummond to

Myrtle (Doney) Timmerman, Louise (Doney) Logan, Jessie (Doney) Trafford and Robert Trafford.

Ovando according to the *Silver State Post's* June 27, 1889, issue: "Mr. William Doney, an old resident of Montana, has made all necessary arrangements to establish a stage line from Drummond to Ovando and Helmville, making his first trip on July 9, 1889."

Bill began to feel his mortality when his brother Edward died January 18, 1908 near Ovando. Bill wrote a letter to his daughter Myrtle Doney in Nebraska stating "I am living all alone on my homestead four miles from town or from any person. I am very lonesome…I am likely to be found dead at any time. I wish you would be sure and answer this letter so that I can let you know some of my business."

In 1910 he built a new house for himself and tore down the old one. In September 1910, Bill became a member of the Society of Montana Pioneers. At that time, he listed his home as Pikes Peak and his occupation as a miner. On December 31, 1911, *The Missoulian* ran an interview with "Major Bill" that was later published in Arthur Stone's 1913 book *Following*

John P. Weidenfeller holding John F. Weidenfeller and Arthemise Isabelle (Doney) Weidenfeller (sister to William J. Doney).

Old Trails.

In 1914, Bill's son-in-law and daughter, George and Myrtle (Doney) Timmerman, along with their daughters Pearl Elizabeth (born November 10, 1910) and Ruby Margaret (born September 5, 1912), came to Montana and homesteaded approximately 20 miles from Roundup in central Montana – Pearl remembered her grandfather Bill visiting their homestead that first year. Three more children were born to George and Myrtle in Montana – Grace Alice (November 9, 1914), Lelah Louise (November 1, 1916) and Clara Ann (December 6, 1918). After raising only one crop of wheat in 7 years, and after their daughter Grace died on October 8, 1919, the family moved back to Nebraska in 1920.

Edward D. Doney. Brother of William J. Doney.

Bill remained active and lived on his claim until his death. While riding his horse near Gold Creek on his way to visit friends in Missoula on February 27, 1921, he died of heart disease. His body was taken to Deer Lodge for the funeral and he was buried in the Deer Lodge Hillcrest Cemetery, near his parents, William Henri and Marie Olivia (Buatte) Dannis, a sister Arthemise Isabelle (Doney) Weidenfeller, and other relatives and friends.

Bill Doney was known as one of the jovial, good-hearted placer miners of the Gold Creek area and one of the old landmarks of the county. He was affectionately known as "Major Bill" and the "Mayor of Pikes Peak."

Doney Lake, located in the hills above Pioneer, was named for him and Doney Cabin, located nearby, can be rented through the Forest Service.

Bill answered "The Call of the West" and was one of many pioneers that helped to settle Montana. Some of his descendants still proudly call Montana home.

Benjamin Henry Dudden

Submitted by William Paul Hartz, Great-Grandson, and Ida Gregory Hartz, Great-Granddaughter

Benjamin Henry Dudden was born in Hamburg, Germany, on November 22, 1838. He immigrated with a group of German men and arrived in the Deer Lodge Valley in 1864.

Benjamin and Johanna Folchen (some in the family say Tochman), were married in December 1869. Johanna was born in 1854 in Conlienziel, Germany. She immigrated to German Gulch in 1869 coming overland by covered wagon pulled by oxen from Ogden, Utah. They were the parents of 12 children, some who died in infancy or early childhood. Margaret was the first born on August 3, 1871; Annie on November 18, 1872; Mary on

Dudden home at Silver Bow, Montana, with William Dudden on a horse. The Dudden home became the Hotel for several decades and stood beside the Northern Pacific Railroad. The Hotel was torn down when Interstate 15 was built in 1960.

September 17, 1876; Harry in April of 1878; Benjamin A. on August 3, 1879; Altie was born in May 1883; Adeline in August of 1885 (Adeline lived to be 100 years old); twin girls Annie and Alice in 1894; William in March 1897 and Clara, date unknown.

The Duddens owned mining claims in and around Butte and we are told they once had one where the corner of Park and Main Street is now. The family home and farm was built and completed in 1888 at Silver Bow. It covered part of the area that is now Interstate 15.

The Dudden children attended the old Silver Bow School, which was located just below the present Interstate 15 across the creek from town. The children learned the English language and taught it to their parents.

After the death of her husband in 1901, Johanna had the family home moved to the town of Silver Bow where she operated it as a hotel and rooming house. It was located near the railroad station. A sign painted on the side of the building read "Hotel – Meals 25¢." It was torn down in 1960.

Johanna (Folchen) Dudden passed away at the age of 70 on March 5, 1922. Her ashes are scattered at the family farm.

Benjamin was present at the Masonic Temple meeting when the Vigilantes were organized. He passed away on January 22, 1901, and is buried in Butte, Montana, along with most of his family.

Margaret "Maggie" Dudden was married to Paul Henry Hartz on June 29, 1893, at Silver Bow Junction, Montana. Paul and his father, Peter Hartz, and three brothers, Peter, Matthew, and Theodore, emigrated from Prussia, Germany, to the Deer Lodge Valley in 1870 and lived on a farm at Pioneer, Montana. Paul and Maggie were parents of four sons, Paul Benjamin, Raymond John, Harry Henry, and Benjamin Alfred all born at Silver Bow. A daughter, Margaret, was born in Helena, Montana, in 1914. Paul Hartz worked at the Anaconda Brewing Company and the Diamond Ice Company in Anaconda. They moved to Helena in 1909 and he was Brewmaster at Kessler Brewery. The family moved to Butte in the 1930's and he worked as a Brewmaster at the Butte Brewery until his death on August 20, 1940. Maggie passed away on December 20, 1951.

Family members who were and are members of the Sons and Daughters of Montana Pioneers include: Raymond J. Hartz and his son William Paul; Benjamin A. Hartz; Ida Hartz Gregory, daughter of Paul Benjamin Hartz; and Evelyn Hartz Hamill, daughter of Harry H. Hartz.

Pierre Napoleon DuMontier

*Submitted by Albert L. DuMontier, Grandson,
and Dorothy DuMontier Ford, Great-Granddaughter,
Members of the Sons and Daughters of the Montana Pioneers*

    Napoleon DuMontier was born November 2, 1840, in Quebec, Canada, and left Quebec as a boy of fourteen to come west to Montana. He joined the Hudson's Bay Company, and while with this famous company, he had many interesting and dangerous experiences. These involved the old Forts: Steele, McKenzie, McLeod, Hall, Union and Benton. He later spent some time in the Red River Valley. Later he located at Virginia City, and then at Deer Lodge, where he formed a lasting friendship with men who started the "Pioneer Club." W. A. Clark was president of the Pioneer Club. Mr. DuMontier took an active interest in this club and never failed to attend a meeting or banquet.

    In 1860 he drove a freight team of oxen for Johnnie Grant between Fort Benton and Deer Lodge. He later worked for Dent, Stewart & Company of Deer Lodge, and for Worden Mercantile Company of Deer Lodge. He went to the Bitterroot in 1862 and erected a hand-hewn log house that stood long after his death. While in the Bitterroot Valley he met Miss Esther Matt, sister of the late Alec Matt, also a well-known pioneer of the state. Pierre and Esther were married on June 25, 1867. About the time of his marriage he made a trip across the mountains with eight head of horses for "X" Biedler, the famous Vigilante. He was also given a package for delivery, and did not know what it contained. Upon his arrival in Deer Lodge found that he had safely delivered several thousand dollars worth of gold dust. For his good work Mr. Biedler gave him his choice of the horses for his own to make the return trip. He chose a beautiful roan that he prized as long as it lived.

    After his marriage he lived a more quiet life in the Bitterroot Valley. Fourteen children – eight daughters and six sons – were born to this union. All but two of these children were baptized in the first church erected in Montana, which is still standing at Stevensville and is known as St. Mary's Mission.

    This church was one of the landmarks loved by Mr. DuMontier. His personal friend and companion Father DeSmet erected it. The Father made two trips across the same part of the country as Mr. DuMontier. One time the Father was able to save the lives of the entire party. A horseman became lost when looking for the horses and wandered into an Indian camp. He pretended to be crazed thinking the Indians would not kill a crazed man. However, by his presence the Indians knew there was a camp of white men nearby. After locating the camp, the Indians fired upon them. They probably would have all been killed, but Father DeSmet was able to make peace by giving the Indians blankets, tobacco, and small trinkets.

Pierre Napoleon DuMontier

Mr. DuMontier was a scout during the Nez Percé War of 1877, and spent much time mining in Alder Gulch, Cedar Gulch, and Virginia City. He knew all of the well-known characters such as Sheriff Henry Plummer and Tin Cup Joe. One time when carrying a message, he ran into a civil war between two Indian tribes. It was necessary for him to hide in the bushes for days until the battle subsided so he could proceed without being seen.

Esther Matt DuMontier passed away October 14, 1898, before Mr. DuMontier left the Bitterroot. She is laid to rest beside her small son in the Stevensville Cemetery.

At age 84, Napoleon DuMontier fell ill with pneumonia and heart failure. He was able to get to the home of his old friend, A. L. DeMers, and ask for aid. The children were summoned and he was taken to the home of his daughter where he died on December 18, 1924, just 24 hours after he was stricken.

His was the useful and happy life of the pioneer, and during his time he made many true friends, was admired for his bravery, and respected for his noble character.

Services for Mr. DuMontier were held at the Catholic Church at the old Jocko Agency in Arlee where he was buried. Father Taelman, who was a friend of the pioneers as well as the Indians, officiated.

Napoleon DuMontier was the father of Alfred "Fred" DuMontier (1877-1948) of Stevensville and Arlee, the grandfather of Albert L. DuMontier, born 1904, and great-grandfather of Dorothy DuMontier Ford of Arlee and Missoula.

Francis R. (Frank) Ellis

Submitted by W. Robert Ellis, Grandson

Francis Richard (Frank) Ellis was born on January 23, 1842, in the small mining district of Zennor about six miles south of St. Ives on the West Coast of Cornwall, England. His parents, Thomas Ellis and Grace Richards, were married September 10, 1826, in Zennor, Cornwall, England. There were ten children born to this marriage: Ann born November 5, 1826, Mary Richards March 15, 1829, John born June 27, 1831, Thomas Ellis born June 1, 1835, Robert Richard born November 20, 1836, William born in 1839, Francis Richard born January 23, 1842, Grace born in 1845, Ruth born in 1848, and Nancy born in 1849. All ten children were born in England. The three cities where the family lived, Zennor, St. Ives, and Madron were mining towns located in the area known as Lands End, Cornwall, England.

The 1851 census showed the family living at Barvella or Baruella, Parish of St. Ives, Cornwall, England, Ecclesiastical District of Halsetown. The head of the family was listed as Thomas Ellis, age 50 years, occupation miner. Grace Ellis, wife, listed as homemaker, was 44 years old. The eldest daughter, Ann, 24 years old, was working as a servant but still living at this address. Mary was not listed at this address but her age would have been 22 years old. What happened to Mary is unknown. John who was 19, Thomas 16, Robert 14, and William 12, were all living at this address and their occupations were miners. Francis, aged nine, listed as a scholar, as was his sister Grace aged six. Francis and Grace along with Ruth aged three and Nancy aged two were all living at this address.

In the years following 1850, the United States began mining copper and tin ore faster and cheaper than could be produced in England. England could no longer compete with the United States in the world market.

Cornwall tin and copper mines began to shut down leaving up to 80 percent of the families out of work. Thomas Ellis could no longer support his large family. He was a violinist and had a pleasant singing voice, so he found work entertaining in the local pubs, but unfortunately, it was not enough to support him much less the entire family. Francis' brothers looked to other countries to support themselves. John and Robert went to the United States, Thomas was reported to have gone to South Africa, and William and Francis were taken abroad on sailing vessels with their mother's brothers, the Richards. Francis was paired with his namesake, Francis Richards. William went with another uncle, but this uncle's name is unknown. According to family hearsay, the ship that William was on sunk at sea and all hands were lost.

Francis "Frank" Ellis

Captain Richards, Francis' uncle, was also known as Captain Jack, and Francis was to become known as Frank. Reasons for the name changes are unknown, but the name Frank stuck with him for the rest of his life. Frank was around nine or ten years old and was being raised as a sailor, learning the ways of a seaman and the operations of a sailing vessel. The ship became his new home.

Captain Jack knew the importance of an education, so when Frank was not on the ship he was required to go to school in New York City. New

York was one of the chief ports used by Captain Jack. Frank and Captain Jack made many trips across the Atlantic Ocean to many shipping ports in Europe. They made several trips around Cape Horn of South America and up the West Coast of South and North America. Most of their shipping in the late 1850's and early 1860's was up and down the East Coast of the United States. With the coming of the War Between the States, Captain Jack was carrying supplies to both sides of the conflict. Since his ship was of foreign registry, he could offer his services to both sides without having to declare allegiance to either. It was on one of these supply missions that Captain Jack's ship was either sunk by the States war effort or sprung a leak and sunk near the harbor of New York City. It is unknown if Frank was aboard the ship, but Captain Jack made sure that his crew was safely on shore, and as traditional, he went down with his ship. With his uncle dead and his home on the bottom of the harbor, Frank was on his own. Frank knew his way around New York City and having inherited his father's singing voice, he soon found work singing in the local bars.

In the early 1860's Frank was contacted by his brothers in Michigan and was informed of the need for sailors on ore ships sailing on the Great Lakes. Frank went to Buffalo, New York, and was hired on an ore ship as its Captain. He sailed from Buffalo to Port Huron where the ore was loaded, and then returned to Buffalo where the ore was processed. Frank's brothers were working the mines where the ore was mined.

Frank's brothers introduced him to William Corkill who was mining with the Ellis brothers in Michigan. William was a miner from the Isle of Man, an island located between England and Ireland in the Irish Sea. Frank and William developed a friendship that lasted a lifetime. During this time, the Ellis brothers, John and Robert, decided that working for someone else offered little future. With their experience in the mines of Cornwall, England, not forgotten, they decided to head for the gold fields in California, where a miner could mine for himself. Before John and Robert left the mine in Michigan, Frank had agreed to meet them in Grass Valley, California, after they scouted out the area around the gold fields in Grass Valley. William Corkill decided to also go to California when Frank was ready to go. Frank did not like sailing the Great Lakes. Many ships were lost due to the rough choppy water, short high waves and heavy ore loads that caused the vessels to set low in the water.

After spending a couple of years sailing on the Great Lakes, Frank returned to New York City where he was hired as a common seaman on a ship going to South America. William Corkill left his mining job in

Michigan and headed for California, going overland. The two men agreed to meet in the gold fields of California.

When his ship reached the Isthmus of Panama, Frank left the ship and walked overland to the West Coast. There he caught a ship bound for San Francisco. It is not clear whether Frank hired on as a crewmember or paid his way.

By the time Frank reached Grass Valley all the claims were taken and no one was interested in taking on partners. William Corkill it seems had not reached the area. It is not known if Frank's brothers got to Grass Valley in time to get placer mining claims or if they purchased them from someone else or even reached the gold fields. Frank apparently never heard from his brothers. Frank arrived in Grass Valley in either late 1863 or early 1864.

Frank, after checking out the gold fields and seeing that there wasn't much opportunity left to find gold, decided to return to San Francisco for he knew that shipping merchants were looking for experienced seamen. He had no trouble being hired on a ship that sailed down the coast to South America and back to San Francisco. The more trips he could make the more money he would receive. One trip found him racing another ship when he misjudged the tide and ran the ship aground off the southern coast of California. Fortunately, this wasn't considered his vessel since he was only hired as skipper, so he was not bound, as traditional, to go down with the ship. After putting his crew and himself ashore, the year being 1866, Frank headed for Grass Valley where he now knew that William Corkill had arrived and was looking for him. How Frank got from southern California to Grass Valley is unknown. After meeting William it was obvious that there was no longer much chance of finding gold there. The word was out that Montana was the place to find the mother lode. After much thought the two men decided that Last Chance Gulch in Montana Territory would be their last chance, so they headed for Montana. William again overland, and Frank headed for a seaport where he either hired on as a common sailor or paid his way to Seattle, Washington Territory. This would end Frank's career as a mariner.

After inquiring which was the best route to take, Frank began his overland journey, walking in the direction of the Montana Territory. He reached Last Chance Gulch, now known as Helena, in late 1866 or early 1867. He bought a third partnership with two men for $250. The mining claim was located where Broadway and Last Chance Gulch now meet. Parchen Drug Store would later be built on the site. In the first year, Frank had cleared more than $7,000 and had his gold molded into a brick. The partners sold their claim to a group of Chinese. This would be an end to Frank's career as a placer miner. William Corkill had not reached Montana at this time.

Frank Ellis was a thinking man and could see that Montana offered many opportunities. The area was not over populated like the East Coast was becoming. The land was for the taking and offered free range for the raising of livestock. The land surrounding Helena and a large valley just over the hills to the east grew tall native grasses, often as high as a horse's belly. There was plenty of clear running streams and rivers, a perfect place to raise animal stock. When Frank was making his trek to Last Chance Gulch he had passed the place where the Snake River joins the Columbia River and near this area he noticed the good looking cattle being raised in what is now Walla Walla, Washington.

In early spring of 1868, Frank bought an old white burro to pack his bed, supplies and gold brick and started off for Walla Walla, Washington. He was not far from Last Chance Gulch when he was stopped by a group of law officers. They demanded to know where he obtained the burro and what his business was. He finally convinced them that the burro was not stolen nor were the supplies. Frank was never quite certain if these men were law officers, road agents, or Vigilantes. Not long after his run-in with the law, several Indians who wanted money stopped him. He satisfied the Indians with a few coins and continued on without any more delays. It is not known which route Frank followed through Western Montana, Idaho, and finally into Washington.

Frank had planned to buy cattle, then return to Montana and establish a ranch and make his living by raising beef cattle. In Walla Walla, Washington, he cashed his gold brick and bought two hundred and fifty head of Oregon Short Horn cows. The Oregon Short Horns were a cross between Short Horn bulls and Texas Long Horn cows. The cattle were bred to survive the cold winter months and forage for themselves on the open range. Frank obtained the stock for $8 per head with spring calves included. He hired some friendly Indians to help drive the cattle from Walla Walla to Montana. The drive started in May and took until late September to complete. Some time during the drive, William Corkill met them and joined the drive the rest of the way to Montana. William's reason for not joining Frank in Montana was that he did some prospecting along the way without finding any gold leads. William did not expect to find Frank driving cattle, but after Frank explained to him his future plans and that he would like to have William join him, William decided this didn't sound like a bad way to go as he was getting tired of moving all over the country looking for that gold strike. They reached the Missouri River at a place called Ogden, about 40 miles east of Helena. Ogden was known as the place to ford the river, which later became known as Bedford and where the first flour mills in Montana Territory were located. There is a red brick silo still standing at the site. After paying the Indians, the partners set about finding a place to ford the river. The plan was to cross the river and winter their cattle on the East Side. For some reason, the river was overflowing its banks, although normally at this time of year it would be at it's lowest. The men were having trouble getting the cows to ford the river and were short-handed, as they no longer had the Indians to help.

William Gordon, Almond Lincoln, and Hank Frazer were partners starting a ranch on the Musselshell River near the town of what is now known as Martinsdale. The ranch would later be known as the old Frazer Ranch. By chance the three men met Frank and William as they were attempting to ford the river. Seeing that they were having trouble and since they were looking for cattle to buy, they made Frank and William an offer of $14 per head including the spring calves. Since they were not getting the cows to ford the river and had spent little money getting the herd this far, and $6 per head was a good profit, they sold the herd to the Musselshell partners. The Musselshell partners got their start in the ranching business with this herd.

Frank and William thought this was not such a bad way to make money and began to plan another trip to buy more Oregon Short Horn cows. They conferred with the Musselshell partners and learned that the cattle were thriving and were foraging for themselves on the open range. It was in the spring of 1869 when they packed the old white burro with supplies and saddled up for the return trip to Washington Territory. They felt that if they could not fund buyers for the cattle, they could always go into the ranching business for themselves. When they reached the other side of Lewiston, Idaho, just across the Washington border (as is known today) they found a herd for sale. They paid $7 a head with the spring calves included; this made a herd of 250 cows with calves. They again hired Indians to help with the drive back to Ogden and the ford on the Missouri River. The drive took the best part of the summer and after paying the Indians they began looking for a buyer. There was no buyer this time and with winter approaching, the men had to begin to prepare for winter. They were able to ford the river just a few miles down the river from what is known today as Townsend. From here they moved several miles further down the river and picked an area known as Duck Creek, which is on the East Side of the river. They made a dugout in the hillside for shelter during the winter, and the cattle foraged on the river bottomland. Frank and William enjoyed this kind of life and knew that this was what they wanted so they began scouting the surrounding area for a permanent site. Over the mountain range to the east they found good grass, plenty of water and no one to compete for the wide-open range. The large valley is known as the Smith River Valley. There was only one resident and a military post at the northwest end of the valley.

Early in the spring of 1870, the cattle were moved over the mountains to where Newland Creek empties into the Smith River. This site is about 5 miles down the river from a log cabin built where the hot springs are located, now the site of White Sulphur Springs. The military post, the other settlement, was located about 10 miles down the river from where Newland Creek empties into the river. The post was established to keep watch on the Indians, assist the settlers by loaning them equipment to clear the land, erect buildings, and provide whatever services were available at the post. The partners took advantage of the military services and borrowed a team of oxen, a wagon, hand tools, army rifles and ammunition for protection against the Indians. They began constructing a dugout in the side of a small hill with a pole roof covered with sod and dirt as a temporary shelter. They hauled poles and fence posts from Lime Kiln Gulch so they could fence the property on all sides as well as make corrals and a barn for the saddle horses and oxen. The military posts also supplied them a mower and rake so they could cut the wild grass and rake it into piles to be stored in the barn. The wild grass was not only used for their animals, but was shared with the post as payment for use of government equipment. The Indians would often stop and use the grinding stone to sharpen their knives. The Indians were never a problem to the partners.

The first couple of winters were mild and the cattle wintered well. But after two winters in the dugout, they got busy and built themselves a decent cabin. They spent valuable time making improvements on their ranch. Having neglected getting supplies for the coming winter, which came early with heavy snowfall and cold temperatures, the partners ran short on supplies. They had spent so much time on the building project that they failed to make their regular trip to Helena for their winter stock of rations. The men had no choice but to try getting to Helena with packhorses. They knew that with deep snow in the mountain passes that the only way was with saddle and packhorses. The trip was very difficult. There was even more snow on the mountain pass than they had expected. Once in Helena the weather turned even worse forcing the partners to spend the remaining winter there. It was late spring before Frank and William could return to their ranch.

Their ranch house and out buildings survived the winter with little damage. However, their cattle were scattered all over the valley. Deep snow and cold temperatures along with the wolves had claimed quite a few. As Frank began to find, count, and gather the cows together, he found that a large number of cows had wandered into a group of mountains known as the Dry Range in the northwest part of the valley where Smith River flows through the large canyon that separates the Belt Mountains in the north. Another large mountain stream, known as Rock Creek, flowing from the west enters the Smith River. To the south of Rock Creek and west of Smith River lies the Dry Range. The cows that Frank found that had wintered in the Dry Range were in much better condition than those that hadn't, so Frank decided to make a check of this area. He found that because of a lack of water in this range of mountains, only two small springs, summer grazing is limited without access to water and whoever controls the water supply controls the grazing in the Dry Range. The wild grass-eating animals made this area their winter range and moved to other areas during the summer months. Frank could see great possibilities by having the free grazing of this high productive grass growing range. Frank was to keep this area in mind.

The partners continued to make improvements on the ranch. They increased the size of their cabin. They fenced an area where wild hay was grown and cut for storage in the barn for their saddle and workhorses. The partners had returned the oxen to the military post and now depended on horses to do the ranching chores. They used workhorses to build ditches for water irrigation and pulling wagons for whatever needs came up. The partners established the policy of selling only steers that had reached the age of four. Some of these animals weighed as much as a ton.

Susan Ann Buckingham was born February 27, 1856, in East Newlyn, Cornwall, England. Her father, Abraham Buckingham, was born in East Newlyn, 1824, his wife, Martha Buckingham, was born in 1826 in Sparnok, both in Cornwall, England. They were married May 23, 1847, at Kea Parish, Cornwall. The couple had the same last name, as they were first cousins. Susan Ann came with her parents, older brother, Abraham, younger brothers William and Joseph, and sister Ellen Nellie to the Territory of Montana in 1874. Abraham worked as a tin-dresser and in the smelters, but when the mines shut down there was no more ore to be processed. Like the miners he had to leave Cornwall to find work. How the family found their way to Montana Territory is unknown. The family settled in a mining camp called Diamond City in the Belt Mountains northeast of Helena, which was the County Seat of Meagher and a very rich gold field. Abraham established a livery stable and a freight business. Frank Ellis met the Buckingham family in Diamond City when he stopped there on business trips to Helena.

Frank had applied for citizenship to the U.S. District Court of the Third Judicial District of the Territory of Montana in Helena. Frank was granted citizenship in 1879.

Frank and Susan were married in Diamond City on July 15, 1876, by J.E. Murray, Probate Judge, and witnessed by Susan's brother, Abraham, and Sarah Winston. Frank built a new house for his bride on the property that William and Frank had claimed but did not have legal title to. The couple furnished their home with first class furniture.

The valley was beginning to draw settlers. A town site was forming at the old trapper's log cabin, where the hot sulphur springs were located, about five miles to the southeast of the partners' ranch site and fast becoming a trading center.

By 1879, Frank and Susan had two children, Francis Thomas, their first born and named after his father and grandfather, was born in 1877. Grace, the couple's second child was named after Frank's mother and was born in 1878. With a growing family to care for, Frank could see that he and William should acquire legal ownership of this property.

William felt that Frank should become the owner. To purchase the property, Frank needed to file an affidavit of preemption claimant and pay $1.25 per acre to the land office in Helena. His land purchase was recorded as cash entry No. 741. Before he could obtain clear title to the land, Frank needed to have two witnesses testify that he was a person of respectability, that he had lived on this land for a certain period of time, and that he had made improvements. Both witnesses had to record and sign a preemption proof form. John H. Freeser, the first witness, occupation was listed as stock raiser, James Mayn, second witness, signed the forms for Frank. Frank did not have a homestead filing on any property on Newland Creek, but he did patent 160 acres as preemption on March 4, 1882. William Corkill and Frank Ellis dissolved their partnership in 1882.

William moved to a parcel of land where he built his own place. His new ranch included bottomland that the Smith River flows through and lies about three miles due west of White Sulphur Springs. William brought his nephew from Missouri to help with the ranch. William's nephew was named after his uncle but he was called Billy. The Corkills were very successful ranchers. In later years Billy married one of Frank's daughters. William died in 1910 and Billy continued to run the ranch until his death. The break-up of Frank and William's partnership did not change their feelings for one another, and they remained friends.

In 1883, Frank Ellis, William Gordon, Hank Freeser, and two other ranchers from Lavine, Montana, rounded up a herd of steers from the open range to be driven to the railroad station in Corrine, Utah, where they would be loaded on railroad cars to be shipped to eastern markets. The herd consisted of around 900 steers four years old or older, and the drive began in early August. At a crossing on the Yellowstone River at Fort Colson near Billings, nearly 300 of the steers were lost either from drowning or breaking away from the herd while trying to ford the river. It took the ranchers several weeks to get the runaway steers back together in the original herd and to make a count of the drowned steers. It was the middle of October before the drive reached Corrine. The drive was such a failure that they never tried another drive.

Every fall the ranchers would hold an annual round-up. Working together they would take turns driving the wagons that carried their food as well as bedrolls and other supplies. A round-up could take up to a month to gather the cattle into herds and then not always getting all the cattle. The men on horses would drive the cattle into groups at a designated area where the cattle would be checked for ownership and after determining ownership, the owner would usually determine from seeing his cattle in one group, the cows that were not producing calves. Cows too old to survive the coming winter or have more calves would be shipped along with the steers. The fall round-up would probably be the only time of the year that the owner would see all his cattle in one group. Having cut out the cattle that were to be sold, they next had to be driven to shipping points. Over the years, Frank shipped from many places such as Corrine, Utah, Billings, Great Falls, Townsend, Ringling, Armington, Dorsey and White Sulphur Springs. From these shipping points the cattle would be loaded on railcars and sent to eastern cattle markets. Each year Frank shipped around 300-400 head of cattle, the majority being four-year-old steers. The steers were so heavy that they would often break the floor of the railcar requiring the railroad to bring in extra cars. The beef price varied from year to year usually ranging from $50-200 per animal.

One year Frank had rounded up a herd of steers to be shipped from

Dorsey. Dorsey had a station on the Jaw-Bone Railroad, which would later become the Milwaukee Railroad. Frank and his hired men kept the steers in a holding pen waiting for the train to arrive. When the train engineer entered the station, he blew the whistle. The whistle frightened the large steers and they stampeded, tearing down the holding pens and demolishing the stock yard. The steers then headed for the surrounding hills. It took several days to gather and drive the steers back to Dorsey. The railroad used the time it took to round up the steers to rebuild the holding pens. The engineers never blew the train whistle again entering Dorsey.

The years between 1880 and 1912 were good years for raising cattle on the open range. With mild winters and wet summers, there was plenty of feed, which kept animal loss to a minimum, and Frank's herd was growing as well as the other ranchers. The competition for the free range was still small, but each year there were more ranchers taking advantage of the free range. Having more cattle forced the cattle to cover larger areas. Frank could no longer keep track and cover the large area that his cattle now covered. He had to hire help, anywhere from two to four men, more in the winter months. A cowboy who looked after the cattle on the open range was a special person, he had a love for country and animals. During the years of the open range, bulls ran with the cows at all times. A new calf could be born at any time during the winter or summer months. Calves born during the winter months required more attention than those born in the warmer months. Young cows often would have trouble birthing their first calves, so the cowboy's help was needed. The new calves needed to be marked or branded, to prove ownership, and this usually required two men. First a fire had to be started to heat the branding iron, then one of the men would rope the calf around the neck and hold it until the second man could wrestle the calf down and tie its legs. If it was a bull calf castration was necessary, by this time the branding iron was hot enough to put Frank's mark on the animal. One of the biggest problems was keeping the calf's mother from hurting the men while trying to protect her calf. All these jobs were performed on the open range not in corrals or sheds that added protection. There was always the threat of wolves, mountain lions, and other wild meat-eating animals. A large portion of the herd was lost to these predators. A new calf was an easy meal for a pack of wolves. The bulls and two-year-old steers were usually safe because of their size, and that they stayed in larger groups for protection. Killing the wild animals to protect the cattle was a requirement for the hired help. Frank made sure the bounty collected, which could range between $5 and as high as a $100 went to whoever killed the predators. The hired cowboys worked from sun-up until sundown thirty days a month. There was no such thing in those days of a forty-hour workweek. Frank would supply room and board for the hired men and their salary was based on experience and tenure, with salaries ranging from $30-60 per month. Raising cattle on the open range was not easy work, for it required long hours in difficult weather, and dangerous working conditions when dealing with wild cattle. The most trusted employees were sent with the cattle on the train to the market area that was usually Chicago. They were responsible for the care of the animals while on the train. The animals would be unloaded at different stations to be fed and have water. The train trip could take as long as two weeks to reach Chicago from Montana.

During the fourteen years that Frank and Susan lived on the ranch on Newland Creek, Frank acquired legal ownership of the property and had acquired a 160-acre desert claim that bordered the Newland Creek property. He had a herd of cattle that numbered anywhere from twenty to twenty-five hundred head. Their family had grown to include not only Francis and Grace, but Susan named after her mother and born in 1880. Martha or Mattie, as she was called, was named for Susan's mother and was born in 1882. The last girl was named Edith and was born in 1885. William Robert, the last child born on May 9, 1890, was named after Frank's brothers. All of Frank and Susan's children were born on the ranch.

Soon after the birth of William in 1890, Frank and Susan were divorced. In the divorce agreement, the children were to stay with their mother. Francis, the oldest child, was twelve years old and William was a baby. Susan would be given the ranch and all improvements on Newland Creek along with 250 cows with spring calves and operating money for a period of time. Susan, with six children to care for, soon found that she could not run the ranch and take care of her cattle on the open range. She sold the ranch to Dave Folson, and apparently Folson bought the cattle also. Susan moved her family to White Sulphur Springs where the children were educated and grew to adulthood. By 1900 Susan had spent all her money from the divorce settlement and was having trouble providing for her two youngest children. Frank moved to his desert claim, where he built a one-room cabin and ran his cattle ranch from his temporary home.

The Homestead Act brought into the valley a lot of new settlers who were fencing their property to keep open range animals off their land. This was forcing the open range ranchers to either buy ranch land or cut the size of their herd. Frank was one of the ranchers with a large number of cattle that were being shut out of the free range. In order to keep a large herd,

Frank filed for homestead rights in 1897 on property where Rock Creek flows into the Smith River. This is the same land that he had found where so many cattle had wintered during the bad winter that William Corkill and Frank spent in Helena. Frank built his ranch house facing south looking up this large canyon, what is known today as Ellis Canyon, that controls access to the Dry Range. Frank also purchased a railroad section that Smith River flows through that bordered his homestead property. Frank kept his desert claim on Newland Creek. Frank now had around 40-50 sections of grazing land that he could graze his cattle on, free open range that no one else could use because of the lack of water. The cattle continued to graze on the high, productive grassland of the Dry Range producing healthy calves and larger steers. During the winter months there would be enough snow on the north slopes for water, and during the summer, water was supplied by Smith River or Rock Creek. The Dry Range, with its mild winters with little snowfall, did have its shortcomings. Large numbers of deer, elk, wild horses and other grass-eating animals would migrate there for the winter followed by the wild meat-eating animals. The great loss of stock to the meat-eating wild animals was always a problem.

During the years of 1890-1912, Frank had so many cattle that he was shipping a large number of steers and older cows to market each year. He was probably one of the last to have a large number of cattle still forging on the open range. However, Frank did realize that the free open range would not last forever. It was becoming evident that there was more stock competing for the free grass and many of the ranchers were cutting back on the number of cattle in their herds because of a lack of open range.

In 1910 the Federal Government set aside most of the land that wasn't claimed as homesteads, railroad property, or owned by private citizens. This land was to become public lands and was to be controlled by a new branch of government called the Federal Forest Service. The Dry Range was divided with every other section of public land. Frank could no longer graze his cattle on Federal lands unless he was willing to pay a fee per animal. Free open range was to be no more. In the fall of 1912, Frank rounded up 1500 head of cattle, steers, bulls, and cows with calves, and sold them to Roy Minty and Duff Prit, local cattle buyers. He kept about 500 head and grazed them on property that he owned or leased. The ranching operation remained the same with the cattle forging themselves and Willy putting up enough hay for saddle horses. Willy, Frank's youngest son, was to handle the everyday duties and supervision of caring for the stock with the help of one or two hired men. Every fall, Frank shipped several railcars of beef to market to pay the hired help and meet expenses. Frank never gave up his ranching interest and was actively making decisions up to the time of his death.

Frank, now past seventy years old, found that he spent more time in town or on his desert claim and was spending more time taking care of his investments. He had bought several city houses that he rented and had purchased city water and sewer municipal bonds. His money was in several banks, however most of his every day banking was with the local bank. He kept a tight rein on his money and was not quick to spend it on the comforts that it could buy. Over the years, he remembered his children and grandchildren on special occasions. Two brothers who were friends of Willy, were trying to establish a ranch and were in financial trouble. The brothers asked Willy if he could loan them $2,000. Willy did not have the funds to help them, but suggested they ask his father. The brothers contacted and asked Frank for the loan. Frank said he would loan them the money and for them to meet him at 8 o'clock the next evening at the springs. White Sulphur Springs has a hot water sulphur spring and local people would gather there to drink the water believing the spring water had healing powers. Frank asked the brothers if $2,000 was enough. They agreed it was and promised to pay Frank back whenever they could. The next morning the brothers hurried to the local bank to deposit the money. The banker inquired if the brothers knew what Frank had done with the rest of the two hundred thousand he had withdrawn the day before. Apparently none of Frank's family even knew that he had withdrawn the money or what he did with the rest of the money. Some of the brothers' heirs still live in Meagher County and are cattle ranchers.

Susan Ann Ellis, with the children raised, filed for homestead rights on property that was in the Newland Creek drainage fifteen miles northeast of White Sulphur Springs and later married Constance LaChat whose homestead bordered Susan's. Constance and Susan lived on their homesteads until age forced them to give up ranching. They retired to White Sulphur Springs where Susan died on March 3, 1936, and is buried in the Mayn cemetery.

Francis Thomas was employed by the *Rocky Mountain Husbandman*, the local newspaper. He later went to Park City, Montana, where he owned the local paper. He was a talented musician, playing the cornet with a local band that had the opportunity to perform for Teddy Roosevelt in Miles City, Montana. Francis married Edna Duncan from Townsend, Montana, and they had no children. Francis died in the mid-1950s and is buried in

Park City, Montana.

Grace married Thomas Edwards and lived on their ranch in the northwest section of Meagher County. Grace's wedding dress was made by her mother and the dress is nearly 100 years old and still intact. Grace and Thomas had five sons, Russell, Alfred, Walter, Harold, and Lawrence (who died at a young age). Grace was the first of the Frank Ellis children to die. She died in 1934 at the age of 56 and is buried in the Mayn Cemetery, While Sulphur Springs. Two of Grace's children lived their entire lives in Meagher County.

Susan married John Bryne and they had a ranch near her sister, Grace, in the northwest Meagher County for a number of years. The Brynes' had sheep on their ranch. Susan was known for her extraordinary cooking ability. The Byrnes' had three children, Edward, Ramona, and Lurlene. Their daughter, Lurlene, became one of the first licensed female pilots in Montana. In later years, the family moved to Chateau, Montana, where John ran a plumbing shop. Susan died in Billings, Montana, in the early 1960's and is buried in the Mayn Cemetery in While Sulphur Springs.

Martha (Mattie) married Billy Corkill. Billy was the nephew of William Corkill, Frank's early day partner. Mattie spent her entire life in Meagher County. She lived on the ranch that was started by William and later became Billy's after the death of William in 1910. Mattie and Billy had three children, Marvin, Leslie and Julia. One of the Corkill's sons is still living in White Sulphur Springs. Mattie died In White Sulphur Springs on June 7, 1961, and is buried in Mayn Cemetery.

Edith married Ernest Falen in White Sulphur Springs. They soon moved to Orofino, Idaho, where Ernest worked in the timber industry. The Falon's had four children: Ellis, Kenneth, Vera, and Bernadine, one son is still living. Edith and Ernest were divorced and Edith moved to Seattle, Washington, where she remarried. Edith died in Seattle and was brought back to Orofino where she is buried.

William (Willy) finished the eighth grade and at thirteen years of age went to work for his father as a hired man. Twenty-six years later at the time of Frank's death he was still running the ranching part of Frank's estate. Willy married Ella Chambers in 1925 in White Sulphur Springs. Willy and Ella had three children, W. Robert (Bob), John W., and Ruth B. All of Willy's children are still living. Willy spent his entire life in Meagher County. Willy died in 1945 at the age of 55 from injuries he received from a ranching accident four years previously. Willy is also buried in Mayn Cemetery.

As Frank got older he would often be singing when riding, walking, or leading his horse. When going to his ranch on Rock Creek with the many limestone cliffs, his voice could be heard for miles as it echoed off the cliffs. Frank enjoyed his pipe and would only smoke after his evening meal. He bought plugs of chewing tobacco and would shave off strips of tobacco with his pocket knife placing the shaving in a container on the back of the stove to dry before smoking. This habit followed him from his days as a seaman.

Frank spent most of the years after his divorce from Susan alone. He did spend a lot of time with his old partner, William Corkill. Frank's three daughters lived on ranches in the same area that many of his cattle roamed and while checking on the animals he would often spend time with them. Two of his grown children had left Meagher County. His youngest son, Willy, spent more time with his father, working for him, than any other of Frank's children. Willy married at age 35, but this was not part of Frank's plans for his son. Since Willy was not going to live alone, neither was Frank. He married Maggie Jenkins. Maggie was the widow of John Jenkins who had a ranch on Tenderfoot Creek where it enters Smith River about ten miles down Smith River from the mouth of Rock Creek. The match turned out to be a mistake. Frank forgave Willy for getting married. Willy was back running Frank's ranch and Frank was in the process of divorcing Maggie when Frank died at age 87 on January 2, 1929.

Funeral services for the remains of Frank Ellis were held at the I.O.O.F. Hall with the Reverend Hamilton officiating. The services were attended by many of his old time friends in the valley and from many outside points. The funeral was delayed for their arrival. Frank is buried in the Mayn Cemetery.

Frank died a wealthy man and his estate was considerable for the time. His widow received 2/3s of the estate and the other 1/3 was divided among his six children. Each child received $60,000. Willy took possession of the ranch and the few cattle that remained as part of his inheritance.

Jennie W. Ennis Chowning

Submitted by Winifred Chowning Jeffers, Daughter

Jennie W. Ennis was born in Oneida, Ohio, August 13, 1863. Her father was in the Madison River Valley filing on a homestead on the day she was born.

William Ennis had taken his wife, Katherine Shriver Ennis, to her father's home to await the baby's birth. He proceeded west to Bannack and Virginia City, with his freight outfit loaded with goods that would be needed at the gold camps.

In the late fall of 1864, Mr. Ennis took his freight outfit to Omaha, left it with a trusted employee, and joined his family in Ohio. In early 1865, the freight wagon arrived in Alder Gulch from Omaha, Nebraska. The trip took 96 days to complete.

Jennie Winifred (Ennis) Chowning

In August 1863, William Ennis built a fairly large log cabin on his homestead. The cabin had a dirt roof, no floor, and a window. It is said to have been the first cabin built in the Madison Valley.

The Ennis family lived about a year in Virginia City. Mrs. Ennis taught school while Mr. Ennis continued to freight. In the spring of 1866, they moved to the cabin Mr. Ennis had built in the Madison Valley in 1863. Mrs. Ennis fastened buffalo hides to the ground with wooden pegs to make a more comfortable floor.

After finishing the grades provided in local schools, Jennie attended

Home School in Virginia City to prepare for entrance into St. Mary's Hall, an Episcopal high school for girls in Fairbault, Minnesota. She had taken piano lessons in Virginia City and continued them at St. Mary's. Her father went to the Centennial Exposition in Philadelphia in 1876 and bought her an upright piano in the Steinway rooms at the Exposition. He had it shipped to Corinne, Utah, from there it was freighted by wagon to the Madison Valley. The piano is still in the family in Bellevue, Washington.

After finishing at St. Mary's, Jennie entered the University of Michigan at Ann Arbor where she studied during the course of a year. She taught school for two terms after returning home. Jennie helped in her father's general store that opened in 1877. She also helped on the ranch and with the housework.

As a child, Jennie rode calves as all ranch children did for excitement. When she was four, her mother put her on a gentle horse and she went to the river bottom to drive in the milk cows. As she grew older she enjoyed fishing and bird hunting.

In 1891 Jennie taught herself the Morse Code of Telegraphy and was licensed as a telegrapher. The telegraph line from Virginia City to Norris ran part way, via the foothills located west of Ennis. Ennis was granted permission to hook on. This mode of communication with the outside was used until the telephone replaced the telegraph.

Jennie met Charles W. Chowning when he came to the valley as a surveyor and land classifier for the Northern Pacific Railroad. They were

Jennie Winifred (Ennis) Chowning. Age 82.

married June 7, 1893, in her parent's home. They made their home in Helena. Their first child, Winifred, was born August 7, 1895. Two other children died at birth. In 1898, they were in Ennis when her father, William Ennis, died.

Mrs. Chowning inherited the store, a few cattle and horses, and some real estate from her father. She was appointed postmaster to succeed him. She continued in the office for forty-two years, when she retired. In about 1905, the Chownings enlarged the general store into one of the finest country stores in the state.

Jennie Ennis Chowning was an Episcopalian and a charter member of Trinity Guild, a charter member of Madison Valley Woman's Club, and the clubs past president. She was a member of the Society of Montana Pioneers and also a member of Sons and Daughters of Montana Pioneers and held offices in both organizations.

The schools held her interest and she supported consolidation. She was convinced a larger school would provide more benefits for the pupils. She was school clerk for over twenty years and the present grade school in Ennis was dedicated The Jennie Ennis Chowning School in her memory in 1953.

She visited the sick and in the absence of a doctor telegraphed or telephoned the symptoms to the doctor in Virginia City who sent medicine out on the stage. The patient usually recovered.

Because of Mrs. Chowning's active interest and participation in community affairs, all businesses in Ennis closed for her funeral. She died on November 11, 1951, at the age of 88 and was buried in the Madison Valley Cemetery.

Katherine Shriver Ennis

Submitted by Winifred Chowning Jeffers, Granddaughter

Katherine Shriver was born in Columbiana County, Ohio, the daughter of John and Rachel Summer Shriver April 2, 1835. She lived on the farm of her parents while attending public school in Oneida. In 1861, she and William Ennis were married at Oneida. Mr. Ennis was freighting into Pikes Peak, Colorado. Mrs. Ennis accompanied him on some of his trips.

In March of 1863, Mrs. Ennis returned to her father's home while Mr. Ennis prepared to go to Bannack, Idaho Territory, to the gold diggings.

He sold his ranch and small store in Colorado, loaded up with 80 tons of freight and moved west. He arrived on about June 10, 1863.

Mr. Ennis filed a homestead in the Madison Valley on August 13, 1863, the exact day his wife gave birth to their first child, a daughter, Jennie Winifred, in Ohio. He built a one-room cabin on the homestead, and in 1865, brought his family to Alder Gulch. In 1866, they moved to the cabin on the Madison where a son, William John, was born, January 29, 1867.

In 1868, a four-room log house was purchased in Virginia City and moved to their land in the Madison Valley for a roomier home. This house had two stories, and a "lean to" was added for a kitchen. Mrs. Ennis often kept large amounts of money for Mr. Ennis. She hollowed out a place in the log wall, put the money in, and pasted paper over the place so it looked just like the rest of the wall.

Katherine (Shriver) Ennis

In 1872, Mr. and Mrs. Ennis took their children and, accompanied by the family of William I. Marshall, went on horseback to see the wonders of Yellowstone Park. The two Ennis children rode double. It is suspected they were the first white children in the park.

In 1881 or 1882, the Ennis family built a large home of 13 rooms, with 11-foot ceilings. Mrs. Ennis designed the home and it had a large masonry cellar beneath the kitchen. A hand-driven well, supplied water with a pump in the kitchen. Materials for this home were hauled from Franklin, Idaho, as well as the fine furniture that furnished the five bedrooms, parlor, sitting room, and dining room. The home burned in 1917 but some of the furniture was saved.

Mrs. Ennis was widowed in 1898. She continued to run the part of the ranch that Mr. Ennis willed to her. She was a woman of true pioneer spirit and nothing daunted her. She was not afraid of Indians. Some made regular trips throughout the valley and were her friends. She loved to milk, and in spite of entreaties by her family; she kept a cow until she broke her hip on a visit to Washington State in 1919. The doctors were amazed that the hip began to knit. She was not put into a cast, and was able to massage her hip, which she did with regularity. When she was allowed to return home by train, she sat on a straight chair and was transferred from train to train, as necessary, sitting on the chair. In a few months, she was on crutches, which she used for about a year. She was able to use a cane around the house or on a level walk. Eventually she walked with just a cane, but that leg was a trifle shorter.

Mrs. Ennis was confirmed into the Episcopal Church, the church of her husband, and was a charter member of Trinity Guild. The ministers who came to hold services in the valley were most often her guests – but preachers, or ministers, of any denominations were welcome in her home. She was an excellent cook and a fine seamstress and did fine needlework. Her dining table was always covered with a hand-hemmed, linen cloth - yet she could do most any of the ranch tasks, and did if the occasion required it.

One neighbor told of coming to visit Mrs. Ennis and finding her out in the corral. She was holding a horse's head to the ground, which Mr. Ennis had thrown in order to get some part of the breaking harness on.

On many occasions Mrs. Ennis served as a midwife and helped nurse the sick. She was a long time member of the Society of Montana Pioneers and attended the yearly meetings if at all possible. On her birthday, she held open house assisted by her daughter Mrs. Chowning, and her niece Mrs. Hattie Angle. She especially liked to meet the new schoolteachers.

She donated land for the school, the Methodist Church, the Forest Service Buildings on Hugel Street, and the V.F.W. building.

Mrs. Ennis attended the Pioneer meeting in August 1931. Her death followed on November 4th. She was 96 years old.

William Ennis

Submitted by Winifred Chowning Jeffers, Granddaughter

One of the honored pioneers of Montana and Madison County was William Ennis, born in County Down, Ireland, March 17, 1828, of Scottish parentage. John and Mary Stuart McKee Ennis had come to Northern Ireland to avoid religious persecution. There were 11 children and William was the sixth. At the age of 14, William came to America with his father and attended school in Holyoke, Massachusetts. He later moved to Detroit, lived with an uncle, and entered the railroad machine shops where he learned the trade. He was first a conductor on a gravel train, then on passenger trains, and was promoted to roadmaster of Chicago & Rock Island Railroad where

William Ennis. Founder of Ennis, Montana.

he had charge of such things as the erection of bridges. It was while railroading that he met Miss Katherine Shriver of Altoona, Iowa, whom he later married. In 1858 he left railroading for Kansas where he freighted. He moved to Central City, Colorado, where he took up land and opened a general store.

On August 5, 1861, he and Miss Katherine Shriver were married at her father's home in Oneida, Ohio. In the spring of 1863, Mrs. Ennis returned to Iowa. Mr. Ennis bought 80 tons of freight in Omaha, such as sugar, flour, bacon, and other groceries, and some miners' tools. With his 100 head of oxen, some mules and a few saddle horses, he headed his freight outfit toward Bannack, Idaho Territory. He arrived on about June 10 and sold quite a bit to miners. He proceeded to Alder Gulch and arrived June 22. He sold as fast as gold dust could be weighted out – this procedure taking about three days. Bacon that cost six cents a pound sold for 60 cents. Flour sold for $50.00 per 100 pounds that had originally cost him $5.00. Sugar had the same profit.

With so much livestock, Mr. Ennis needed feed. He was directed to the Madison Valley, but the townspeople of Virginia City did not think he could get over the Tobacco Root Divide, since there was no wagon road. On July 5, 1863, he told his teamsters to hitch up and start up through Daylight Gulch. They climbed to the Race Track and went down Freiler Creek to the south side of Moore's Creek. Then they went out onto the bench, east across the bench, dropping off about where the brick kiln used to be, and then down the plateau, about where Joe Brion's place used to be. Then due north along Moore's Creek to where Main Street in Ennis is now located. He called a halt and he stopped there. The men were set to work cutting the lush river grass that sold in Virginia City for $100 to $125 a ton. About the middle of July he returned to Virginia City with about 20 tons of grass.

Before leaving, however, he had men cut cottonwood logs on the east side of the river in a grove. They then brought them across the river and set up a one-room dirt floor, dirt-roof cabin which is said to be the first cabin in the valley. When he arrived back in Virginia City, Mr. Ennis took a "squatter's right" on the land he had chosen. On August 13, 1863, he claimed it as a homestead. He made three or four more hay trips and returned to freighting.

In the late fall of 1864 he went to Ohio, leaving his freight outfit with a trusted employee in Omaha. In early 1865 Mr. Ennis returned to Omaha to prepare for the trip west. His wife and little daughter Jennie who had been born August 13, 1863, joined him in May. The load consisted of groceries, miners' tools and other farm tools. On May 6, 1865, they started for Alder Gulch. The trip took 96 days. The first winter they stayed in Virginia City. Mrs. Ennis taught school, and at times was assisted by Mr. Ennis.

In the spring of 1866 they moved to the cabin in the Madison Valley and Mr. Ennis freighted again. In 1868 a two-story log house was purchased in Virginia City and moved to the valley for their dwelling. In 1873 Mr. Ennis built a log building and went into the general merchandise business. He was made postmaster in 1881, when the Ennis Post Office was established. In 1881–1882, a large residence of 13 rooms was built and furnished throughout. The materials were hauled from Franklin, Idaho.

Mr. Ennis owned over 2,000 acres at his death – a good many under ditch, surveyed, and constructed by him. He was extensively engaged in stock raising and originated and used the "Rising Sun" brand. He continued with these works until his untimely death on July 4, 1898, from a gunshot wound at the hands of a former friend, Martin Peel. Feelings ran high over the cold-blooded murder. He was buried in Virginia City and was moved to the Madison Valley Cemetery after his wife's death.

Charles Alexander Evans

Submitted by Brenna Leigh Dorrance, Great-Great-Granddaughter of Charles Evans

Charles Alexander Evans was born on February 27, 1848, in Iona Township, Michigan. He enlisted in the Northern Army during the Civil War. However, because of a bad leg caused by childhood tuberculosis, he was mustered out while marching to the South for combat. The doctor said that a dry climate would help the leg, and at age 19, he decided to make the trek to dry Montana with Jim Titus and his family. They left Michigan together on May 5, 1867, and traveled by wagon train where Charlie spent many nights watching the stock for the group by night.

On one particular night he fell asleep while riding his little cow pony but the horse knew what she was doing and herded the stock herself. Every night from then on Charlie relied on the horse that he came to call his friend, and she was given the job of keeping track of the stock.

After some time on the wagon train, the Titus family and Charlie became concerned about the speed that the train was moving – they were afraid they would not make it to Montana before winter. They held a meeting and with a few others broke off from the wagon train and ventured forth to Montana. On October 10, 1867, they reached Ethel Maynard's stock ranch on the Madison River and stopped for the winter. Charlie worked for the Maynards as a herd breaker.

Through the following years he tried his hand at several occupations including that of a trapper, a ranch hand, and a horse breaker. He once camped with a group of friends by Old Faithful, while it was still pure wilderness. A year later it was declared Yellowstone National Park.

In May of 1880, he married Mary Jane Carter, and they settled across the river from Salesville. This area is now known as the Gallatin

Gateway near Bozeman, Montana.

On May 5, 1882, they had their first son, Harold Duncan Evans. He was lovingly called Dunk by the family, and was named for Charles's brother who had died in Michigan in 1863. Duncan served as a freighter with a 14-horse string, and later operated sawmills in the Judith Gap area. He died on May 15, 1939, at 57 years of age. He never married. The family buried him in the Moore, Montana, cemetery.

Charles and Mary had their second son, Warren Ellis Evans, on April 29, 1884, at Salesville, Gallatin County, Montana. On October 26, 1916, he married Hazel Charlotte Franklin in Living Springs, Montana. They had one child, Marimavis, born on June 9, 1918, at Living Springs.

Charles A. and Mary J. (Carter) Evans – May, 1880.

Marimavis married George Alan Dorrance and currently lives in Billings, Montana. Together they have three sons: Paul, Craig, and George Alan, all of who reside in Montana. Marimavis remembers her grandfather for his twinkling blue eyes and his keen sense of humor. At age 91, in October of 1975, Warren Ellis Evans died in a Billings, Montana, nursing home. His body was cremated and his ashes are buried on his farm near Judith Gap in the Snowy Mountains.

The third son, Charles Burt Evans, was born July 21, 1886, in Salesville. He was called Burt by the family, and wrote several books about the early pioneer experience in Montana. He married Clara Peterson on December 18, 1913, and they settled in Spokane, Washington. He died on January 12, 1976, at age 89, and is buried in the Spokane Memorial Gardens.

The fourth son was named George Roy Evans, and was born January 4, 1889, at Cottonwood, Fergus County, Montana. He never married and ran a sawmill. He took time off only to serve in World War I. He died in Judith Gap, Montana, at the age of 58 and is buried at the Moore Cemetery in Moore, Montana.

Mary and Charles' fifth and final son, John, was born on February 19, 1899, at Little Cottonwood Creek, Montana. He married Florence Geyer on April 22, 1935, at Livingston, Montana, and together they had two children. He died in the April 1970 at the age of 71, in Judith Gap, Montana.

Charles had always dreamed of becoming a cattle rancher and he moved his family toward the future Great Falls, Montana, to find suitable land. He ended up running the Little Rock creek stage station north of Lewiston for a number of years. He built a log cabin on the land across the road from the station. It was here in this cabin that the family lived until the boys were nearly grown. In January 1905, he left the family for a visit to Michigan. That February the rest of the family came down with la grippe that eventually killed Mary before Charles could return. John was only six at the time.

Charles hired a series of housekeepers until he met and married Minnie Taylor around 1907. About this time, the boys had acquired about 1,700 acres of land from the government, and Minnie and Charles sold the log cabin and moved to be with the boys in what later became Judith Gap, Montana. His leg bothered him from the childhood tuberculosis for the last several years of his life, and he was forced to use a cane. His youngest son John was with him when he fulfilled one of his life's greatest ambitions, shortly before he died. He played the fiddle at the Pioneer's Convention held in Great Falls, Montana. After finishing the old fiddler's contest he turned to his son John and said, "I'm through. I've realized all my ambitions." Not long after that he took ill and died peacefully in the Lewistown hospital in the spring of 1932. The family buried him with his beloved wife, and later three sons, in the Moore Cemetery, Moore, Montana.

Charles Alexander Evans was a member of the Society of Montana Pioneers for a number of years. His son, Burt, or C.B. Evans, has written two books concerning the life of his father.

Charles is remembered by the Old Pioneers monument in Garneil, Montana, and will never be forgotten by his descendants – all of whom are truly proud to be related to such a great Montana pioneer.

Colonel and Mrs. W. H. Ewing

Submitted by R.C. Smith and James H. Smith, Great-Great-Grandsons

Colonel William H. Ewing was born in Millersbough, Bourbon County, Kentucky, on July 11, 1818. His ancestors were early settlers of Virginia and Maryland, and his forefathers on both his paternal and maternal sides were participants in the Revolutionary War. Colonel Ewing's father, William M. Ewing, was born in Hamilton, Ohio, in 1796, and was married in 1817 to Mary Reed, a native of Pennsylvania, born in 1799. After their marriage, they resided in Kentucky for a time, two of their children being born there. From Kentucky they moved to Ohio where two more sons were added to their family. William M. Ewing died in Ohio in 1824. His widow survived him until 1852 when she passed away at the age of 53.

Col. William H. was a West Pointer and a Southerner. Having taken the oath of allegiance to the government of the United States at West Point, he would not fight against it nor would he fight against his beloved South. He owned several slaves who were loath to be left behind, so he brought them to Montana about the time of the beginning of the Civil War. The weather was too cold for them in Montana, so he took them to Oregon. He freed them at this time and one of them, Knute by name, later returned to Montana where he died.

Col. William H. Ewing was a veteran of both the Seminole and Mexican Wars, and one of Montana's highly respected pioneers. Young

Ewing was just merging into manhood when trouble arose with the Seminole Indians in Florida. He enlisted for service for the war and went to the seat of the action. He served under Colonel Zachary Taylor and Colonel Dick Gentry. On Christmas day, 1837, they fought the battle of Okechobee and won the battle with the loss to the United States being sixty men. A Colonel and seven men were killed in Mr. Ewing's company.

Mr. Ewing remained in Florida until October when he returned north. A few years later when the trouble with Mexico arose, he again enlisted. But previous to this, he was employed as clerk in his uncle's store in London, Missouri. It was in Colonel Willick's Battalion, Company I, that Mr. Ewing entered the ranks for the Mexican War. Soon after, he received the appointment of Colonel's Bugler, in which capacity he served until after the American victory at the city of Kansas. He served for some time in New Mexico, where his term of enlistment expired and where he re-enlisted in

Sarah Ella (Goodwin) Stranahan, granddaughter of William H. Ewing. Taken at Fort Benton, 1955.

Company C, Santa Fe Battalion. They continued in New Mexico until October of 1848 and then marched to Independence, Missouri, where he was mustered out in November of 1848. He participated in the battle at Touse and also the battle of Santa Cruz. He was with the forces that wintered on the Rio Grande, and it was there that they received news that the city of Mexico was taken and hostilities ended. Before this news reached them, however, they had gone on forced marches to Santa Cruz and had captured that city. The war over, Colonel Ewing returned to Independence, Missouri, and was honorably discharged.

Soon after the Mexican War, William H. Ewing started from Missouri across the plains to California and landed at Los Angeles on Christmas in 1848. He went to the mines at Rough and Ready below Nevada City, and in a short time made about $12,000. From there he went on the Gold Lake stampede and lost most of his money. He continued to trade and mine until 1854, when he returned to Santa Fe, New Mexico. The following year he went on to Missouri and from there to Kansas opposite the city of Leavenworth. He located a tract of land on his Florida War warrant and resided there for several years selling the land for $6,000.

In 1856 he was married to Mrs. Sarah Ellen (Taylor) Hill, a widow with three children. Sarah had three children, Mary Rebecca, Sallie L., and adopted son Phillip. Of her children, we record that Mary Rebecca, formerly the wife of David M. Goodwin, and later Edward Crawford, resided near her stepfather; Sallie L., was the wife of J.W. Hopkins; and the adopted son, Phillip, lived in the Flathead country in Montana.

It was in 1864 that Colonel Ewing crossed the plains the second time, this time coming in an ox train. His outfit consisted of four wagons and a carriage which brought his wife Sarah and son, Phillip. Sarah's other children were left to attend school. Colonel Ewing, his wife, and son arrived in Virginia City on September 7, 1864. The Colonel brought with him a lot of goods, a part of which he sold at a good profit in Virginia City. The following spring he brought the rest of his goods to Helena, where he disposed of them. He then engaged in the livery business in Helena, and from the fall of 1865 until 1871, did a successful business. In 1871 he sold his horses and carriages and rented his building, and the following year the building burned, his loss being several thousand dollars. In 1868 he purchased a squatter's right to 820 acres of land in the Prickly Pear Valley, four miles north of Helena, this tract costing him $1,500. Later Col. Ewing purchased 160 acres more, for which he paid $400. This later piece of land he gave to his son when Col. and Mrs. Ewing made a trip to California, remaining in the Golden State from July until December. They then went east and spent the rest of the winter returning to Montana in the spring.

Although he had bought his farm in 1868, it was not until the spring of 1872 that he moved to it. Here he resided, and his career as a farmer was a successful one, his principal products being hay and grain, which always finds a ready market in Helena. In 1890 he sold 100 acres of his farm for $75 an acre and rented the rest of the land. The income from the land together with the interest on his money afforded him a comfortable support. He also received a small pension for the services he rendered during the Mexican War.

Mrs. Sarah Ellen Ewing died on December 19, 1888, of pneumonia and was buried in Helena, Montana. She was a most estimable woman, and during their pioneer life as well as later years of prosperity, she proved herself a helpmate in the truest sense of the word.

On December 8, 1890, the Colonel married Mrs. Mary E. Bates Stranahan. Mary did not remain in Helena long, but went to California to be with her daughter, Esther, from her second marriage. The Colonel had two nieces who came from Missouri who took care of him in his old age. He died in Helena around 1905 and was buried in Helena.

Colonel Ewing was a life-long Democrat. A veteran of two wars, a pioneer of several states, and a man who traveled extensively, he had many pleasing reminiscences that he related in a manner that was instructive as well as entertaining. Few of the pioneers of Montana had a larger circle of friends than Colonel Ewing.

Andrew Fergus

Submitted by Andrew J. Fergus, Son

Andrew Fergus entered Virginia City, Montana Territory, as a youth of 14 years, on August 14, 1864. He had trekked from Little Falls, Minnesota, with a party that included his mother Pamelia, sisters Frances Luella and Lillie. A third sister, Mary Agnes, came with her new husband, Robert S. Hamilton. There they were reunited with James Fergus, Pamelia's husband, the children's father. James had arrived two years earlier. All would aid in the development of what would one day become the state of Montana.

Andrew, born on July 2, 1850, was the third child of four and the only son. He came by his name through the Scottish tradition of naming the first son Andrew. Through much of the following 38 years, he was a quiet support to his energetic father. This support allowed his father additional freedom to devote energies to agricultural improvement, writing, reading, and public service. Though a close associate with his father, Andrew was a man in his own right. He was known throughout his life for his integrity and as a true gentleman.

The family moved from Moline, Illinois, to Minnesota Territory when Andrew was about 4 years old, first to St. Anthony and then soon to Little Falls. While in Little Falls, especially the last four years there, his father was either much occupied with the business or was in the West seeking livelihood. So it was necessary for Andrew to take on increasing responsibility. Now his activities tended to go from boyish activities, like swimming across the Mississippi River, to seeking stray cows when unfriendly Indians were in the area. As to the cows, his instructions were, "Don't come home until you find them." This meant, on at least one occasion, he had to spend the night out in the woods where he found a woodsman who took him in for the night. Of more delight was being included in a bear hunting party with Little Falls men.

Andrew enjoyed the trek from Little Falls to Montana, except for the fact that one of the men hired to help the party had ridden his pony so hard Andrew was afoot.

Because of lack of regular school and the timing of the several moves, his elementary schooling was somewhat sketchy. This was contrary to the standards that James and Pamelia had desired for their children. James wrote from Montana urging the reading of good books and the girls avoiding novels. While his older sisters had schooling in Moline during 1860 and 1861 the younger Andrew stayed to help his mother. Little Falls had little to offer. One year there was a three-month term with a 20-year-old female teacher to teach 63 pupils. However, his sister Luella tutored Andrew and his younger sister Lillie. Both his oldest sister, Mary Agnes, and Luella were offered teaching positions. Luella was only 14 at the time. It is possible he may have had the opportunity to attend classes given by Prof. Thos. J. Dimsdale during 1864 in Virginia City as his sisters did. Andrew's further school attendance in Helena and with a school of part-Indian boys is reported in *The History Of Montana*.

After considering several ventures and the poor prospects of mining, Andrew's father turned to agriculture obtaining the place known as the Bradley and Prewitt Ranch near Helena in 1866. Hay was raised and additional milk cows were obtained in order to produce butter during the winter for sale in Helena. In addition, chickens were raised for eggs and livestock for meat for the market. The next year vegetables were grown. After nearly five years the family moved on to the Malcom Clark Ranch. Progress in family fortune at this time was due not only to the foresighted industry of James, but to the support and hard work of his wife Pamelia and son Andrew.

In Robert Horne's biography of James, Horne writes:

"James' only son Andrew, twenty years old in 1870, proved to be a great help to his father after they settled in the Prickly Pear Valley. In fact, the prosperity James came to enjoy during the decade of the 1870's and thereafter in Central Montana could be traced, in large part, to the help provided by Andrew, though of course James also contributed a great deal. Though they worked together on the same ranch and then ran two or three more, they apparently had no formal agreement until 1868, when James sold Andrew 'one undivided one third (1/3) of all the cattle, or cattle stock now owned by me, whether branded or not . . .' for one dollar."

In 1870 James Fergus bought the Prickly Pear ranch of Malcom Clark, now the Sieben Ranch. At this juncture, father and son operated two ranches totaling 480 acres. Two years later they owned three ranches, operating two and renting the other.

The Valleys of the Prickly Pear by Floyd Synness Peterson, mentions two events in Andrew's time in the Prickly Pear area. One illustrates that it was not all work for Andrew as shown by his participation in the famous foot race of 1874. The contestants were David Hilger, son of Judge Nicholas Hilger, Horace J. Clark, son of Malcom Clark, William (Billy) Johns, and Andrew. The race took place on the main wagon road between Benton and Helena. The course was one-quarter mile from John's station to a fence corner by the road and return, a total of one-half mile. It was an endurance test. Fifty years later the four contestants had a reunion and had a group picture taken. At that time, there was dispute as to whether Andrew or Horace won the race. David Hilger commented that because of his weight he was not a serious contender. The second item reported is that Andrew was the original owner of the Gates of the Mountains Ranch, which he sold to Nicolas Hilger in 1873. This transaction plus J. K. Ralston's mention, in *The Voice of the Curlew* by J.K. Ralston, of Andrew Fergus and Ralston's father making a reconnoiter trip to Judith Basin in 1877 would indicate that their move to Central Montana in 1880 was considered well in advance.

Moving to Armells while difficult proved to be well timed, for the winter of 1880 proved to be the harshest and coldest since settlement started in Montana. The losses of 300 head of cattle from a herd of 900 was less than if they had remained in the Helena area. Losses from the herd of 100 horses were kept to a lesser amount by care in sheltering against the weather and the Indians. One Indian was found attempting to remove horses from the barn near the house.

After moving and building two base camps before winter sent in came Andrew's challenge of weather, inefficient help, and hungry Indians. Though there were still some buffalo in the general area, the Indian's horses were in poor condition and many died. At an economic loss, Andrew traded beef for robes but considered it better than other possible consequences. He considered that, in addition to the cattle that died and available to the Indians, a portion of their losses were due to Indians killing cattle. At times as many as 600 Indians were in the area. Andrew reports hearing the Indian drums at night from a camp three miles away. He attempted to keep good relations with them.

The winter of 1880-81 was tough for everyone. One incident involved a large band of hungry Indians and his hired men. Andrew came to the ranch to find his crew preparing for a fight. Contrary to Andrew's instructions, the men had rebuffed the Indians requests for food. Andrew immediately ordered hams, sacks of flour, and other food to be put in his rig and drove into the Indian camp. The band of Indians traveled on soon after.

During the first year at Armells before winter set in, Andrew had started cooking his supper. He had had a hard day's ride and put his gun belt on the bed, his Winchester was behind the door of the small cabin. A war-painted Indian slipped into Andrew's cabin and positioned himself between Andrew and his weapons. Andrew continued cooking his supper as he was being jostled by his larger, uninvited visitor. Two of the "visitor's" companions watched through the opened door. About the time that Andrew had had enough, his jostler found himself suddenly being thrown out with the door slammed behind him. When Andrew armed himself and opened the door he saw three braves whipping their ponies for maximum speed. Afterward he related, "I was laughing so hard I couldn't have shot if I had wanted to."

Andrew's homestead was in the northern foothills of the Judith Mountains on Box Elder Creek, a short distance south of where William Fergus would locate three years later. What was to be known as the Armells home ranch location was about five miles northwest at the confluence of the east and west forks of Armells Creek and on the Carroll Trail. Fort Maginnis was about 15 miles distant on the south side of the Judith Mountains.

The headquarters house at Armells was built somewhat as a stockade with security as well as utility in mind. During the early 1930's, the building site was marked by a stone monument. It was erected through the efforts of Ellen (Nellie) Fergus Romundstad, Andrew's cousin. She gathered stones from historic Montana sites for most of it. The petrified tree trunk adorning the top was found by Andrew J. Fergus on the ranch. Tom Hamilton, Andrew's cousin, contributed the memorial plaque. It reads:

JAMES FERGUS
FATHER OF FERGUS COUNTY
WITH WIFE PAMELIA AND SON ANDREW
LOCATED THIS RANCH
1880
CAME TO MONTANA 1862
WITH CAPTAIN FISK EXPEDITION

While Andrew's father was occupied with the actual building of the ranch headquarters, Andrew was involved in fencing as well as continuing to take care of other range work. By the fall of 1881 Andrew's mother, Pamelia, came to grace the new headquarters, and in 1883 the arrival of James half-brother William Fergus and his family, contributed further to temper the initial sense of isolation.

In the summer of 1883 Andrew took wagons to Carroll Landing

Armells Ranch House, built 1881 – circa 1914.

meeting the steamboat that brought his Scottish immigrant uncle and cousins to their new location. William Fergus' wife was fearful of wild animals when staying in a tent on the trip. Though wolves were in the area she came through safely. Now Andrew would have an association with a group of young people nearer his age. This was to be a lifelong influence on him and may have been one factor in his marrying later in life.

When the initial land surveys were made, it was done by private contract and not in detail. Andrew was involved in some of the later more detailed survey of lands of interest to their ranch, later he was often called upon to locate survey corners.

Andrew Fergus – circa 1895.

Andrew was involved in the vigilante action of 1884, organized by neighbor Granville Stuart and supported by James Fergus. At the time of this writing little is known of Andrew's involvement except for the stories Andrew related to his son and in Granville's letter of June 24, 1884, to James Fergus stating, ". . . Andrew and Stuart are with them and well and hearty." Andrew related this incident. He was a guard to some of those 'held for further action.' One of Andrew's assignments was to hold a woodcutter who had been living with his family on the Missouri River bank. While some in the vigilante group considered everyone along the river as being guilty of range crime, Andrew took a different view. Upon talking with the woodcutter, he was certain that he was innocent. As the woodcutter was in danger of being hung when the main party returned, Andrew had this conversation with him, "Can you swim across the river?" "No! I can't swim well." "Then you'd better go down and get a log and kick like Hell. If you get across the river and go, you will be safe. Your family can find you later."

So the decade of the 1880's brought more change. During much of this time, James was absent due to his involvement with politics of the Territory as well as making a trip with Pamelia to the Pacific Coast and California. In 1886 Andrew's mother developed cancer and died in October of 1887 while Andrew was with a cattle shipment to Chicago. More land had been acquired and Andrew's responsibilities increased as James' physical activity decreased.

Through Andrew's adult years he wore a full beard in the Van Dyke style. It may have been, in part, due to a childhood facial burn scar. During the final years of his life it was snow white – free from stains of tobacco use.

The 1890's saw the peaking of the cowboy era along with continued improvement of the ranches. A telephone line connecting the Armells home ranch with both the outside world and several other ranches was installed. Ditches and roads were developed or improved, fences built. Yet all was not serene. England's Boer War at the turn of the century increased demand for horses in Canada. This resulted in increased border running of stolen horses. Determined thieves would attempt – in daylight – to run off whole herds of horses. The expansion of the '90's gave Andrew more freedom to see the world and to consider romance. Before this time in his 20's and 30's although enjoying social activities, his opportunities for serious romance were limited. Now with business trips east, Ada entered his life. She was the socialite daughter of Andrew's father's old friend and business associate, George Stephens, of Moline, Illinois. Their correspondence shows a romantic connection. Andrew encouraged a visit by Ada and her father. They did not come though Andrew offered to take her "to the top of a mountain where she could see forever." And, "with a light rig and a change of horses, the trip from the railroad at Benton could be easily made in two days." Even though letters were exchanged for a number of years, distance and differences in their ways of life would prevent the romance from coming to full bloom. One example of the these differences is in a letter Andrew received after a hard ride to the ranch during a roundup. She tells of the fun she and her friends have horseback riding and playing tennis. Then she asks, "Do cowboys like to play tennis?" The Ada connection, the attention of his several younger nearby female cousins, coupled with his closeness and duty

Hazel (Akeley) Fergus, Agnes A. and Andrew Fergus – circa 1910.

to his parents were to be factors in Andrew not marrying until several years after his father's death on June 25, 1902.

By 1909 Andrew was a well-to-do business man, well liked and active in community affairs. He was a member of the Elks and the Odd Fellows Lodges. Several years earlier he had been attracted to Hazel the daughter of one of the family friends, Freeman Akeley. Andrew and Hazel were married on August 1, 1909. Andrew was 59 and Hazel 20 years old. His female cousins were much involved and helped arrange the wedding at Steilacoom, Washington.

From this union three children were born. Agnes Abbie on June 22, 1910; Pamelia June on June 2, 1914; and Andrew James on September 2, 1916.

On rare occasions, the poet in Andrew surfaced. One was about the loss of the children's pet dog run over by a passing car. Another to his wife was found written as a draft on an old envelope. It most probably was written while Hazel visited her parents in California about 1918:

>Hello, sweetheart, precious thing,
>
>You are my angel without wings
>
>And to my heart comfort brings
>
>And if you have a lingering thought
>
>Cherish my love and lose it not!

Andrew loved his wife and enjoyed his children. However, it must have been challenging to become a father at 60 years old and the husband of an active, vivacious, young wife.

His first car was a 1910 Franklin, costing $3,000 – the windshield was $30 extra. Hazel soon displaced the chauffeur. She became the first woman in that area to drive a car, no mean feat in those days with having to clean spark plugs and change tires along the way. Andrew did love and enjoy his children, as they grew so did his responsibility. In 1916 the eldest, Agnes, was ready for the first grade. Andrew hired a school teacher from the East to teach Agnes and the several neighborhood children. The school was held in rooms in a dance hall building at the town site at the Armells railway station, a short mile from the ranch house.

1910 Franklin Car. Front: Chauffeur and Andrew Fergus. Back: Hazel A. Fergus.

Further change came with the inrush of homesteaders. As the ranch was on the main road, which followed the old Carroll Trail, many homesteaders came by. Most expected, or hoped, for free meals and animal care. It is reported by one such traveler that he encountered a charge at the Armells Ranch. With the increased flow of homesteaders, Andrew may have posted a charge, contrary to the usual ranch hospitality to friends and the usual casual visitors. Indeed with much less traffic James Fergus had posted a charge for these services. Andrew was more generous than his father. It is said during the winter when the dinner bell rang that men sprouted from all the bunkhouses and barns! One related incident showing Andrew's character was reported by Robert J. Fink in *Homestead Shacks Over Buffalo Tracks*, a

History of Northeastern Fergus County. Fink related that in the spring of 1916, his father and two uncles arrived at the Armells Ranch in midmorning after walking most of the night from the Roy area. They were a sorry sight, tired, shoes bound with rawhide, and of course hungry. Andrew asked the three what they wanted. They replied that they were looking for work. Andrew then said, "Work we got. Have you had breakfast?" The answer was, "No." Andrew turned and hollered to the cook, "Put on breakfast for *nine* men!"

By the end of the second decade of the 20th Century, many of the homesteaders trickled their way out. Both James and Andrew had a vision for the need and value of conserving the spring runoff with reservoirs, both for crops and for increasing the utility of the range. Andrew would delight to fly today over the ranges he knew and see the many man-made lakes and ponds.

The period of 1910-1920 was one of prosperity and change. While both sheep and cattle were raised, some properties were leased for crops, a steam tractor was purchased to increase crop production during the labor-short WWI years. Andrew also became a shareholder in local state banks, which were organized to serve the rapidly expanding homesteader population. In the depressed period following the war these investments proved to be a financial mill stone. The tractor became uneconomical and the banks failed with shareholders not only losing their initial share cost but were libel for an equal additional amount. The coming of the railroad in 1914 was no real blessing. Freight was cheaper, but the railroad right-of-way came through the ranch on some of the best land. Furthermore, it was a serious fire threat. During the dry season a constant fire watch was necessary. In 1921 locomotive sparks set off a fire that burned the barns and the original log headquarters. These factors and falling prices placed a financial strain on the ranch resources. Andrew weathered these changes as well as other private challenges. The scale of operations was reduced and Andrew did much of the work with the assistance of his wife, one associate, and in the summers his children.

Coping with these changes, Andrew continued. In his last year of his life, he prepared the irrigation dams and managed the irrigation of the hay meadows. At age 78, he was able to ride horseback and to do necessary ranch chores. On July 18, 1928, he died of complications of what today is a relatively simple operation. He was buried in the Lewistown Cemetery after Presbyterian and Odd Fellow services.

The several times that he was described in print the same picture is portrayed of a gentleman of the old style, honest, generous, and civil. One observer said, "In spite of having spent most of his life on the range he gives the appearance of a businessman when met on the street." He had a fine sense of morality. Andrew was noted throughout the country for his integrity and courage. These qualities held whether it was in business or personal relationships, hunting lost cattle as a boy, handling potential Indian problems, or confronting and disarming a drunk-crazed cook wielding a

Andrew Fergus – circa 1924.

meat cleaver. One somewhat less exciting example occurred while attempting to drain a reservoir dam at a remote location to prevent winter damage. Due to a broken part it was necessary to open the drain inside of the dam under several feet of water. Appraising the situation, Andrew declared to his companions, "Get the fire going!" He stripped down, taking the hand wrench and a rock for ballast. jumped in through the skim ice and opened the valve.

Andrew told his son the following stories, over 30 years after they happened:

Andrew continued the breeding of fine horses begun by James in the 1870's. One day near the turn of the century, Andrew was driving a fine team of Hamiltonian coach horses from Lewistown to his home ranch. At the edge of town he came upon a man walking in the same direction and offered him a ride in the buggy. The man turned out to be the "Galloping Swede", well known for his prowess in walking, running and wagering.

The Swede declined the ride with a bet that he would reach the Armells Ranch before Andrew. The distance was nearly thirty miles, an easy wager for a man driving a fancy team. As Andrew trotted his team down the road, the Swede cut across the fields at a steady gallop. Andrew, considering the odds were in his favor, exchanged greetings and news with those he met on the road as usual. But when he pulled up to the ranch house, there sat the "Galloping Swede" on a bench in front waiting to collect his wager and enjoy the acclaim of the ranch hands. Just another case of the tortoise and the hare – and a fast, wily turtle at that! Another earlier event of certain odds was target shooting with an Indian. The Indian came by the ranch and wanted to shoot at a mark. He would put up a fine pair of beaded buckskin gauntlets against a sliver dollar. Andrew, with little doubt of hitting the same mark he habitually bullseyed, readily agreed. He then stepped into the house to get ammunition and wager money. His rifle was in its usual place at the door. When they shot the Indian won. Most of Andrew's shots were off target. After the Indian went down the road, Andrew did some checking. His rifle sights had been jimmied while he was gone to get the silver dollars!

Pioneering and early development of Montana took many stalwart men, Andrew Fergus was there and took his place in the process.

James Fergus

Submitted by Andrew J. Fergus, Grandson

James Fergus was the first president of the Society of Montana Pioneers, preceding the organization of the Sons and Daughters of Montana Pioneers. Upon assuming the post he said he considered it to be a greater honor than to be president of the United States.

Seeking to make his way in the gold fields, Fergus arrived at Fort Benton, Montana Territory, on September 5, 1862, with the Captain James L. Fisk party. He continued on through the Prickly Pear and Deer Lodge Valleys, arriving at Bannack on October 13, 1862. From then until his death in 1902, the territory, and the state of Montana that followed it, benefitted from his enterprise, labor, and public service. Furthermore, it was exposed to utterances and writings of his personal and political views.

Much has been written about James Fergus. This sketch attempts to very briefly outline his life with some additional family folklore and comment. For a fuller appreciation of the life of James Fergus, the reader is referred to Robert M. Horne's excellent detailed biography, *James Fergus, Frontier Businessman, Miner, Rancher, Free Thinker*. Horne drew much information from files James kept of both incoming and outgoing correspondence.

A help in understanding James Fergus is a look at his early life and at the roots of this pioneer. He was born October 8, 1813, on Shawton Farm, Glassford Parish, Lancashire, Scotland. His father was Andrew Fergus, a well-to-do, strict, Presbyterian farmer. James mother, Agnes Bullock (Andrew's first wife), died before James left home. His father remarried. James was educated in the Glassford Parish Schools, which served to nourish his inborn thirst for understanding and knowledge of the world. As his knowledge grew, James sought to learn more. He desired to apply it. Both courses were to lead to conflict with his father who was an unbending man, rigid in his beliefs both religious and secular. He rejected his son's attempts to improve their farming practice, as well as his seeking answers to his questions of religion. James' efforts to find understanding from local religious leaders was unproductive and compounded relations with his father. Because of this and his view that there was little opportunity for him by staying in Scotland, he left in 1833 at age 20. He stated, "I left my father's home in Scotland willingly and without expulsion."

Throughout James' life he would be affected by the actions of his father in demanding that James conform to his way. This relationship only strengthened James' quest to seek and apply knowledge, and his drive to succeed. Because he had been blocked by what he felt was an unrighteous authority in his bid to understand, he matured into his own thinking. He later adopted the free-thinking ideas of the time. The actions of his life show that he kept some of his father's regimens of purpose, but hid what were truly basic Christian principles under a cloak of free-thinking. One of his outstanding characteristics was his integrity; he would not believe anything he did not understand. Opportunity for overall growth waited in North America.

Soon after his 1833 arrival in Canada, he became associated with the Quaker settlement north of Toronto. The three years he spent there becoming a craftsman (carpenter and millwright) was another step in preparing him for his future role as a pioneer. His recounting of this time is characteristic of his way of life.

"I was unfortunate in not going into a trade until I was 20.

To catch up with others I had to give it my whole attention.....I studied books, learned to draw and the result was in one year I raised from six to thirteen dollars a month, in two to 75 cents per day and board; the highest wages then paid journeyman millwrights, and finally I went up to three dollars per day, the highest wages then paid."

James, now equipped with a trade and a determination to succeed, headed west for greater opportunity. As he moved westward, he built saw mills in Illinois and Iowa Territories. At Savanna, Illinois, he built and managed a gun powder mill. In October 1842 he received his highly prized United States citizenship at Jackson County, Iowa Territory. He would later describe his ten years of working and moving around as "fitting himself for the new calling by becoming adapted to his adopted country." He said, "...I read, I studied, traveled, and mixed with her citizens from all countries, and thus acquired knowledge that could not well be obtained by remaining in one place."

In the spring of 1844, James moved to Moline, Illinois, to work with D. B. Sears in building and operating a flour mill. This led to his partnership in a foundry. The Christmas of 1844 he was invited to the home of George Stephens, with whom he was working. There he met Pamelia Dillin, who became his bride on March 16, 1845.

He was now financially successful, but by 1853 the foundry work affected his health. In 1854 he moved 300 miles from Moline, to St. Anthony, Minnesota Territory, and soon to Little Falls. As a partner and resident manager of the Little Falls Manufacturing Co., James helped the company establish a town and mill at Little Falls, Minnesota Territory. It was powered by water from the dam they built on the Mississippi River. By this time there were three children in the family all born in Moline, Illinois. They were Mary Agnes, April 11, 1846; Frances Luella, November 23, 1848; and Andrew, July 2, 1850. A fourth child, Lillie B., was born in Little Falls, December 28, 1857.

In 1857 disaster struck, coupled with the poor crop conditions of the frontier, there was a national economic depression. For James this was compounded by a river flood that damaged the dam and mill and caused a loss of their supply of logs. There were further troubles with other members of the Little Falls Manufacturing Co. who questioned his ability and integrity. James replied to these charges openly. Then with little prospect for a livelihood in Little Falls, James looked to other ventures.

As the Civil War approached, the patriotic anti-slavery minded

Fergus attempted to join the 5th Minnesota Company for the Union, but he was rejected for service as being too old (47). In 1860 he went to the gold fields of Pikes Peak, leaving Pamelia in Little Falls to look after their property and family. (See *Gold Rush Widows of Little Falls* by L. Peavey and U. Smith for more of Pamelia.) This proved to be unprofitable, except that the hard work in the mountain air improved his health. James wrote that he had never worked so hard, for so long, for so little return. He returned to Little Falls to his family and the problems there, but also with an eye to other ventures.

With the need to seek support for his family in desperate times, he looked further west to newer gold fields. He took the opportunity to join the Captain Fisk expedition. The size and makeup of the party was insurance for safety. It was a group of 117 men and 18 women. They left Fort Abercrombie on July 7, 1862.

After 61 days they arrived at Fort Benton, Montana Territory, on September 5, 1862. From there James traveled through the Prickly Pear and Deer Lodge Valleys and on to the Bannack diggings. Here he did all right, but in the spring of 1863 he went on to Alder Gulch 75 miles away. Here again he hit pay dirt. However, news of Sioux uprisings in the Minnesota

Gold balance owned by James Fergus. Used 1862 to 1865 in Virginia City, Montana Territory.

country worried him, and was concerned about the safety of his family. Though Pamelia would have preferred to stay in the more civilized Iowa area, James felt he could do best in Montana.

He decided to have his family join him. In the spring of 1864 arrangements were made with one of his partners to go to Minnesota and help them make the trip. The family arrived in what is now called Virginia City, on August 14, according to writing by his daughter Luella Fergus Gilpatrick.

In the spring of 1865 James and his family moved to Last Chance Gulch, now known as Helena. Though he obtained a claim and other holdings in the immediate area, he left these behind to move further from the settlement and start in agriculture. Hay was raised and cows and chickens were acquired. Produce was sold to the miners and those in the town. James continued to expand his holdings, acquiring the Malcolm Clark Ranch in the Prickly Pear Valley. Horses and cattle were raised along with the garden crops. A stage station was also maintained to serve the traffic on Benton Road that went by the ranch. There he remained and prospered until the move to Central Montana in 1880.

By this time his son, Andrew, was a partner with him. With the marriage of his youngest daughter, Lillie, to Frank Maury on September 2, 1876, all of his daughters were married. Mary Agnes married Robert S. Hamilton on March 23, 1864, before leaving Minnesota for Montana, and Frances Luella had married S. F. Gilpatrick on January 1, 1867.

After a decade on the Prickly Pear, James started looking to the range country opening up. Earlier in 1873, Andrew sold one of the three ranches they operated. In 1877 Andrew made a trip looking for range. He traveled through the Judith Basin in Central Montana. Granville Stuart going through the same country may have reinforced thinking in the direction of that area.

It was decided to go to a location on Box Elder and Armells Creeks on the north side of the Judith Mountains. During July 1880 the move was made. James took part in moving the stock, 900 head of cattle and 100 horses. After some preparation, James returned to Helena in the fall. Andrew remained to do what he could to establish the ranch and care for the stock. This proved to be a task. The winter of 1880-81 was the coldest the settlers had known. James counted about 300 head of cattle lost to the weather and the Indians. The latter were plentiful, and the buffalo scarce. The Indians suffered much due to loss of horses to the cold weather and deep snow. Over all, James considered their losses less than if they had remained in the

Prickly Pear.

With spring, James returned to the ranch at Armells and Andrew. There he directed and helped build the log home and ranch headquarters. In addition, he did all of the critical carpentry in cutting out the doors and windows and making frames for them. James made posts for Andrew's fence that required considerable labor. The all-wood fencing consisted of three legged 'jack posts' setting on the ground. The largest leaned and supported rails to form a barrier fence. It was still in use 50 years later. Father and son continued to work together in a partnership (James Fergus and Son) until the end of 1884, with James as President. Andrew continued to take a greater part in the operation, with James doing the bookkeeping and otherwise maintaining the headquarters. This allowed James to devote more time to writing and public service.

James' good friend from the Virginia City days, Granville Stuart, was running a cattle ranch on the south side of the Judith Mountains about 15 miles away. James and Granville enjoyed the opportunity for a renewed association. James often made the weekly mail and supply trip to the new Fort Maginnis near Granville's home. Both men were well read and had similar religious views. They had further association "for the good of the range."

Along with the settlers in Montana came the inevitable *outlaw*. James wrote letters complaining about the cost of taking suspects or those persons caught red-handed the 90 miles or so to the county seat of Meagher County, White Sulphur Springs, only to be turned loose! James noted this

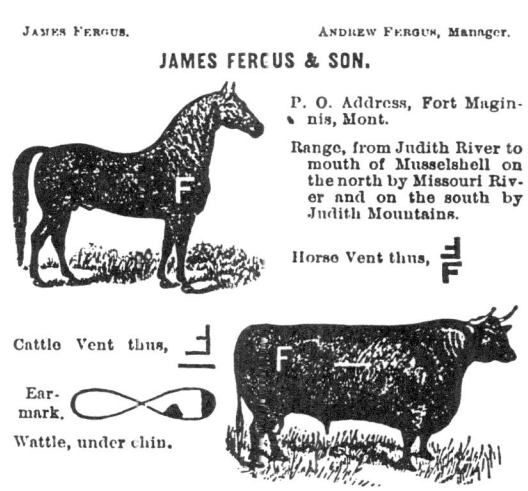

James Fergus and Son, Brand – 1886 Brand Book of Montana.

apparent lack of justice and that he was left holding the bag for the expense of capture, feeding, and sending escort.

In the eighties the range of the Fergus brand, the F Bar, was from the Judith River on the west to the Musselshell River on the east and from the Judith Mountains on the south to the Missouri River on the north. This Moccasin and Cone Butte Association range covered about 3,500 square miles. The DHS brand, on the south side of the Judith and the Maginnis Range, was of similar size. These wide ranges looked inviting to the criminal element that had taken over the badlands of the Missouri River. Most of these were tough men drifting to their ways because of the decline of buffalo-hide hunting and the reduced need for steamboat wood. Neither the county sheriff nor the military, based at nearby Fort Maginnis, could or would act to prevent this growing lawlessness. Ranchers, tired of having their herds preyed upon, took action.

James and Granville consulted on the action to be taken – Granville was the mastermind of the operation. He was an effective leader who gathered information on the location of the suspects and identified the individuals involved in the crimes. Ranchers, led by Granville Stuart and accompanied by a U.S. Marshal, raided badlands haunts and "took care of the problem."

This was done in secrecy for several reasons. One was to effect the element of surprise, another was because it was an extra-legal action. Soon after, James, a Republican on his way to a legislative session, was approached by a newsman for information. James replied that there wasn't much he could say about it beyond that there were several less Democrats in the county. Some considered this a breech of secrecy.

As a member of the Montana Legislature, he sponsored a bill for a new county. One of the reasons cited was the distance to the Meagher County seat at White Sulfur Springs. For some residents in the northeastern section of the county it could mean a trip of as much as 200 miles. Fergus proposed Judith as the name for the new county. The bill was amended to name it Fergus County. The only dissenting vote for the bill was James. He also was farsighted enough to see the value of moving the county seat from Maiden, the most populous town in the county, to Lewistown, a central location with growth potential. The change came about through his influence.

In October of 1887, James' wife, a sturdy, patient support through the years, died. James kept on acquiring books to study, and periodicals to read and send his opinion to. In addition, he continued his correspondence

James and Pamelia (Dillin) Fergus – circa 1880.

and public service.

After Pamelia died, his health reduced his physical activities. However, he did thirst to go to a new frontier – to Alaska with the Klondike gold seekers. He did give one of his grandsons support for the young man's Alaska venture. His decline in physical activity did not slow up his stream of letters to friends and the press. In 1895 a family organization was formed, Fergus Livestock and Land Co. James kept pushing on the frontiers until his failing health and eyes forced him to slow down. For an avid reader to see his library and anticipate the usual flow of reading materials, it was, for James, like a starving man restrained from a banquet. The end came at Armells on June 25, 1902. He was buried in Helena beside his wife Pamelia.

It is well to note some facts about James in addition to his determined pioneer spirit. He didn't use tobacco, drink, or swear. There is no record that he used a gun. While much of his life was spent on the frontier, he was well read in books and current news. He was a craftsman, but willing to make his way in other endeavors. He was a free-thinker with high principles, a restless pioneer. Above all he was a determined man with integrity.

From the time James obtained his citizenship in October of 1842, he was involved in public service and politics. Reasons for this were his desire to see public office serve the public need, and his desire to voice an opinion and act upon it. Also he was willing and capable to do the clerical side as necessary. He was known for his judgment and fairness in all matters.

While in the Montana gold fields in the early 1860's, James became aware of the wonders of what is now Yellowstone Park. Characteristically, James wrote to his friend Ignatius Donnelly, a Minnesota Congressman, of the wonders of the area. Of course, it contained suggestions for its use. In 1872 much upon his suggestions, Congress created Yellowstone National Park as the nation's first park.

In Foster's *James Fergus* he notes mention in the *Fergus County Argus* that James "was one of the most consistent members of the first miners' court, and was chosen as the first judge and won honor by his rulings and decisions."

He has been described as a 'liberal Republican.' His anti-slavery views drew him to the New Republican Party while in Little Falls. There in 1856, he was elected Judge of Probate for Morrison County, Minnesota Territory. Two years later he served a two-year term as County Treasurer for the same county.

He was respected for his character but also because he kept a course.

An event in the Montana gold field is an indication of what he expected – and received. One day a fellow miner hailed him from across the stream with, "Hey, Jim," with no answer, he repeated. Again, no answer. Finally he went around and crossed over to where James was and asked, "Couldn't you hear me!" James answered, "My name is <u>James</u>."

In 1869 Fergus was appointed to fill a vacancy as county commissioner of Lewis and Clark County. In 1878 he was reelected to the same position. He also served terms as Republican precinct chairman. In 1878 he was elected to a seat in the Territorial House of Representatives for Lewis and Clark County. James also served in this body representing Meagher and Fergus Counties. One time there was a question about having a chaplain to open the legislative session. James said he would serve, but instead of a prayer he would read an appropriate selection from Shakespeare!

From his 60's James used a cane. This was due to an injury that came about years before. He was challenged to a contest of strength with a larger Irishman. Contestants would sit with feet together and grasp a rod with both hands. The object was to pull the other over. James held his own until his back snapped.

James' reaction to his bachelor brothers' offer of a significant legacy has appeared in print more than once, often with a little different slant. This author feels he should report the story as he heard it from James' grandson, S. F. Gilpatrick, in 1933. The condition was if James, the infidel, would just acknowledge Jesus Christ as the Son of God, James would be given their wealth, otherwise it would go to the Presbyterian Church. This was a difficult financial time for James, but his reply in essence was, "Not for all of Scotland will I subscribe to something I do not believe." The rest of the story is that a woman who had cared for them during their dotting old age was left nothing. When a letter came requesting James give money for her support he sent enough to keep her. At this point I was asked, "You tell me who the Christian was?" Things are not always what they seem.

James was aware of the support that his wife Pamelia was through two-thirds of his life, and his son, Andrew, the last 35 years While a strict parent, he loved his children and both enjoyed a wonderful association in their adult years.

After retiring from state public politics, James continued to write for the public and to his associates. These associates of the Bannack and Virginia City days were stalwart pioneers. They played important parts in the development of the State of Montana.

John Fifer

Submitted by Mary M. McKain, Great-Great-Granddaughter

John (Jake) Fifer (Pfeiffer) was born October 28, 1812, at Stanton, Virginia, to John Fifer (Pfeiffer) and Agnes Van Trump, the daughter of Daniel Van Trump. Jake was born while his father was serving his country in the war of 1812. When Jake grew to maturity, he moved to Ohio. It was there that he met and married Zelda Jane Saphrona Philomela Meride Morton Anderson Smith, the daughter of Lewis and Hannah Smith, on February 8, 1838. After a short time in Ohio, the family and grandparents moved to Scotland County, Missouri, where Jake was the county judge.

Meredith S. Fifer, son of John "Jake" and Zelda Fifer.

Jake and Zelda had twelve children. John Lewis Turner was born on August 8, 1839, and moved to Payette, Idaho. William M. was born on January 23, 1842. Meredith S. was born on January 12, 1844; he spent his life at Butte, Montana. Henrietta H. was born on January 26, 1846; she married George W. Lee and lived at Butte, Montana. Alvira Virginia was born on June 22, 1848, married William M. Wilson in 1897 and lived most of her life at Deer Lodge, Montana. Lavinia Jane was born May 26, 1859, and was married three times – William Hartley living in Deer Lodge; James Levi Collins living in Deer Lodge; Lewis (Smokey) Daggett living in Choteau, Deer Lodge, Black Leaf, and Plains. Benjamin F. was born on December 14, 1860, and lived at Race Track. The rest of the children died young.

In 1850 Jake left his family and went to California in search of gold. He remained in California for three years. He returned to Missouri in 1856 and stayed three years. In 1859 Jake again was seized with a desire to go west. He started out for Pike's Peak, but instead continued on to California. Both times he made some money, but when he returned the second time to Missouri in 1862, he came with only $600.00. He remained in Missouri until after his father's death.

Alvira Virginia (Fifer) Wilson, daughter of John "Jake" and Zelda Fifer.

Jake's father died in August 1863 at age 87 years at Scotland County, Missouri. Jake's mother died at 78 years, also at Scotland County, Missouri.

In 1865, still having a desire to find gold, Jake sold the farm and started toward California – this time taking his family with him. After a few days travel, he decided to go to Montana. In 1865 Jake, his wife Zelda, and their six children arrived in the Deer Lodge Valley.

He purchased 480 acres of land at Race Track on Lost Creek in the Deer Lodge Valley. Zelda died February 28, 1891, and Jake died on June 18, 1894. Both are buried at Hillcrest Cemetery in Deer Lodge.

Both Jake and Zelda were original members of the Society of Montana Pioneers. A granddaughter, Mollie J. Fifer Kline, daughter of Meredith and Mary Fifer, was president of the Society of Montana Pioneers in 1929-1930. Mollie was one of the "covered wagon babies."

Mollie J. (Fifer) Kline, granddaughter of John "Jake" and Zelda Fifer.

M. R. George Filson

Submitted by Marvelyn M. Wick, Great-Granddaughter

The patriarch of the Filson family was John Filson, a lowland Scot who emigrated from Ulster to East Fallowfield Township, Chester County, Pennsylvania, prior to 1740. His last will and testament was on record as of 1751. He and his wife, Jane (surname unknown) had five sons and three daughters. John, with some of his neighbors, established the first Presbyterian Church at Doe Run (now called Buck Run) on Strasbourg Road, near his home. There were eight children born of this union.

As the westward movement began his grandsons left Pennsylvania. One of his namesakes, John Filson, was instrumental in surveying and mapping Kentucky and is credited with establishing Losantaville, now

Cincinnati. Indians killed him and his body was never found. Another grandson, Samuel, was a soldier in the War of Independence. Samuel's first wife, Elizabeth Herron, bore him five children before her death. Samuel's second wife was Mary Cooper, whose father was killed at the battle of Cowpens in the Revolutionary War. There were eleven children from that union. Samuel moved his family to Fleming County, Kentucky, where their home became known for its hospitality. One notable thing about his marriage was the "flowery" names Mary attached to all her children, e.g. Maxwell Robert George Filson, my great great grandfather, born Aug. 19, 1816, in Fleming Co., Kentucky. He died April 4, 1898, at his Montana homestead.

Maxwell Robert George Filson

Maxwell Robert George and his wife, Sarah A. (nee Phillips), eloped and, tradition says, were married by a riverboat captain en route to Missouri. The story goes that she packed her few belongings, stuffed in a pail that was supposedly used when picking peas. The couple remained in Missouri until 1858 when they moved across the state-line into Doniphen County, Kansas, where their last daughter was born in 1862.

M. R. George Filson and his wife, Sarah, and their family, arrived first at Virginia City, Montana Territory in 1864. They then went to Alder Gulch, and finally secured land in the Beaver Creek area, near Winston, in Jefferson County (which is now Broadwater County.) They later donated land for the erection of a schoolhouse. After the Canyon Ferry Dam was constructed and began filling, the Government volunteered to pay for removing bodies from the Beaver Creek Cemetery into Forestvale Cemetery, in Helena, Montana. George and Sarah's two-story house was moved into Helena to escape the dam's waters. It still remains in Helena, off Montana Avenue.

M.R. George Filson died in 1898. Upon his death, Sarah moved to her daughter Mary Frances (Filson) Carpenter's cabin, where she remained until her death in 1909. She outlived her son-in-law, Benjamin F. Carpenter, who died in 1890. This cabin remains standing on the Leslie Davies land now owned by his son, Allen Davies.

Sarah A. (Phillips) Filson

M.R. George Filson and his wife, Sarah A., are buried in Forestvale Cemetery among many of their descendants.

Little is known about the couples' three eldest sons: Clay, Wayne, and Lewis, but they did not move westward with their family, it is assumed they died while still in Missouri. The next son, Daniel Boone Filson, was in Price and Beauregard's Army for one year, and then went to Denver, Colorado, where he met and married Catherine Hammons in 1876. She was a native of Colorado. Six children were born to them.

Daughter, Mary Frances (Filson) Carpenter Cronkite, was born in 1851, in Buchanan County, Missouri. She was married first to Benjamin F.

Carpenter, who was born in 1845, and died January 1890. Benjamin F. Carpenter arrived in Virginia City, Montana Territory, also in 1864. Nine children were born to them. Her second marriage was to a divorced man, Alonzo Cronkite, in 1898. This ended in divorce prior to Mary's death in 1919. There were no children from this marriage.

Another son, Albert Sidney Filson, born in 1856 in Missouri, married Emma White and they had four children. He was able to achieve a degree of fame as a violin maker in California.

Mary Frances (Filson) Carpenter Cronkite

The next daughter, Corda B. Filson, born in 1858 in Missouri, married Andrew Thompson. They had one son. They moved to the West Coast, in Oakland, California.

The last Filson daughter, Virginia D. Filson, born in 1862, married Charles Leffler. She died in 1944. They had four children.

There are many stories of the adventures and misadventures experienced by these early settlers. One story tells about the time Daniel Boone Filson was out putting up hay along Beaver Creek and a bear, intent on attacking him, came charging out of the brush. He discharged his rifle to no avail and upon hearing Daniel's rifle shot, his brother-in-law, Benjamin F. Carpenter, came to his assistance. Benjamin fired his rifle, and instead of hitting the bear, it hit Daniel Boone and wounded him severely enough that he had to remain bedridden for several months.

Another story explains that when the family planted their corn crop they always planted rows right up to the bedroom windows. In the event of an Indian attack, they would escape through the windows into the corn to hide.

There is also a story about some outlaws who had robbed a stagecoach. Pursued by Vigilantes, they hid in a shack. It is believed by many that they hid their loot somewhere close, but it has never been found. The Vigilantes caught them and strung them up. The shack and surrounding hollow is said to be haunted and there is a noticeable coolness in the surrounding area. Whether or not it is from the deep hollow that does not get much sunshine, you can judge.

John Thomas Flaherty

Submitted by Carma Jean Gilligan and Madeline Heer, Great-Granddaughters

John Thomas (John T.) Flaherty emigrated from County Donegal, Ireland, to America during the potato famine on May 1, 1851. His father, John Flaherty Sr., who emigrated in 1848, was a shoemaker and lived in VanBurensburg, Illinois, from 1855 to 1865.

John T. Flaherty, 19, headed west and arrived at Ft. Leavenworth, Kansas, where he engaged in "teaming" through the summer. In the fall he returned home to Illinois to help his ailing father. His father died in 1865. John T. headed west again by way of Salt Lake City, Utah, with an ox team. He arrived in Virginia City, Montana, on October 22, 1866, (supposedly with Grandma Yates, step-grandmother to John T. Flaherty's future wife, Elisabeth).

In 1867 John T. joined the stampede to the Salmon River district in Idaho, via Bannack and reached his destination on February 11. He started diggings at Leesburg, Lemhi County, Idaho, where he worked in the mines until August 15, 1867. On August 15 he headed for Montana, through Salmon City. In the company of 14 others, he worked at placer mining in Homestake Gulch. He remained there for two months, had fair success, and then headed to Virginia City, Montana.

The first day, the party camped on the ground where General Gibbons had fought the Nez Percé Indians. The party separated and John started off for Highland Gulch. He made his way to Virginia City, Montana, and arrived on October 24, 1867. He also worked at the Ore Cash Mine for another two months.

From there John T. headed for the North Boulder Valley where he met his brother William at the Cardwell Ranch. They both worked on this ranch until 1868.

Granny Yates stopped at Cold Springs on the North Boulder where she took up a ranch, which was supposedly taken over by John Flaherty. Elizabeth Murray, a step-granddaughter to Granny Yates, came west in Granny Yates's wagon train around 1869. She was to work one year for Granny to pay for her trip west. Granny Yates made 13 trips across the plains from Missouri bringing her family members to Montana.

John Thomas Flaherty

In 1869 John T. purchased the Cottonwood Ranch on the North Boulder Creek where he farmed and did general stock raising — he wintered about 500 head of cattle and 100 horses. John was one of Montana's earliest settlers and erected the first human habitation between Virginia City and Helena.[1]

The Flaherty homestead cabin had narrow slits for windows that held their rifles in the rear of the homestead cabin — they were used to spot Indians. Another family source writes that there was a tunnel from the homestead cabin to the river. This was their escape route should the Indians attack (a canoe was always hidden in the bushes).

The Flaherty ranch had a wooden water flume running from a ditch above the house to the kitchen door, making a turn to go underground to

---

1. *Progressive Men of Montana*, Anonymous, p 628.

the nearby creek. The flume was used in the preparation and washing of vegetables, for cooling milk and churned butter, and for water for the weekly washing. Edward, a bachelor, was babysitting a niece and the baby needed some cleanup so Edward used the flume for that too – it was a favorite story.

In the winter months, card parties were held at the various homes. They played cards to raffle off live turkeys. Winners would grab their live turkey, put it in a gunnysack, and head for home.

The Flaherty ranch (Cold Springs Ranch) was an early stagecoach stop. Freight haulers on the Virginia City-Bozeman route could stop there to feed and rest their horses overnight. The drivers usually played cards all night, received a hearty breakfast, and then went on the next day. Mail came by stagecoach through Willow Creek from Virginia City to Helena by way of Boulder, Montana. Stage service was $6 to $10.

Elizabeth "Betty" Ann (Murray) Flaherty

The Cold Springs Ranch was also a post office from July 7, 1886 until 1922. Horses brought the mail three times a week. All the neighbors would come to the ranch for their mail, which was 25¢ a letter.

The Flaherty property had a buffalo jump near it. This jump is still in pristine condition but inaccessible for tourist traffic. After the buffalo were stampeded over the cliff and killed, the Indians would skin the buffalo and remove all the hair with a sharp bone. Then every trace of meat and fat was scraped from the inside. A chunk of soft limestone was then pulverized and mixed thoroughly with coarse salt and added to the brains and intestines. This mixture was rubbed by hand into the skins. The squaws sewed the tanned hides into clothes using a bone needle with sinew thread to sew buffalo capes for the winter months. The Indians used practically every part of the buffalo – nothing was wasted.

John T. Flaherty married Elizabeth (Betty) Ann Murray on October 13, 1872, in the Boulder Valley. They had eight children: Edward Bradford, John T., Ida May, William Alfred, Charles David, Richard Marvin, George Franklin, and James Solomon.

William Alfred Flaherty and Marie Lelah Shedd, my grandparents, were married in 1907 and were homesteaders on the North Boulder. They had seven children: Elizabeth (Toots) Isabelle, Lillian Marjorie, Dorothy Hazel (my mother), Gwendolyn Marie, Madelyn, Billie Darlene, and the only boy, Robert Desmond.

John wanted his eight children to have an education, so he built a school on their property around 1882. It was built west of their house, and had wooden benches and desks. The boards weren't planed and were full of splinters. That first schoolhouse was soon too small, as the neighbors had started to send their children. John Flaherty hired and paid the teacher for the first school. Before too long, another school was built and a school district was formed, and everyone then helped to pay for the teacher's wages. John T. served many years on the Jefferson County School Board. Marie Shedd was one of those teachers – that's where she met William Alfred Flaherty.

In 1903 John T. Flaherty was elected to Montana's Eighth Legislature for the House of Representatives. He was a Democrat for Jefferson County, and served only one term. He introduced two bills. One of the bills was HB 35, which was to make the education of the deaf and blind compulsory. HB 35 was tabled and made into law the next year creating the Boulder School for the Deaf and Blind. The second bill was HB 82, which was to protect the owners of horses and was referred to committee. Bill HB 240 was a revision of HB 82 and was voted into law.

In August 1919, John and Betty attended the 36th session of the State Convention of the Society of Montana Pioneers at Butte, Montana. Betty and her granddaughter, Billie Darlene, had their picture taken as the oldest and youngest members attending the convention.

Betty died in 1922 of gastric cancer and John T. died at their home during a fire in 1924. They are both buried at the Boulder Cemetery in Montana.[2]

1987. The Flaherty and Shedd/Williams Family Tree, by Carma Mitchell Gilligan, p. 531.

John Henry Freeser

Submitted by Doris Lyons Kendley, Granddaughter

John Henry Freeser was born January 9, 1843, in St. Charles, Missouri.

When I was a little girl, I sat on my grandfather's lap and listened to his stories of the early days in the mining camps of the vast unsettled west. Others listened too, as John Freeser told of his experiences during those years when our nation struggled to develop its western territories into a civilized and law-abiding system of government and states. Others have

John Henry Freeser – 1900.

written about my grandfather and his accomplishments. The following was taken directly from his handwritten journal:

"Left St. Louis for Atchison, Kansas, and from there with one four-mule team, loaded with merchandise, went with the train of Erfert and Busch. Forty wagons in outfit. No trouble with Indians. Wagon Master traded for horses with Indians. That night they started to steal them back. The night herder gave the alarm and they did not succeed. When we got to Green River, half of our drivers quit. We left half of our wagons and doubled teams on the others, and then came on to Virginia City. We were three months on the road. Arrived July 14th, 1864. They were placer mining there. They paid the miners six dollars a day. Miners received good pay as long as the work lasted. They asked us to carry them through the winter, which we did. That winter Silver Bow, German Gulch, French Bar, Ophar and Helena were struck, and miners went to the four winds of heaven, and so did the money they owed us. Next spring I started out to collect on horseback.

"The first trip I collected two hundred and fifty dollars. That fall I started out again and did not make my expense. Came home and burned up my books for which I have been sorry ever since. Then I went down to Salt Lake and bought some bull teams and started freighting. Freighted to Virginia City, Helena, Deer Lodge and Ophar. Freighted two years, then settled on the Missouri River at the mouth of Beaver Creek. Went into the cattle business, and have been in that business for fifty-five years. Moved my cattle to the Musselshell in 1874 and '75, and bought my ranch near Twodot in 1887. Flathead the Nez Percé Indians hunted for buffalo during summer months in this valley every year."

In 1878 John Freeser married Louisa Fink of Chicago, in Helena. They raised four daughters – Minnie Lyons, Marie McCarthy, Laurie, and Adele Freeser, and two sons, James and William.

John Henry Freeser, Daniel McCarthy and Doris Lyons – 1922.

John Freeser was involved in the direction and operation of several banks – Helena, Harlowton, and Lewistown. He was very active in the civic affairs of Helena, where he maintained a home until the family moved to the Musselshell in 1906. Fraternally, he was a charter member of the Virginia City Chapter of Royal Arch Masons. He was a member of King Solomon's Lodge, A.F. and A.M. of Helena and a 32nd degree Scottish Rite Mason. He wad also a member of the Society of Montana Pioneers.

John Freeser died July 21, 1927, at his ranch home near Twodot. He was buried in the Ft. Benton Pioneer Cemetery, Helena, Montana. His surviving grandchildren are Nancy Capser, Harlowton, Montana; Doris Kendley, Polson, Montana; Laurie McCarthy, Townsend, Montana; and Jeanne Prlain, Portland, Oregon.

Michael Lewis Geary

Submitted by Rita Gibson, Great-Great-Granddaughter and Shirley Herrin, Great-Granddaughter

Michael Lewis Geary was born in Kilrush, a village located near the mouth of the Shannon River in County Clare, Ireland on April 12, 1843. He was the son of Daniel John and Margaret (O'Dea) Geary. His parents, Daniel and Margaret, emigrated to the United States in the early 1850's, along with their daughter Maria, and two of their sons, Edmond and John. (His father, Daniel, died of a sunstroke in the state of Tennessee and his mother, Margaret, remarried a gentleman by the name of Kinney.)

Michael Lewis, age 14, and another brother, William Francis, age 13, joined them later after they had completed their term of school in the fall of 1857. According to the history of their journey, as described by Michael and published in the *Helena Independent* on February 17, 1938, the ship they were sailing on, the Southampton, encountered a very severe storm which blew them off course and they landed in Mobile Bay in the winter of 1857, after a journey of six weeks. From that point they went to New Orleans, then made their way up the Mississippi to St. Louis, remaining there only a short while before proceeding to Huntsville, Missouri by way of the Northern Missouri Railway. He lived in various places in the state of Missouri prior to commencing his journey west in 1864.

When he reached the age of twenty-one Michael and his brother William joined a small wagon train headed to the new mining camp of Virginia City, Montana Territory. A merchant of Vienna, Missouri, John

Byrnes, had made plans to take two wagons of supplies to Montana and when Michael learned of his plans he made arrangements to accompany the party as a driver of one of the three-ox teams. The train left Vienna, Missouri in Macon County on May 4, 1864, with the Geary brothers, John Byrnes, George W. Reed (who had his own three yoke ox team) and Reed's wife and four small children as members of the party.

Michael Lewis Geary – 1865.

The route they followed was through Nebraska along the Immigrant Trail up the Platte River through South Pass, over the Old Oregon Trail. They crossed Hamms Fork after making their way through South Pass, and then over the Divide to Bear River, following the stream down to Soda Springs, where they rested their cattle for a week. Upon leaving the Bear River the party traveled in a northerly direction, crossing the Snake River by ferry. They followed the Snake River for awhile, leaving it to follow the main road to Virginia City. They arrived in Virginia City on September 15, 1864, after a journey of more than four months.

Upon arrival in Virginia City Michael's first employment was to cut a set of logs and build a General Merchandise Store for John Byrnes. Byrnes had brought a good supply of clothing and a quantity of medicine for which there was a great need in the booming gold camp. With that work done Michael found employment working for a company of eastern men for a short time before the word came of a big rich strike in Emigrant Gulch.

Michael soon was off with two friends from Missouri to try his luck in placer mining. On their trip to Emigrant Gulch, he and his two friends packed their equipment on a wheelbarrow because "a pony cost $60 and we could buy a barrow for $30." They nicknamed the barrow "Jeff Davis" and the trio estimated they pushed and pulled the barrow about 150 miles to Emigrant Gulch and then back to Virginia City. Michael said in an interview that "wading the Madison and Gallatin Rivers was not the pleasantest part of our trip and carrying the wheelbarrow over didn't make the crossing any easier." They were only away from Virginia City a little more than a week, stopping in Emigrant Gulch only a day or two. He said he then joined another stampede to Confederate Gulch in the latter part of October, 1864. There were seven in the party that went to Confederate, but they returned to Virginia City after a short stay. He was quoted in the *Helena Independent* as saying " There was so much excitement and so many reports about big strikes from all over the mining country that it was hard to stay at any one place."

Then in December the next report was a very rich strike in Silver Bow, so Michael along with six men hitched up a ox team and left Virginia City. He said they experienced some of the severest weather he had ever witnessed in Montana. Not having much luck in Silver Bow they only stayed for two or three weeks before returning to Virginia City. Michael

Michael Lewis Geary Family. Back Row: Mabel, Margaret, Will and Emma. Front Row: Michael Lewis, Ella, Irene and Amanda Malvina (Hardgrove) Geary – nickname "Vine".

spent the rest of the winter of 1864-1865 at Pine Grove, a camp about eight miles up Alder Gulch above Virginia City. He said that Pine Grove was quite a camp, having a hurdy-gurdy house and all the other excitement of the mining camps of that time.

In the spring of 1865, in company with Ben Douglass, Walt Flannagan and Jim Allan, Michael left Virginia City for Last Chance Gulch in Helena going over the mountains on foot with crackers being the only provision they were able to purchase before leaving. Upon arriving in Helena they found the entire cash wealth of the party was just one dollar, which was spent on a pie they had seen in a bakery window on Main Street and sent Michael in to purchase. The quartet then went to work for Major Davenport at his claim in Grizzly Gulch, one and a half miles south of Last Chance Gulch. They later camped in the same area at Oro Fino Gulch and lived for six weeks on a diet of beefsteak and salt, as flour was a rare commodity in both Alder Gulch and Last Chance Gulch. According to Michael they put on weight instead of losing it.

After working for Major Davenport, Michael went prospecting on his own. On May 24, 1865, he, along with John Harris, George McGraw, James Faller and John Allen discovered gold one mile north of where the Prickly Pear Creek joins the Missouri River that they named "Black Horse Lode". The very next day they made a second discovery, just east of "Black Horse Lode" and named it the "May Flower Lode". This lode was discovered by Michael along with John Harris, George McGraw, John Allen and Edward Scroggons. This creek is now covered with the backwaters of Hauser Dam all the way to Lake Helena.

Michael later went back to Helena and formed a mining partnership with John Allen and Ed Stillwell, starting mining operations in the summer of 1865. It was during that time that one of the party took out a nugget valued at more than $2,200 – and almost threw it away because it looked like iron ore until a glistening mark was seen where a pick had scratched it.

Michael was one of the first miners to go over into the Cedar Creek country in 1870 where Superior, Montana is now located. He said that he had stampeded there with sixteen other men only to get news of a rich strike at Bear Gulch some four or five miles distant. "There were two men at Cedar Creek who knew the trail over the hills to Bear Gulch, but didn't want to go, so the men all gathered around their camp fire until they froze them out and practically made them go. In the rush through the timber they lost the trail and the party was nearly a day and a half reaching the new excitement, finding nothing there to get stampeded over." One of the members of their original party had staked a claim at Cedar Creek that turned out to be pretty good so Michael spent about a year working in that vicinity and did fairly well. He went on to say that when they first reached Cedar Creek there were fifteen men there trying to get their claims recorded, every man yelling his name to the recorder to get his name on the claim book first. It was finally all worked out and there were claims for all that were there at that time.

After he got through with his Cedar Creek claim, he went to Nelson Gulch, northeast of Helena, and secured a claim that he worked until 1878. While he was in Nelson Gulch he met and married Amanda Malvina Hardgrove, the daughter of George Hezekiah and Emily (Crews/Cruse?) Hardgrove, on July 28, 1872 in Helena. Michael and Amanda were the parents of seven children – Margaret, who married George R. Colvin and had 11 children; Emma, who married Charles E. Warren and had six children; Mabel, who married Lewis Ramsey; Ella, who married John N. Bryson and had eight children; Irene, who married Oscar Milot and had one son; and William Francis, who married Sarah Thompson and had one son; another son, John Edward, twin to William Francis, died at one and a half years. Margaret and Emma were born in Nelson Gulch and the other five children were born on their ranch in the Helena Valley.

Michael took out an egg shaped nugget valued at $1,100 during his mining operations below the mouth of Christmas Gulch. He then sold out his claim in 1878 and purchased a ranch in the valley about twelve miles east of Helena near the present site of Lake Helena (which covers most of the property today). In 1905 when the Hauser Dam was completed, the backwater covered three-quarters of the ranch property. It was then that Michael sold the part not under water and moved to Helena where they resided at 1303 No. Benton (which has since been torn down). In 1906 he purchased a home at 418 12th Avenue which he made his home until 1928. He also purchased a ranch from the Clark brothers one and half miles north of East Helena, which he operated until finding that the hay and stock were being poisoned by the emission of toxic air from the lead smelter in East Helena.

Michael recaptured his experiences in Helena with the statement "I have seen Helena when the town was alive with newcomers and the streets were filled with stage coaches and freight outfits and the long ox trains that pulled supplies from Fort Benton and Corinne, Utah. It was the frontier then." He summed up his life in the interview in the *Helena Independent* by saying "At this time I am 94 years old and still find much pleasure in living. I have my children near me and their children, my health is excellent for my age..." He continued "I have seen the country when it was indeed a wild land and now see it a place of homes and schools and the things we like in a land where we are to make our homes. I have tried to do my share in the work of making it such a place." Michael died on February 16, 1938, at the age of 94, and is buried in Forestvale Cemetery in the Helena valley, as is his wife, Amanda.

John Craig Guy & Amanda (Green) Guy

Submitted by Georgia Branscome, Great-Great-Granddaughter, and Jim Guy, Great-Grandson

In 1849 John Craig Guy, age 26, had crossed the plains by way of New Mexico and Arizona to the Mariposa mines in California. This was a trip that had taken ten months and ten days. He worked and mined there for three years, then returned to Missouri where his parents, John, born in Ireland, and Mary (Baskin) Guy, born in Virginia, had settled after leaving Augusta County, Virginia, with their family around 1833.

John Craig Guy

John C. Guy married Amanda Green in her beloved Missouri on February 3, 1852. Amanda's sister had married John's brother, Robert. Amanda's parents, James Green and Elizabeth (Proctor) Green, were pleased when Amanda married him. She was 24 in 1852, when John and Amanda had gone to Dallas, Texas; there he drove cattle for three years. Their daughter Sophie (Mrs. Charles Dyer) was born while they were in Texas. Upon returning to Missouri, their son, Robert James was born in 1857.

After they left Missouri to join the original Gold Rush to Pikes' Peak, they settled on a farm on the Platte River in Colorado in 1859. Amanda's brother, Benjamin Green, accompanied them to Pikes' Peak. The discovery of gold had caused thousands of hopeful miners to dash to Pike's Peak. Denver was founded as prairie schooners, mules and horses bearing the gold seekers flooded to the mountains. John and Amanda built a hotel on Guy's hill between Denver and Central City. Two more sons were born to the couple in Colorado. Mason Green Guy was born in 1860 and Jefferson Davis Guy in 1861.

Amanda (Green) Guy

In 1863 John and Amanda traveled with their four children: Sophie 9, Robert 6, Mason 3, and Jefferson Davis 2, to what was to become Montana. The road across the plains via Fort Bridger (Wyoming) to Virginia City had not been easy. Amanda's brother Benjamin again accompanied them to Montana. With a thankful heart for the safe journey, John proclaimed, "I will always remember September 1863 and our arrival in Virginia City."

Highland Gulch was where they decided the miners needed rooms. It was a busy year in 1864, building a hotel. However, it was not much of one, as the gold seekers came in droves and left the same way. Amanda placed the older children in school. John became an original member of Alder Gulch Vigilantes participating in all of the activities of the Vigilantes. But Virginia City was not to be their home. In the fall the family moved by wagon train to the Gallatin Valley. Believing in the future of the country, John bought many lots and sold them as the immigrants came into the valley. Less than 100 residents lived there and the house he built was considered grand for the times. The Guy family farmed, raised cattle, and fine strawberries.

In May 1864 Montana became a territory with John voting for it. The Civil War ended in 1865, President Lincoln had been killed, and as the country mourned, Montana Territory moved forward. Just as the country had been divided between loyalties to the North and South so had the Guy family. Family members had fought on both sides.

Gallatin Lodge No. 6 was organized in 1866. John became an original member. He was the first elected Sheriff of Gallatin County and served from 1867 through 1869, and again in 1871 through 1875. John would have been sheriff during the construction of Fort Ellis and the establishment of Yellowstone Park March 1, 1872. John experienced many adventures during his terms as sheriff including an escapade that left three dead and bringing two back for trial. During his first term in office, he and Amanda built one of the first hotels in Bozeman on the northwest corner of Main and Black naming it "Guy House." It became the social center of town. On Christmas Eve 1868 a Grand Ball was given as a formal opening.

Guy house. First hotel in Bozeman, Montana – 1868. Later renamed Northern Pacific.

Tickets for the affair were ten dollars, and people from all over the valley were in attendance.

The hotel was a log structure boarded up on the outside, and a large porch in front. For chairs, they used three legged stools. Most of the furnishings were homemade except for the horsehair furniture in the parlor. Amanda's room had the hotel's only carpet. Hotel rates were $17.00 per week for room and board. Music was provided for entertainment.

The Territorial Legislature established the first counties in 1865, and designated Gallatin City as the county seat. The governor appointed the first commissioners. Bozeman was organized in 1864 at the opposite side of the county, and it grew rapidly. The county seat was changed to Bozeman in 1867. In 1869, needing a jail, John Guy and D. Wilson raised the money and John built Bozeman's first jail. Bozeman reorganized as a corporate body in 1874, and John was appointed to act as a commissioner. In 1872 John and Amanda sold the "Guy House" which was renamed the Great Northern. John served out his second term as sheriff in 1875.

In the spring of 1877 John, his son Robert, Wiley King, Silas Ralston, and a Frenchman, left Bozeman with four yoke of oxen and enough supplies to last all summer. They wanted to settle in a valley many miles east of Bozeman. Wiley returned before they reached their destination. The remaining party traveled on and found Fort Pease close to the Yellowstone River. Before winter set in, Silas Ralston returned to Bozeman where he was

Bozeman, Montana – 1875.

elected Sheriff, and a few months later, was killed. John and his son Robert lived in a tent and planted a crop of potatoes. Late in the year 1878 Wiley King came to Pease Bottom, also Amanda and Mrs. Allen. They were the only white women in the area.

The family property was located on the Yellowstone near Fort Pease, and the site of battles with the Sioux. They built a steamboat landing and wood yard on the riverbank close to their home in 1882. Boats stopped to unload cargo for the settlers. In the same year he built a post office, general mercantile store and a stagecoach station. In time, George Hyde built a hotel, Sam Kappel a restaurant, and Williams and McLean became liquor dealers. Amanda named the small town Etchetah, the Crow Indian word for horse. John later served two terms as Commissioner of Custer County.

John and Amanda's son, Robert, worked with his father and took out a homestead. Mason went to Seattle and became a purser on steamships. Robert also went to Seattle for a few years and had a store with Mason on 3rd and Pike in Seattle until Robert returned to Montana and followed in his father's footsteps in becoming Sheriff. Sophie lived in Seattle with her husband Mr. Dyer. Jefferson Davis attended agriculture college, but drowned at the age of 18.

Montana became the 41st state in 1889. Ten years later, in 1899, Amanda and John moved to Seattle, Washington, where they built a new home. John died on February 18, 1909, at the age of 86. Her daughter, Sophie, then cared for Amanda. Amanda died at the age of 91 on September 27, 1919. Both John and Amanda are buried in Mt. Pleasant Cemetery in Seattle, Washington. "Gone but not forgotten."

Guy homestead near Etcheta, Montana, in Custer County – circa 1878.

Robert James & Alice Blanche Higgins Guy

Submitted by Georgia Branscome, Great-Granddaughter, and Jim Guy, Grandson

Robert James Guy was born September 1, 1857, in Green Field, Missouri. In April of 1863, at age six, Robert along with his parents, John Craig Baskin and Amanda (Green) Guy, his older sister Sophie, and two younger brothers, Mason Green and Jefferson Davis, set out in a wagon from their home near Denver to move to Virginia City, Montana. In September 1863 they had finally arrived at Alder Gulch, Montana. Robert looked at his mother as she threw her bonnet in the air. It was then he heard his father shouting "Amanda, look over the ridge, see...we are almost there, Virginia City!" It had been a long trip across the plains via Fort Bridger, Wyoming.

Miners were everywhere, so they hastily built a hotel. Robert's father, John, had built a hotel at Highland Gulch, but it was not nearly as fine as the one he had previously built on Guy Hill near Central City, Colorado. They all missed the farm on the Platte River in Colorado, but his mother Amanda said they would make a new life and new friends. Robert was glad when his parents said they were going to the Gallatin Valley, as his father said they would have a farm again.

Robert was ten years old in 1867, and he was proud of his dad being elected Sheriff of Gallatin County. In 1868 his parents built a hotel naming it "Guy House". People said how grand it was and they came from all over for the grand opening. The "Guy House" became the social center of the town of Bozeman. Robert did well in school and made many friends.

Robert spent time as a clerk and salesman in a general store, and as a clerk and bookkeeper in his father's hotel. In 1872 after his parents sold the Guy House, Robert helped work the family farm. There were three strong boys and the work was shared. In 1875 his father finished out his last term as Sheriff.

After hearing about Pease Valley, east of Bozeman, Robert, his father John, along with three of his father's friends loaded four yoke of oxen and headed to this new territory. The Indians had forced the closure of Fort Pease and there had been battles with the Indians under the leadership of Terry and Custer. Robert knew there was danger, but then he had grown up accustomed to it. His father had been Sheriff many years and he had heard the stories how his father with the Vigilantes had captured and hung skinners and outlaws, and saw how he had broken up numerous bands of horse thieves. At twenty years old, Robert looked forward to the adventure.

Robert's parents took up a homestead in the Pease Valley. Working together, the family built a steamboat landing and wood yard on the riverbank. Later the same year, a post office and a stage coach station. Other enterprising men built a hotel, restaurant, and saloon. The family operated a general mercantile store under the name of "Guy and Sons." The family home was built and Amanda named the town Etchetah. Etchetah means horse in the Crow Indian language. Robert and his Uncle Ben Green gave the first dance. Ben helped provide the music. Meat was plentiful as Robert hunted from the large buffalo herds in the area. As steamboats would arrive freight needed to be loaded and unloaded.

Alice Blanche Higgins was born in Missoula, January 25, 1865, to a noted pioneer family. Her father, William Booth Higgins, arrived in Montana in 1860, and her mother, Lucina Worden, came to Hell Gate prior to 1863. Lucina was the sister of Frank Worden, the founder of Hell Gate and Missoula.

In 1878 Alice's family was returning from visiting back east, when

Robert James and Alice Blanche (Higgins) Guy.

Robert James Guy (seated), first Sheriff, Rosebud County, Montana, (1902-1910) with Deputies.

they heard of an Indian uprising. Because of the uprising, the family did not return to Missoula but traveled to Pease Bottom. Alice was 13. At age 14 she began teaching school at the first school in Rancher District No. 2. The log school building had a dirt roof and floor. The students sat on planks laid on top of the end pieces of the logs sawed off during building construction.

Alice Higgins and Robert Guy married in 1884 and homesteaded on the quarter section next to Robert's parents. Ten children were born to the couple: Edna, Herbert, Robert Bruce, Olive, John, William, Emily, Frank, Blanche, and Edwin. Robert worked in Etchetah at the general store now called "John Guy and Son" and later built a livery stable in Meyers. Alice worked as post-mistress and was active in school affairs. In 1892 they lived in Missoula, and in 1894 they moved to Seattle where Robert and his brother Mason had a store on Third and Pike Street. In 1896 they left Seattle for Drummond, Montana, and returned to Etchetah in the summer of 1897.

Robert was elected as the first Sheriff of Rosebud County, and served from 1902-1910. There is an interesting story connected with the first election that led to a fistfight. The election was tied. A recount was called that ended with the same results. The county commissioners were appointing Robert, a Democrat. This was just the beginning of a battle that went to the state courts for a final ruling.

The Democrats accused the Republicans, and the Republicans accused the Democrats of getting outside votes, which was later proven to be true. During the court battle another man held the office until the commissioners boldly placed Robert behind the badge. Robert lost the court battle but he refused to give up the position. That is when it came to blows; nevertheless Robert remained sheriff. In 1904 the voters had had enough and he was ousted and the Republican put in the position. But the voters re-elected Robert for the term 1906-1910. Years later his son-in-law, Phil Isaac, was elected Sheriff and at his death, his wife Edna, Robert's daughter, was appointed Sheriff.

Alice died on November 11, 1919, at the age of 54, at Meyers, Montana, and is buried near Meyers. Robert, at age 78, died in Kalispell, on December 8, 1935, at the home of his son Herbert (Bert). He is buried in the Conrad Cemetery in Kalispell, Montana.

Ira Monroe Hanna

Submitted by Roy D. Weston, Great-Grandson

Ira Monroe Hanna was born at Highpoint, Missouri, on February 4, 1836, where he lived until 1852. He and a few friends crossed the plains for the gold fields of California, where he worked as a miner. He did not strike it rich and for several years was engaged in packing supplies and guiding parties into the mountains.

Ira moved to Oregon, and in 1856 he enlisted as a private with Capt. Wm. Chapman's Co. I, 2nd Regiment, Oregon Mounted Volunteers. This unit saw a lot of action and suffered several casualties in the Rogue River Indian Wars.

In about 1858, Ira headed for Montana over the Mullan Trail. He made his way to Ft. Benton where he worked freighting supplies to Yellowstone Park. In about 1865, Mr. Hanna moved to the Flint Creek Valley and settled near Hall, Montana, where he met and married Miss Sarah Alice Carns. Sara had crossed the Plains from Illinois. Records in an old family bible state that when she was about 5 years old, Sarah was found living with Indians in Canada. She was adopted by the Carns family in Illinois.

Ira Monroe Hanna

Ira and Sarah raised ten children: Mrs. Fanny Milligan, Mrs. Martha James (mother of Martha June (James)Weston), Mrs. Julia Callahan, Mrs. Katy Gordon, Bill Hanna, Mrs. Emma Grant, Mrs. Annie Engel, George Hanna, Mrs. Nellie Grant, and Mrs. Alice Bruton.

After Sarah died in 1886, Ira sold his ranch and moved to Drummond where he lived near his daughter Martha until his death in 1922. In 1902, Ira was granted a government pension of $8.00 per month for his military service in Oregon. This was raised to $30.00 per month in 1913. When Ira received his pension check each month, he would enjoy walking to downtown Drummond and sharing some cheer with old friends. When Ira passed away, he was buried in the Flint Creek Valley Cemetery in New Chicago, Montana.

Ira became a member of the Society of Montana Pioneers in 1916. He would be proud to know that his granddaughter, Martha June (James) Weston, has continued to be active in the Sons and Daughters of the Montana Pioneers and is a past Historian and President.

George Hezekiah Hardgrove

Submitted by Rita Munson Gibson,
Great-Great-Great-Granddaughter

Hezekiah was born September 26, 1819, in Pulaski County, Kentucky, the son of John W. and Susannah (Beason) Hardgrove. He married Emily Crews (Cruse) on March 5, 1840, in Macon County, Missouri. Emily was born on October 9, 1821 in Macon County, daughter of Anderson and Nancy (Lynch) Crews (second wife). Hezekiah and Emily had two sons; John William and James and three daughters, Francis Ann, Amanda Malvina and Nancy Ellen.

Hezekiah Hardgrove

At age 45, Hezekiah and his son, John William, age 21, left their home in Macon County, Missouri, as a part of an unknown wagon train taking the Immigrant Trail to Montana in 1864. They arrived in Helena on September 15, 1864.

They prospected in southwestern Montana and settled in Christmas Gulch. John returned to Missouri and married Ellen Simpson on October 30, 1867. In 1871 he came back to Montana with his mother, his wife, and 13 month old daughter, his younger brother, James, and three sisters; Francis Ann, Amanda Malvina, and Nancy Ellen. They took the Immigrant Trail to Corrine, Utah, and then the stage to Helena. On July 28, 1872, Hezekiah's daughter, Amanda Malvina (born February 25, 1849) married Michael Lewis Geary, an Irish Immigrant from County Clare. (See separate

Hezekiah and Emily (Crews) Hardgrove – mining claim, Christmas Gulch.

biography).

When the mining gave out, Hezekiah and Emily moved off the claim and lived on "the old mill place" which was located just north of the Michael Geary Ranch in the Helena Valley. Emily died on Valentine's Day in 1891 at her daughter Amanda's home. Hezekiah passed away at daughter Francis Ann's home on May 15, 1894. Both Emily and Hezekiah are buried in the Hardgrove Cemetery, located in the Prickley Pear Valley north of York Road and off of Lake Helena Drive. This property previously belonged to their son, John W. Hardgrove, who purchased it on April 16, 1884. It is currently part of the Fox Ridge Golf Course.

Adelaide Price Berry Harris

Submitted by John Harris III, Grandson

Adelaide "Addie" Price Berry was born at Alder Gulch near present day Virginia City, Montana Territory, on May 14, 1867, to Mary Elizabeth and James F. Berry of Mexico, Missouri. In 1864 her parents joined the gold rush to Virginia City, Montana, and remained there until 1867.

Late that summer Addie Berry, her twin sister, Anne, and an older sister Jenny Lee were brought to Ft. Benton by stagecoach. Berry himself did not accompany them at this time, only the mother and the three children made the trip together. At any rate, they boarded a steamboat with Mexico, Missouri, as their destination. Departure from Ft. Benton was delayed at the time by the drowning of acting Governor Thomas Meagher on July 1, 1867.

At Cow Island, about 170 miles downstream from Ft. Benton, the steamer (Gallatin) sank and the passengers had to make camp on the south side of the river. A few buffalo robes and blankets had been salvaged from the wreck. Crude mackinaw boats were then constructed and the journey continued on to Bismarck. From that city, passage was obtained onto Mexico, Missouri.

Adelaide Price Berry Harris
— February, 1885.

In the spring of 1880 Addie Berry returned to Montana with her mother, then widowed, and her two sisters, taking passage on the steamboat "Red Cloud." Her late father, Jim Berry, had died suddenly on October 21, 1877, near Mexico, Missouri.

May 27, 1880, is a date to be especially remembered as it marked the arrival of the steamer Red Cloud at the Ft. Benton levee after a continuous voyage of 77 days coming up the river from St. Louis, Missouri. The Red Cloud, of the I.G. Baker line, was one of the largest boats on the river and one of the most palatial. A stern-wheeler, it measured 225 feet in length with a 34-foot beam. Upon this trip the boat was very heavily loaded with freight and carried some 200 passengers, most of them bound for the port of Ft. Benton. The long journey was partly due to the excess weight as the boat drew over four and one-half feet of water and was consequently hard to manage in the narrows and when negotiating rapids. Without its load aboard, the boat had a draught of just over twenty inches.

As for the cargo, it might compare to that of Noah's ark. They had aboard almost everything one could imagine: cattle, horses, mules, pigs, chickens, ducks, and turkeys. It was reported that they had three good meals aboard each day. The menu included: bacon, beans, salt pork, and all kinds of dried fruits. Several times they had deer, antelope and buffalo meat. They saw herds of buffalo and Indians almost every day until they arrived at Ft. Benton.

On reaching Ft. Benton Addie and her family moved to the Highwood area where her mother's brother, Charles W. Price, had located a homestead relinquishment, which they bought. Addie's mother had brought up river a team of horses and a cow, also some equipment with which to start ranching that could help support her family. There were practically no residents on Highwood Creek at that time other than a Mr. James Arnoux and a John Harris.

On February 28, 1885, Adelaide Price Berry and John Harris were married at Highwood, Montana. Mrs. Harris had retained the land on Highwood Creek originally owned by her mother (Mary), which is still part of the Harris ranch today.

There were three sons and four daughters born to this marriage: Nell Margaret (1889), Mary Edward (1891), Barbara (1893), Howell (1895), Anna (1897), Edward William (1900), and John.

Addie Price Harris died on September 1, 1954, at Ft. Benton. She is buried in the Harris family plot at the Riverside Cemetery near Ft. Benton, Montana. Her husband, John Harris, died on January 7, 1932, and is buried at the same location. Both Addie and her husband John Harris I were members of the Society of Montana Pioneers.

Evan J. Harris and Amelia M. (Davis) Harris

Submitted by Rita Gibson, Great-Great-Granddaughter

Evan J., age 21, and Amelia M. (Davis) Harris, age 19, came to Montana as newlyweds. They were married on March 8, 1864, in Mills County, Iowa, and arrived in Virginia City sometime during that year. It must have been quite an adventure for a newly married couple. Amelia was born in August 1845, in Mills County, Iowa, to George Sterling and Mariah Davis. The Davis line reaches back and connects with the Richardson line, both from old New England families that emigrated from England in the 1600's. Evan J. was born July 22, 1843, in Warren, Putnam County, Indiana, son of Noah and Christiania Harris originally from Tennessee and Virginia.

Evan and Amelia had lived in Council Bluffs, but there are few details of their westward journey. They arrived in Virginia City, Montana, in 1864. By 1868 they had left Virginia City and were living in Diamond City, where Evan mined. Their daughter Jennie was born during this time (1865/66) and by 1868 another daughter Mary E. (1868-1921) had also arrived. Evan made his living as a teamster and post trader at Fort Logan. Five other children were born to the Harris family between 1869 and 1888: Wilson (1869-1937), Noah Evan (1872-1885), Rosella (1874-1885), Joe (March 1886-August 1886), and my great grandfather, Oscar (1888-1924). Three of these children died within nine months of each other. Noah, age 13, and Rosella, age 11, died within 12 days of each other during a diphtheria epidemic. Joe was just a baby of five months when he passed away in August 1886 – nine months after his older brother and sister had died. The oldest child, Jennie, also passed away in December 1880 at the age of 15. There was a diphtheria epidemic in the Helena area at that time, according to the local papers, so it is suspected she succumbed to it. All of the children are buried in Forestvale Cemetery in Helena, Montana. Three out of seven children survived to adulthood. My great grandfather Oscar was one of them.

Oscar married Hazel Sparrell (granddaughter of another of my pioneer ancestors, George Henry Sparrell) on February 4, 1913. He died in a runaway cage that was being hoisted into a sheave of the Mountain Con Mine, Centerville, Butte, Montana, on November 27, 1924.

The Harris family had lived in Helena since 1878, and around 1900 Evan became involved in real estate. According to the Helena City Directory, the Harris family lived on 637 Highland in 1891, at 1026 – 11th Avenue, in 1893, and by 1894 they lived on 736 E. 6th Avenue. This was the family residence until sometime after 1917.

On Sunday, April 26, 1903, at 2:00 a.m., Evan J. Harris, age 59, was found unconscious on a sidewalk, on the corner of Main and Broadway in downtown Helena. He died without regaining consciousness five hours later in St. John's Hospital. Because of the mysterious circumstances surrounding his death an inquest was called. The doctor who treated him stated that death was caused by brain concussion. An early theory suggested that Harris had been intoxicated and merely fell down, but witnesses denied that he was drunk. Additional evidence proved that he'd fallen backward, not forward, as is common if one is drunk. Other witnesses stated some young men had surrounded Harris, one hit Harris, and then they split up. On April 27, 1903, Edward Roy Jones, a property man for Butte's Broadwater Theatre, and Raymond Moore, were arrested in Butte. The young men were part of a group of men who came to Helena with the Overland Minstrels. Another of the group, Benjamin Timmons, said Harris was drunk and tried to pick a fight with them by attempting to hit Jones. Jones hit Harris "with force." Jones denied the accusation and said Harris fell backwards on his own and they left him.

According to the *Helena Independent* headline, June 12, 1903, "Edward Roy Jones Not Guilty of Manslaughter – Shortest Murder Trial on Record" in Lewis & Clark County – no longer than three hours. It was determined that Harris got in between two groups of boys who were yelling at each other and he thought they were yelling at him. "Harris then struck…Jones slapped or struck him and Harris stepped back and tripped, his heel catching…and he went down striking the back of his head." According to his obituary, he was buried in Forestvale Cemetery.

Amelia lived three more years until November 6, 1906, passing away of heart failure at age 61. She, too, is buried in Forestvale, according to her obituary.

John Harris I

Submitted by John Harris III, Grandson

John Harris was born in St. Louis, Missouri, on November 20, 1849. His father, William Harris, was born around 1800 and was a native of Wales. It is thought that his father was a miner by profession. His mother, Margaret Edwards, was born July 13, 1821, in Carmarthenshire, South Wales. William Harris and Margaret Edwards were married on July 4, 1843, in Wales and immigrated to this country in the 1840's. John Harris also had an older brother by this marriage, Howell Harris, born April 21, 1846 in St. Louis, Missouri.

According to John's brother, Howell Harris, the lure of gold fields in California and elsewhere probably caused his father, William Harris, to head West alone in 1850 or early 1851 to seek his fortune. In any event, in

1853 William Harris, after two years out West, supposedly sent word for his wife, Margaret, and the two children in St. Louis, Missouri, to come to California across the plains by way of Salt Lake City, Utah Territory. The family started out from St. Louis in June 1853, via Ft. Leavenworth, Kansas, to Salt Lake City by oxen or mule team. On reaching Ft. Leavenworth, the government authorities stopped their group until a large enough party could be formed to protect against the possibility of encountering roving bands of hostile Indians, which inhabited the plains at that time. They apparently reached Utah without any serious problems that same year. Margaret and the two boys wisely decided to stay there with others of the party until spring because of reports of Indian massacres and attacks further west.

John Harris I – February, 1885.

The story as repeated by John Harris is that they arrived in Salt Lake City and stayed over the winter waiting for their father to return for them. He supposedly started out for Utah the following spring of 1854, but while halfway on his journey he received a report that the Indians had massacred his family, so apparently he immediately returned to California. Even though their mother tried all possible means to locate him, nothing apparently was ever heard from him again, even though it was vaguely reported that he may have lived his life and died near Placerville or Sacramento, California.

John's mother's name, Margaret Harris, surfaced again on May 2, 1855, when it was recorded that she had married a William Williams Thomas on this date in Box Elder Ward, Weber County, Utah Territory. John Harris would have been 5 1/2 years old at the time.

Eventually Margaret Harris Thomas had six other children born to Mr. Thomas between 1855 and 1866. Their children's birth dates are spread out between this period, all of whom were born in either Utah or Southern Idaho which would explain why they spent at least part of the next eight years in that region. In fact, it was believed that they may have farmed or ranched in the Malad City, Oneida County, area of Idaho during this time.

It is also apparent that the family ventured North into the gold mining camps of Bannack and Virginia City, Montana Territory. John Harris, at the age of 13, was involved in that stampede to Bannack, Montana, in June 1863 and later to Virginia City. Harris and his family were members of a prospecting party at Bannack when in July of that year, hearing of a great discovery of gold at Alder Gulch near Virginia City, immediately moved there, staying until late in the fall of 1863. Owing to the rough and unsettled condition of the country with outlaws and murderers, they went back to Southern Idaho for the winter. Harris reported that he frequently saw the notorious Sheriff Henry Plummer who was hanged by the Vigilantes and around whose life is written a considerable part of Montana's early mining history. The family returned to Alder Gulch the following spring in 1864 and remained until 1867. Harris managed to obtain odd jobs around these early gold mining camps and also assisted his stepfather as a miner at Bevins Gulch near present day Virginia City, Montana. In 1868 the family relocated to the Upper Deer Lodge Valley about 20 miles from the town of Deer Lodge, Montana, where John's mother and stepfather had established themselves as fairly prominent ranchers.

John Harris at the age of 18 went to work mining in French Gulch and various other places in the vicinity of Deer Lodge. In 1871 he came to Ft. Benton, the head of navigation on the Missouri at the time, and it is said he went hunting in the nearby Highwood Mountains. It is also said that he was very impressed with the land and nature of the area.

In 1873 John Harris came back to Ft. Benton. With his brother Howell, the two embarked in a freighting business for two years between Ft. Benton and Helena, but In 1875 John retired from freighting. His brother Howell continued in the freighting business for many years, but mainly on the Whoop-Up Trail, which led from Ft. Benton to Ft. Macleod. Howell later settled on a large stock ranch of his own near High River, Alberta. Eventually, Howell sold his holdings, moved back to Ft. Benton, and passed away there in 1921.

In 1876 John Harris returned to Deer Lodge where he purchased his mother's herd of cattle from her estate (700 head) driving them from the Deer Lodge Valley to a point near the Great Falls of the Missouri. On reaching the Missouri River, the cattle were driven across at the "Old Indian Ford" which was just up river near the present day Great Northern Railroad Bridge that now spans the river at Great Falls just above the dam.

In that same year, Harris took up "Squatter's Rights" or a homestead on Highwood Creek about 10 miles south of the present town of Highwood, Montana, and began a cattle operation that is still in the family today – 120 years later. He was 26 years old at the time. His homestead was the second in that region, his predecessor having been a Mr. James M. Arnoux. His nearest neighbors were at Ft. Benton 30 miles away and at Sun River Crossing 50 miles distant. Mr. Harris built a cabin from scratch out of cottonwood logs containing two small rooms. He had a chimney, not a stove, and cooked his meals and heated the rooms from a fireplace. He and Mr. Arnoux were the first to experiment with farming, though his chief interest was his cattle. It was a wonderful region for wild game so there was no need to resort to his cattle for a source of food. There were other early settlers on Highwood Creek at about that time, Horace Clark and "Red" Buckland.

John Harris lived during a period when Indians were more numerous than white men, and he always carried a rifle for personal protection. On several occasions, Mr. Harris had skirmishes with Indian parties that were in the area or just passing through. His homestead was on the trail of the Piegans who passed through when going to the Judith country for their annual berry picking. The Crows quite often passed through also, while on horse-stealing expeditions.

In 1882 John Harris consolidated his cattle with herds of Charles E. Conrad, William G. Conrad, and Isaac G. Baker, all early day Ft. Benton merchants who had come there to establish trading posts at the head of navigation on the Missouri River. Together they incorporated the Benton and St. Louis Cattle Company (later known as the Conrad Circle Cattle Company) into one of the largest in the state at the time, of which Mr. Harris was the general manager. The company conducted a large and prosperous cattle business north of the Missouri on the Marias River reaching to the Sweet Grass Hills and onto the Canadian border. The company had about 35,000 head of cattle at one time scattered throughout this region. The business was in operation from 1882 to 1909 when the cattle operation was disbanded due in part to the inflow of homesteaders into the area. With the rapid settlement of Northern Montana, the Conrad Circle Cattle Company closed its books on the business with a final meeting at the Rainbow Hotel in Great Falls, Montana, on April 13, 1921, after distributing more than one and a half million dollars in dividends to its stockholders. This ended the era of the open range and began the period of the homesteader in Montana.

John Harris held the position of Superintendent and General Manager of that corporation for 28 years. When the company sold its cattle holdings in 1910, its officers and directors prepared a resolution that became a matter of record stating the following:

"Whereas, the Conrad Circle Cattle Company has this day wound up its affairs by disposing of the last of the lands and personal property; and whereas, this corporation and its predecessor, the Ft. Benton and St. Louis Cattle Company, have been engaged in the business for about 40 years, and during that time have distributed to their stockholders more than $1,600,000 in dividends, and whereas, the success of the Conrad Circle Cattle Company and the Ft. Benton and St. Louis Cattle Company has been in a large measure due to the faithful and loyal service of John Harris, its superintendent for many years, a service which many times involved the risk of his life and requiring a high degree of both skill and courage, which service was performed by compensation in money less than a hod carrier demands and receives today, now, therefore, be it resolved by the board of directors of the Conrad Circle Cattle Company that a vote of thanks be and hereby is tended to John Harris for his faithful service to this corporation, and that these resolutions be spread upon the minutes of the books of the corporation and an appreciation of what the company owes him for past services." Signed: Joseph A. Baker, President, A.F. Conrad, Vice-President, and J.H. Edwards, Secretary, Conrad Circle Cattle Co."

During this time, the company changed its grades of stock from the range type of animal to the Hereford breed and developed one of the finest herds of cattle in the Northwest. As cattlemen, their chief market was the government. Large numbers of cattle were required by the government to supply the garrisons at Chinook, Browning, Ft. Peck, and to help feed Indians on the agencies or reservations. The usual price for steers in the 70s and early 80s was four cents a pound.

After the Great Northern Railway was built through Ft. Benton in 1888, many shipments were sent to Chicago for sale at the large stockyards there. Mr. Harris most always accompanied the first shipment of stock to that city each year. The shipment usually went to the oldest and best-known commission houses at the Chicago Stockyards, usually the commission firm of Rosenbaum Brothers and Company. The average price paid for Montana stock ranged around three and one half to five cents a pound, so the average steer brought between $35 or at best $40 a piece. In later years prices increased somewhat and Mr. Harris sold cattle on the open market as high as twelve cents a pound.

Mr. Harris as a ranch superintendent had the supervision of many cowboys. The cowboy were usually paid about $40 a month, including bunkhouse accommodations, eight horses kept for the use of each man, and use of regular equipment of roundup necessities such as wagons, tents, and cooks. The roundups were held twice a year in the spring and in the late fall. The branding of the calves was done principally at the spring roundup. In the fall the stock was driven together and separated among its owners, chiefly to afford an opportunity for shipping to market.

Roundups, said Mr. Harris, were periods of hard work interspersed with a great deal of rough merry-making. Usually some liquor reached the camp, and the familiar scenes of the wild west were reenacted. The Harris led outfit was generally noted for its peaceful inclinations. It seems that Mr. Harris, even though he had an assortment of rough fellows to deal with, maintained a firm grip and insisted on good order.

In 1911, after disposing of his interest in the Circle Cattle Company, he returned to raising cattle on his Upper Highwood Ranch, although continuing to make his home in Ft. Benton.

John Harris, besides his cattle interests, was a stockholder and served on the board of directors of the Stockman's National Bank in Ft. Benton. He also was a stockholder in the Conrad National Bank of Great Falls. He helped organize the Montana Stockgrowers Association and was a member of the State Livestock Commission in Helena for a number of years.

Besides owning a large home in Ft. Benton, he was active in the Ft. Benton real estate market as well. He helped finance the first Benton Opera House and Lyceum Co. and assisted in building the first Electric Light Company, which later sold to the Montana Power Company. He served a number of years as a Chouteau County Commissioner between 1878 and 1882.

Even though Mr. Harris never sought the honors of a politician, he was known to have refused several nominations for the legislature. He was considered to be a staunch Democrat by persuasion and in his various political views. He was a member of the Episcopal Church and the Independent Order of Odd Fellows as well as serving on the local school board for a number of years.

John Harris was married at Highwood on February 28, 1885, to Adelaide (Addie) Berry, whose parents were Mary Elizabeth Price Berry and the late James Berry of Mexico, Missouri. Mrs. Harris, a twin, was born at Alder Gulch, near Virginia City, Montana Territory, on May 14, 1867. Seven children were born to this marriage, including three sons and four daughters. The sons names were: Howell, Edward, and John. The daughters were: Nell, Mary, Barbara, and Anne.

John Harris died on January 7, 1932, in Ft. Benton, Montana, at the age of 82. His death was due to conditions associated with advanced age. He was buried in the family plot at Riverside Cemetery near the above community. Harris, a true "Montana Pioneer," came to Montana Territory in 1863 as a boy of 14 with his mother and stepfather. He was a resident of Montana for 69 years, ranched at Highwood for 59 years, and a resident of Ft. Benton for 40 years.

Harris has nine grandchildren: John H. Patterson, Edward B. Patterson, William H. Patterson, Ned R. Clarke, Donald Clarke, Marjorie Lynch Gray, Mary Jo Harris Walker, John F. Harris, and Carol Lee Harris Russell.

John Harris I was a member of the Society of Montana Pioneers and attended a convention held in Lewistown, Montana, in 1908 and one in Great Falls, Montana, in 1915.

Margaret Edwards Harris Thomas

Submitted by John Harris III, Great-Grandson

Margaret Edwards was born July 13, 1821, in Carmarthenshire, South Wales, to John and Ann Edwards. She married William Harris on July 4, 1843, probably in Wales. They immigrated to this country sometime prior to 1850 and settled near St. Louis, Missouri. She had two children:

Howell, born April 21, 1846, and John born November 20, 1849, in St. Louis Missouri.

In 1851 leaving his family in St. Louis, William Harris traveled west to California's gold country arriving at or near Sutter's Mill where the great gold rush was centered. It appears that William Harris sent word to his family in St. Louis to come to California. In the spring of 1853, Margaret and her children traveled overland by wagon train to Salt Lake City, Utah. Because the threat of Indians still remained in the Salt Lake valley, Margaret along with her children, Howell and John, stayed the winter in Salt Lake City waiting for William Harris' return or word from him. It apparently never happened, even though Margaret Harris made numerous efforts to locate him, nothing was ever heard from him again.

On May 2, 1855, Margaret Edwards Harris married William Williams Thomas in Box Elder Ward, Weber County, Utah Territory. From this marriage six children were born. William Henry Thomas was born September 25, 1855, at Brigham City, Utah, and died October 16, 1935, at Highwood Montana. Mary Ann Thomas was born in 1857 in Utah, and married William Norton. Margaret S. Thomas was born in 1860 in Utah, and was buried in the Norton (Gregson) Cemetery, Anaconda, Montana; the age on her headstone is 17 years, 3 months. Rachel E. Thomas was born in 1861, in Utah, and married Griffith Earhart. Morgan E. Thomas was born in 1863 at Malad, Idaho. David W. Thomas was born in 1866 at Malad, Idaho.

William and Margaret Thomas first came to Bannack, Montana, in 1863 where they remained a few weeks, after which they moved to Virginia City, Montana, where Mr. Thomas prospected until December 1, 1863. Mr. Thomas was also working a claim in Bevin's Gulch. They then went to Brigham City, Utah.

In the spring of 1864 they moved to Malad City, Idaho. Mr. and Mrs. Thomas were the first settlers of that town. On May 1, 1868, they went to Salmon River, thence to Horse Prairie, Montana, on their way to Deer Lodge, Montana, arriving in the Deer Lodge Valley on October 1, 1868. In 1870 Mr. Thomas located a ranch of 160 acres in the Deer Lodge Valley and afterward increased his property until he accumulated 480 acres.

On June 5, 1879, Mr. Thomas died in Deer Lodge County, Anaconda, Montana, and is buried in the Norton Cemetery near Anaconda. He left the property without a will. Mrs. Thomas lived on their property letting her farm be worked on shares. She also owned six or seven hundred head of cattle, which one of her sons took care of for her near Fort Benton.

Margaret Edwards Harris Thomas died at the age of 77 on February 8, 1898, in Deer Lodge County near Anaconda, Montana. She is buried in the Norton Cemetery, close to present day Fairmont Hot Springs, which is near the town of Anaconda, Montana. On her grave marker is written, "A Pioneer Who Came to Montana in 1863." (Please see photo on Page 448.)

The Norton Cemetery is located about one mile west of the present day Fairmont Hot Springs. It is located on a hill north of the railroad tracks and is about one acre in size. There are no well-maintained roads that go to the cemetery and access appears to be across private property only.

Margaret Thomas' two sons by her first marriage, Howell Harris and John Harris, went on to become prominent citizens of the region and are buried along with their families at Riverside Cemetery near Fort Benton, Montana.

Howell Harris

Submitted by John Harris III, Grand-Nephew
An Autobiography of Howell Harris – dated December 18, 1908, Lethbridge, Alberta, Canada

I was born on Gravoy Road, three miles from the town of St. Louis, Missouri, at that time, but what is now practically the center of the city, on April 21, 1846. In 1853 my father, who had gone west three years previous, sent word for my mother, my brother, John, and myself to come to California across the plains by the way of Utah.

We left St. Louis in June 1853 and arrived in Ft. Leavenworth in due time, being held there by the government authorities until a large enough party could be formed to protect ourselves against the roving bands of hostile Indians which inhabited the plains. We reached Utah without any serious trouble, but mother decided to say there with others of the party until spring on account of reports of Indian massacres further west. In the meantime she had notified father of our sojourn; and he started for Utah the following spring, but while halfway on his journey, he received a false report that we had been massacred by the Indians, so he immediately went back to California; and he has never been heard from since, although we heard later that he had gone to Australia when the gold fever was at its height there.

Mother tried all possible means to locate him, but her efforts proved unavailing and concluding that he may have been drowned on his trip to Australia, she remarried on May 2, 1855.

We lived in Utah and then Idaho, and in June 1863 came to Bannack City, Montana Territory, which was the only mining town in the area at that time excepting Gold Creek in Deer Lodge County. In July the same year, hearing of the great gold strike at Alder Gulch, we moved there and stayed till fall. Owing to the rough and unsettled condition of the country, Montana at that time being filled with outlaws and murderers, we went back to Idaho for the winter.

The following spring I came back to Montana alone and mined at Alder Gulch, Bevans Gulch, Lincoln Gulch, and Silver Bow. (The latter named being now the present site of Butte). I mined in various camps till 1869, the last being the American Bar near Helena which proved to be such a failure that I got disgusted and gave up mining for good.

Howell Harris – June, 1901.

We then went down the Missouri River with three rafts of lumber belonging to Whit Tenant to Ft. Benton. An amusing incident occurred on this trip. Mr. Tenant and I had charge of the first raft. While floating down the river, a bear swam out and caught hold of the bow. Our guns and skiff were on the second raft so we tried to club him off, but the bear finally got on in spite of us. Mr. Tenant and I had to jump into the river and swim to shore leaving the bear in full charge. He proceeded to knock everything lying around loose into the river, stood up on his hind legs and paced the deck like a captain in full charge. In the meantime the boys on the second raft came out in the skiff and took us aboard. The first raft finally ran aground on a sandbar, so we landed the second and third rafts below it. As it was quite dark by this time, we decided not to molest the bear till daylight, by which time he had disappeared, so we proceeded on our way after working all that day getting the raft off the sandbar. On arriving at the mouth of the Sun River, we had to portage our lumber below the falls on the Missouri, which occupied about two weeks, and we finally landed in Ft. Benton after several exciting encounters with the Indians. I might state that there were 1600 lodges of Indians camped in the flat around Ft. Benton on our arrival there.

I then entered the employment of I.G. Baker and Bros. as a bullwhacker and went to Ft. Peck. There were four trains in the party. One Diamond R train, one Garrison and Wyatt, one I.G. Baker and Bros., and one train composed of small freighters. We reached Ft. Peck two days before the steamer arrived. While waiting for the boat, we herded the cattle on the hills back of the fort, eight herders on horseback and four including myself on foot. While on herd duty a man, whose name I can't recall but who was afterwards postmaster at Missoula for a number of years, went out hunting contrary to our advice. When he had gone about a mile from the fort and a half a mile from the herd, he was surrounded by a small party of Indians and in their endeavor to secure his gun, it went off, killing one of the mounted Indians. About this time, two of the herders had started out to look for him, and they reached the brow of the hill just as the Indian was shot. The Indians, thinking there was a larger party of whites after them, took to their heels, and the two herders rode up, then the man mounted behind one of the herders, and they started for the fort at full speed. The Indians on discovering there were only two men instead of the large party they supposed, started after them and passed within a hundred yards of myself and the three others on foot, the balance of the herders having deserted us on seeing the Indians. In the meantime, the shooting and yelling had attracted the attention of the men at the fort, and they came to our rescue in the nick of time. The Indians realizing that they were too late to affect a successful capture emitted a yell of disappointment, wheeled around and disappeared.

On the second day of our stay at Ft. Peck, the boat arrived and we loaded up the trains and started on our return journey. Forty miles out, a night herder for the Diamond R train, by the name of Cook was killed by a solitary Indian while on duty. We had no further mishaps till we got about 150 miles up the river, when one night an Indian sneaked up on the corral guard and aimed to shoot him in the temple with an arrow, but it just grazed his forehead leaving an ugly gaping wound; but otherwise not seriously injured. His evident intention was to kill the guard and steal the horses in the corrals, but the guard let out such a yell that he woke the whole camp and the Indian took to his heels. Nothing unusual occurred from that time till we reached Ft. Benton.

It now being late in the fall, Mr. Baker paid the whole outfit off. Two of the bullwhackers and myself bought an outfit from I.G. Baker and went down the Missouri River to a place called Three Islands and cut wood all winter for the steamboats.

The Indians were very bad this winter. One band of Piegans was on the warpath, killing stray freighters and hunters. It was this band that killed Malcolm Clarke, a West Point cadet, who stood very high in government circles, also seriously wounding his son.

Col. Baker was sent out by the government to bring this band to account for their depredations. It is well known history how Mountain Chief moved camp after Col. Baker's scout, Kipp, had located him and another band of Indians under Low Horn had moved into the camp vacated by Mountain Chief with the result that 300 of Low Horn's band were killed instead of Mountain Chief group.

The Indians being scattered by the soldiers committed depredations right and left, and it was absolutely unsafe for us to stay on the island, being only 50 miles below the point where the battle occurred. We broke camp and went to Ft. Benton accompanied by George Baker, one of the brothers of the firm of I.G. Baker and Bros. On our way, we met three wolfers on their way down the river. McDonald, Antelope Charlie and Frank Pouleat. We advised them to return with us, but there were determined to proceed. We afterwards learned they were all killed by one Indian named Bearding, who had captured their guns while they were gathering fuel and shot them down one by one as they returned to camp.

The following year in 1870, I was put in charge of I. G. Baker and Companies' trains as wagon master hauling freight from Benton to Helena and Butte, and for all other mining camps throughout Montana during the season of open navigation. In the winters I built several trading posts in Montana and Canada for I.G. Baker and Co. (1871-1872).

Since that time, my work has been chiefly in Canada in fur trading and freighting for the Royal Northwest Mounted Police and am now engaged in stock raising.

Post Script from Submitter:

In the early 80's, Mr. Harris was engaged in the livery stable business in Fort Benton and a few years later acquired a ranch and livestock interest near Lethbridge, Alberta, Canada, which then became his home. In 1881 Mr. Harris was married to Miss Emma Babbage of Fort Benton. He died on August 19, 1921, at Warm Springs Hospital near Anaconda, Montana. Mr. Harris had suffered from mental ailments for some time and after several months was taken to the state hospital for treatment. He died two days before his 75th birthday.

Edward Sherman Hayes

Submitted by Donel G. Hayes, Grandson

Edward and Elizabeth (Speaks) Hayes began their westward journey from Missouri in 1864 with two yokes of steers and one yoke of cows, crossing the plains on their way to make a new home in the west. Arriving in Salt Lake City, they elected to stay the winter and continue their journey in the spring. While in Salt Lake City on January 23, 1865, Edward Sherman Hayes was born.

With his parents, young Ed Hayes moved from Salt Lake City to Montana when he was a few months old. They stopped at Washington Gulch near the head of Nevada Creek at a town called Finn. This is about 14 miles north of Avon along State Highway 141. Washington Gulch was later to become a rich gold strike studded with placer mines. For four years while at Finn, the Hayes family operated a boarding house and saloon serving miners and cowhands.

In 1869 they moved to the Missoula area and settled along the Bitterroot River near where the McClay Bridge now stands. Ed Hayes grew up here on the farm his father developed and lived the remainder of his life in Missoula County. In June 1887 Ed's father, who also operated a ferry across the Bitterroot River, was swept off the ferry and drowned while attempting a crossing during high water.

When he was 19 years old (1884), Ed entered the sawmill industry and for the next 56 years operated lumber settings in Missoula County. His first mill was set at Hayes Creek along the Bitterroot River a few miles upstream from the family farm. This creek was named for him and still bears his name. He also operated settings at Clinton and near O'Brian Creek, four years at Miller Creek, two years at Nine Mile, one at Bearmouth, and two years at Dead Man's Gulch a couple miles above Hayes Creek. An old sailor who worked for Ed passed away and was buried there, hence the name Dead

Man's Gulch.

For twelve years Ed operated on the Flathead Reservation near St. Ignatius, which was then a part of Missoula County. His last sawmill venture was in Pattee Canyon, where he retired in 1938. After the equipment was removed from Pattee Canyon site, the buildings were given to the Girl Scouts.

As can be imagined for someone who spent so much time in the woods, Ed knew a lot about what grew there. He was fond of huckleberries and knew all the best spots for picking. His closely guarded secret was the location of the "white" huckleberries. As reported in the *Missoulian* in August, 1938:

"White or albino huckleberries have been picked from a few carefully guarded bushes on the Ranch of Ed. S. Hayes, Missoula pioneer residing far up in Pattee Canyon. Mr. Hayes, who has lived in this region since 1865, says that the huckleberry bushes have been producing the Albino berries each year, a distinct novelty, as huckleberries attain a dark blue or purple color upon ripening."

Ed attended school at the Buckhouse School, which was built in 1874. In later years, Ed took an active part in the gold rush to Welcome

Edward S. Hayes at Hayes Homestead along the Bitterroot River near the site of the McClay Bridge – cicra 1920.

Gulch along Cedar Creek. That was in 1883, the year the railroad first came to Missoula.

Ed was joined by a sister, Mary A., and two brothers, John William and Mathew Charles. He delighted in telling his grandchildren of stories of their childhood. He recalled in 1872, when he was seven years old, of riding with his father in a team and wagon and fording the Missoula River (Clark's Fork) because there was no bridge at that time.

Another of his favorite stories was in 1877 when the Nez Percé Indians came over the Lolo Trail on their famous flight toward Canada. The farmers and settlers got word of their coming and hid all of their valuables in the grain fields, then hustled their families into Missoula and took refuge in the basement of the partially completed Missoula Mercantile Company Building. After nearly a week of hiding, they got word that the Nez Percé went South up the Bitterroot, and in a few days fought the army in the battle of the Big Hole. Everyone was able to return to their homes, but there was much talk of speculation and excitement for a while.

Ed Hayes Family. Left to Right: Back Row: Carl S., Earl Herbert, Samuel Luther, John Monroe and William Lloyd. Middle Row: Charles Edward, Maud S. (Brechbill) Hayes, and Edward S. Hayes. Front Row: Mary Edna and Ruth Eileen – circa 1927.

He told of the visit to the farm by Father Ravalli, who announced that he was there to vaccinate the children. Ed overheard this and not knowing what vaccinate meant, ran and told his sister and brothers that something terrible was going to happen to them. Ed, John and Mary started to run and got away, but poor Mathew got caught so he was vaccinated.

He also told of another visit from the priest who was going to baptize the children in the river. Seeing the dunking his siblings were getting, Ed snuck off and hid until the priest left, so, he says, he was never baptized.

Ed married Maud S. Brechbill on July 24, 1890, in the first Florence Hotel in Missoula. Maud, the youngest daughter of Samuel L. and Martha J. (Freeman) Brechbill had lived in Stevensville from the time she was five years of age until her marriage at the age of 16. She had five older brothers and one sister. Maud used to say Ed told her, "If you marry me, you'll never have to put your hands in cold water again." But, she would add, I think he also said, under his breath, "unless you're too damn lazy to heat it."

Ten children were born to them, eight of which grew to adulthood. They were Charles Edward (1893-1933), William Lloyd (1895-1956), Mary Edna (1897-1967), Earl Herbert (1900-1967, John Monroe (1903-1961), Samuel Luther (1905-1983), Carl Speaks (1910-1979) and Ruth Eileen (1915-present). Ed saw to it that all eight children were enrolled as members of the Sons and Daughters of Montana Pioneers.

Ed Hayes passed away at his residence in Missoula on January 19, 1948, just five days short of his 83rd birthday. His wife, Maud, passed away in Missoula on January 20, 1967, at 91 years and 8 months of age.

As later generations, we are proud to keep the pioneer spirit of the Hayes family alive.

Daniel S. Herrin

By Keith William Herrin, Great-Grandson

Daniel S. Herrin was born at Canaan, Maine (Somerset County) on June 24, 1832. He was the son of Henry and Rachel (Starbird) Herrin and Great-grandson of Daniel Herrin, I, who originally emigrated from Ireland. He was married to Mary F. (Jewett) Herrin, who was also born in Maine. He was engaged in farming prior to coming to Montana with his wife and children; Henry H. (born January 25, 1859), Anna M. (born April 7, 1860), Milford D. (born November 3, 1861) and Harland Joseph (born May 31,

1863) who this author is descended from. All of the children were born in Canaan, Maine.

The family came by steamboat up the Missouri in 1866 to Fort Benton, Montana; then to Helena by ox team. They settled in Clancy, Jefferson County, where Daniel conducted a hotel and also engaged in raising cattle. His sons were employed as drivers on the stage route between Butte and Virginia City, Montana. In 1880 he moved to the Blackfoot Country, near Lincoln, Montana, and continued the same line of enterprise on an extensive scale.

In 1883 he formed a partnership with two of his sons, Milford D. and Harland J. in the business which continued until the spring of 1887 when, by mutual consent, they made an equal division of the land, cattle and horses that amounted to 320 acres of land, fifty-three head of cattle and twelve horses for each of them. Daniel then went into a partnership with his son Milford and that partnership continued.

Daniel S. Herrin died on July 27, 1904, in Chicago, Illinois. His son Harland J. and his wife accompanied Daniel's body back to Helena, Montana for burial.

William C. Hickey
Nellie (Hickey) Moran

Submitted by Bill O'Keefe, Great-Grandson and Grandson

"William C. Hickey – For many generations the ancestors of Mr. Hickey lived in Ireland and contributed to its advancement and improvement. His parents, Thomas and Katherine (Curran) Hickey, emigrated therefrom in 1828, settling in New York state, where our subject was born October 1, 1846. They were the parents of eight children, of whom six are living, namely William C., Thomas, Edward, Michael, Margaret and Johanna. The father died in 1875, and the mother in 1894." (Progressive Men of Montana, 1893)

In 1866, Bill came to Montana and located at Butte for two years, then relocated to Helena area where he stayed until 1909, where he devoted his time to placer mining, until buying into the Empire Lode, a quartz mine, which was "just over the hill from Tom Cruses' Drumlummon", near Marysville on December 3, 1879. Mr. Hickey's success in mining and real estate operations has been very gratifying to him and his friends.

Meanwhile his brothers, Edward and Michael, had located and

named a number of valuable mines in Butte, namely the Anaconda, Mountain View and St. Lawrence mines. Another brother, Thomas, brought his mother and his sisters, Julia and Margaret to Butte in 1882.

On July 16, 1876, he was united in marriage to Miss Matilda White, a native of England. They were the parents of three children: Nellie, Frances and Myrtle. Mrs. Hickey died September 28, 1884, after eight years of happy wedded life. The girls were placed in St. Peter's Missionary, near Cascade between 1885 until July 1892, This Ursuline boarding school at St. Peter's Mission was probably a "Godsend" for everyone concerned, as the girls received a better education, board, room and laundry for $12.50 a month per child. School was held 10 months a year, which allowed the girls to visit their father during July and August each year and allowed their father to be freer to attend to his many mining and real estate interests during the rest of the year.

On August 22, 1888, Mr. Hickey contracted a second marriage, his choice being Miss Agnes Moran, (born 1870) a native of Montana and daughter of Patrick and Katherine Moran, natives of Ireland, who first came to America in their early married life, locating first at Cincinnati but removing to Montana in 1863. The father was engaged in freighting and also conducted a hotel on the road to Bozeman and Gallatin, in both occupations he was fairly successful.

Bill Hickey, by his second marriage, is the father of six children: William, Edward, Irene, Benita, Flora and Zella.

Bill moved his family back to Butte in 1909, where he passed away in 1911 and is buried in St. Patrick's Catholic cemetery in Butte. Agnes Moran Hickey died on June 27, 1957, in Seattle, Washington. All of this generation of Hickeys is buried in St. Patrick's Cemetery in Butte.

Will and Nellie (Hickey) Moran

Submitted by Grandson Bill O'Keefe

When Nellie married her stepmother's older brother, Will Moran, on October 5, 1898, in Helena, it made the family tree somewhat confusing — but legal. They remained in the Helena area for much of their early lives. While living in the Helena area, Nellie gave birth to eight children, seven daughters and one son. Will and his younger brother, Thomas, owned and operated the Helena Meat Market and raised beef on the Spokane Ranch, until it was sold to the Myles family in 1904 (current owners).

Will and Nellie moved to Butte in 1912, where Will found work as a carpenter at various mines and occasionally as a butcher. During 1913 three of the children, Larene, William, and Winnifred, died with a fourth child, Mary, dying in 1916. Nellie operated a boarding house for many years to help make ends meet. After the remaining four children, Helen, Gladys, Frances, and Agnes, finished school, Will and Nellie moved to Avon, Montana, in the late 1920's. Summer months would find them near Blackfoot City prospecting for gold – returning to Avon during the winter months where Will worked part-time as a butcher.

It was at Avon, during the summer of 1938, that I, at age seven, first stayed with my grandparents. My 75-year-old grandfather's daily activities were quite limited – working a few morning hours at the Parker's Meat Market, and napping every afternoon. During these quiet afternoons and early evenings, Grandma Nellie taught me to play cards with cribbage being her game of choice. Often when my attention with cribbage waned, Nellie would make entries in the Moran/Hickey family tree and attempt to explain the various relationships to me. This penciled record was kept on a large roll

William Moran and Helen "Nellie" (Hickey) Moran.

of wrapping paper. Today, this faded and barely legible record is in the care of Will's nephew, Father Edward Moran of Butte. Most of my Moran and Hickey family histories can be traced back to Nellie and her dedication in preserving them and love of family.

Will Moran passed away on May 16, 1946, and is buried in the Hillcrest Cemetery in Deer Lodge. Nellie joined Will on December 28, 1959. Two of their daughters, Helen and Gladys, are buried there as well.

William Booth Sheldon & Lucina Semantha (Worden) Higgins

Submitted by Georgia Branscome, Great-Great-Granddaughter, and James Guy, Great-Grandson

William Booth Sheldon Higgins, son of Robert and Esther (Hamilton) Higgins, was born September 22, 1834, in Anslow, Nova Scotia. (He was of Irish descent). He left home at 16 and spent 18 months in Truro as an apprentice of the carriage trade. In the spring of 1852 William left Nova Scotia for Boston, Massachusetts, where he learned the carpenters trade.

In 1856, he left Boston for the "Great West," and in St. Louis took passage on the steamer Julia for Kansas. He went to work for a merchant named Boney Wood when he reached St. Joseph. They crossed the plains for California and his duty was to count and look after the stock. Their wagon train consisted of three family wagons loaded with women and children, first Boney Wood and family, then came seven Murphy wagons with five yoke of oxen pulling wagons loaded with provisions.

Behind the wagons came 300 head of loose livestock. A few cattle were lost by alkali and murrain, and when they crossed the desert, three of the men were wounded when struck with Indian arrows. Not one of the 25 was lost to sickness or death, and they landed in Placerville, California, in good health after a hard six-month trip over the trail.

From Placerville, William took the coach for Grisley Flatts and arrived at Uncle David Hamilton's home in the mines. For about six months, William remained with him and learned to prospect and mine for gold. In the spring of 1857, they joined the great stampede from California for Fraser River British Columbia. Taking a steamer at San Francisco, they landed in Whatcomb-Bellingham, Washington. There they found

Californians congregated and waiting for the floodwaters of Fraser River to subside so they could get to the mines in skiffs. In the meantime, a town of log houses, stores, dwellings, and gambling houses was being built.

William tells in his journal of building skiffs and selling them to the miners. After some unsuccessful attempts at prospecting, his uncle went to Yuma, Arizona, and William went to Fort Gamble (Washington) until the spring of 1858. William stated,

> "In the spring of 1858 I left Olympia by coach for Coulitz Landing on the Columbia River thence by Steam Boat to Fort Vancouver where I remained as carpenter in Government employ for one year. In 1860 I was employed by Captain Kirkman to build a Wharf Boat at Fort Walla Walla. On the 5th day of July 1860…John Owen, an Indian named Gregory, and I left Walla Walla for the Bitter Root with horses."

William Booth Sheldon Higgins

In 1860 Major John Owen, a United States Indian agent for the Flathead Nation, hired William now 26 years old. They arrived at Fort Owen on August 16, 1860, by way of the Mullan Road. William assisted in building the first sawmill on the Jocko Reservation. He worked on the building of Fort Owen, putting up the well house and other carpentry work. John Owen's journal states, "Feb. 8: Mr. Higgins today finished a fine writing desk for me and put it in the office. It is a beautiful piece of furniture it reflects much care on the builder."

William went to Fort Benton and brought back a Howitzer where it was mounted and fired five times. It was the first cannon shot in the Bitter Root.

Gold was discovered on Gold Creek near Deer Lodge in the spring of 1862, and William mined at Pioneer Gulch. When gold was discovered on Grasshopper Creek, he built a sawmill some miles above the mining town of Bannack.

William served on the first jury held in Montana in March 1862, at Hell Gate, and voted in the 1864 election making Montana a Territory. In 1883 he served on the grand jury held at Miles City. He was elected in 1884 to serve as a Representative, and he also served as a county road supervisor.

Lucina Semantha Worden (a descendant of John Billington, a passenger on the Mayflower) was born December 14, 1843, in Vermont, to a prosperous Welch couple, Rufus and Susan Powers Worden. She kept home for her brother Frank Worden (co-founder of Hell Gate, and later Missoula) when the Vigilantes from Alder Gulch came and hung "Skinner and the outlaws."

In 1864 Lucina married William. He assisted in building the first mills in Missoula and numerous other buildings. The family lived in Missoula until relocating to Pease Bottom around 1878. Five children were

Fort Owen – circa 1908. (William Booth Sheldon Higgins arrived at Fort Owen on August 16, 1860.)

born to the couple: Alice, Herbert, Esther, Gertrude and Frank.

The family was active in setting up the first school in what later became Treasure County. Their daughter Alice (Guy) taught at the school at the age of 14, another daughter Gertrude later became the Superintendent of Schools.

The Higgins' were a musical family and a music school was held in their home. Their melodeon was used to teach the students new songs and hymns.

Lucinda Semantha (Worden) Higgins

In 1880, William, John C. Guy (founder of Etchetah) and Robert Guy (who married Alice in 1884) went to Miles City where they picked up two tread-powered threshing machines. The machines had been shipped by steamboat from the factory in Pennsylvania in time to start the threshing in the fall. Their cost was $500 and it took a team of six to complete a threshing job.

In 1899, ten years after Montana became a State, the Higgins' moved to California because of ill health, and purchased an orange grove. William Booth Sheldon Higgins died in his sleep in 1906. His obituary states, "The casket rested beneath a beautiful certificate given by the Montana Pioneers." He remained an intimate friend of Col. Wilbur Sanders until his death.

Lucina then returned to their home in Rancher, Montana, where she lived until her death on May 15, 1916.

William was a member of the Montana Historical Society. Both he and Lucina were Grand Pioneers.

Eliza Foster Carlton Holden Lavey

Submitted by Cheryl Holden Rice, Great-Great-Granddaughter

Embarking from what is now Kent, Ohio, but what was then Franklin Mills, down the Ohio River to St. Louis, Missouri and then by steamboat up the Missouri River to Fort Benton, Montana, the Holden family hit the two-year-old Montana Territory in the spring of 1866. In a wagon train of twelve wagons, they followed the newly constructed Mullan Road through Hellgate, established in 1862 west of Missoula, to the captivating Bitter Root Valley. Their oxen-drawn wagon proved useful because the cows were milked and all were used in carving out their future in homesteading. The family settled on a mountain stream south of Lolo. It became known as Carlton Creek, later Carlton, Montana, named after Eliza's oldest son traveling with her, Robert McMurdick Carlton.

Matriarch Eliza Foster was born on June 3, 1820, to Samuel and Elizabeth Foster in Foster Rhode Island outside Providence, Rhode Island. As a young girl she relocated with her family to Franklin Mills, Ohio named after the flour mill that still stands in downtown Kent, Ohio. By age 36, she was already widowed twice, with the loss of her first husband Sherman Carlton, then by the loss of her second husband, Col. James Holden. Mr.

Carlton Church. Built 1884 at Carlton, Montana, on land donated by Robert and Mary Carlton.

Carlton is buried in Mantua, Ohio, and James Holden is buried with his first wife, Sarah, and his mother, Alice Holden, near the original Franklin Mills.

Sherman Carlton died on February 20, 1851, leaving Eliza with sons Charles, Nelson, Robert and twins Forrest and Francis "Frank" Carlton. A neighbor, Col. James Holden, also lost his wife Sarah that same year, leaving James with adult children James Amidon, William Lewis, Morris Dewayne and Ormond Clinton. That December 21, 1851, Eliza and James married in Franklin Mills, Ohio. Born August 26, 1791 Col. James Holden was 29 years older than Eliza.

A year later on December 28, 1852, a son, Ruben John Holden, Sr. was born. His brother, Morris James, arrived in 1855. Morris was named in memory of his half-brother, Morris Dewayne Holden, who died of natural

Ruben John and Mary E. Holden – 1925.

causes the previous year in April 1854. Unfortunately, Col. Holden died of natural causes in Franklin Mills on August 10, 1856, leaving Eliza with two young sons.

With the Homestead Act of 1862, the designation of Montana Territory in 1864 and the discovery of gold, the 45-year-old widow Eliza ventured with her brood to the Bitter Root Valley of western Montana to start life anew. With her were sons Robert, Forrest and Frank Carlton and Ruben and Morris Holden. Ruben was thirteen. Robert, 22, brought his young wife, Mary Lavey Carlton and their infant son, Robert F. Carlton. Accompanying them were siblings to Mary: bachelor Lawrence "Larry, the Piper" Lavey, Oliver "Ole" and Bridget "Beady" Lavey Jackson and Bartholomew "Bart" and Margaret " Molly" Lavey Campbell. Mr. Campbell's mother's maiden name was Kelly. Other Kelly family members also traveled with the group. This is the same Kelly family for whom Kelly Island is named near where the Bitter Root River feeds into the Clark Fork River west of Missoula.

From 1867 to 1907, when the Carlton homestead sold to Peter Hendrickson, three generations of Carlton/Holden/Lavey family established in 1867 and maintained a Carlton Creek – powered sawmill and gristmill, stage station, livery stable and trading post known as Carlton, Montana

Lavey-Holden Sawmill on Sweeney Creek south of Florence, Montana. Left to Right: Larry Lavey, Lewis Holden, Ed Magee, Ruben Holden, Sr., with hand on hat, Morris Holden, Ben Duffy, Alta Johnson, Larry Holden and Reuben Holden, Jr. – circa 1900.

Territory. As this frontier community developed, it also had a post office (1883), church, school, railroad depot and cemetery. Above it in the Bitter Root Mountains, the 1886 Carlton Lakes Dam fed by Lolo Peak watershed is still the oldest irrigation storage in the Bitter Root, although it was rebuilt in 1948.

During the Flight of the Nez Perce in 1877, bypassing Fort Fizzle and U.S. cannons in Lolo Creek canyon, a weary Chief Joseph and what remained of his Nez Perce nation spent their first night in this benevolent Bitter Root Valley on the Carlton homestead. Father D'Aste of Montana's first Euro-American settlement, St. Mary's Catholic Mission in Stevensville, wrote in his notes on July 8, 1877, that the Nez Perce "had come out from Lolo Canion (sic) and were camping at the Rob Carletiery place that they had not intended to fight the citizens but only the soldiers. What shame for the U.S. government. The soldiers were camping yet at Lolo watching the rocks."

The Nez Perce camped in a draw below a little bluff on the Carlton place near an area now known as the Sun Valley Ranch. In 1884, Bob Carlton donated land on this bluff for the Florence-Carlton Community Church and Cemetery. Eventually, the Carltons spent their last days in California.

On the journey west with the family, Larry Lavey stopped in Pioneer, Montana, near Philipsburg to mine gold. In 1868, he trekked the

Ruben John Holden, Sr. with load of logs for sawmill.

Indian trail over the Skalkaho divide through the Sapphire Mountains on horseback to settle with Eliza on 160 acres she had purchased from Squire Parker and his Salish Indian wife. By 1870, the widow Eliza Holden married Larry Lavey. He was 20 years younger than Eliza, making a difference of 49 years between the ages of her second and third husbands. With the place paid off by 1878, the creek through their place became his namesake, Larry Creek.

Born in Ireland in 1840, Larry "the Piper" Lavey loved to entertain with bagpipes and Irish jigs. He especially enjoyed amazing his Carlton nieces and nephews and Holden step-grandchildren and the young Salish children who gathered 'round his lively performances. He also raised funds for the Holden School with performances.

Although the first Holden School was built of logs in 1885, a frame school erected in 1893 still stands in the year 2001 along Highway 93 south of Florence between Sweeney Creek and Larry Creek on Hoblitt Lane on the Ruben Holden homestead. Hoblitt Lane also was put in by Ruben

Holden School – 1893.

Holden as were many of the early roads because he served as the first road superintendent from the Florence, Montana area.

Logging and farming, Holden and Lavey each took out homesteads near Larry Creek. The Laveys also bought the John Eichoff and the John and Eliza Rodgers Sweeney homesteads. In 1879, they were also the first to sell land to Missoula industrialist Andrew B. Hammond. Then in 1912, Allen and Naomi Tevis Hoblitt bought the original Holden homestead. In the late 1940's their son, Billy Hoblitt bought the Holden School because the community became consolidated with Florence-Carlton. It is currently privately owned and vacant. Billy Hoblitt lives directly across Highway 93 from it. To this day the area school is still called Florence-Carlton School.

Also in 1879, in Stevensville's St. Mary's Mission, Eliza witnessed the marriage of her son Ruben to Mary Elizabeth "Liz" McNaughton. Born in 1858, Liz arrived from Mt. Vernon Alabama, now a suburb of Mobile, in 1877 with the U.S. Army assigned to build Fort Missoula. Her Irish immigrant blacksmith father, Francis McNaughton, had been killed during the Civil War, leaving her French immigrant mother, Emeline, a widow. Liz met Rube as he hauled lumber down the Bitter Root Valley for the fort's

Morris Holden's Funeral Day in front of his parents' home, the homestead of Ruben Holden, Sr. Left to Right: Back Row: Reuben, Jr., Emma, Ruben, Sr., Anna, Bertha (Grenfell) Holden, Mary Elizabeth, Marguerite (Harper) Townsley in her mother's arms, Ida (Holden) Harper and Charles Holden. Front Row: Lawrence, Robert, George, Clarice, Rose and Lewis – April, 1907.

construction. With no buildings completed, Liz was living in a tent with a Fordham family at the fort.

As Eliza took Catholicism seriously, so did her son and daughter-in-law Rube and Liz Holden. For years, Florence's St. Joseph's Catholic Church was affectionately known as the Holden Church because they and their eleven children, all born between 1878 and 1903 in the Holden district south of Florence and Carlton, made up most of the first congregation. These children were Ida, Morris (a.k.a. Maurice) James, Lawrence, Reuben John, Lewis Orman, Emma Eliza, Charles, Robert McMurdick, George Francis, Clarice and Rosana. Reuben John Holden, Jr. was baptized at St. Mary's Mission having been born on July 4, 1884 before St. Joseph was erected.

The native Salish were good friends as is evident in the fact that Eliza stood as one of two witnesses to nearly a hundred confirmants, mostly Salish, as again recorded at St. Mary's Mission by Father D'Aste in 1878. When the American government forced the Salish from their Bitter Root homeland north to the Jocko River Valley, the family was distraught. Neither their protests nor the protests of the priests or membership of St. Mary's did any good. The Salish walked miles to the Flathead Reservation in October, 1891, forming the Confederated Tribes of Flatheads, Pend d'Oreilles and Kootenais by government order.

A short ten months later on August 15, 1892, Eliza Lavey passed away on Larry Creek. She lay in rest at the Missoula home of her in-laws who came west with her, Bart and Molly Campbell, whose son, a few years later, became Montana Supreme Court Justice Hugh Campbell.

Left a widower, Larry Lavey then married a woman 25 years younger than him thus making a difference of 45 years between the ages of his first and second wives. He is buried in Missoula's St. Mary's Catholic Cemetery.

For seven generations the family of Eliza has lived in her beautiful Bitter Root Valley – leaving a significant heritage. Nevertheless, nothing carries her name but her tombstone. Known as a fairly big woman, the family has no pictures of her. Few people know about her. However to this day, the Florence-Carlton Community Church and Cemetery, the school and Carlton Lakes, Dam and Creek carry the name of her son Robert Carlton and therefore indirectly her first husband, Sherman Carlton. The terribly weathered Holden School carries the name of her son Ruben Holden and indirectly her second husband, Col. James Holden. Larry Creek and the U.S. Forest Service Larry Creek Campground carry the name of her third husband, Larry Lavey. Yet what we have in remembrance of Eliza

Foster Carlton Holden Lavey is best revealed on that tombstone in Missoula's old St. Mary's Catholic Cemetery:
> Christian brothers, as you are now so once was I
> As I am now soon you will be.
> Prepare for death and pray for me.

Gregory J. Hollenback

Submitted by Robert (Great-Grandson) and Debby Hollenback

Gregory J. Hollenback was born in Germany on March 5, 1843, in the province of Schleswig-Holstein. On May 26, 1846, at the age of 3, he arrived with his family at the Port of New Orleans on the Brig Tuskan, which had sailed from Bremerhaven, Germany. On board the ship with him were his parents, Joachim and Martha Elizabeth Hollenback, who were listed as farmers from the city of Steinbach. They were both born in Prussia. Also with Gregory were his sisters Martha, age 9, Anna Elizabeth, age 8, Regina, age 6, and Amelia, age 6 months. There were a total of 99 people listed on the ship – all immigrating to America. In many places, Gregory is also listed as "George".

Gregory Hollenback family. Back Row: Thomas and Joseph. Front Row: Margareth, Gregory and Kathryn.

After arriving in the United States, the Hollenbacks purchased land in Grant County, Wisconsin, in 1849. Six more children were born to them. Joachim became a citizen in 1857.

In 1862, Gregory crossed the plains for the West and worked as a placer miner in Alder Gulch. In 1866, he returned to his home in Wisconsin and married Margareth Schrieber, who had been born in Luxembourg Germany, and had come to the United States the previous year. They made their home on a farm four miles from East Dubuque, Iowa, and then they moved to Kossuth Co., Iowa, having arrived with about 40 other Luxembourg families in 1871. Gregory owned land, a hotel, was postmaster and helped start the Catholic Church at St. Joseph, Iowa.

Gregory and Margareth had six children: Thomas James born September 8, 1867, Joseph, Kathryn, Mary, Caroline and Susan. In 1877, cholera struck the family and three of the daughters died – Mary, Caroline and Susan. Kathryn survived but was deaf. She never married and lived with her parents.

In 1879 the family again traveled to Montana where their daughter Elizabeth was born. In 1882, they returned to Iowa. Another daughter, Rosi, was born that year. However, in 1885 they returned to Montana and

Hollenback home, Gold Creek, Montana. Left to Right: Richard, Lena, Josephine, Susan, Thomas, Marguerite and Marion – circa 1913.

Scene from Pioneer, Montana.

Pioneer Society Meeting, Helena, Montana. Gregory Hollenback: first row, right side, long white beard.

settled on a ranch at Gold Creek. Their daughter Rosi died in 1887 and Elizabeth died in 1892.

Gregory was engaged as a miner during the early years of his residence in Montana. In later years he worked in farming and raised stock. He sold his property in Gold Creek to his son, Thomas, and for many years Gregory owned and operated a ranch near Kessler's in Helena but in his later years joined his son Joseph in farming near Birdseye.

Many of Gregory's siblings also resided in Montana. His sister Elizabeth married Agnatius Briggeman and many of their descendants are in the Deer Lodge area. His sister Catherine married Frank Kaiser and lived in the New Chicago area. Brothers Godfrey, Joseph and Leo also made their homes near him. His youngest brother, Adam, lived in Helena.

Gregory's son, Thomas (also known as T J), married Susan Richard in 1889 and continued operating the ranch in Gold Creek. They had five children – Marguerite, Lena, Josephine, Richard and Marion. President Wilson appointed Thomas Postmaster in 1913. He used his home as the post office with the help of his daughters, Marguerte and Lena, until he established a store on his property.

Thomas and Susan Hollenback – 1889.

*Thomas Hollenback,
Montana Militia.*

Ed Moore (father of Catherine Moore Hollenback) working as bullwacker in Pioneer, Montana.

Thomas' son Richard married Catherine Moore (the granddaughter of Arthemise Isabelle (Doney) and John Weidenfeller of Pioneer, Montana. Isabelle's brother William J. Doney was a member of the Pioneer Society). Richard took over the operation of the ranch and Thomas' daughter Lena and husband Bernard Sauber ran the store and post office. Thomas' daughter Marion married the son of a neighbor, Dave Hogan, and daughter Marguerite married John Rogers. Thomas and Susan's daughter, Josephine, became Sister Alexine in the order of the Sisters of Charity of Levenworth.

Thomas' grandsons continued operating the ranch that is today owned by John and Carole Hollenback, Keith and Jennifer. His grandson Robert and wife Debby operate the Country Village Travel Mall in Deer Lodge where they raised their four children: Philip, Elizabeth, Meridith and Josie.

Gregory was a member of the Pioneer Society and attended their yearly meetings. He was also a member of the St. Joseph's Verein Society. He died on December 20, 1915, at the age of 72. The Montana Daily Record heads the column with "Grim Reaper Visits Many".

His funeral was held at St. Helena Cathedral with burial at the Resurrection Cemetery beside his wife Margareth, who passed away in 1908.

Gregory Hollenback was an adventurous man – interested in the development of Montana Territory. He was proud to be a member of the Pioneer Society.

Myron D. and Florence Switzer Jeffers

Submitted by Mrs. Fay B. Jeffers, Daughter-in-Law

Myron D. Jeffers, (M. D.) was born September 18, 1833, and was the eldest of nine children of Jefferson and Martha (Patty) Burton Jeffers of Hadley, New York. He spent his childhood on his father's farm in Saratoga County, and attended local schools. He also attended the Academies of Cooperstown and Charlottesville, and completed a technical course in Civil Engineering.

When 21, he headed west to Iowa and remained a year. Rico, Colorado, was his next stop and he worked as a civil engineer. Going to Nebraska he joined a government survey crew. The year of 1859 found him in Pikes Peak, Colorado, where he did some mining. He could then have purchased Denver himself!

In 1864, he went to Alder Gulch, and followed freighting for five years with temporary headquarters at Deer Lodge, Virginia City, and Madison Valley.

Mr. Jeffers went to Texas in the spring of 1869, purchased a herd of cattle, trailed them to Montana Territory, and sold them at Bannack. He was the first man to bring a herd over that route in a single season. The next year he did the same.

He went to Texas again in 1871 for cattle and kept this herd for himself. His diary states that 1,894 head of cattle and 37 head of horses were road branded. He had 14 riders, a cook, and a cook's helper in his crew. The trip took a little over seven months and established him as a stockman.

Myron D. and Florence E. (Switzer) Jeffers.

In 1883 he purchased a band of sheep in Oregon. Thereafter he was always engaged in stock raising.

Mr. Jeffers and his brother Burt entered into a partnership located on Jordan Creek in 1872. They built a house, barn, and shed.

In 1876 M. D. located his home ranch at the place he called "The Yellow Barn Ranch". Here he put up wild hay to feed his stock in the winter. He and his brother dissolved the partnership in 1880.

In 1881, Mr. Jeffers, Burt Jeffers, E. A. Maynard, and other Madison Valley stockmen organized a cattle pool, leased land on the Yellowstone, and trailed cattle there. The winter of 1886-87 was extremely severe on the open range in eastern Montana and many head of cattle died on the range. That winter on the Madison Valley was a normal winter. The cattle pool was dissolved in the early 1890's and the Yellowstone herd was sold.

On December 5, 1878, Myron Jeffers and Florence E. Switzer, the eldest daughter of Mr. and Mrs. Andrew W. Switzer were married. Mrs. Jeffers had crossed the plains with her parents at age eight in 1865. She grew up in the valley and was schooled there, later taking some advanced courses in a private school in Virginia City. She taught school in the valley one term. Mr. and Mrs. Jeffers made their home at the Yellow Barn Ranch where their five sons were born: Jefferson Clifford on October 1, 1879; Walter Clarence (Tas) on January 29, 1881; Paul Myron on November 25, 1882; Fayette Burton on July 26, 1885, and Austin Pierpont on December 16, 1894.

When the older boys were ready for high school, Mrs. Jeffers moved to Bozeman for the school year and lived in a home outside of town that is still standing on Eighth Avenue – the town having grown to encompass the area.

A large home of 12 rooms was being built about one-quarter mile south of the village of Jeffers when Mr. Jeffers died in May 1900. When the home was finished in 1902, Mrs. Jeffers and her sons moved in and remained until the ranch was sold in 1919.

In recognition of Mr. Jeffers three successful cattle drives and his contributions to the formation of the stock industry in Montana, he was elected to the Cowboy Hall of Fame in 1961.

Mrs. Jeffers was a member of the Episcopal Church of Jeffers and a charter member of Trinity Guild and a member of the Society of Montana Pioneers. She was past president of the Madison Valley Woman's Club and its historian at the time she prepared a report to the Club now called "History of Madison Valley" by Mrs. M. D. Jeffers. Mrs. Jeffers died in 1940. Both Mr. and Mrs. Jeffers are buried in the Valley Cemetery.

John Jones

Submitted by Cindy Jones Kittredge, Great-Granddaughter
(Portions excerpted from Jacob Hardesty Jones *by Freda Jones in* Mountains and Meadows *and from research by Janet Jones Ivie.)*

If there is one word that describes the history of my father's family, it is *westering*, that fascination with the lands that lie west toward the setting sun (Kittredge, 1996). Like other early American pioneers who were susceptible to the urge to move west to greener ground, this family found their way to the new world from the British Isles, then pushed across the

Alleghenies onto the Great Plains finally settling in the Rockies.

John Jones was born April 8, 1817. He was a graduate of Hanover College in Ohio and taught school in Kentucky for fourteen years. John married Elisa Allen (born November 20, 1808) and they had five children, William Benjamin (born 1840, died 1852), John Samuel (born September 21, 1842, died November 8, 1914), James Gustavis (born 1846), Robert (born November 22, 1847, died 1854) and Frances Lavinia (born June 23, 1850, died May 28, 1851). Elisa died in 1851, and John married Rebecca Hardesty (born March 20, 1832) on March 21, 1852.

In 1859 seeing the gathering clouds of an armed conflict between the states, he gave up the profession of teaching and went to Central City, Colorado, filing on mining claims and sluicing for gold. He built a home and became judge of the first Miners' Court. In 1861 he returned to Salem, Kentucky, and moved his wife Rebecca and children Jacob Hardesty (born February 14, 1853 in Covington, Kentucky), Thomas Benjamin (born July 27, 1854), Edward Washington (born July 30, 1857), Sarah Frances (born September 30, 1859), Emma Lue (born October 14, 1861) and Martha Ina (born August 20, 1866) to their new home in Central City. In covered wagons, they followed the route of the low-banked Arkansas and Platte Rivers from Missouri to Colorado.

According to family oral history, John Jones became upset at having to sentence a man to hang for stealing a mule. In the fall of 1863, he traveled to Virginia City, Montana-Idaho Territory, in order to examine mining and business prospects. It was during this stay that John wrote letters to his wife describing the Virginia City of the day. He also bought a running mare that had belonged to Jack Slade, the last person hung by the Vigilantes. The purchase was made at the auction held by Mrs. Slade after her husband was hung. The mare became the seed stock for the horses raised (until the late 1980's) on the Richard H. Jones ranch near Cascade.

In February 1864, John Jones returned to Central City and with his four brothers-in-law, John, Edward, Thomas, and Jackson Hardesty, he moved Rebecca and the children to Virginia City. To prepare for this venture he outfitted his ox-train with provisions and saleable goods bought in Denver. He readied his family and set out for the booming gold camp. The trip took 76 days. His son J. H. (Hardy) Jones recalled that on this trip they had anticipated trouble with the Indians on the Snake River because Army Officer Conner and his men had massacred an Indian group there. Reprisals against the whites were expected. However, after a friendly conference with some Indians they did encounter, the wagon train went safely on its way.

Although he was only eleven years old on this trip, J. H. (Hardy) Jones always remembered another lively experience. This memory was the vying of the Jones-Hardesty ox-train with a mule-train that was following the same route. When the going was fair, the mule-train advanced quicker. When the going was rough, the ox-train led. Just by chance, a day's travel away from Virginia City, heavy rains fell and the roads on the long pull over a mountain became a bog, making them almost impassable. The ox-train slowly pulled past the mule-powered wagons and led the way into town.

Protection of their oxen also led John Jones to create the family's brand, the Wagon-Rod, which became one of the oldest registered brands in the state of Montana. Concerned with the prospect of possibly losing his oxen through confusion or theft, he removed the tie-rod from the back of a wagon box. Using the ring of the rod as a circle, he bent the rod to form a stem at the base of the circle, creating a brand that, though simple, could not be easily altered.

Once in Virginia City, John Jones established a trading center with the nucleus of goods he had brought from Denver. The family remained in Virginia City one year, and in 1865 they moved to the Prickly Pear Valley near Helena, Montana. There John Jones had bought the rights on the land of two squatters and began ranching operations. Evidently gifted with practicality, John Jones prospered in the ranching business. He also became interested in the early government of the state and is listed as one of the legislators elected to the 1869-1870 Legislative Assembly of Montana Territory.

John Jones died on July 19, 1879, in the Prickly Pear Valley near Helena, Montana. Rebecca died on January 29, 1894, in Helena, Montana. They are both buried in the Helena Forestdale Cemetery.

John's son, Jacob Hardesty (Hardy) Jones was the eldest of John and Rebecca's children. He was born in Covington, Kentucky, on February 14, 1853. Though part of the historic movement west, he grew to manhood in Helena. In his late teens, he became interested in settling in Choteau country, but rejected the idea because of the raw and violent winds he experienced when visiting there. In 1874 he and a party of hunters came from Helena to Ulidia (near current day Cascade, Montana) to hunt buffalo. They shot no buffalo, but they loaded their wagons with antelope and deer.

Apparently, he liked the country for he returned to Cascade in 1879 with Joe Bickett, his brother-in-law. Each filed on a 160-acre timber claim, although other information suggests he took up a desert claim of 640 acres five miles from Cascade. In either case, he was a busy man dividing his time between the Prickly Pear, which was under his operation since his father's death, and the Chestnut Valley ranches. This double duty continued for two years before he moved his family to the ranch near Cascade to make a permanent home.

Hardy Jones was one of the first growers of alfalfa in Montana and was one of the first purebred Hereford breeders in the state. One author wrote of him, "In fact, his genuine interest in good horses and cattle, and in good ranching practices made his name synonymous with those terms in a wide area." However, perhaps the most forward-looking of Hardy Jones' endeavors was the five miles of irrigation ditches he engineered for the purpose of watering his hay lands. This feat not only required great effort but also knowledge of irrigation engineering. The work was done without scientific surveying tools and was accomplished by horses and men. Teams and slips were used for the work, and the natural engineering gift of Hardy Jones was the moving spirit.

Hardy Jones' holdings, before the financial and natural disasters of the early twenties, grew to encompass a number of ranches. They included the home ranch presently held by Jean Nicholls; the Whitmore Ranch now owned by John Rumney; the Adel, Weiderhold, Coulson, Morley, Monroe, Brodock, and Lockray ranches, now owned by Seiben Ranch Company; and portions of the current Armstrong and Gollaher ranches.

He served for years as a member of the Cascade school board, being instrumental in the development of the town's high school. He also served as President of the First State Bank in Cascade, was a member of the Masonic Order, and was an active member of the Methodist Church, being instrumental in the building of its church that still stands to serve its congregation.

Hardy Jones married Bessie Hannah Bunnell of Galt, Missouri, (daughter of James and Elizabeth McAfee Bunnell) on January 1, 1888. She was also a member of a pioneer Montana family, who settled in various parts of Montana, including Helena, Cascade, and Bozeman. Although her family had not come west as early as the Jones family, their forebears had come to the U.S. in pre-Revolutionary times. They were part of the movement of Scots who, disenfranchised from their native Colonsay, settled first in Northern Ireland, finally coming to the American colonies where they became contemporaries of Daniel Boone in the push through the Cumberland Gap. In fact, Bessie's great-great grandparents, Robert and Jane

McAfee, left Ireland for the new world in 1739.

J. H. Jones died in Helena, Montana, on November 11, 1941, at the age of 88. He and Bessie, who died in 1931, are buried in Helena. Their children were Thomas Leslie, Mable Rebecca, Robert Lloyd, Charles Shelton, Mary Elizabeth, Russell Bunnell, Richard Hardesty and Helen Maxine. Richard, who lived to 96, ranched adjacent to the Hardy Jones home ranch outside of Cascade, Montana. The ranch that Richard and his wife Freda developed is now known as the Bird Creek Ranch and is run by their daughter Cindy, her husband James Kittredge, and their son Stephen.

J. H. (Hardy) Jones' half-brother, John S. Jones, also accompanied his father John to Central City, Colorado, and then to Montana in the 1860's. There he was associated in mining interests with his father, but sold them. In 1865 he filed on a homestead in the Prickly Pear Valley, and in 1867-68 he successfully engaged in freighting from Fort Benton to Helena.

In 1881 in Missouri, he married a widow, Mary E. (Mollie) Bunnell Shanklin, who had three children. They moved to Montana Territory for a time, returned to Missouri, then finally moved back to Montana in 1893. They ranched near Helena and then in 1894 settled on a ranch near Cascade. John Jones, along with his half-brother Hardy, figured prominently in the building of the Chestnut Valley irrigating canal that supplied water for the valley. He designed and helped build the rock retaining wall that is still traveled over on the Sheep Creek Road. He died in 1914, and Molly passed away at her home in Cascade in 1942.

Adam Agustus LaLonde

Submitted by William M. Caplis, Grandson

Adam A. LaLonde was one of the worthy pioneers of Montana and an honored citizen of Missoula County. He raised livestock and gave attention to the development of the fruit-raising resources of the state. He grew much fruit on his fine ranch, located six miles west of the city of Missoula.

His career was eventful with many interesting points. Mr. LaLonde was born near the city of Montreal, Canada, on May 21, 1839. His parents were Augustus and Amelia (Walker) LaLonde, natives of Canada. They had one son and three daughters. Their son, Adam, was the only one to locate in the United States. In the agnatic line, Mr. LaLonde traces back to French and English origin. His maternal lineage is French and Scotch.

Adam A. LaLonde resided in Canada until he was 18 years old. He received educational advantages of the public schools. He spent four years on steamboats on the St. Lawrence river and was a captain at 18. In 1861 he crossed the international boundary and made his way to the great Mississippi River. It was here he became identified with the steam boating business, first as watchman, and later as master of a river packet. He navigated nearly the whole length of the Mississippi River for five years during the period of the Civil War. Once, on the White River in Arkansas, his boat narrowly escaped capture by a Confederate officer, General Sterling Price. After the close of the war Mr. LaLonde engaged in freighting on the Mississippi for one year.

In 1868 he came up the Missouri River to Fort Benton where he drove freight teams between the great supply point and the mining camp at Virginia City. In the winter of 1868, Adam went to Helena, or "Last Chance," as it was then designated, and obtained a position in the 1XL quartz mill for about 18 months. He then opened a bakery and lodging house, which proved to be one of the popular resorts of the busy little mining city.

He conducted this business for three years, until the building and contents were destroyed by fire, entailing a complete loss. Not dismayed,

Adam A. LaLonde Family. Left to Right: Back Row: Sarah Naomi, Rebecca "Reba" J., Ova Louise, Ada Minerva and Lucy Mae. Middle Row: Emily Gertrude. Front Row: Adam A., Ruth Charlotte and Lucy (Wells Bisson) LaLonde.

however, he found another medium for success, and went to Cascade County and located a claim on Cedar Creek, No. 75, and devoted his attention to farming and raising cattle for three years.

He associated himself with Louis Barrett, Daniel Stewart, Frank Houseman, H. Nightingale, and others to prospect for gold. The party was eventually successful and discovered a lode of the precious metal on Nine Mile Creek. They patented a claim two and one-fourth miles in length and worked for three years with varying success.

In 1876 Mr. LaLonde came to Missoula and rented the ranch now owned by J.R. Lattimer. Two years later he purchased the land of his present ranch and remained for 23 years. He had 200 acres of well-improved land and was devoted principally to raising cattle and hogs, and cultivating fruit. The ranch is located six miles west of Missoula and is one of the attractive and valuable places of the county.

Politically, Mr. LaLonde was a Populist and a zealous advocate of the party's principles. He was held in high esteem both as a man and a pioneer. In 1886 Mr. LaLonde married Miss Lucy Wells Bisson, a native of Pennsylvania. Lucy already had one daughter, Elisabeth A. Bisson. Together Adam and Lucy had one son and seven daughters. Their son was John A., and their daughters were Ada Minerva, Rebecca "Reba" J., Sarah Naomi, Lucy Mae, Emily Gertrude, Ova Louise, and Ruth Charlotte.

Judge William I. Galbraith, Missoula, Montana, naturalized Mr. A. A. LaLonde in District Court of the Second Judicial District, Montana Territory, on November 17, 1881.

In March 1918 at the age of 78, Adam LaLonde died a quiet death as a result of sugar diabetes that he had become ill with some years earlier. Both Adam and his wife Lucy are buried in Frenchtown, Montana.

John Largent

Submitted by Bridgett Oliver, Great-Great-Granddaughter

John Largent was born in Hampshire County, West Virginia, on March 10, 1839, the son of Mr. and Mrs. John Washington Largent. He was a direct descendant of revolutionary stock; his grandfather, Major John Largent, was born in North Carolina in 1770. When he was ten years old his parents moved to Peoria County, Illinois.

In the spring of 1862 at the age of 22 years, John Largent engaged with the American Fur Trading Company to come to Fort Benton, Montana. They came up the Missouri River on the steamer Spread Eagle. It took 90 days to make the run from St. Louis, Missouri, to the land of Fort Benton. The boat did not carry him all the way to Fort Benton by any means, in fact, everyone on the boat tugged and pulled the boat much of the distance. About 24 white men comprised the entire force at Fort Benton.

While John was working for the American Fur Trading Company, he was paid $19.50 per month. Later he helped Major George Steell build and supervise a new trading post called Fort Andrews. At that time his wages were raised to $40.00 per month. During the building of the post, their food and ammunition ran short during the winter. They lived partly on wolf meat and corn. They ground the corn in the coffee mill into meal and made bread out of it. The mice had eaten the kernel, or heart, out of the corn and it was impregnated with mice pepper, but it filled the hollow stomachs of everyone at the fort.

They had several encounters with the Indians while hunting for fox meat. One day John and Bill Oliver, known as Canada Bill, went out to rustle fox meat. They saw Indians on foot, but Bill mistook them for being friendly. They waited until they approached and Bill shook hands with them not knowing they were on a warpath. John and Bill could have been

John Largent Family.

murdered at any moment. The Indians (or Bloods) took John's horse, gun, and knife, but Bill wasn't treated in this manner. They held John hostage until they reached the Fort and asked the American Fur Company to give them blankets, coffee, tea and tobacco for John's life. George Steell gave them their goods in return for John. John felt indebted to the company since goods were very expensive. John was happy to be back at the Fort but still very angry for the way the Indians treated him.

They had a number of scrapes with the Indians at this fort. George Steell, who was in the trading house, discovered the Indians intentions and armed his men before they were all murdered. One morning an alarm was given and someone shouted "hostile Indians in the corral!" John noticed a party of Indians leading away his favorite saddle horse. John forced his way to the horse and took hold of the rope attached to the horse's neck and made a sign to the Indians that he loved this horse and would not part with him without a fight. The Indians motioned John to let go of the rope, but John refused. One Indian strung his bow and pointed the arrow at his breast but John would not let go. He then struck John in the breast with the arrow. John felt the blood running down his body. John, forced to let go of the rope, vowed if he ever got the opportunity, he would make a good Indian out of the fellow. This same Indian was killed about two years later by a party of white men out hunting Crows.

It was easy for those that knew John to understand why the American Fur Company depended upon and trusted so much in him. John was six feet, two inches in height, rawboned and of sanguine temperament. He was known for his honesty, trustworthiness, and good judgment. In his earlier days he was a remarkably good shot with the rifle and few men equaled him. He was well versed in the language of most of the northern tribes of Indians and was feared and respected by them. It was a fact that many of the young warriors feared him because he was so quick and accurate with his old "Kentucky rifle."

John married Miss Sarah E. Hughes on March 10, 1869, in Illinois. She came with him to Montana and settled in the Sun River Valley. Mr. and Mrs. John Largent had five children: Sarah, Eva, Mary Jane, John, and Ida. John lived and prospered at his Sun River home. He later built a brick hotel named the Largent Hotel. John built the first log cabin that was 154 feet in length. This cabin was used for a store, saloon, hotel, and living quarters. He also served as Sun River's first postmaster. Sarah died in 1912 and is buried at Sun River.

John had a tree at his ranch. When it needed to be cut down to make a railroad right-of-way, John pleaded to leave the tree standing. Inspired by this event, Robert Vaughn wrote a poem called "Right of Way Man Spare This Tree."

On June 17, 1919, John passed away and was laid to rest at Sun River. His work was well done and after years of hardships, privations, and overcoming the perils of a new country, he left a permanent record in the history of Montana. He was known as the man who was not afraid and knew how to do things. John Largent's passing took one of the oldest of the pioneers of this section, if not the dean of them all, for he came to Montana in 1862. He gained membership in the Montana Society of Pioneers because of his long-time residence. That is regarded honor enough by those who are fortunate enough to wear the emblem of the pioneers. John wasn't affiliated with any other societies or organizations at the time of his passing.

This is the poem written about the tree Mr. Largent wanted spared. I thought it would be great to add this with the story.

Two Pioneers: John Largent and his Tree.

Right-of-Way Man Spare This Tree
By Robert Vaughn

Oh, right-of-way man, I pray you,
   Spare this pioneer tree,
In eighteen hundred sixty-two
   This monarch sheltered me.

When this part was a desert waste
   An old fur trader with me,
Camped through many a frosty night,
   Under this dear old tree.

In our blanket bed we laid
   The old pioneer and I,
Gazing through its spreading boughs
   At the silv'ry moon on high.

Look at its height, its giant form
   It has passed the century score
'Tis hard for me to think that soon
   'Twill not be seen any more.

Why not go back to yonder curve
   And make a new survey,
Remove those stakes, and build the road
   A little more that way?

The right-of-way through all my land
   Will be deeded to you free,
If, in return, you kindly spare
   My own, old cottonwood tree.

We looked into the matter thoroughly
   Have made a new survey.
The tree is saved, I assure you
   And off the right-of-way.

Aime Lepine

*Submitted by Ruby Michel, Granddaughter,
and Gloria Sundquist, Great-Granddaughter*

Aime Lepine, whose full name was Edward Aime dit Lepine, was born in Green Bay, Maine, on January 15, 1843. He was the youngest of twelve children, and the son of Francois Berard dit Lepine.

Aime Lepine was a descendant of the Acadians; they were the French people who settled Acadia in 1604. In 1775 when the British took over Acadia, they renamed it Nova Scotia (New Scotland), seized all their possessions and deported the Acadian people in small groups through the British Colonies, which are now the United States.

At an early age, he moved with his family to Quebec. At age 15 he left alone for Boston. There he worked for a construction company. He shortened his name to Aime Lepine. Wanting to move farther west, Lepine went to Chicago and then to St. Joseph, Missouri, where the wagon trains were preparing for the long journey to Washington and Oregon by way of the Oregon Trail. He joined a wagon train, pulled by oxen, and took off across the prairies for Montana. The trail followed the Platte River and the North Platte west to Wyoming. Though the travelers described the muddy

Aime Lepine Family. Left to Right: Sara, Sara (Marcotte) Lepine holding Aime and Edward, Aime Lepine with Adeline and Camile in front.

water as "too thick to drink but too thin to plow" they were aware that they could not have crossed the dry prairie without its ample supply of water for both people and livestock.

They endured several Indian attacks along the way and they lost two men to them. This was approximately the time the Civil War started. They arrived in Soda Springs, Idaho, and from here Aime went on to Alder Gulch. He arrived there in 1861. He staked a claim and spent several years mining at Last Chance Gulch. Mr. Lepine also mined in the Grasshopper and other diggings. He spent time as a trapper along the Yellowstone and Madison Rivers. He also trapped beaver in what is now known as Yellowstone Park. In the early 1860s he took charge of building a road to the Stinking Water for Henery Maurier. These were Vigilante days and several times Mr. Lepine saw men who had been strung up by the committees and the bodies left hanging as a warning to others. In 1866 he went to Helena, Montana, and spent about four years working for Wilcox in the mines and cutting wood. He also worked in Frenchtown, Cedar Creek, and Bozeman for a time. The next several years were spent at Fort Ellis cutting cordwood, trapping beaver and wolves on the Big Horn near the present sight of Billings. Deer were also plentiful.

In 1871 he was in Yellowstone Park country and worked for Major

Aime and Sara Lepine, Edward Lepine and Herman Schultz at home on the Teton River – circa 1905.

Pease, taking up adobe brickwork and erecting houses for the Indians to live in when they came to trade at Fort Pease. In 1874 with Oliver Bernier, of Augusta, he made his first trip to Fort Benton. They took wolf pelts to Bozeman by packhorses.

In 1876 Lepine was employed by I.G. Baker and Conrad Companies. He later went into business for himself freighting from Fort Benton to Fort McLeod, and later to Helena and Butte. At first he used oxen and soon changed to horses. In 1880 he returned to Fort Benton, and on August 9 of that year he married Sara Marcotte. Sara, who was born in 1860, had moved with her parents from Three Rivers, Quebec, to Ft. Benton.

They took up resident on the Teton River. Their home was made of lumber, two stories high with a winding stairway and a lean-to kitchen with a shingled roof. Most of the houses of the day were cabins with thatch roofs and in many cases the walls were also thatch.

There were five children born to Aime and Sara Lepine. Mr. Lepine knew many people from all over the country, and many times they stayed over with the Lepines while riding through. Cold-weather straw mats would be put on the kitchen floor for them to sleep on.

There were quite a few settlers along the Teton at this time. Many were bachelors and quite a few took Indian women for their wives.

One day, while Lepine was resting in a saloon in Ft. Benton, an arrow came through the window and killed the man who was sitting beside him and was talking to him. The man died almost instantly. They never did find out who did it.

Mr. Lepine died in February 1931. He was a resident for over half a century in Chouteau County. He spent around 69 years in the state, and was probably the oldest pioneer in Chouteau County. A pioneer in every sense of the word, Mr. Lepine blazed many trails and followed many callings. He was survived by his wife Sara, daughters Sara Maurer, Adeline Neubert, and Camile Price. Two children preceded him in death, Aimee and Edward. He was buried in Riverside Cemetery in Fort Benton. Sara Lepine died in 1936 and is also buried in Fort Benton, Montana.

Peter Levengood

Submitted by Billie Ratcliffe, Great-Great-Great-Granddaughter

Peter Levengood's story would provide good material for a novel or Hollywood film. He was one of the diminished band of men who hewed their way into the wilderness that was once the Wild West.

Peter was born December 17, 1832. He came from pioneer stock, his father being one who settled old Kentucky, when it was called "the Dark and Bloody Ground." In 1859 socio-economic and political forces were changing forever Peter's familiar world and causing the Civil War to begin.

Peter married Mary Elizabeth McCandless at Levengood Station in Kentucky in 1850. They had two children, Mary Catherine born December 15, 1851, and an infant son, unnamed, born and died on September 20, 1853. His wife Mary died on the same day and was buried in Pendleton County, Kentucky.

On February 1, 1857, he married Elizabeth Anna McPherson. They had the following children: Nora May (died in infancy), Elizabeth Ann (Ella) (November 6, 1859), Hattie (August 5,1861), Jefferson Jas (Jeff) (January 28, 1865), Carlos (Cal) Peter (July 31,1864) Grace (April 15, 1870), Harriet and Cora (January 11, 1869).

In search of new freedom, while trying to reconcile his political leanings, he moved his family to Missouri, becoming a general store owner. Peter didn't believe in fighting against the government, nor his "brothers," so neutrality was the obvious answer. But there would be no respite, with situations worsening in the border states. He, along with others, was accused of Rebel sympathies and was jailed. Perhaps the statement "Hurrah for Jeff Davis," questionably attributed to his feisty wife, hastened the decision. The charges couldn't be proved, but emotions ran high enough that one of those jailed was shot through an open window and died. Upon release and in fear of his life, Peter headed north to Vernon, Iowa, never seeing Missouri again. His wife and children stood by while the store and its contents were ransacked or stolen. They subsequently joined him in Iowa.

He sought means of providing for his family and worked as a store clerk. Understandably, his vision of their future as an employee of another was not satisfactory. He was again looking West, this time to the Idaho Territory. Word had spread about the opportunities at the rich gold strikes in Virginia City, so in April 1864 he left from Omaha, Nebraska, via wagon train. His family returned to Kentucky to await whatever fortune was to be his lot.

Since he had no livestock but his horse, his apparent leadership qualities gained him the wagon boss position. The Platte River route was subject to many hazards, including hostile Indians. Travel by foot and ox team was excruciatingly slow. A smaller, faster train with horse drawn wagons joined them, but within in two to three days they became impatient and pushed ahead. A few days later they came upon the burned wagons and the dead from that wagon train where they were left by the hostiles. All they could do was bury the remains. His train, being better prepared defensively, was never seriously threatened. After three months on the trail, he arrived July 15, 1864, at Virginia City that was now in Montana territory.

Peter Levengood

His arrival was two years after the original gold strikes and desirable claims were gone. He again was working for others – this time in a placer mining capacity. The wetness and cold weather triggered asthma and rheumatism so he moved down to the Ruby Valley, working in ranching and logging, still driven to find his own place so his family could reunite. While traveling to the Deer Lodge Valley, his search ended.

A few miles west of present day Anaconda he established the Levengood Ranch, an area of fish and game, profuse wild hay, thick stands of pine and fir, and well watered pastures. He was ready for his family.

Elizabeth and the children went to St. Louis and boarded the stern wheeler "Fort Benton," ironically also their destination, in April 1867. For eleven weeks they endured the dangers coming up the Missouri River arriving July 2. The apparition that greeted them was unexpected. In three years the man of gentlemanly appearance, with trimmed facial hair, was now in a worn blue woolen shirt, heavy boots, and full beard. The younger children weren't quite sure of this "stranger."

The trip back to Deer Lodge via horse and wagon took approximately ten days. Upon arrival he started building what eventually became a nine-room log home that over ensuing years saw extra duty as stage stop, post office, church, and wayfarers food and lodging. None left hungry – either paying then or when they could.

Peter's involvement in civil affairs was legendary. He served as postmaster, voter registrar, and stage stop operator among others. A lifelong Democrat, he was philosophically involved politically though he never sought or was elected to office. He became a "living encyclopedia" of Anaconda, knowing the hottest and coldest days, years of the "big snows," and the names of every local office holder from 1867 until his death. He also was a member of the Pioneers of Deer Lodge County, Montana.

His morals and sense of values were sorely tested in later years. Marcus Daly's smelter operation had so polluted and destroyed plant life that he and others formed a "smoke-farmer" group to sue against the smelter smoke. Peter mortgaged the ranch to help in the fight. They eventually would have won, were it not for their lawyer "forgetting" to appeal and letting the suit default. There were thousands involved, and their lawyer was ever after "well off." So add this to his list of one more accomplishment "early day environmentalist."

After losing the ranch he was forced to move to a small cabin built for him on a daughter's land. At age 83 he broke his hip and eventually became bedridden. On the night of June 6, 1923, at 11 p.m., his son-in-law, Charles Sparrow, checked to see if he was comfortable and straightened his quilt. The next morning at 5:30 am, Peter was found dead just as he had been left except for one hand above the covers as if reaching out to something. So passed this six-foot two-inch "giant" of a man of over 90 years. He was buried at Hill Cemetery in Anaconda, Montana.

His was the hardy independent pioneering spirit that would not be subjugated or dominated by any law, save that of his own conscience and God.

Edward A. Lewis

Submitted by Elizabeth Tabor Kehmeier, Great-Granddaughter, and Rosemary K. Siemens, Granddaughter

Edward A. Lewis was a native of Cambia County, Pennsylvania. He was born on May 18, 1837, the son of Alma and Lydia Lewis of New York and Pennsylvania. Edward was one of eight children born to Alma and Lydia.

Alma Lewis was principally a farmer by trade, though at one time operated a sawmill. He also was an active supporter of the Whig Party during its ascendancy. Alma eventually moved his family to Iowa where he devoted the remainder of his life to farming. Alma passed away in 1872 and Lydia in 1885.

Edward Lewis received his early education in Iowa in the common schools and assisted with the farm work. He remained at his parent's home until 1854 when he secured work on a steamboat on the Mississippi and the Missouri rivers. His first employment was as a deck sweeper and later was promoted to deck hand.

Left to Right: Joe Moran and Edward A. Lewis at Sullivan Valley in the St. Peter's Mission Area.

In 1857 Edward Lewis came up the Missouri by steamboat to Fort Benton, Montana. He was hired out to the American Fur Company in St. Louis and worked on the "Star of the West" steamboat that made it as far as what is now Culbertson. The boat was loaded with goods to pay the Indians their annuities for the treaty they had made with the government. From Culbertson the men had to build Mackinaw boats (flat boats) to take the goods on to Fort Benton. They had to tow those boats up the river, so it took 65 days to get to Fort Benton. Most of the traveling was done at night because of hostile Indians.

One adventure Ed Lewis had on the Missouri River was a trip he made with two friends, Mr. Armel and Bill Fatherland. They volunteered to take a dispatch for the American Fur Company to Omaha. They went down the Missouri in a cottonwood boat that was 12 feet long with nothing but dried buffalo meat for provisions. They had no problems until they got to the Mandan Village. There they found a Sioux Chief with many warriors who were bitter enemies of the whites. They decided to pass the village at night when they saw the reflections of the campfires in the village. They waited until late night when the Indians were asleep. They floated close to the bank not making any noise with their oars, but as they got past, one of the Indian guards heard them and raised the alarm. They really worked those oars, and being hidden by the thick brush along the bank, they finally were out of danger. They came back to Fort Benton on the steamboat.

Later the company sent them to the Highwood Mountains to cut logs to make Mackinaw boats. This was another narrow escape with the Indians. In fact, they were captured and their horses were stolen.

In 1860 Major Blake, along with a detachment of troops, came up the Missouri River to Fort Benton and was bound for Fort Colville. Blake and his troops came on the steamboat *Chippewa*. Edward Lewis was also on this boat. The *Chippewa* was the first steamboat to land at Fort Benton. Marjor Blake was very anxious to know the whereabouts of Captain John Mullan, who was then somewhere west of the main range of the Rockies building a wagon road from Walla Walla, Washington, to Fort Benton. Major Blake sent Edward in search of Captain Mullan to give him a message. Ed traveled up the Prickly Pear Canyon where, at the Deer Lodge River, he met an Indian who spoke some English. Captain Mullan was camped across the river and it was spring run-off time. Ed didn't know how he was going to get the message across the river, but the Indian said he'd do it. The Indian put the message in his mouth and proceeded to swim the river even though it was cold and swift. It had taken Edward eight days to make this trip.

In 1861 their supplies were coming on the steamer *Chippewa* when it blew up and all the goods lost. So they had to get more supplies from Fort Union. Ed Lewis, accompanied by others, was sent to haul the goods over land. They left Fort Union with several wagons and carts drawn by oxen and horses. A war party of Crow Indians came and demanded goods. They had trouble with these Indians. One Indian was killed trying to get into one of the wagons. Now they were in big trouble because a large band of them came to demand all the goods. A band of Gros Ventres Indians came and saved them just in time.

Ed Lewis had many adventures during the time he was employed by the American Fur Trading Company. Fort Benton was a great fur trading point until most of the buffalo and other fur bearing animals disappeared.

In 1864 Ed formed a partnership with Malcolm Clarke to build a road through Prickly Pear Canyon. They did not do this but sold the charter to James King and W. C. Gillette. It was at Malcolm Clarke's that Ed met his wife, Sy-ca-was-ta-ca-pa, a cousin of Mrs. Clarke. Ed and his wife were living at Silver City near Helena when a daughter, Isabell, was born. Through the intercession of the Great Spirit, she lived. Several of their children died as infants.

After doing some mining at Silver City near Helena, Ed took up a

Left to Right: Neighbor, Edward A. Lewis and wife Sycawastacapa.

preemption claim on land near the then-abandoned St. Peters Mission in 1869. At St. Peters Mission, Mr. Lewis raised vegetables and a variety of farm produce that he sold to the people at Fort Shaw. Ed and his wife were good friends of the Jesuits and Ursulines at St. Peters Mission. This is where he lived out his life, and passed on in 1914.

Montana ranch children had little opportunity for education in frontier time. Outside of towns there were few schools even of the one-room variety. As late as 1878 there were only 88 schoolhouses in the territory. Seven of which were in the Lewis and Clark County. Mr. Lewis gave his children a better education than most in spite of the difficulties encountered. There was no school near their home, so Isabell was sent to school at Sun River, and lived in the home of friends there. Later she attended St. Vincent's Academy at Helena in charge of Mother Xavier. She was there during the years 1878-1880, and studied law.

Ed and Sy-ca-was-ta-ca-pa were able to raise another daughter, Mary Anne (Molly). Molly Lewis was one of the first students at the St. Peters Mission Girls School. The Ursulines came to open a girl's school through an invitation from the Jesuits who had an established boy's school at St. Peters Mission. This was a wonderful chance for pioneer education close to home. Isabell had to go to Helena to school that was a long stagecoach ride away.

In July 1880, Isabell Lewis married John P. Tabor, a native of Kentucky, who had a fine ranch in the Sullivan Valley. The ceremony took place in the little log chapel of St. Peters Mission, with Father Peter Prando officiating. Mrs. Tabor became a convert at this time, as did Ed Lewis, father of Isabell. They had two children, Mary and John Leo. John Leo Tabor married Catherine Marie Hollenbach Jan. 4, 1909. To this union were born nine children: John Edward, Trannie Isabell Bertsch, Thomas, Agnes Ione Olds, Mary Ann Lee, James Leo, Minnie Rachael Remsh, Emmett J., and Elizabeth Johanna Kehmeier. Mrs. Isabell (Lewis) Tabor is buried at St. Peters Mission.

Molly was married to Steve Kologi in 1907. Steve worked at the St. Peters Mission ranch. Molly and Steve had five children: Elizabeth Chamberlain, Helen Williams, Stephen, Teresa Norris, and Rosemary Siemens. Stephen preceded his mother in death. Molly Lewis Kologi passed away in 1931. Rosemary Siemens, the youngest of the children, lives on the ranch Ed Lewis came to enjoy until his death.

Mr. and Mrs. Lewis spent the remainder of their lives on the ranch. Mrs. Lewis died January 11, 1906. Both are buried in the St. Peters Mission cemetery.

Edward A. Lewis was one of the first members of the Montana Pioneers Society and took a lot of pride in being a member of that organization.

George R. Lyons

Submitted by James F. Lyons, Great-Grandson

The Lyons Family story in Montana begins with the arrival of George R. Lyons in Massachusetts from his homeland of Ireland.

He was born June 16, 1842, in Connemara County Galway, Connaught Province, Ireland, son of George and Mary Lyons. He came to the United States as a child of twelve in 1854, when he took up farming. When the Civil War began he was caring for his mother and their farm so a substitute was hired to fight in his place. In 1863 he left the east, crossed the Isthmus of Panama, and came to California where he remained for three years.

In May of 1866, he headed north to Last Chance Gulch in Montana. During this period of his life he kept a journal detailing his mining activities in the Nelson Gulch and Diamond City areas. One entry shows "amount of work done by G. Lyons on shaft and rain," with a list of hours worked in the weeks ending October 23, 30, November 6, 13, 20, 27, December 4, and 8, 1869, with the amount totaling 37 hours. The next entry says, "Sold out to Pickering Dec. 10th."

A bill of sale on a back page of this journal may indicate when he went into the freighting business. It is dated October 16, 1870, at Salt Lake City, Utah Territory. He bought all he needed for this business, four mules, a Schutler wagon, two sets of harnesses, and a camping outfit, for the sum of $600. At one point in his freighting days he had to sell one of his two saddle horses. He put his arms around the horse's neck and cried and promised he'd never become so attached to an animal again. His freighting days lasted until 1874, when he obtained his own mine in the Diamond City area and stayed with it until Diamond City began to die in the late 1870's and he was tired of the mining camp life.

He returned to Massachusetts and married his former schoolmate, Mary Orr, on March 10, 1880. He and a friend, Perry Moore, moved their families into the Mussellshell Valley, where he spent his life ranching and raising his children, a son, George R., and a daughter, Helen.

His days on the Mussellshell produced interesting stories of Indians looking in windows, a neighbor's cabin that was broken into, and chasing the Indians who escaped through an unknown pass in the Snowy Mountains.

He was an avid horseman and, at one point, paid five dollars to learn "the horse subduing process as taught by a Professor Wright." It was basically a device to trip fractious horses. Friends wondered why he needed it since "he was never afraid of a horse in his life." Friends recalled it was dangerous to ride in a buggy with George. When he came to a ditch he eased the front wheels in, and then he would slap the reins and holler at the horses.

His love for spirited horses probably had a great deal to do with his death on July 9, 1914, at age 72. The Twodot paper said his death was caused from being thrown from his carriage by an unmanageable horse! George was buried in White Sulphur Springs, Montana, where his wife Mary was laid to rest after her death on July 22, 1939.

George Lyons was a member of the Masonic Lodge and one of the first directors of the Montana Stockgrowers Association.

Mr. Lyons' great-great-great-grandchildren call the Mussellshell Valley and Montana their home today.

Catherine "Kate" McDonald

Submitted by Jeanette Larson, Great-Granddaughter, and Donald MacDonald, Grandson

Catherine "Kate" Emerson McDonald was the second daughter born to Francis "Frank" and Bridget Halprin Emerson on May 8, 1858, in Omaha, Nebraska. The surname is actually Ammerson, but was spelled incorrectly in New York when Frank arrived in the United States. Frank and Bridget both immigrated to this country from County Cork, Ireland, around 1850. They were married in Iowa and lived in Council Bluffs and then moved to Omaha, where their three girls, Mary, Catherine, and Elizabeth were born.

The Emerson family left Omaha in 1864 by ox train for Oregon, and on their journey west heard about the discovery of gold in Montana. They traveled down the Oregon Trail to the junction of the Soda Springs route and headed to the goldfields of Alder Gulch. A son, Charley, was probably born along the trail.

Early one morning, the three little girls left the train and went down to the creek to play and the wagon train left without them. It was not until noon that the little girls were discovered missing, and a party of men went back to look for them. It was feared that the Indians might find them first, but they were found playing happily at the creek unaware that they had been left behind. Needless to say, the people on the train were very unhappy with them because they had lost an entire day of travel.

Kate's father died about two months after their arrival in Virginia City on September 1, 1864, from lung fever, and is buried in Virginia City. Her mother was left with four small children to support and worked as a seamstress for the miners, usually stitching leather patches on their pants and selling fresh bread.

Catherine "Kate" (Emerson) McDonald

Bridget later married Stephen Cahill and they all moved to a ranch on the Ruby River where seven more children were born: Ester, Stephen, Nicholas, Ambros, Albert, Henry, and Fannie.

In 1880 Kate married John Hugh MacDonald, a Scotsman from Alexandria, Ontario, Canada. Because of her Irish heritage, they spelled their name McDonald. After their marriage they moved to a ranch near Sheridan and later bought a ranch near Alder.

Nine children were born to John and Kate – two girls and seven boys. A baby girl died at birth. One daughter, Flora, married Julius Firpo and had one son Donald. Charley married Alvida Lindgren and had two sons, Robert and Donald. John married Irene Kelly and they had no children. Stephen married Anna Rew, the granddaughter of George H. Gohn, and they had a son Donald Rew and a daughter Frances Marie. Robert, Hugh, Oscar and Albert never married.

Kate was an original member of the Society of Montana Pioneers and is listed in the *1899 Montana Pioneer Index*. She loved the Pioneers' Society and attended their annual meetings until her health prevented her from journeying to their conventions. She declined to hold an office in the Society, because of her limited education and the feeling that she wasn't qualified for the job.

Kate lived all of her life in the Ruby Valley and died in 1945. Her husband John died of pneumonia in 1922, and they are both buried along with their sons Robert and Oscar in the Laurin Cemetery.

The dust that Kate shook from her shoes as a child pioneer walking down the Oregon Trail billowed up into endless opportunities for all of her descendants. She was a true pioneer all of her life.

Patrick and Winifred McKnight

Submitted by Lillian Patricia Reller, Great-Granddaughter

Patrick McKnight and wife Winifred (Green) came from Iowa City, Iowa, to Denver, Colorado, traveling across the plains by ox team in 1864, and settling in Virginia City, Montana Territory. They were among the immigrants who were spared trouble from Indians. In Virginia City, Patrick carried on his trade of blacksmithing until they moved to Helena in 1866, where he was a blacksmith until 1870. After that until 1879, he had a blacksmith shop in Diamond City. They purchased a ranch in the Missouri Valley in 1875, built a beautiful home, developed the property, and resided there until his death in 1895.

Patrick and Winifred had two sons, George and William, and four daughters: Isabella (Mrs. Wm. Manley), Katherine (Mrs. Fred Callaway), Mary (Mrs. Anthony Dunleavy), and Frances (Mrs. Thomas McCormick). George McKnight received his education in Diamond City and Townsend Schools. He never married and lived his life on the homestead, taking a very active part in all community and religious affairs. George was the first to welcome the Bishop to the valley – Bishop O'Connor, who had come from Omaha to confirm a class at Canton. William was always interested in blacksmithing, operating shops in White Sulphur Springs and later in Townsend. He served as Undersheriff in Meagher County and later in

Townsend as Deputy Sheriff. William was married to Maude Dean, a pioneer family member from the Deep Creek Valley. Isabella and William Manley had two sons, William and Harold, and a daughter who died at an early age. Katherine and Fred Callaway had one son, Adrian, who was killed by lightning while a young man on the McKnight ranch. The history of Mary and Anthony Dunleavy is unknown to us. Our grandmother, Frances McKnight, married our grandfather Thomas McCormick, November 27, 1895, at Canton Missouri Valley.

The McCormick Family originally traveled from Missouri and settled first in Centerville in 1879 – and as soon as Townsend became a reality, moved there.

Thomas was taken in as a partner with his cousin Ficklin McCormick in the livery and stable business. They had a large enterprise in feed supplies for livestock, had facilities for heavy freighting, and offered transportation in the horse and buggy days.

After the turn of the century another service was offered – the Wagonette. This was a wagon seating 10 to 12 people, enclosed with windows on all sides, opened in the rear with a door, and steps for the passengers. For 25 cents it served as a taxi-on-call and to meet trains. They owned one of the first hearses with horses well matched to be on-call for the proper dignity on the occasion of a funeral.

They also owned a bar that was turned over to J.M. Schmidt in the early 1900's.

Thomas and Frances (McKnight) McCormick had two daughters, Lillian (Mrs. William Kieckbusch) now deceased; Mae (Mrs. Ernest Palmquist of Helena); and one son, Paul, who worked for the N.P. Railroad and lived in Livingston, now deceased.

Our mother and father, Lillian (McCormick) and William (Bill) Kieckbusch, had one son, Tom (now deceased); and two daughters, Mary Frances (Mrs. Pat Hooks of Townsend), and Lillian Patricia "Patsy" (Mrs. Dale Reller of Thompson Falls).

They lived and worked the Kieckbusch ranch in the Deep Creek Valley until after the death of Bill in 1948. The family then moved to live with Frances McCormick – mother and grandmother to Lillian, Tom, Mary, and Patsy.

Angus McMillan

Submitted by Judith M. McNulty, Granddaughter

Angus McMillan was born in 1843, in Glengarry County, Ontario, Canada. His grandparents had come to Canada from Scotland in the late 1700s and early 1800s. Angus worked in the woods of Minnesota. In 1866 he came to Helena, Montana, with the fourth Fisk Expedition. He went to Virginia City but did not like working in the mines. He settled on the Prickly Pear, where East Helena is now located, and raised garden produce for the miners. In 1872 he quit gardening as many Chinese were raising produce.

Angus McMillan

He then began freighting and it is believed he headquartered on the Blackfoot River. In 1880 Angus McMillan and a partner located a place in Central Montana. They had two men put up hay and went to bring in a band of sheep. One of the men putting up hay broke a leg, and the other man took him to receive medical care. Very little hay was put up. During the hard winter of 1880-81 they lost most of the sheep.

Angus built his cabin and other buildings on Beaver Creek about eight miles southwest of the present town of Lewistown. In 1884 he returned to Canada and married Annie McMillan, born in 1856. This was a marriage within the clan. Their children were John McMillan (1885-

1970), Florence McMillan Otten (1887-1934), Mary McMillan Hollenback (1890-1976), Anna McMillan (1892-1964), Ina McMillan Yaeger (1895-1995), Judith McMillan (1900-1907), and Donald McMillan (1902 -).

After a number of years living in the log cabin, Angus bought one of the officers' quarters from Fort McGinnis, dismantled it, then rebuilt a nice frame home on his place. In 1890, he bought 100 head of shorthorn cattle. His grandsons, Angus and Tom McMillan, are still raising shorthorn cattle at Glengarry, Montana.

When the railroad was being built into Lewistown, the survey crew took room and board, and had their office in the McMillan house. The station built near the McMillan home was named Glengarry as Angus had come from Glengarry County, Ontario, Canada. Mr. McMillan donated land for a church and new school in Glengarry.

Previously, Angus had been active in helping to get grade schools for the children. During the first few years, the McMillan children went a distance of three or four miles to either the Beaver Creek School or the school in the town of Cottonwood. Later a school known as the McMillan School was built on the hill above the McMillan home. Teachers received board and room by staying with the families of pupils. My mother said the

McMillan Family. Left to Right: Back Row: John Tresch (neighbor), Annie, Donald, Angus, Gaylord Eccles (railroad), John. Front Row: Laura Dawes (teacher), Anna, Judith, Mary, Ina, Elberg Ray (railroad) and Florence – 1903.

children put on programs and charged to help earn money to pay the teachers. She also told of a term when one teacher had 40 pupils.

Mrs. McMillan and a neighbor, Fred Jenni, Sr., were instrumental in getting the Presbyterian Church built in Glengarry. This church was also used as a community hall for everyone in the area.

Angus and Annie McMillan also did much to promote the building of the Saint Joseph Hospital in Lewistown. The nuns stayed at the McMillan home while soliciting funds in the Glengarry area, and Annie accompanied them on several trips to more remote areas of the Judith Basin helping them find prospective donors and hospitality on the overnight journeys. I believe Angus furnished a team and double buggy that a bachelor neighbor, Felix McGinn, drove on those trips.

Angus McMillan died in 1906 and is buried in the Lewistown City Cemetery. The following year, the youngest daughter Judith died. Annie McMillan continued to live on the ranch until her death in 1946. She is also buried in the Lewistown City Cemetery. Their oldest, John, and daughter, Anna, never married and lived their entire lives at the McMillan home on Beaver Creek. John operated the place for over 60 years, and then turned it over to his nephew, Angus McMillan.

At the time of this writing, Donald McMillan, age 96, is the only surviving child of Angus and Annie McMillan. He lives near Glengarry and still tends a small flock of sheep and raises a large garden.

There are many descendants of Angus and Annie McMillan living

McMillan Ranch Home.

in Montana and many more are widely scattered. The following are members of the Sons and Daughters of the Montana Pioneers: Donald McMillan (son), Judith Hollenback McNulty (granddaughter), BettyDon McMillan Ross (granddaughter), Janet Yaeger Walling Lewellen (granddaughter), and Mary Ellen McNulty Schnur (great-granddaughter).

Theodore Barstow Merritt

Submitted by Juanita Pearl, Great-Granddaughter

Theodore B. Merritt was born March 1, 1830, in Honsdale, Pennsylvania, the youngest of six children born to Gilbert Helvington and Sarah Rose Merritt. When he was six years old the family moved to Marion, Ohio, where he spent time in school. At the age of fourteen the family moved to Dubuque, Iowa. It was here that he met his future wife, Ellen White, whose family was originally from Alden, New York. They were married on October 8, 1851, in Dubuque, Iowa. Their first three children were born in Iowa. Theodore's trade was in cabinetmaking.

On May 1, 1864, they loaded everything they had into an ox-drawn cart and left Dubuque for the Montana Territory accompanied by Theodore's brother. Theodore and Ellen's children, Fannie Maria, Laura Katherene, and George Barstow, were aged eleven, nine and six when they made their trek across the plains and mountains. Everyone had to walk as the oxen couldn't pull all the belongings and the people too. They were headed for Virginia City to make a new and better life for themselves and families.

As they crossed the plains they saw many Indians but were never bothered. However, they did come across wagon trains that weren't as lucky. At one massacre they found a man who was still alive. Gus had been scalped and buried to his armpits. He told them the wagon train was composed of German immigrants. Theodore doctored him and they brought as many of his belongings as they could include. In his things were two cut glass horns of plenty. Many years later he gave one of them to Theodore's youngest daughter, Mary Ellen "Mamie", on her thirteenth birthday and the other to her best friend whose birthday was on the same day. Gus lived the remainder of his life with the Theodore and Ellen and worked for them.

When Theodore and Ellen reached the crossroad that headed for Oregon, Theodore and his brother parted company – Theodore for Montana and his brother for Oregon. They never saw each other or heard from each other again. Contact was hard to keep up and as was found out many years later they each thought Indians had killed the other. When Theodore's daughter, Mary Ellen "Mamie" Merritt Ross, was in her sixties and in Portland, Oregon, visiting with her daughter, Harriett Ross Torkins, she was looking in the phone book for a company that repaired corsets. She found Merritt Corset Company and when she arrived at the place of business found out they were cousins. The Montana Merritt family was believed massacred. In those times no one checked out information that was believed to be bad.

Theodore and his family moved on toward Montana, traveling over Bridger Pass/Bozeman cutoff. They stayed in Bozeman before continuing on – arriving in Virginia City on September 1, 1864.

Theodore again engaged in cabinetmaking and Ellen was a dressmaker and homemaker. In the spring of 1870 Ellen loaded Ida Mae, age 3, her fourth and youngest child at the time, and headed for Dubuque, Iowa, alone and pregnant. She studied medicine with a local doctor, remaining there until the following spring, having had a baby girl, Nora Bell, born on November 8, 1870. As she traveled back across the plains – again by oxtrain – she helped to save several people while taking care of her own two children. This very brave lady was tiny – only about 4' 11" and most likely not over 100 pounds. But she was mighty and someone to look up to.

Ellen (White) Merritt at the original Merritt home in Prickly Pear Valley, Montana – 1866.

Ellen was a top dressmaker. She could make any type of clothing for men or women. She also made beautiful quilts and other handcrafts. Her daughter, Laura Katherene, was given earrings made from the first nuggets that came out of the Last Chance Mine. These earrings have been passed down and are treasured by the family.

Ellen was a wonderful horsewoman. She would swing up on the horse as it went at full gallop. One time she and some other women were in a cabin (in Prickly Pear Valley) making soap in large iron vats. Some young Indians came to hassle the women. The Indians were painted and hooping it up. Ellen and the other women pulled the vats up to the loft and waited to see what the Indians would do. When the Indians came in the cabin and started breaking things up and making a mess, the women dumped the hot soap on top of them and they went running for the woods. From that day on not one Indian would come close to the cabin and it was a safe haven for settlers even when the Indians were bothering others.

Ellen also doctored a lot of Indians, as not many other healers would go into the Indian camps. They thought she had powerful medicine after the hot soap incident. She learned how to gather herbs and roots from the Indians.

One day Ellen headed into Helena with her daughter, Mary Ellen "Mamie," in the buggy. As they got just outside of Helena the horse spooked, got the bit and ran away right into Helena before she could control the horse. When she did, she stood up in the buggy, turned it around, and

The Merritt Ranch in Prickly Pear Valley, Helena, Montana. Part of this landscape was later flooded by Hauser Dam.

made a very tired horse run back through Helena all the way to the spot it had spooked. There she turned him around again and they went back to Helena and did their shopping. The horse never ran away again.

Texas cattlemen brought herds of cattle to Montana in early spring and summer – sometimes getting caught in snowstorms. Mary Ellen "Mamie" would tell of cattle and calves dying all along the trails as they froze. She said everyone would go out and try to help as the cattle passed. Her father saved several head of calves that the Texas cattlemen had left behind. Theodore never understood why anyone would bring cattle so far from home without knowing more about Montana weather. Ellen would wrap abandoned calves in blankets and keep them in the kitchen trying to keep them alive. Theodore would sell the surviving calves and give the money to his daughter, Mary Ellen "Mamie." Once she bought a dress and had her photo taken in it. The photographer put the photo in his front window where her father saw it along with several other men. Was she ever in trouble! He took the photo and burned it and Mary Ellen "Mamie" could not go anywhere but school for some time. She did save a copy of the photo.

Ellen was called at all hours of the day or night to deliver babies, tend the sick, or stay with the dying. She was also a wonderful poet, having written many short stories and poems. Mary Ellen "Mamie" was only 19 years old when both her parents died. (Her parents were both in their fifties when she was born.) She married and left at age seventeen so really didn't have much time with them, but she had a wonderful childhood and so much love and caring. One winter when the snow was up to the second floor windows, her father dug tunnels from the house to all the outbuildings. He also made a play area for her and her girlfriend.

Theodore homesteaded in Prickly Pear Valley close to Helena. In 1866 he moved the family to the homestead that had 320 acres with 160 acres of fine meadowland. He engaged in farming and raising fine horses. As his son, George Barstow Merritt, grew to manhood, he joined his father in the farming business.

Raising horses was how Mary Ellen met her future husband, Huitt E. Ross. He delivered some horses to her father from Washington State. When she was seventeen they were married at the farm on January 25, 1898. Her dress was made of wool spun so fine it felt like silk. It had long sleeves and a high neck. It was cream colored, had no train, and could be worn after the wedding for formal outings. Huitt and Mary Ellen loaded all of her things into a wagon and headed for St. John, Washington, which was

Huitt's home.

Mary Ellen would tell her children about hayrides with families from the surrounding farms and going Christmas caroling from one farm to another, of potlucks at one farm and then another, of sewing bees and quilting bees. Of how your neighbors would look out for you and always be there to help when asked and even when not asked they would come anyway. Of how their home was always full of the Pioneers of 1864, of listening to their stories. She was very proud of her Montana heritage and made many trips back to Helena and Virginia City to visit her many family members.

Theodore Merritt had good health until the day he died August 6, 1899, at the age of 69. Experiencing stomach and chest pains, a doctor was called but, finding nothing wrong, left. At 6:00 p.m., as the Helena paper said, "this pioneer soul passed across the Great Divide."

There was a big turnout for the service as most everyone and all the pioneers knew him. At the time of his death, his wife, Ellen, was bedfast and dying of colon cancer. She lived until March 21, 1900. Their second daughter, Laura Katherene Merritt Cook, died September 7, 1899, after becoming sick with a bad cold at her father's funeral from which she never recovered. Theodore, Ellen, and their daughter, Laura Katherene, are all buried in the Forestvale Cemetery in Helena, Montana.

Ellen White Merritt composed the following verse as she lay on her deathbed with colon cancer:

<u>It's Never Quite the Same Again</u>

A humble cottage neath the hill,
Where children romp and laugh at will.
With parents tender love and care,
How could their life be else but fair?

O' let them be glad today
For swift the years will pass away.
And when they are women and men
It's never quite the same again.

Together all their tasks are done,
Their interests are all as one.
The self-same board they gather around,
And at one altar all are found.

The same dear song, the same dear prayer,
The same old Bible all may share.
But when they leave the home O' then,
Its never quite the same again.

The wedding bells may surely ring,
And glory be on everything.
But where one leaves the dear old nest,
It's lonelier for all the rest.

And if they one by one shall leave,
How can the parents help but grieve?
All come and go and love – but then,
It's never quite the same again.

In other houses as dear and sweet,
Will be the sound of childish feet.
In many homes instead of one,
There will be frolic, laughter, and fun.

The old love may be true and deep,
But sometimes it may sigh and weep.
For something gone, somewhere, somewhere
And it's not quite the same again.

Ah? Well perhaps its' better so,
That deeper meaning we may know.
There is no loss, no grief, no pain,
That may not be its own sweet gain.

And in the blessed land above,
There'll be again one house, one love.
Then one in heart and one in name,
At last, it will ever be the same.

Thomas Odber Miles

Submitted by Dorothy (Miles) Pitcock, Granddaughter

Thomas Odber Miles was born December 6, 1844, near the town of Maugerville, Sanburg County, New Brunswick, Canada, to Thomas O. and Nancy A (Perley) Miles. He was the fourth child of a family of twelve. In March of 1866, at the age of twenty-one, he thought he would branch out in the world and go west. His father did not approve of his leaving and offered him no financial assistance thinking it would force him to stay home. With ten dollars of borrowed money in his pocket, he started out. Before the money ran out, he met a friend who was going to Montana who offered him all the financial aid he needed. They journeyed westward by rail reaching St. Joseph, Missouri, on April 6, 1866. There they purchased a mule team, wagon, and provisions including bedding, firearms, and other essentials.

Thomas Odber Miles

On April 10 they crossed the Missouri River into Kansas and headed for Montana. They joined two more wagons owned by C.W. Blodgett bound for Montana. Along the way they joined other wagons going to Montana. Tom's diary tells of the struggles traveling the Bozeman Trail – lives and equipment lost and animals drowned when crossing rivers. They arrived at Fort Laramie on May 12 and found some 5,000 Indians gathered to make a treaty. Fearing a possible Indian uprising, they decided to get as far away as possible. They got into Arapaho Country close to Fort Reno on the Powder River. On May 22 they arrived at Fort Reno and there they found Winnebago and Pawnee Indian scouts with some American officers. The travelers were the only white people they had seen in eighteen months. There was a celebration that night and Tom's dog "Artemus" was used for the feast.

Leaving there, they reached the Big Horn River on May 31. They would cross many streams before reaching the Yellowstone River and arrived near present day Billings on June 15. On June 25 they camped near Old Fort Ellis, drove through Bozeman, and on June 29 arrived at Virginia City. Tom went up to Summit the next day and surprised his two brothers, George and T. Clowes Miles. He mined at Summit in Alder Gulch and stayed there until June of 1870 when he came to Silver Bow and placer mined at Silver Bow Canyon.

Agnes (Goddard) Miles

In 1872 he and his brother, T. Clowes Miles, took up land and the Warren Placer claim ten miles west of the Butte mining camp and began what was afterwards known as the "Miles Ranch." Tom raised hay, sheep, cattle, and Percheron horses. His ranch was one of the first and best in the Deer Lodge Valley because of the availability of water from Silver Bow Creek and the large quantities of hay raised in the meadows along the creek. It is recorded that in 1885 Tom received an excellent price for hay at $50 a ton. The place became known as "Miles Crossing" as the stagecoaches from Cottonwood (Deer Lodge) to Bannack crossed Silver Bow Creek there.

At one time, Tom decided to go to Virginia City and take a young lady to a dance. He rode his horse a full day to get there. The second day he acquired a buggy and escorted her to the dance. The third day he rode his horse home again and exclaimed, "That's enough of that!"

Tom left for New Brunswick in June of 1880 arriving on July 12 to find that his father had died on July 1. While there, he met Agnes Goddard and they were married on October 13, 1880. Tom was 36 and Agnes was 33. Her wedding band was made of the gold he had panned from Silver Bow Creek. Agnes was a very refined lady and accomplished on the piano. She found life in the West hard, but Tom afforded her the life she was used to. She was always terrified when Native Americans came to the ranch to ask for a "a litty bitty salt and a litty bitty sugar." They raised three children: Thomas Odber IV, an adopted daughter Hazel, and John Fredrick, my father. Agnes was very ill with diabetes in her adult years and died January 31, 1909, at age 62. Before her death, Tom promised to take her "home" to St. John, New Brunswick, to be buried. He could not accompany her body at the time of her death but returned at a later date and planted a rose at her grave.

Tom played the fiddle, was well known, and well liked. He was a non-drinker, known for his honesty and as an Episcopalian. A newspaper article is quoted as saying he was "a patriarch in appearance, his countenance portraying an ideal sturdy man of the West, yet with a heart as tender and sympathetic as that of a child and with a hand that is generous."

He was prominent in politics for many years, attending all the Republican county conventions as a delegate except one, and most state conventions until 1913. He was a member of the Society of Montana Pioneers. For twenty years, he had been a member of the school board of his district, and on the Republican legislative ticket twice. He retired in 1916, passing the ranch on to his son, Fred, but resided there until his death April 13, 1923. The property remained in the family until 1994 when the last 40 acres were sold.

Thomas Odber Miles is buried in the Mount Mariah Cemetery in Butte, Montana.

Nick L. Millen

Submitted by Nick Shrauger, Great-Grand-Nephew

A first time visitor heading up Helena's Last Chance Gulch about 1868 would have lots to observe in the narrow, busy street. It would have been packed with horses, wagon teams, and people. And there were signs for businesses, all competing for attention. A tin coffee pot was in front of John Kinna's hardware store, next to the Wells Fargo Company. Pioneer "Cheap John" had two signs for his mercantile store. Sam Hauser's bank sign was simple – BANK.

Then there were barber poles and clocks to see. The Montana Post even hung a banner across the street. But the sign that would catch the most attention was Nick Millen's boot store at 34 Main. This metal sign, a red cowboy boot about 16 feet tall and eight feet from heel to toe, was the signature of Nick Millen's boot shop. W.F. Wheeler writing about Montana

Nick and Louisa (Kessler) Millen – 1881.

in *The West Shore* stated in April 1883:

"Just when that sign first made its appearance it is difficult to say, but it is currently reported that Joe Meek, who went to Oregon 'when Mount Hood was a hole in the ground,' passed this sign on the way, and that it was full grown at that time. Some even maintain that at the time of the creation, when the command was given, 'Let there be light,' the first object dimly outlined against the surrounding gloom was Nick Millen's boot."

The boot became the center of a controversy when the City of Helena demanded that Nick remove the sign. Nick's sign, according to the newspaper, was "one of the old land marks and Mr. Millen intends to strenuously oppose its removal." Indeed there was a jury trial and Nick hired three lawyers "to fight it through."

George Millen. Arrived Virginia City, Montana Territory – August 18, 1864.

The size of the Big Boot suggests that Nick Millen was a successful businessman. Nick was born at Waldbillig in the Grand Dutchy of Luxembourg, Germany, in 1833. His parents were Michael and Anna Maria Millen. It is not known when he arrived in America, but he came to Virginia City, Idaho Territory, from Colorado, in July of 1863.

He set up a cobbler's shop in a tent and made good money. However, he had a passion for mining adventures and that quickly used up his profits. After two years, he moved his business to Helena where he opened a boot and shoe establishment. His store was located at #47 Bridge Street in 1866, but by early 1867 he moved it to a large space next to King and Gillettes' stone block on Main Street. The *Helena Herald* of February 28, 1867, listed Nick as proprietor of Gurney & Co., one of five boot makers in Helena, four of which were located on Main Street. Nick was an active businessman and was a founding member of the Helena Board of Trade and one of its directors.

Fire was a major problem for the Helena business district. There were nine fires between 1869 and 1874, three of which were especially large and destructive. The Big Boot survived all of them, including the major fire on April 28, 1869, which consumed Nick's store.

In 1870 the call of mining again claimed Nick Millen's attention. He leased his store to D. H. Weston for a two-year period and went to the Cedar Creek Mines in Missoula County. There he again opened a shoe store in an active mining camp. When his lease with Weston expired, he returned to Helena and remained there in business until his death in December 1883. Nick married Louisa Kessler on June 21, 1881. They had no children.

Who won the sign battle? Apparently there was a compromise. The sign could stay, but it had to be placed on the roof rather than hang over the street.

Three of Nick's siblings also came to America. His brother George, born on June 9, 1836, in Luxembourg, was also an Alder Gulch pioneer as he states in his application to the Montana Society of Pioneers:

"having departed from Troy, New York, route traveled from St. Joe, Missouri, on California road to Landers cut-off by Soda Spring to Snake River to Virginia City, Montana Territory, date and place of arrival 18 Aug 1864."

George first engaged in freighting and mining. By the mid 1880's he was ranching in Beaverhead County near Beaver Head Rock with his address at Blaine. George married Leah Lucinda Harbaugh on March 30, 1880. She died five years later. They had no children. George passed away while living at the Masonic Home in Helena on January 7, 1929.

Two more Millen children came to America. A brother settled in Troy, New York. Their sister Catherine married George L. Staudaher, another Alder Gulch Pioneer.

John Clarkson Moore

Submitted by Robert and Debby Hollenback

John Clarkson Moore was a native of Holly Grove, West Virginia. He was a Civil War Veteran and pioneer rancher. During the Civil War, Mr. Moore, a sergeant in the 7th Illinois infantry, was wounded while engaged in scouting in Missouri – after which he was discharged because of a disability. He remained in Missouri until the war ended.

Soon afterward he headed west via St. Joseph, Missouri, and Salt Lake City and arrived in Virginia City, Montana, in 1866 where he worked the placer diggings for several months. He moved to Last Chance Gulch in May 1866, worked a number of mining claims and then sold them for considerable money. He then moved to Carpenter's bar where he lived until 1877.

Mr. Moore married Flora Ann Manwarring of Terre Haute, Indiana in 1864. While she was young, the Manwarring family moved to Tuscola, Illinois. Flora was a pioneer nurse. At the age of 13 she learned the skills of nursing during the Civil War. She treated illnesses with herbs and roots and went long distances to doctor Indian women.

In 1877 John and Flora Ann settled in the Blackfoot Valley – one mile west of Helmville. The Honorable John Moore was elected to the Montana Territorial Legislature in 1875.

The Moores were the parents of the following children – James C., Clark, John L., Albert, George, Flora and Edith who married David Raymond in 1902. There are many descendants of David and Edith Raymond in the Helmville area.

Their oldest son, James C. Moore, was a blacksmith and rancher in the Avon vicinity. He was an active member of the Montana Pioneers. In 1893, he married Louise Isabel Weidenfeller, daughter of John Peter and Arthemise Isabelle (Doney) Weidenfeller. They had six children: John Clayborn, Walter, Edmun, Edith, Willis and May Loretta who married Arthur Anders. All the children of James and Louise Moore were members of the Sons and Daughters of Montana Pioneers.

James and Louise's son, John Clayborn, played a large role in Butte's World Museum of Mining that opened in 1965. He was President of the Blackfoot City Historical Society.

Flora Ann Moore passed away in 1899, after which time Mr. Moore lived with his daughter, Mrs. David Raymond, until his death in 1919.

Mr. Moore's funeral service was held at the Methodist Church in

Helmville, Montana, and he is buried next to his wife in the Helmville Cemetery.

Pat and Katherine "Kate" Moran

Submitted by Bill O'Keefe, Great-Grandson

On May 26, 1864, Montana became a Territory. On or about this date my great grandparents Patrick and Catherine "Kate" (Mulligan) Moran (Irish immigrants), with their five children, began a three-month journey to Montana from Omaha, Nebraska. By following the Oregon/Mormon Trail to South Pass and taking the Lander Cutoff Trail, they arrived in Virginia City, Montana Territory, on September 12, 1864. My grandfather, William "Will" H. Moran, at age 18 months, was the youngest of five Moran children making the trip. His older siblings were Edward, Loretta, Annie, and John.

Helena, Montana Territory. Main Street looking north from the Wood Street area. Freight wagons. Driver of the mule team (wheel horse rider) is identified as Will Moran – circa 1870's. Courtesy of the Montana Historical Society, Helena, Montana.

Pat, although bitten by the "gold bug," needed a place to settle and raise his family. This long search is traced by the births of Thomas in Virginia City on August 12, 1865, Arthur "Niche" at Moran Creek in Madison Valley on February 19, 1868, and Agnes in Helena on April 1, 1870, and by the following land deeds. Pat bought his first mining claim in Lewis & Clark County on May 12, 1868, and his last when he purchased the "Lulu Lode" on September 30, 1886. Pat and Kate purchased the 480-acre "Spokane Ranch" in Jefferson County (now Broadwater County) for $1,000 on July 31, 1872.

Pat and Kate ran a stage station, halfway house, at this location that was called the "Spokane House." Pat raised and butchered cattle for meat markets in Beaver Town (later Placer, then Winston) and Helena. Pat became adept in making bricks from a clay soil deposit (called Claysoil today) on his property. Moran bricks constructed many homes in Helena and the local area. His sons quickly learned to drive freight wagons and haul bricks to these sites.

Meanwhile, Kate operated their nine-room log constructed "Spokane House" for stage passengers on the Helena/Bozeman Road. This stage station also served passengers going to Confederate Gulch, Diamond City, and Fort Logan. Completion of the Northern Pacific Railroad in 1883 signaled the end of stage stations. The following signaled the end of Pat!

"Patrick Moran Dies from Suffocation in a Mine," From the *Helena Weekly Herald*, 9/20/1888:

"The funeral of the late Patrick Moran of Beaver Creek, was held today from the Catholic Church in Helena. His death occurred in a singular manner. He had a mine near his home at the Spokane House and has been engaged in developing it for over a year. The shaft was down about 150 feet but further work was prevented by foul air. Last Friday he came into Helena and purchased some piping to ventilate his mine. This he got in place yesterday and ordered his men down the shaft to prosecute work. The men having had a previous experience with the suffocating gas in the mine refused to go. Where upon Mr. Moran, thinking his ventilating apparatus had done away with the danger, descended the shaft himself. In a few moments he was hoisted out utterly overcome by the noxious gas and soon after reaching the surface expired.

He was an old timer in the territory and is well known as the proprietor of the Spokane House on the Bozeman road. His death will be mourned by a large number of friends. He was a man of about 65 years of age and leaves an estimable wife who will inherit a considerable estate."

Kate passed away in 1896 and is buried along side of Pat and their oldest son, John, in the Resurrection Cemetery in Helena, Montana.

The Moran boys had a local freight business, and Will hauled freight between Fort Benton, Helena, and Virginia City. Railroads soon took most of this business. After their father's death in 1888, Will, Tom, and Niche continued raising and butchering cattle for their Helena Meat Market and other meat markets in the Helena/Winston area. The "Spokane House" and land was sold in 1904 to the Myles family, who still owns it. The 32-horse barn still stands today.

Will was the youngest member of the Society of Montana Pioneers when he signed up during the first organizational meeting in 1884.

In 1898, Will married Nellie Hickey, the oldest daughter of Wm. C. Hickey of Marysville. This marriage was blessed with Helen, Winnifred, Gladys, Larene, Frances, Agnes, Mary and William Jr. Winnifred, William and Larene died in 1913 and Mary died in 1916 – all are buried in Butte.

Will Moran passed away on May 16, 1946, and is buried in the Hillcrest Cemetery in Deer Lodge. Nellie joined Will on December 28, 1959. Two of their daughters, Helen and Gladys, are buried there as well.

Of the two remaining children, only Frances, my mother, and Gladys lived to have any children of their own. Gladys married Carl Carlson in the early 1930s and had Jean Ann and Carl Jr. Frances married Remy O'Keefe of Finn, Montana, in 1925 and they had Emmett, Gloria, Edward, William, Robert (Pat), Dan and Don. After my father, Remy, died in 1938, we moved from Maxville to Deer Lodge, where we all attended school. In 1947 Frances married Peter Beck – they had Barbara in 1948. Pete Beck died in 1956 and Frances in 1963. Frances is buried in the O'Keefe plot at Helmville, alongside of Remy, his brothers Emmett and Arthur, their parents Edward and Margaret (McConville) O'Keefe and my sister Gloria Corcoran

Several of the remaining grandchildren, great and great-great grandchildren still live in Montana.

Daniel Bohan Noble

Submitted by James R. Freeman

Daniel Bohan Noble was born in West Bloomfield Ontario County, New York, March 13, 1822. Daniel was the son of Bohan Noble, a farmer, and Cynthia Goodsell Alger, daughter of Daniel and Abiah (Dean) Goodsell. He was educated in the East Bloomfield Academy, and at the age of 18, went to Delaware County, Iowa, where he farmed and worked in lumbering. In 1860, he went to Pike's Peak, Colorado, and remained for three years engaged in mining and milling.

Daniel Bohan Noble

Fortune not favoring him fast enough, he then went to Virginia City, Montana, in 1864. At first he worked with two other men in supplying meat for the miners in Alder Gulch. He hunted the game in the section around Waterloo. Romulua Brown hauled the meat to Virginia City, and Jim Engals ran the butcher shop. Mr. Noble located a farm and sawmill on Indian Creek, and returned to Iowa via the Yellowstone River in a scow boat. In 1865 Indians killed his brother Albert on the Yellowstone River.

In 1868 he returned and established a mine and mill at Nobleville on the south fork of Wisconsin Creek. The mine was very successful and produced a great quantity of ore. At one time the mine was sold to an eastern corporation for a large sum of money. This corporation, inexperienced in mining operations, sank a deep shaft and ran out of ore.

They then decided to cancel the deal, claiming the previous owner knew the gold ore was running out when he sold it to them. Mr. Noble, being an honorable man, told them to take back their money, which was still in escrow. He took back the mine and continued this occupation until his death on September 19, 1899, at Sheridan, Montana.

On April 27, 1846, at Farmersville, New York, Mr. Noble married Minerva Peet. She was the daughter of Levi and Eunice (Carpenter) Peet. She was born October 31, 1821, in Farmersville, Cattaragus County, New York, and died November 13, 1895, at Sheridan Montana.

Minerva (Peet) Noble

Their children were all born in Iowa. Eunice Ann was born March 8, 1847. She was married on December 31, 1874, to James Selway, a stockraiser in Beaverhead County. Cynthia Eliza was born March 6, 1848. Cynthia was married on December 3, 1866, to James Madison Robinson, Edgewood Iowa. Minerva Jane was born March 4, 1849. She was married in September 1868, to Sherwood Blakeman Robinson, Edgewood, Iowa. Robert Worthington was born on November 11, 1851. On July 1, 1880, Robert married Mary (Minnie) Brooks. Mary Delocia was born on April 10, 1852. She married on August 31, 1874, at Omaha, Nebraska, to Theophilus Berginer Craver of Iowa. Theophilus Berginer later became a sheep rancher in Beaverhead County, Montana. Daniel Herbert was born August 25, 1855. He married on October 27, 1877, to Millicent Ferris. Flora Angelina was born December 31, 1860. She died February 18, 1867, at the age of six.

Mr. Noble had an interesting lineage. He was a direct descendant of Thomas Noble, who immigrated to America from England about 1650 and was a settler of Springfield and Westfield, Massachusetts. Two other ancestors, Silas Noble and his son Medad, served in the American Revolutionary War. Through his grandmother, Lydia (Frary) Noble, wife of Medad, Daniel Noble was descended from Charles Chauncy, the second president of Harvard University and from the Reverend Peter Bulkely, a founder of Concord, Massachusetts. Through these two illustrious persons and their wives, Mr. Noble's ancestry can be traced to King Edward I of England, William the Conqueror, Alfred the Great and Charlemagne.

Mary Delocia (Noble) Craver, my grandmother, would load her children in the buggy and go to Sheridan to help her mother Minerva who was very frail. You can imagine how long a trip that would be from Medicine Lodge to Sheridan in a buggy. Theophilus and Mary (Noble) Craver had eight children, but only three lived to adulthood. They were Flora Elizabeth, born July 12, 1875; Oleta Eda born April 15, 1888; and, Thomas Arthur born April 12, 1897.

Oleta Eda married James R. Freeman on July 24, 1915, at the home of her mother at Medicine Lodge. Five children were born of this union: James Richard Ross Freeman, 1916; Claude Craver, 1917; Thomas Lynn, 1919; Mary Eda, 1920; and Margueritte Ellen, 1922.

Noble home on Indian Creek in Sheridan, Montana.

Thomas John Robert Patterson

Submitted by Frances F. McDonald

Thomas John Robert Patterson was born in Scotland, circa 1835, where he spent his boyhood. As a young man he migrated to America to seek his fortune. He came to present day Montana with the earliest placer mining men. Patterson traveled by saddle horse with a pack mule into the yet unnamed Lincoln area via the Dalton Mountain Trail in 1862. A group of miners of the Gulch called a public meeting on August 31, 1865, and chose the name Abe Lincoln Gulch. A set of laws covering the claims, their operation, and methods of government were drawn up and unanimously passed. This hand-written recorded journal from 1865 to 1870 was signed by Mr. Patterson, D. W. Culp, John Lewis, John Lowdell, and James Giles and is presently preserved at the State Historical Library in Helena, Montana.

In the following years, Patterson and Culp worked in partnership in placer mining. After some difficulty and two unsuccessful attempts, they finally reached bedrock with their third shaft and had a promising lead. A substantial fortune was taken from the workings and Mr. Patterson returned to Scotland a wealthy man in 1872.

In his native land he was married to Miss Anna May Walker on

Early Miners in Abe Lincoln Gulch. Thomas Patterson is sixth from the left.

March 26, 1873. She was a native of Paisley, Scotland, born on March 16, 1847, the daughter of Thomas Walker and Ann Grant. Thomas Sloan, a fellow Scotsman, had accompanied Thomas Patterson back to Scotland. Sloan was married to Mary McCallum around the same time as the Pattersons. Both couples returned to America by sailing around the Cape of South America landing in San Francisco, California, where Anna May's sister and family lived. From there, the two couples went directly to Lincoln Gulch, near present day Lincoln, Montana, taking out a homestead at Stonewall Gulch. Thomas later became a member of the Society of Montana Pioneers. Homesteading in the Wild West with Indians still 'loose' must have been a harrowing experience for the young brides. Fort Lincoln was built and maintained for the protection of the women and children.

Anna May (Walker) Patterson

Although actual Indian raids were infrequent, many bands passed through as the old Indian migration trails crossed the area. Blackfeet and Piegan bands were the most common. Indian bands had a reputation similar to gypsy bands in the Old World – things seemed to pass along with them. Early settlers feared thievery, even of children. Whenever Indians were sighted, an alarm was issued and families rushed to the fort where they remained until the band had passed through. If there was insufficient warning the families hid where every they could. On one such occasion, two Patterson boys were hiding under a washtub on the homestead. A scuffle between the boys resulted in an Indian lifting up the tub to see what the commotion was. Fortunately, no harm came to the scared boys.

Thomas and Anna May Patterson's six children were all born at Lincoln Gulch, Montana Territory. John February 1, 1874; and in the following four years Thomas July 6, 1875; Mary August 22, 1876; David July 30, 1877; and Martha September 7, 1878. Grace was born June 10, 1881, just 2 months before Martha died of a fever. Martha is buried in the old Lincoln Cemetery. Thomas died March 1, 1899, at his Stonewall Homestead near Lincoln, Montana, and is buried in the Forestvale Cemetery in Helena, Montana. Anna died February 12, 1935, and is also buried in Forestvale Cemetery beside her husband.

Patterson homestead on Stonewall Gulch – 1900.

Life of the early pioneers was filled with hardships and very few luxuries. But as travel became easier, more goods were available within a decent price range.

The Pattersons enlarged their small log cabin into a spacious two-story house on Stonewall. The young children each lived the typical life of the times – plenty of hard work, a limited formal education, well seasoned with merriment at community socials that were enjoyed by the entire community.

Near Stonewall homestead. Left to Right: Hugh McDonald, mother Mary (Patterson) McDonald and Grace Patterson – 1910.

Mary (Patterson) McDonald, Hugh McDonald and D. H. McDonald at Lincoln, Montana – 1910.

John Peter Pfeifer

Submitted by Shirley A. Groff, Great-Granddaughter

Political upheavals of various magnitudes in the mid-eighteen hundreds caused massive migrations from Germany to lands of more opportunity. They immigrated to all parts of the world, seeking chances to start over and make fortunes in Australia, North America, and South America – the so-called lands of opportunity. The favored place was the United States. Although it was suffering from the pains of Civil War, there were lands to be developed, cities to be built, people to feed, gold and other minerals to be found and mined. These people had the talents and skills to do all of these things.

This is where John P. Pfeifer and his wife Barbara (Beck) entered – fresh from Germany and living in a German settlement in Keokuk, Iowa. John was born in Wurttemburg, Germany, in 1825 and Barbara was born in Germany in 1835. Word of gold in the western states spread like wildfire. John and Barbara had two daughters, Ida Barbara born in Iowa in 1861 (Mrs. George C. Fitschen, Mrs. Palmer Jacobs) and Mary A. "Molly" born in Keokuk, Iowa, on February 13, 1863, (Mrs. Howard Smith, Mrs. Hayes Cannon). With their two small daughters, this couple started west to find their fortune. Their first stop was Austin, Nevada, where they were blessed with a third daughter Louisa (Louise) Pfeifer (Mrs. Gus Fitschen), born May 22, 1865, and supporting themselves by working at trading livestock, brewing beer, and running boarding houses.

In the spring of 1866, along with others anxious to reap the riches of the Montana goldfields, they started their migration north. Traveling in oxen-drawn wagons with chickens, cattle and horses, they ventured forth on the long arduous trek from Austin, Nevada, to Highland City, Montana, via Bannack. The trip could take up to six months. The whole train was held up for an entire day when Louisa got lost in the sagebrush in Nevada, so the story goes. Chickens were trouble too as they got loose and had to be chased and caught.

Barbara was plagued with morning sickness as she was expecting her fourth child. She must have been of very hardy stock, as she never complained of the hardships of that trip. Just lifting the crocks and cook pots, not to mention doing the laundry with homemade soap on a wash board, tending small children and cooking in such primitive circumstances would have killed many of us.

Traveling from Austin to Corrine, Utah, via the Virginia City,

Montana, road they crossed into Montana over Bannack Pass (probably using DeLacy's Map of 1864) to Horse Prairie and on to Bannack where just two years before the Vigilantes had cleaned up the notorious road agents headed by Sheriff Henry Plummer. Records show that they then went to Nissler Junction to Helena and back to Highland City, Montana Territory.

The winter of 1866-67 was spent in Highland City, a then thriving gold strike. There are no details, but there is a grave of a Pfeifer child in the old Highland City Cemetery. The family was very private and they did not talk about losses and sadness. On September 21, 1867, a fourth daughter, Pauline Pfeifer, was born in Highland City (my grandmother).

John Peter and Barbara (Beck) Pfeifer.

The family engaged in various mining and agricultural enterprises eventually moving to the South Boulder, Jefferson County, area. John P., seeing that the climate was similar to his home in the state of Wurttemberg, Germany, sent to the old country for apple trees and other seeds. He planted the first apple trees in the area.

It was there that the Nez Percé Indian chief tried to buy daughter Ida (she had snapping black eyes, a right beautiful teenager) but her father would not sell. The Indians tried to rope her off the horse as she rode out to bring in the milk cows. She said she felt the ropes hit on the back of the saddle. The neighbors organized a posse and the Indians moved out in the night.

Later the family ran a boarding house, stage stop, and an Inn at Nissler Junction. The younger girls were sent to St. Mary's Academy in Deer

Lodge to be educated. There they learned the fine art of making hairpin lace, tatting, crocheting, painting, and all of the graces that would help them become proper young ladies. Pauline made layers of lace for her wedding petticoat. The petticoat was around for years. There still exists a piece of the lace sewn into a tablecloth owned by my sister Louise. They were at Nissler Junction during the time of the August 1877 Battle of Big Hole. Fearing Indian attack, they took their horses to Browns Gulch to hide them.

Hartwig home near Glen, Montana – 1917.

It is interesting to note that the family owned and operated the Nevada Saloon on Nevada Street, Butte, Montana. The family prospered in this area until the Utah and Northern Railroad reached Silver Bow in 1880. The three younger girls stayed in this area, married, and lived their lives there. Two (Louise Fitschen and Mollie Cannon) are buried in Butte, Montana. Pauline Hartwig is buried in Dillon, Montana. John P. and Barbara, along with daughter Ida B., later made their permanent homes in Boise, Idaho where all three are buried in the Morris Hill Cemetery and Pioneer Cemetery.

It was in Boise, Idaho, that my grandparents, Pauline Pfeifer and Julius Hartwig, were married at the family home on Warm Springs Avenue on September 28, 1892. Pauline and Julius made their home in the Glen area in the early town of Willis, Beaverhead County, Montana, where their four children were born: Ida Barbara Hartwig (Mrs. John W. Hand, my mother), Louise Mae Hartwig (Mrs. Frank Kambich, Mrs. Russell Hirst), Peter John Hartwig (died at 10 years of age), and Julius Frederick Hartwig.

The home at Glen was always a warm, welcoming place. In summer, there were all of the activities of a working farm and ranch. Julius always started his bedding plants in a hot bed near his blacksmith shop early in the spring. To heat it he used green horse manure covered with a layer of sand and then a layer of his good soil. All of this he covered with glass. His garden was about two acres in size and he raised enough food for everyone. Pauline kept turkeys, chickens, ducks, and geese. At times, she had peacocks and guinea fowl. Several hives of bees kept the family in honey. The aunts, uncles, cousins and other relatives came from Butte on the train to help with the harvest, get ready for the holidays, and help with other work that had to be done.

Pauline (Pfeifer) Hartwig, Ida Barbara (Pfeifer) Fitschen Jacobs.

The kitchen at the Hartwig home was very modern for those times. A very large wood range, a walk-in pantry with four large bins for flour, sugar, oatmeal, dried beans, etc., and pass-through cupboard from the kitchen to the dining room. Behind the range was a very large woodbox that was filled before supper every evening. The kitchen was always warm, fragrant, and inviting. The dining room was a place where all meals were eaten and politics, religion and other things were discussed. On cold evenings the family would sit around the table and read by kerosene lamps. Homework was done there too. Sometimes the math facts were practiced on butcher's paper. The good paper was for perfected lessons.

It was in this setting that my parents (John W. Hand and Ida B. Hartwig) were married at the family home on April 11, 1917. The stories go that it was a real celebration, true to character of my grandparents.

Grandma sent to Butte and bought yards of linen to make the tablecloths. Some of this linen is still in the family.

Many stories have been handed down by word of mouth for several generations – stories of burials for beloved pets, birds, and all other kinds of occasions that were important to the kids; or when Grandpa went to town on the train and never came home without molasses candy, known as monkey candy, and other things for the kids. There were seances where the answer came in the form of two knocks on stovepipe and card games that lasted into the wee hours of morning.

Louisa (Louise) (Pfeifer) Fitschen, Mary A. "Mollie" (Pfeifer) Smith Cannon.

Before the holidays they would peel tubs of apples to make mince meat (the recipe is still in the family). To keep it from spoiling they put it in big crocks, laced it with lots of good booze, and poured hot lard over it to seal it until it was time to use. They polished the silver, ironed the yards of linen tablecloths, told stories, played cards, and thoroughly enjoyed one another. The Christmas goose was decapitated on the evening of the twenty-third of December and placed in the woodbox to be plucked and drawn after supper by the women of the house. Everything was a celebration.

Christmas at Grandma and Grandpa's was a magical time. The kids were not ever allowed to see the Christmas tree until after the big Christmas Eve dinner. The big doors were opened and the candles would be lighted. With all of the glistening glass ornaments and the candles it was the most beautiful sight a child ever did see even if it only lasted for three minutes.

The packages brought by Santa Claus were beautifully wrapped in white tissue paper and tied with red and green string. They contained books and things that kids needed. There were some toys but mostly necessities.

The culture and customs that came from Germany have been passed down to the younger generations. Several generations later the family members are all still innkeepers so to speak. The whole family loves to have company come and everyone is invited to Christmas celebrations. No one is ever left out no matter what their means.

There are so many warm and fond memories of family, friends, and celebrations. Everything was always done in a big way. It was, and still is, a disgrace to run out of food at Christmas or any other festive time. A great-great-grandson is a Christmas ornament collector and has collected many of the same kinds of ornaments that were on the Christmas trees at "Aunt Polly" and "Uncle Julius" house, as all who knew them affectionately called my grandparents. Never was a person turned away without a meal. Grandpa always said that we never know when someone in the family might be hungry sometime and he hoped that someone would feed them.

John Pfeifer passed away in August 22, 1911, and Barbara (Beck) Pfeifer had passed away on March 30, 1900, in Boise. Both are buried in the Pioneer Cemetery in Boise, Idaho.

With hard work, tradition, family values, and just good old survival skills, these people were amazing. They accomplished so much without all of the conveniences we now enjoy. How can we honor all their efforts better than keeping their memories alive by writing down what we know for future generations lest they will never know that their very own relatives were part of the history of this great state of Montana and the United States westward movement?

Quinlan Family Pioneer History

Submitted by Elaine (Burch) Miles, Great-Great-Granddaughter

In Ireland in 1844 the Devon Committee, composed entirely of alien landowners, recommended Ireland disallow all tenant-rights, consolidate small farms, and encourage emigration. By 1847 the pursuance of the recommendations had caused the Great Famine. In that year, more than one half million people died of famine and fever. By 1851 over a million and a half people had died and another million had immigrated to the United States, many of the families having been ejected from homes.

Our Quinlan family consisted of Henry, born about 1829, John, born about 1830, Patrick, born about 1831, and Anastasia, born about 1832, to Thomas and Catherine (Cullrene) Quinlan in Waterford City, Waterford County, Ireland. We have learned very little about Thomas and nothing about Catherine.

The oral history from both the John and Henry Quinlan families state that they and their brother and sister, Patrick and Anastasia, met and traveled with the David Powers family from Ireland. If this is the case, we can document their journey from Ireland in early 1852 upon the "Asia" from the Port of Waterford to New Orleans. From New Orleans they traveled on the Mississippi River Packet "Uncle Sam" with Robert Smith, Master, to St. Louis, Missouri. It is said that Thomas Quinlan died while they were traveling on the Mississippi River and was buried in Arkansas. On the Missouri River they took a riverboat to Galena, Illinois.

John Quinlan

In the 1860 Illinois census, we find the Quinlans farming in the Menominee District of Jo Daviess County, Illinois. It was there that Henry met and married Margaret Grace, and John married her sister Mary. They were the daughters of James and Alice (Cleary) Grace. The girls were born in the early 1840's in Jo Daviess County, Illinois. Alice (Cleary) Grace was born in Ireland in 1817 and died and was buried in Deer Lodge, Montana, in 1884.

In March of 1864, John and Henry sold their farmland, and started their trek west with their families. They visited the Sinsinawa Seminary, with fellow travelers aboard the "Asia," including Father Louis Powers, a priest and instructor at the seminary, and his sister, Mother Emily Powers. Mother Emily Powers was the first Mother General of the Order of the Dominican Sisters. They crossed the Missouri River on planks at Dubuque, Iowa.

The Quinlan's traveled by wagon train with a team of oxen to pull their wagons. The wagon master was a man by the name of Syoms. They crossed the plains over the Platte River route and arrived in Virginia City, Montana Territory, on June 14, 1864.

For a time they engaged in mining at Alder Gulch, and later at Lincoln Gulch. The brothers were in the Registry to vote at Nevada City, Montana Territory. The vote was to determine whether Montana should become a state or remain a territory.

John and Mary (Grace) Quinlan daughters. Left to Right: Back Row: Margaret Alice Remigia (Quinlan) Laundreville and Ellen Catherine "Nellie" (Quinlan) Mero. Front Row: Mary Ann (Quinlan) Lowery.

In the spring of 1865 they moved to the Deer Lodge Valley and homesteaded, establishing their ranches on the Dempsey Creek. They engaged in stock raising and ranching. The firm of the Quinlan Brothers stood high in financial and solid business circles. Their brands are registered in VanDersal & Conners "Stockgrowers Directory of Marks and Brands for the State of Montana 1872-1900. The brand for Henry and John Quinlan was "Q" on the right hip. Their horse brand was "+" on the right shoulder. Patrick's brand was " Ò" The three brothers are in the *Registry of Montana*

Pioneers, as well as the *Society of Montana Pioneers, Vol. I.*

In the District Court, Second Judicial District, Deer Lodge County, Montana Territory, the Honorable Judge Hiram Knowles granted citizenship to John Quinlan on May 1, 1878.

Henry Quinlan married Margaret Grace in Galena, Jo Daviess County, Illinois, before their trip to Montana. Their union was blessed with six children: Alice (Mrs. Tom Sugure), Kate (Mrs. James Foley), John J., Joe P., Hallie (Mrs. George Johnson), and Harry. Henry died on August 21, 1900.

Father Remigius DeRykere married John Quinlan and Mary Grace in 1870. To this union came daughters Ellen Catherine (Nellie), born March 27, 1873; Mary Ann, born February 8, 1875; and Margaret Alice Remigia, born August 30, 1879. Mary Grace Quinlan died on February 25, 1883, at the age of 36, leaving John to rear the three girls. The girls spent some of their time with their Uncle Henry and Aunt Margaret, and some of their time as boarders at St. Mary's Academy to attend school, when they were not at home with John. Margaret was an accomplished artist, this talent being nurtured by the Sisters at the Academy. There are still several paintings in existence that were done by Margaret. John died of pneumonia at the age of 90 on December 4, 1920.

Patrick Quinlan remained a bachelor and lived with Henry and Margaret. He was in ill health much of his life and was nearly blind in his later years. He died on August 1910, at the age of 81.

Anastasia Quinlan – In *"The New North-West"* Deer Lodge City, Friday January 27, 1870, was the obituary: "Died, Quinlan, In the Deer Lodge Valley, January 19, 1870 of consumption, Anastasia Quinlan, aged 43."

Nellie Quinlan (John and Mary's daughter) married Fred Mero. They had nine children: Aggie (Mrs. Roy Sager), Helen (Mrs. Fred Pascoe), Margaret (Mrs. Robert Neilson), Kathleen (Mrs. Byron Lindquist), Ray, John, Marvin, Frank, and Charles. Nellie and Fred ranched "The Mero Place," a part of the John Quinlan homestead. Nellie died in January of 1937. At this time she had 14 grandchildren.

Mary Ann Quinlan (John and Mary's daughter) married Mike Lowery, who was from Galena, Illinois. They settled on what is known as "The Lowery Place," a part of the original John Quinlan homestead. Mike and Mary Ann had eleven children: Vin, Gerald, Edward, Loretta (Mrs. John Robinson), Evelyn (Mrs. Matheson and Pardue), June (Mrs. Guy and Mrs. Carl Demos), Juanita (Mrs. Hageman, Pimenta, Wesley Anthony, and

Patrick Thomas), Irene (Mrs. Leeper, and Mrs. Ben Pardue), Gladys (Mrs. Peterson, and Mrs. Lloyd Johnson), Sabina (Mrs. Meagher and Smilonich), and Kate, (Mrs. Jack Kelley). At the time of Ann's death, October 7, 1949, they had 36 grandchildren and 20 great grandchildren.

Margaret Alice Quinlan (John and Mary's daughter) married Peter Joseph Laundreville, son of Joseph and of Lucy DeZourdi dit Moreau, at Race Track on December 13, 1905. They were married by the Reverend D.M. Foley. They lived at the home place, the "John Quinlan Place." John had divided his land among his three girls. John lived with Pete and Mag until his death in 1920. Pete and Margaret had six children, two died in infancy, Mary and Eli, Edith Irene (Mrs. Matthew Strizich), Madelyn Lucille (Mrs. Wilbur Slaughtner), Marceline Margaret (Mrs. Andy Burch), and Lincoln Glenn. Margaret became a member of The Sons and Daughters of Montana Pioneers on August 27, 1936. At the time of her death on August 5, 1955, she had 13 grandchildren and eight great grandchildren.

Of Margaret and Peter Laundreville's children: Edith and Matt Strizich had nine children, Helen, John, Delores, Joyce, Matt, Jr., Kay Marie (who died at one month of age), Shirley, Peter, and Cathy. At the time of Edith's death on August 21, 1990, she had 34 grandchildren, and 34 great-grandchildren. Madelyn married Wilbur Slaughtner. They had no children. Marceline (Marcie) married Andy Burch. They had two daughters, Joan Lee and Elaine Marceline. Joan married A.L. (Hap) Jennings and they had six children: Stephen, Leigh Ann, Lynn Marie, Dana, Susan, and Terry. Hap and Joan have 14 grandchildren.

Having come from Ireland at a time when they did not have freedom of religion, or freedom to pursue an education, they were very concerned with helping to establish both. They were among the early residents who asked that a resident priest be sent to the valley. The property for the first Catholic Church was acquired from the Quinlan, Grace, and Brown families on Third (Main) Street. This log building was succeeded by what is known as St. Mary's Hall. The Quinlan brothers hauled rock for this building. The first baby baptized was John Quinlan, son of Henry and Margaret Quinlan, in 1866. The old Quinlan schoolhouse still stands in the Deer Lodge Valley.

When they located in the Deer Lodge Valley, wild game of every description abounded. It was a favorite hunting ground of the Indian tribes. John lived to see the valley transformed into a fine agricultural community with modern cities and towns growing in the valley.

Robert Smith

Submitted by Phyllis W. Jakovac, Great-Granddaughter

My pioneer story really begins in Ireland during the potato famine. Great grandfather, Robert Smith, arrived with his family in St. John Newfoundland in 1848. He was 15 years old. They settled in Montreal, Canada, and he soon learned to be a baker. At age 23, Robert moved to Chicago, Illinois, where he met and married a little Irish girl who was only 15 years old, Margaret Shortley. The baker's trade served him well for many years as they traveled first to Louisiana, and then Fort Scott, Kansas, in 1860. Iowa was also listed as a residence, and in 1861, they were in Delaware, Colorado. (This was when the Civil War began).

My grandmother Arvie was born November 18, 1863, in Blackhawk, Colorado, a small mining town near Denver. The year of my grandmother's birth, Robert and Margaret packed up the wagon again when they heard of the gold strike in Virginia City, Montana. Arvie was six months old and it must have been a very long and treacherous trip for the

Robert Smith – circa 1894.

Post Office and Store in Nelson, Montana.

family. They kept no diary but from reading other accounts of overland trips, I can imagine what they endured. Surely there were Indian troubles along the way.

Later in life Grandma Arvie wrote this (her only written history) in her Bible:

"Arvie Josephine Smith. Born Denver Colorado 1863. Crossed plains with parents. Arrived in Virginia City May 6, 1864. Father Robert Smith. Mother born in Montreal. Born Margaret Shortley Smith. Died 1880, 39 years old."

In 1864 Robert was 31 years old and Margaret was 23 years. This was the year Montana Territory was formed. They did a lot of traveling. Robert mined in various places: The Highland Mining District, Helena, Diamond City, and Oregon Gulch. They ran the hotel at the French Bar. In 1871, Robert revisited Colorado, presumably by himself. In 1872, they lived at Yam Hill and ran the Hotel. They then moved to Helena again, Dog Creek, and the Pioneer Montana Mining District where Robert was listed as a stock raiser. They moved to Eldorado Bar, and in 1875 they were back in Diamond City. During all this time, Robert was also listed as a baker, so his trade served to make a living for the family over the years.

In 1880 my great grandmother Margaret died in Diamond City of a brain tumor. She is buried in the Boulder Bar Cemetery. Her headstone is one of the few that remain. Margaret moved all the time and gave birth to five children. At the time of her death, her son Bob was 22 years old. Daughter Recina was 20 years old, and had been married for four years. Arvie (my grandmother) was 17 years old. Ben was five years and Mae three years old. The burdens of life fell upon the two oldest children that were still living at home in wild Diamond City. Arvie learned to be a good cook and baked very delicious cinnamon rolls.

At this same time my grandfather, Cyrus Nelson, arrived in this part of the country as the stage driver from Helena to Diamond City. He was born in Clyde, Ohio, in 1856. When he was 22 years old, in 1878, he left home for Texas. He drove cattle for the Hopper Livestock Company of Texas. He worked as a blacksmith up the Chisholm Trail to Montana.

He met Arvie and they were married in November of 1881. She was 18 years old and this was only one year after her mother's death. Cyrus drove stage for a time, and they ran the Hotel at Diamond City. This was probably a family venture since they all lived together. In 1882 they moved to Fort Logan where they ran Raders Trading Post for four years. In 1886 they left there and moved to York and lived there ten years. By this time there were five children born to Cyrus and Arvie. She was 33 years old. Cyrus still drove stage but now from Helena, Canyon Ferry, York, and beyond about five miles, to a place called Beaver Creek. In 1888, they were able to buy a ranch that nestled in these mountains and straddled Beaver Creek. It had a log cabin and some other sheds and barns. This log cabin was their home for quite a while. Since Cyrus drove the stage, he also

Cyrus Nelson Family. Left to Right: Back Row: Elbert, Bob Smith and Mable. Middle Row: Cyrus, Arvie (Smith) Nelson and Pearl. Front Row: Edith and Myrta – 1899.

brought the mail to this very small settlement. It came to be known as Nelson, Montana.

In 1897 one more daughter was born here at home on this ranch. At 34 years of age, this was my grandma Arvie's last child. All these children lived happy, long lives, in the Helena and Butte area. The only exception was their son Elbert who died in 1914, at age 28, of typhoid fever.

The Nelson household always had extra mouths to feed. Their lives always included Arvie's brother, sister, and her father. Brother Bob never married and died at age 53, in 1911. He always helped support the family.

Great grandfather Robert Smith died at the ranch on December 28, 1898. Both he and his son Bob are buried at a very old Cemetery at the top of the hill above York, Montana. My uncle Ben had a very nice stone placed to mark the burial of his father and brother, which still remains there.

Cyrus and Arvie lived on the ranch for 55 years, until in 1943. They then moved into town to live at the newly built Stewart Homes. Cyrus died at age 98, in 1954, and Arvie died at age 91, in 1955. Arvie became a member of the Sons and Daughter of the Montana Pioneers at age 74, in 1937. She attended some meetings but probably not very many. She was proud of her heritage. I am the fifth member of our family to join the Montana Pioneers. More have joined since.

Cyrus and Arvie did not travel during their lives. The longest distance they went was to Lewistown where Arvie's sister, Recina Brassey, lived. Cyrus traveled by train to Ohio to attend his father's funeral.

Cyrus was a quiet man who loved to read papers and magazines and talk politics. Arvie was always at home, and kids and grandkids were always underfoot or nearby. They had no money to spend, and there was never anything to spend it on anyway. They were 30 miles from Helena and rarely left home. A daughter and family (my parents, Edith and Owen Warren) lived one and a half miles up the road from the ranch, since about 1923, when they moved to Beaver Creek to work for the Montana Power Patrol Station. At this time Owen also worked the ranch and Cyrus and Arvie were always loved and cared for. Their three daughters were married and lived in Helena and they also gave them lots of tender loving care over their remaining years. Cyrus and Arvie lived to celebrate their 72nd wedding anniversary together.

George Henry Sparrell and Augusta Hull Piggott Sparrell

Submitted by Rita Gibson, Great-Great-Great-Granddaughter

"George H." as my mother's family refers to him ("George T." is his son) arrived in Virginia City, June 1864, from Massachusetts. George Henry was a carpenter and millwright by trade, in a family of shipbuilders. The sea had always been a part of their lives, but by 1850 most of the timber along the river where the Sparrell's lived, had all been cut down. The larger-sized ships couldn't be launched from where they resided, so the family trade developed into carpentry.

The Sparrell's descend from Elder William Brewster of the Mayflower. Some members of the family had died at sea. I wonder what George Henry thought of our Montana mountains? He must have been content because he brought his wife and children from Massachusetts, through Omaha, Nebraska, in 1861, and apparently never went back. In my attempt to trace my ancestors, I have contacted the Sparrells "back east". They said they'd always wondered what happened to their relative who went west; guess he didn't keep in contact. Now they know.

George H. was born May 10, 1831, in South Scituate, Plymouth County, Massachusetts. His parents were James Newton and Desire (Barrell) Sparrell. Yes, Barrell! Desire is our connection to William Brewster.

George married Augusta Hull Piggott, born May 14, 1835, daughter of George Washington and Catherine Allen Howland (descendant of a younger brother of the Mayflower Howland) Piggott, on April 17, 1853, in New Bedford, Massachusetts. The couple had four children, one named Augusta died young, seemingly before the family left Massachusetts. I descend from their oldest son (George Turner, born April 21, 1855). In 1861 the family – including their children Abbie Louise (born 1853), George T. (born 1855) and Edward Howland (born 1859) – left Massachusetts for Omaha, Nebraska. Traveling with children all under the age of seven had to have been a continual test of endurance! It is believed that in the fall of 1863 they arrived in Salt Lake City by ox-drawn wagons over the famous Overland Trail. George left Augusta and the children in Salt Lake City with her parents to winter there, and went on ahead to the new gold diggings of Alder Gulch, just above Virginia City. Augusta and the children arrived, again by ox train, to the new home he'd prepared in April of 1865.

A story reported in *Pioneer Trails and Trials,* by Mrs. Mary Tallman (neighbor of George's son, Edward) and also in George's daughter, Abbie

Louise Mason's obituary, relates that in an unfinished building George was constructing in Virginia City for W.W. Morris, an execution of five bandits took place.

According to the Montana Historical and Architectural Survey Form for the Virginia City Project the description of the hanging is as follows, "The log building on the corner of Wallace and Van Buren Streets was only partly finished, but to support the roof, it was equipped with a large, heavy beam across the center. On January 14, 1864, the Vigilantes captured five men accused as road agents. A brief trial was held in front of the Virginia

George Henry Sparrell in front of Morris State Bank Building in Pony, Montana – 1900.

Hotel (diagonally across the street – later called the OK Corral). The five were marched to the unfinished building on this site, forced to stand on boxes in this order, left to right (west to east) Frank Parish, Boone Helm, Jack Gallagher, Haze Lyons and Club Foot George Lane, and hung by ropes from the rafters. After the execution the five were buried on Boot Hill by their friends". The five men were reported members of the Sheriff Henry Plummer's Gang.

The building in which the hanging took place was completed and purchased by R. S. Hale soon after he arrived in Virginia City on July 10, 1864. He went to Helena in 1865 but his partner, Clayton, continued to operate the drug store in Virginia City. The firm later became Clayton and Morris and by 1873 it was W. W. Morris alone. Morris later operated a bank in Pony. In 1880 Mrs. Mary Deimling became postmistress of Virginia City and the post office was located in this building.

With the decline of gold mining in Virginia City, the Sparrells moved to Silver Star, in the Ruby Valley. By 1871-72 the family again moved, this time to Deer Lodge. Sometime around 1872 the good prospects of the Pony and Harrison communities lured them. Augusta disappears from any records I've been able to locate after the 1870 census.

George married Elizabeth Evans in Butte on April 11, 1880. They returned to Pony around 1891. George resided there for over 20 years until his death on September 12, 1911. He's buried in the Valley View Cemetery in Pony.

After his mining days, George took up ranching and farming. He was a member of the Pioneers in Butte, a Mason, and joined the Montana Moriah Lodge No. 24, A.F. & A.M. of Butte. He took the first degree March 4, 1884. On September 19, 1901, he became affiliated with the Montana Jefferson Lodge by demit as one of its charter members.

George Turner Sparrell

Submitted by Rita Gibson, Great-Great-Granddaughter

By the time he was ten years old, George had traveled across the United States. Born in New Bedford, Massachusetts, on April 21, 1855, George Turner Sparrell left his birthplace at the age of 6 and, with his family, came west to Omaha, Nebraska. The year was 1861.

Then in 1863, the Sparrell family moved farther west by ox-drawn wagons over the famous Overland Trail. For a boy of nine, it must have been an exciting adventure, especially if he was unaware of the dangers inherent in such a journey. His father, George Henry Sparrell left him, his mother Augusta, his brother Edward Howland, and sister Abbie Louise ("Lue"), to winter in Salt Lake City. He went on to the mining camp of Alder Gulch, above Virginia City, Montana. Augusta and her children journeyed by ox train again in the spring and reached their new home in Montana in April 1865. When the Sparrells left Massachusetts the children were the ages of 6, 5, and 2, by the time they arrived in Montana, they were 10, 9, and 6 years old. Traveling in those days with children so young had to have been more than an "adventure" for mom and dad.

Both boys had middle names that were the maiden names of their grandmas. "Turner" was their paternal great-grandmother, Rachel Turner (1776-1866). She was still alive and they must have known her before they left Massachusetts. "Howland" was their maternal grandmother, Catherine Allen Howland (1812-1887). Catherine and her husband, George Washington Piggott, both died in Salt Lake City in the 1880's, so either the Sparrells came west with Augusta's parents, or grandma and grandpa arrived earlier. I imagine Augusta and the children wintered with her parents the years of 1863 and 1864.

"George T." (to distinguish him from dad "George H.") was still living at home when in 1871 the Sparrell family moved to Silver Star, in the Ruby Valley and then to Deer Lodge. In 1872 they ranched on Spring Creek, and then moved to Willow Creek and Pony where George H. rented a ranch. They planted one crop. Based on the Sparrell letters housed in the Montana Historical Society archives, which originally came from the Virginia City collection, it appears the crop was hay.

George T. worked in various kinds of jobs. He butchered livestock for three years in Silver Star, and ranched on the Cook Ranch in Willow Creek in 1878. He helped capture stray horses, and the money he received from their sale, he gave to the maintenance of the local public school. He even attended it during the winter! For six months he was employed by the Red Bluff Mine. It was located between Fort Bozeman and Virginia City. For seven years he was in the mining employment of J.H. Mallory.

On May 1, 1879, George T. married Florence Sacry (born New Year's Eve, 1862, in Petaluma, Sonoma County, California), in Sappington, Montana. Florence was the daughter of James W. and Marietta (Oman) Sacry, who had arrived in Virginia City in 1876. The Sacry's came from Kentucky. The Oman family was L.D.S. and moved from Pennsylvania to Illinois and then to California.

By 1880 George T. was homesteading on the South Boulder, purchasing the S.D. Bollinger Ranch. He farmed and raised cattle. Their four children were born in this location. They were Albert M. (born March 1880-?); Ella Leone; and twins, Roy and my great-grandmother Hazel (born November 18, 1892). He "erected a commodious and attractive two-storey [sic] brick residence, one of the fine homes of the county." The house is still standing and is located one mile south of Jefferson Island. It is in the process of being listed on the National Register of Historical Places.

George T. was a Republican, served nine years as road supervisor, and two years as school trustee. He passed away at age 68 on December 10, 1923, at his home. He was buried in the South Boulder Cemetery. Among his survivors were his sister, "Lue" Mason, and brother Edward. They both resided in Pony. His wife, Florence died on August 16, 1945, and was buried next to him.

George L. and Catherine (Millen) Staudaher

Submitted by Nick Shrauger, Great-Grandson

George L. and Catherine (Millen) Staudaher were early Montana and Beaverhead County pioneers. Their ranch, called the Pearl Spring Ranch, was located about nine miles north of Dillon near the Beaverhead Rock. It was here that George and Catherine employed many newly arrived immigrants from Austria. Joe Rebich was one of these as was George's niece, the daughter of his sister and brother-in-law, Joseph and Caterine (Staidohar/Staudaher) Butala. Many present day Dillon residents are descendants of those immigrants that George and Catherine helped upon their arrival in Montana.

George was born near Vienna, Austria, on April 23, 1835. He was the son of Michael and Mary (Myers) Staudaher. George had one brother and seven sisters. His parents were farmers and devout members of the Catholic Church.

George left home in 1852 at age sixteen to work on farms near Baden, Prussia, and in Belgium. His wages were $2.50 per month. In 1858 he moved to America and worked for two years on a farm near St. Joseph, Missouri. The 1860 gold discovery at Pike's Peak, Colorado, called George westward. He worked for nearly three years near Blackhawk, Colorado, as a miner on the Bobtail lode. He made $2.50 to $3.00 a day during this period.

In the Spring of 1863 George and three other partners purchased a freight outfit and headed for Bannack and arrived on June 1, 1863. They went on to Alder Gulch where George happened to meet an old friend named Meyers. Both George and Meyers located claims on German Bar. They mined $2,000 in two months. George, Mr. Meyers, and a Mr. Rhine, formed a company of their own. In November they went to Salt Lake City, Utah, by stage. (The eight passengers had $60,000 in gold among them. Stages before them and after them had been robbed.) While in Salt Lake City they exchanged their gold dust for $3,600 in currency. They returned to Bannack and sold their freight outfits and returned to Alder Gulch.

George became ill and returned to St. Joseph, Missouri. There he married Catherine Millen, a sister of Montana and Beaverhead pioneer George Millen, on February 12, 1865. They returned to Alder Gulch where they began married life in a log cabin that George built. Their first child, George J. Staudaher, was born on December 18, 1865. He is among the first of the children born in Alder Gulch. They remained in Alder Gulch until 1867. High wages and poor returns made mining uneconomical. George then moved his family to the Beaverhead Valley in 1867.

George and Catherine's first location in the Beaverhead was near the Point of Rocks south of Dillon. There they took a squatter's claim to a tract of land, built a log house, and turned their energies to farming and stock raising. Grasshoppers destroyed their first crops. During the period from 1867-1870 they had two more children, Nick and John.

They then moved to Prickly Pear, Jefferson County, near Montana City. It was there that their first girl, Catherine Louise was born. It is not known if George was farming or mining at that location.

George and his family returned to the Beaverhead, and by the end of 1876, George received his Homestead Certificate for 160 acres (S29-T5S-R7W) north of Dillon, and about two miles southwest of Beaver Head

George L. and Catherine (Millen) Staudaher with son George J., who was born in Alder Gulch, Montana Territory, on December 18, 1865.

Rock. (The 1870 Land Survey map on file in the Beaverhead County Clerk and Recorder's office lists this as the Beaver Head Rock and not Point of Rocks).

During the next ten years, George and Catherine made several land purchases. One tract that George eventually purchased was described as "about three and one half miles of leaning pole fencing consisting of four poles and jack fencing situated and being upon the Rail Road and school lands, and one cabin and corrals on said Rail Road Land situated on the west side of the Beaver Head River about four miles from the point of rocks on Beaver Head valley Beaverhead County, Montana Territory. Also Cook Stove, Carpenter Tools and Hay Press. Also one cream colored Horse about six years old, One black Horse about fourteen years old, one sorrel Horse about ten years old, and one Cabin used as a butcher shop, and lot and ground upon which the same is situated in Glendale and butchers Tools and account books in said County of Beaver Head for the sum of five hundred dollars."

In 1889 George and Catherine, together with Gerhard Albers, Jack Neely, George Millen, John F. Bishop and the Bliver Live Stock Company, filed a water rights action in District Court against Thomas M. Selway and others. These resulted in an early adjudication of irrigation waters of the Beaver Head River (Case 828).

George and Catherine called their place the Pearl Springs Ranch. Having spent nearly 40 years in mining and ranching, he sold the ranch to John T. Miller of Butte, Montana, on November 29, 1904. John's daughter, Angela, and her husband, John Malesich, began ranching there. The ranch has remained in continuous operation by that family since. George moved to Dillon where he had purchased various lots and tracts of property and spent the remainder of his life managing his real estate.

George and Catherine had nine children. They were George J. (1865-1925), Nicholas Michael (1867-1917), John A. (1869-1945), Catherine Louise "Lucy", (1870-1966), William L. (1873-1938) Anna M. (1875-1882), Agatha L. (1879-1963), Mae Ester (1882-1964), and Francis J. (1891-1962). All their children were born in Beaverhead County, except George, who was one of the earliest children born in Alder Gulch, and Catherine, who was born in Montana City near Helena.

Catherine (Millen) Staudaher was born in Luxenburg, Germany, on June 15, 1844. In 1862 she sailed for America, and landed in New York. She remained there until 1864, when she went to St. Joseph, Missouri. She resided there when she married George. She died of stomach cancer August

17, 1897, after an illness of more than two years. She is buried in Mountain View Cemetery in Dillon, Montana.

On May 9, 1908, George married Mary (Rebich) Kruljac of Dillon. Mary's parents were George and Kata/Katie (Stefonac) Rebich. Her first marriage was to Bartol Kruljac. George was a member of the Society of Montana Pioneers, the Ancient Order of United Workman, and a devout Catholic. He was one of 41 members of the Stock-Growers Association of Southern Montana as listed in 1884.

George L. Staudaher experienced one of the most interesting and quickly changing periods of American history. He arrived in Bannack, Idaho Territory, watched as the Montana Territory formed, and was present when Montana reached its statehood. He was truly a pioneer Montana miner and stockman. George passed away on May 4, 1916, and is buried in Mountain View Cemetery in Dillon, Montana.

Manoah Stone

Submitted on behalf of Irene Stone O'Neill and Pearl Stone Tintinger, Granddaughters, by Audrey Faller O'Neill.

Manoah Stone was born in what was Iowa Territory, now Jefferson County, Iowa, on May 11, 1843. Another source claims the same date for his birth, but reports he was born in Morgan County, Fairfield, Iowa. His parents were Willis Carter Stone and Louisa Thompson Hurt.

Andreas, in his *History of Kansas* (1883), mentions a move to Marion County, Iowa, by Manoah Stone in 1853. He lived until 1860 with his parents. He may have spent some time in Adair County, Kentucky, with his grandparents Permelia and Manoah.

His family had Southern origins, so when Manoah ran away from home at age sixteen and joined the Northern Army, his father brought him home.

In 1863, Manoah, with his father and several others, left for Colorado. Word of a gold strike in Montana prompted them to join a wagon train with the Thoroughman and Bullard families. Manoah's granddaughter, Pearl Stone, recalls Manoah telling her about a small band of Indians that rode along a short distance from the wagons for three days. They arrived in Virginia City in the fall of 1864. He often reminisced about the time they came in and found the Vigilantes had hanged several men in Virginia City.

The search for gold was futile, but the experiences were rich and varied. In 1866, while on a hunting trip, Manoah and his companions were lost in a blizzard for three days. They finally stumbled into a cabin and found Manoah's legs had been badly frozen. His boots were cut away and his feet treated. Upon his arrival in Virginia City it was necessary for parts of his feet to be removed.

Deciding to return to Iowa, the Stones traveled to Helena, and then over the stagecoach trail to Fort Benton. A riverboat took them to St. Louis where his right leg was removed above the knee, as were the toes of the left foot. He was fitted with an artificial right leg, and a ball and toes replacement was made to fit in the left shoe. He never considered himself handicapped.

Manoah Stone

Manoah returned to Iowa where he married Mary McLean (born February 19, 1847, in Morgan County, Illinois) on May 15, 1867, in Knoxville.

Manoah and Mary moved to Nebraska where two of his children, Lillian and Willis George were born. Willis George, sometimes called George Willis or Will, was born in late December 1871.

They settled in Richardson County, Kansas, where Manoah taught school until the spring of 1873, they then moved to Jewell County. He was elected trustee of Prairie Township, and served at least two terms. Among the offices he was elected to were the Registrar of Deeds, County Superintendent of Schools, Judge, County Treasurer, and County Assessor.

They were "engaged in agriculture, having a valuable farm of 240 acres near the thriving town of Jewell City," according to Andreas' *History of Kansas*. Much of his property was lost because of the "national panic of 1893."

Six children were eventually born to Mary and Manoah. One son, Fred, died in infancy from scarlet fever, and Frank died from a football injury. After Lillian and George Willis, a daughter, Louisa Elizabeth (Bessie), was born in 1874. Bessie married James Motes and they had three daughters. Charles Frank (Frank) was born in 1876, and then Loressa Amanda (Dolly) was born in 1880. Dolly married Arthur (Fred) Griffin and had two daughters. Bessie and Dolly's families lived in and around Jewell and Beloit, Kansas. Manoah's wife Mary passed away in November of 1894. Manoah married Harriet M. Curtiss two years later, in 1896.

Manoah's longing to return to Montana was satisfied when he and Harriet decided to join his brother Charles near Cascade. Manoah's son Willis, Harriet's son Harry Curtiss, and her daughter Mary Curtiss, accompanied them. Traveling by covered wagon they arrived at the Charley Stone ranch near Bird Creek on the old Adel road. Manoah had always been interested in that area and in locating his old friend, "Uncle" Bob Thoroughman.

Manoah and Harriet lived in Great Falls where he operated the Montana Feed Yards for some time. In the spring of 1903, his daughter Lillian joined them. Lillian later married James W. Perrine of rural Cascade County.

Various members of the family took up homesteads on and near Castner Coulee. Manoah and Willis filed on the north half of the section lying to the north and west of the Castner Falls School. The school was not built until later. The men in the community built the school. Lillian filed on land nearby.

Having had experience as a rural mail carrier in Kansas, Manoah, saw a need for and established the first rural mail route in Cascade County. He became the first carrier there and carried mail three days a week, over a route of about 63 miles, by horse and buggy on unimproved roads. He did this from December 15, 1904, to May 31, 1908. In winter he drove the route with a horse-drawn sled. Housewives along the route kept soapstones hot to exchange with him to give him warmth in winter. He had a buffalo robe, coat, hat, and gloves that he had from his first trip to Montana. This work is the subject of a paper, *History of Rural Route One, Cascade, Montana 59421* by Joe Zorze, 1968.

Manoah Stone passed away in Great Falls in November 1911. He had been a prominent member of the Mankato Lodge No. 186 I.O.O.F. Manoah was the first person buried in the Castner Falls Cemetery on land that was part of his son Willis' homestead and is now a public cemetery. His second wife, Harriet, died in Grants Pass, Oregon, in 1936.

Granville Stuart

Submitted by Darrell E. Abbott, Great-Grandson

Granville Stuart was born in Clarksburg, Virginia, on August 27, 1834, of Scotch descent to Robert and Nancy Stuart. Brothers James born in 1832, Samuel born in Illinois on August 10, 1836, Thomas born in Iowa on April 13, 1839, and a sister, Elizabeth, born in Iowa on October 14, 1842, made up Granville's immediate family.

In 1837 Robert and Nancy Stuart left Virginia and went to Illinois with their two children Granville and an older brother James. About this time, the government purchased land west of the Mississippi River from the Indians creating Iowa Territory so in 1838 the Stuarts moved to Iowa. During this time, James and Granville attended a school with a red-headed boy of ten or eleven years, a bright intelligent lad named Erastus Yeager, who twenty-one years later was hung by the Vigilantes in Montana for being a road agent with the Henry Plummer gang. It was not until he was hanged did they learn that Erastus was a schoolmate from Iowa.

In the spring of 1852 in the company of his father and brother, James Granville journeyed to the California gold fields. They traveled overland across the vast uninhabited plains then known on the maps as the Great American Desert, forming in later years the states of Nebraska, Kansas, Colorado, and Wyoming. Iowa then was very sparsely settled and there was not a single railroad west of the Mississippi River, and not until 1866 at Atchison, Kansas, was one in existence.

On September 26, 1852, after a trip of two thousand miles, the Stuart party arrived at their destination a few miles from the Sacramento Valley. Granville wrote in his journal that he felt as though he had been transplanted to another planet. There were lofty forests with trees six feet in diameter, three hundred feet high, and from sixty to eighty feet from the ground there was not a limb or a blemish. Tall bearded men were digging up the ground and washing it. In long toms and rockers on the banks by their sides were a sheet iron pan (like a cookie sheet) in which were various amounts of yellow gold.

The gold coins used then were also different than any he had seen. They were coined at the San Francisco Mint and were ten, twenty, and fifty-dollar pieces. The great octagonal fifty-dollar pieces were especially strange to him.

These men had neither tents nor houses. They camped under trees for it never rained there in the summertime. They were strong and healthy and lived a life as free as the air they breathed. No finer specimens of mankind existed anywhere than were these California miners of the days of '49. Men without ambition never started for California. The faint-hearted turned back before they reached the Missouri River. The puny, sickly ones either recovered or perished on the road. Only the courageous determined men crossed the plains and reached the land of gold.

In the years from 1852 to 1857, placer mining in California may be said to have been at its best. On all the streams, in all the gulches and high up in the Sierras to the north clear to the Oregon line every little camp was crowded with miners and gold was being taken out in such profusion as almost to lead one to believe that there would be an over-production and everybody seemed to be trying to find some way to spend all he had.

In the spring of 1857 Granville and James decided to visit their parents and their old home in Iowa. All their preparations being made on June 14, 1857, they started from Eureka, California, on their journey east. En route, on July 18, 1857, Granville was taken ill – so ill that James felt that if he recovered at all it would be a long time before he would be able to travel. James Stuart and Reece Anderson decided to stay with Granville while the rest of the party continued on their journey east. There, on the great Overland Emigrant Road about sixty miles north of the present town of Corrine, Utah, he lay for seven weeks too ill to travel. James succeeded in breaking the fever but not until it had brought him nigh to death's door.

During this time they were delayed, Brigham Young, president of the Mormon Church declared the state of Utah free and independent of the United States. In fact, he had seceded from the Union. United States troops were sent to squelch the uprising.

Due to this delay, Reece Anderson, James and Granville Stuart decided to go to Montana and crossed the Rocky Mountain divide on October 10, 1857, where the Monida station is on the Oregon Short Line railroad. On October 24 they left Sage Creek and crossed the rather high ridge of Blacktail Deer Creek. Having arrived at their destination, the Beaverhead Valley where the wood was plentiful, they remained the rest of the winter living in elk skin lodges, and as there was plenty of game the camp was well supplied with meat. Some fifteen miles down the Beaverhead was another camp consisting of Richard Grant and his son John.

The Indians of the area were mostly Snakes and Bannocks with a few Flatheads. On Christmas Day, Captain Grant invited the Stuart party to dine with him. The menu consisted of buffalo meat, boiled smoked tongue, bread, dried fruit and a preserve made from choke cherries and coffee. This was considered an elaborate dinner of those days. When it was not uncommon to live on a diet of all meat.

Granville Stuart

On April 4 the Stuart party moved and made camp about where the town of Stuart was then. (The town of Stuart existed on a Montana map dated 1902, but not on a map dated 1937.)

On May 2, 1858, the Stuart party consisting of James and Granville Stuart, Reece Anderson and Thomas Adams, who had joined them at Flint Creek, started for Benetsee Creek on a prospecting trip. The prospecting done by the Stuarts was the first prospecting for gold in what is now

Montana. There was gold to be found on a branch of the Hell Gate, now known as Gold Creek. This was Missoula County, Washington Territory, which included all the west side of the Rocky Mountains of the present state of Montana. Missoula County was first organized by the legislature of Washington Territory December 14, 1860. Its northern boundary was Canada, eastern boundary the main ridge of the Rockies, southern boundary the 46th parallel and its western boundary the 115th meridian.

On December 2, 1861, Thomas Adams returned from Fort Benton and brought Granville a new breach-loading fifty-caliber Maynard carbine rifle taking brass cartridges intended to contain forty grains of black powder. This was the first gun of its kind in Montana.

The Stuart brothers were married to Indian women with James marrying March 1, 1862, followed by Granville on May 2, 1862, to Awbonnie, a Snake Indian girl. Granville remained married to Awbonnie until her death in 1888 on the DHS Ranch near Fort Maginnis.

During the early 1860's, Granville and James spent much time at the Johnny Grant ranch, which today is known as the Grant Kohr's ranch near Deer Lodge.

On September 10, 1862, James Stuart gave bonds and took the oath of office having been elected sheriff of Missoula County, Washington Territory. Granville and James Stuart went to the Beaverhead mines to a village that was then called Bannack where Granville Stuart built a butcher shop. This was November 22, 1862. Neither James nor Granville did any mining at Bannack.

Granville reported that it was about this time that Henry Plummer and his gang of road agents began murdering and stealing from the miners until Vigilante action was taken later in 1864 to rid the area of such atrocities.

During Granville's trading ventures he reported that such items as chewing tobacco sold for $4.00 a pound, bacon 40 cents, sugar 60 cents, soap 50 cents, with letters costing $1.00 each to receive and 75 cents on each sent out.

On April 10, 1863, James Stuart, with a party of 15, started for the Yellowstone Valley to prospect for gold. His journal of the Yellowstone expedition of 1863 is published in the Montana Historical Society Contributions. James and party returned in July 1863.

Because of new diggings, the Stuarts moved to Virginia City, the District of Alder Gulch, where they built a blacksmith shop and continued selling goods to the miners. James formed a partnership with W. B. Dance in a general store.

In August 1863, A. J. Oliver and Company started a stage line from Virginia City to Bannack and Salt Lake City. The first newspaper published in Montana was the Montana Post printed by John Buchanan and issued August 27, 1864. On May 26, 1864, the new year saw marvelous changes in Montana. Montana had emerged into a territory with a population of 14,817 souls. The Montana Territory was organized from Northeastern Idaho. The first territorial legislature was in session at Bannack enacting laws for a better government. Virginia City was an incorporated town. Schools were provided wherever six or more children could be assembled.

The Montana Historical Society was organized with Wilbur F. Sanders as President, Judge H. L. Hossner was Historian, and Granville Stuart was Secretary. Granville and James Stuart were two of the incorporators of the society, and in 1875 Granville became its vice-president and served many years in that capacity. In 1890 he became its president, a position he held until he went to South America. After his return, he served on the board of trustees for several years.

There was a strong Masonic Lodge in Virginia City, and during the summer, the organization built a handsome Masonic Hall. A daily mail and stage service was in operation between Virginia City, Bannack, and Salt Lake City. A weekly stage ran from Virginia City to other towns in the territory – carrying both passengers and mail. A great number of steamboats made regular trips from St. Louis, Missouri, to Fort Benton – each loaded to capacity with freight and passengers.

In 1865, the sole medium of exchange was gold dust. The few greenbacks and treasury notes brought into the country by immigrants were a commodity and were bought and sold at a market price. Merchants usually made one last try during the year taking with them the year's accumulation of gold dust, which was to pay their obligations and purchase additional goods.

In 1866 a telegraph line was completed from Salt Lake City to Virginia City, Montana.

From 1865 to 1870 there was an era of great prosperity in Deer Lodge County. During this period the placer mines provided more than $20,000,000 in gold dust. Nelson Story of Bozeman drove the first herd of Texas cattle into Montana in the spring of 1866. Story had purchased these cattle at Dallas, Texas, and arrived in the Gallatin Valley and camped where Fort Ellis was later located.

The first beef cattle driven out of Montana was a small herd belonging to D. J. Hagan of Sun River, delivered to Salt Lake City in the fall of 1866.

In August 1870 L. E. Graham and J. B. Taylor arrived in Deer Lodge Valley with 450 heifers and five bulls of pure Durham blood. The cattle were purchased at Omaha, Nebraska, shipped to Ogden, Utah, and from there were driven north. This was the first herd of thoroughbred cattle brought to Montana.

In 1871 Granville became one of thirteen members of the Territorial Council, the Upper House of the Seventh Session of the Territorial Legislature, which met at Virginia City from December 4, 1871, to January 12, 1872.

Form 1870-1880 there was a period of financial depression in Montana. Until 1870 placer mining was an all-important industry in the Territory, but from that time on, gold production decreased rapidly from all the old placers and there were no important discoveries. Many of Montana's leading citizens thought it was time to abandon the country and left for the States and for the new gold discoveries of the Black Hills, South Dakota.

During the summer of 1880, a co-partnership was entered into between A. J. Davis of Butte, Erwin Davis of New York City, Samuel A. Hauser and Granville Stuart of Helena, Montana, for the purpose of engaging in the cattle business. The capital stock of the firm was $150,000. The brand was "H." The firm's name was Davis and Hauser and Co. The interest was divided into thirds: The Davis brothers – one third, Hauser – one-third, and Granville Stuart – one third, who was also elected superintendent and general manager and was directed to begin at once to look about for cattle that could be purchased at a satisfactory price.

On April 11, 1880, Granville left Helena for a trip to the Yellowstone Country to look for good cattle range. The first part of the trip was by stagecoach. Granville arrived in Miles City on April 17 stating that there were some nice areas but not adequate acreage for what the partnership had in mind. The hotel accommodations at the time in Miles City were not first class. In fact, Granville did not think there were any accommodations. The people that frequented Miles City in those days usually came to town to stay up and see the sights. They did not feel the necessity for a bed or much to eat – they were just thirsty.

At Miles City, Granville invited Thomas H. Irvine, Eugene Lamphere, and L. A. Huffman (a photographer from Fort Keogh) to go with him heading for the Wolf Mountains, east of where Hardin now is.

Eugene Lamphere and L. A. Huffman had to return to Fort Keogh once they reached the Tongue River. By May 6 Granville and Tom Irvine had reached the place of the Custer fight in 1876. They camped between Reno Hill and where Custer and his men were killed. Granville said the field was a ghastly sight.

On May 9, 1880, Granville and Tom had reached the Forks of the Yellowstone and Big Horn Rivers where Granville's brother James had gone on the Yellowstone expedition of 1863. Upon reaching Terry's landing on May 10, 1880, some two miles up the Yellowstone River where a telegraph and post office were located, Granville hired a man named John Roberts to guide them to the Flat Willow Country near where Grass Range is now. The Crow Indians told Granville and his party that the country between there and Flat Willow was swarming with Sioux Indians Granville stated that with their Winchesters, revolvers and plenty of ammunition they would be able to take care of themselves.

Upon reaching the area around the Musselshell River, Granville said the country was black with buffalo. The country, both bottom and hills, was covered with stunted sagebrush and greasewood but little grass. There were petroleum indications all through there and someday Montana would produce oil, but it was worthless then.

By May 13 the party had reached Flat Willow and reported the grass better than anywhere since leaving the Bighorn River. Traveling up Flat Willow about 18 miles to Brown's Trading Post where Bill Hamilton wintered, the little Snowy Mountains up to the Southwest were quite grand. They had a large quantity of snow on them and the tops seemed to be about timberline. To the North were the Judith Mountains but they were not nearly so high or so well timbered as the Little Snowies and had only a few snow drifts on the south side. To the right of them a short distance, standing at the beginning of the plain on rather rolling ridges of little height, rises "Black Butte," which was a beautiful curved top cone. Their journey went northeast crossing the ridge between Fords and McDonald creeks, traveling up Ford Creek crossing back onto a branch of McDonald Creek near the foot of the divide between McDonald Creek and Judith Basin. After camping along McDonald Creek, they crossed over the divide into the Judith Basin and camped between Juneau's Fort and Bowls and Reed's place. Their journey then took them to Cottonwood and Beaver Creeks into Judith Gap and by May 22 they had arrived at Martinsdale at the forks of the Musselshell. Here the rest of the party left Granville to return to the Yellowstone while Granville returned to Helena, reaching there by stage on

May 26. After consulting with his partners, it was decided to continue to search for grazing land. Granville traveled to Sun River then on toward Bowle's Fort and Juneau's Fort on over the Judith Divide, camping for the night of June 24 on a branch of McDonald Creek.

While traveling down McDonald Creek, Granville encountered a party of 50 carts of Red River half-breeds. Upon talking with this party about hayland, streams and the country in general, one of the party, Sevire Hamlin, told Granville he knew just the right place. June 28, 1880, after hiring Sevire Hamlin as a guide, the Stuart party headed toward the Judith Mountains. The next morning they traveled about three miles to a creek on which were small groves of cottonwood trees. Here about two miles from the mountains they found a body of hayland with cold springs all through it. This was the very place Granville had been looking for. The whole country clear to the Yellowstone was good grass country with some sage and all of this country for a hundred miles in each direction was well-grassed, well-watered, and had good shelter.

Granville then returned to Helena to make arrangements to start various cattle herds to the range then hurried back to locate the home ranch, which was about three miles from the foot of the Judith Mountains. In July 1880 Captain Dangerfield Park established Fort Maginnas. The fort being located on the upper end of the hayfield that Granville had selected. Granville said it was annoying to lose the hayground but the fort was a convenience as it furnished a telegraph, post office and a place to purchase supplies. By the first of October Granville had the buildings completed, some range cabins built, and five thousand head of cattle on the ranges with sixty head of horses. When the partnership came to use their brand they found it blotched and was not plain, so it was changed to the "D-S" and the name of the company to Davis, Hauser and Stuart. On the range an established cattle company was "an outfit" and everything pertaining to it was known and called after the brand. From this time on the ranch, cattle, horses and cowboys and owners were know as the DHS Outfit.

In the summer of 1881, James Fergus came to the range and located on Armells Creek. Kohrs and Bielenberg brought in 3,000 cattle and turned them loose on Flat Willow. Power Brothers and Charles Belden brought two herds into Judith Basin. Robert Coburn and Henry Sieben had herds on the Flat Willow. John Davenspeck located on Elk Creek. That spring several outfits on the range "pooled" or worked together as one outfit.

The first meeting was held at the DHS Ranch on May 29, 1882, with Granville acting as Secretary with following members present: James and Andrew Fergus, H. J. Bielinberg, and N. J. Davenspeck. William C. Burnett was elected captain of the spring roundup. It was decided that the spring roundup would start by May 30, fall calf roundup September 1, and the beef roundup to begin on October 1.

In the fall of 1882 Granville was elected a member of the Thirteenth Legislature Assembly at Helena where he was elected President of the council.

August 15 and 16, 1882, the Montana Stockgrowers Association called a meeting in Helena with a membership of 168 stockmen present. The Montana Stockgrowers Association was now one of the most important organizations in the Territory.

By September 1 the DHS had 12,000 head of cattle on the range. By 1883 the railroads had invaded Montana, destroying the Missouri River transportation and the abandoned wood yards furnished splendid rendezvous for horse thieves and cattle rustlers who were becoming so numerous and well organized that they threatened to destroy the cattle business.

In the fall of 1883 the DHS shipped from Custer on the Northern Pacific and had a drive of 120 miles. The beef herd was in charge of William C. Burnett, a young Texan, and the best range foreman that Granville had ever met. He knew the business form A to Z and understood the psychology of range cattle and cowboys. The herd reached the Yellowstone, crossed the river and were loaded and shipped to Chicago where they arrived in first-class condition. By this time there were 600,000 head of range cattle in the Territory and these, together with the horses and sheep, was as much stock as the ranges could safely carry. Between the years of 1880-1883, a rapid change took place. In 1880 the country was practically uninhabited. One could travel for miles without seeing so much as a trapper's bivouac. Thousands of buffalo darkened the rolling plains. There were deer, antelope, elk, wolves and coyotes on every hill and in every ravine and thicket. In the whole territory of Montana there were but 250,000 head of cattle. In the fall of 1883 there was not one buffalo remaining on the range and the deer, antelope. and elk were very scarce.

The story of the Montana cattle ranges would not be complete without a brief description of the Texas Trail. More than one-half of the Montana range cattle were driven over that trail and almost every cowboy that worked on the ranges made one or more drives up the trail.

The Texas Trail started on the Rio Grande and crossed the plains to the Red River. From there it ran due north to the Canadian River and on to Dodge City where it crossed the Arkansas River, to Ogalalla, crossing the North Platte at Camp Clark. From Ogalalla it followed the Black Hills Stage Road to Belle Fouche to the Powder River to the Yellowstone above Fort Keogh. From there to the Musselshell, which was the end of the trail. There were usually 2-3,000 cattle in a trail herd and the outfit consisted of a trail boss, eight cowpunchers, a cook, a horse wrangler, about 65 cow horses and a four-horse chuckwagon that carried provisions and the men's blankets. The food provided was cornmeal, sorghum, molasses, beans, sugar, salt and coffee.

One of the worst things the men had to contend with on the trail was the terrific threat of electrical storms so prevalent on the plains and along the Arkansas and Platte Rivers during the summer months. The greatest responsibility rested on the trail boss who had to know where the water was a day ahead and made the drive accordingly. Conrad Kohrs in 1883 became Granville Stuart's partner on the DHS when Kohrs bought out the Davis and Hauser interests. Kohrs paid those parties $400,000 for their interest.

At the close of the fall roundup in 1883, the tallies showed a considerable amount of stock loss due to rustling. These rustlers were particularly active along the Missouri and Yellowstone Rivers and also the Dakota badlands were great sufferers. A meeting of stockmen was called at Helena on October 16 to consider what to do. The first thing necessary was to discover the leaders and locate the rendezvous. It was then decided to bring the matter before the Stockgrowers Association regular spring meeting. The second annual meeting of the Montana Stockgrowers Association convened at Miles City on April 20, 1884. There were 429 stockmen present. The matters at hand for consideration were overstocking the ranges, Texas fever, and rustling. Granville was elected president.

The civil laws and courts had been tried and found wanting. The Montana cattlemen with $35,000,000 worth of stock scattered over 75,000 square miles of practically uninhabited country wanted to protect their property from thieves. The only way to do it was to make the penalty for stealing so severe that it would lose its attractiveness. Granville opposed open war on the rustlers in that the rustlers were strongly fortified in that their cabins were miniature fortresses. They were all well armed with the most modern weapons, ample ammunition and every man of them was a desperado and a dead shot. In the end the conservative members of the Association carried the day and it was voted that the Association would take no action against the rustlers. In some way the rustlers got information about what was done at the meeting and were jubilant. They returned to their favorite haunts and settled down to what was promised to be an era of undisturbed and successful operations.

There were rustlers' rendezvous at the mouth of the Musselshell at Rocky Point and at Wolf Point. On June 25, 1884, Narciss Lavardure and Joe Vardner stole seven head of horses from a camp on the Judith River belonging to J. A. Wells. While making their getaway with the horses the thieves accidentally met William Thompson, who knew the horses and ordered them to stop. Lavardure fired at Thompson but his horse plunged and he missed his mark. Thompson gave chase, shot and fatally wounded Vardner, captured Lavardure and took him and the horses back to Wells camp. There the horse thief was placed in a stable under guard. At 2:00 a.m. on the 27th an armed posse overpowered the guard and Lavardure was taken and hanged.

On July 3 the DHS crew caught Sam McKenzie in a canyon just above Fort Maginnis with two stolen horses in his possession. That night he was hanged from a limb of a cottonwood tree on Fords Creek between Fort Maginnis and the DHS headquarters. Sam McKenzie is buried at the Fort Maginnis Cemetery.

On July 4 two more hardcases made their way to Lewistown stirring up a fight, which would end up in their deaths. Their names were Rattlesnake Jake (Charles Fallon) and Longhaired Owens (Edward Owen). The fight started when Owen spotted Joe Doney standing in front of Powers store, started across the street and when within a few feet of Doney, Doney pulled a pistol and shot Owen. Owen recovered, joined Rattlesnake Jake, and the fight continued until one citizen was killed and Rattlesnake Jake and Longhaired Owen had received enough wounds to be fatal.

Throughout July the DHS and crew, along with four men James Fergus sent from his ranch (one James's son Andrew), made two expeditions to the Missouri River breaks where some 15-20 more thieves with some 200 head of horses were holed up at a wood yard along the river. These men were dealt with in a most severe manner, putting an end to such depredation in Montana for many years.

The Society of Montana Pioneers began in 1884 with James Fergus as the first president. In 1886 Granville became president, the Society's third.

In the spring of 1885 the DHS incorporated for $1,000,000 and issued 1,000 shares of stock at par value $100 per share. By the fall of 1885, Montana ranges were crowded to the point where a hard winter or a dry summer would certainly bring disaster. The range business was no longer a reasonably safe business but a gamble with the trump cards in the hands of the elements.

During the spring of 1886, a group of eastern capitalists offered to purchase the entire DHS herd but the man who represented the eastern company, Mr. Elkins, died suddenly and the sale was not consummated.

A drought had come over the range with unprecedented heat and it was decided to move at least part of the herd. It was decided to move 5,000 head across the Missouri River to the foot of the Little Rockies. G. P. (Perk) Burnett was given the task of gathering and moving the herd. During this time cattle prices plummeted adding to the disaster soon to come. The fall rains did not come and a severe winter storm hit by November 16. This continued until January 15, 1887, when the thermometer stood at 46 degrees below zero with 16 inches of snow on the level. It was as though the Arctic regions had pushed down and enveloped the range. Everything was white. Not a point of bare ground was visible in any direction. The cattle drifted before the storms with young steers freezing to death along the trails. Following the winter of 1886-87, the DHS's losses were 60 percent of the herd. Other large herds lost even more.

Charles Russell, the cowboy artist, drew a charcoal sketch for an answer to an inquiry of the herd in the Judith basin. This sketch was named "The Last of Five Thousand."

The large outfits were the heaviest losers as they could not feed or shelter their immense herds. Many closed out the remnants of their herds and quit. Granville was one of these. A business that had been fascinating to him before had suddenly became distasteful. He never wanted to again own an animal he could not feed or shelter. Conrad Kohrs then took over the remnant of the herd.

The loss of wealth had been a severe blow to Granville but knowledge and experience on the range gave him hopes of recovering some of the money.

Granville stayed with the stockman and for several years remained President of the Board of Stock Commissioners of Montana. The position carried heavy responsibility and no pay, but under his direction many stockmen were helped to rebuild their business on a different plan and the danger from thieves and cattle diseases greatly reduced.

In 1890 Granville married Allis Brown, who remained his companion the remainder of his life.

In 1891 Granville was appointed State Land Agent and personally selected some six hundred thousand acres of land, which the Federal Government had given the state of Montana for the purpose of providing revenue for the schools.

In 1894 Granville was appointed ambassador to the Republics of Uruguay and Paraguay in South America. He held this position for five years.

In 1904 Granville was appointed librarian of the Butte Public Library and there he began preparation of his journals and reminiscences for the press.

In 1916 Granville was commissioned by the state to write a history of Montana and was at work on this at the time of his death on October 2, 1918, at Missoula, Montana.

Granville Stuart is buried at the city cemetery at Deer Lodge, Montana.

In 1968 Granville was inducted into the National Cowboy Hall of Fame at Oklahoma City, Oklahoma.

The following is a list of the children born to Granville:

- Kate – born at Deer Lodge, Montana, October 9, 1863, died at DHS Ranch, on May 27, 1889.
- Thomas – born on August 22, 1865, died in the mid-1890's.
- Charles – born at Deer Lodge, Montana, November 4, 1867, died in 1952.
- Mary – born at Deer Lodge, Montana, February 2, 1870, died at Lewistown, Montana, in February 1967.
- Elizabeth – born at Deer Lodge, Montana, July 14, 1873, died at Lewistown, Montana, 1903.
- Emma – born at Deer Lodge, Montana, August 18, 1875, died at Helena, Montana, on October 24, 1880.
- Samuel – born at Helena, Montana, August 5, 1877, died in the late 1950's.
- George – born at Helena, Montana, on March 8, 1880, died on April 5, 1880.
- Edward – born at DHS Ranch on July 19, 1881, died on July 4, 1906.
- Harry – born at DHS Ranch, on September 13, 1885, died on June 25, 1906.
- Irene – born at DHS Ranch on September 29, 1888, there is no record of her death.

James C. Stuart

Written by Caroline Stuart Schwerzler, Granddaughter

James C. Stuart was born on May 2, 1839, in Philadelphia, Pennsylvania. He was the son of James and Jennete (Houston) Stuart, natives of the city of Glasgow, Scotland, where they were married. They came to America in 1821. Mr. Stuart traces his ancestral lineage back to the Clan of Stuart. James Stuart (senior) had a successful merchant tailoring business at the corner of 4th and Chestnut Street in Philadelphia until 1847, when his property was destroyed during the religious riots of that year. He often took furs in trade for his tailoring and this proved to be very profitable for him. He moved his family to Dearborn County, Indiana, in 1847 and purchased a farm that was managed and cultivated by his sons while he continued his trade. He was the father of four sons, James C. (Born May 2, 1839), John, Edward and Hugh (1/2 brother), and one daughter, Jennette.

James C. Stuart was eight years old when the family moved to Indiana. He went to public school and assisted in the work at Homestead Farm, the name given to the farm by his mother. When he was old enough to become an apprentice, his father encouraged him to be a cooper. He felt that everyone needed barrels and this should be a profitable occupation. Arrangements were made, but he never followed his trade.

James was 21 years old when he joined the Independent Order of Odd Fellows in Moore Hill, Indiana, in 1860.

When the Civil War started in 1861, he enlisted in the infantry in Company E, Seventh Indiana Volunteer Infantry Division, with the first call for volunteers under Col. Dumont. The regiment was assigned at once to Grafton, West Virginia. Soon his regiment made a night march to Phillippi, West Virginia, and the next day they participated in one of the first battles of the Civil War.

From there they advanced to Cheat Mountain and on to Carrick's Ford on the Cheat River where a battle took place and many of the regiment were killed, including the Orderly Sergeant of the division. His three-month term of enlistment was over. They were returned to Indianapolis and mustered out.

Most of the men reenlisted for a period of three years. James C. Stuart was made Orderly Sergeant of Division A. James was wounded and sent to Mount Pleasant Hospital in Washington, D. C. He remained there for two months. He lost two fingers on his right hand. When he returned to his division, it had been assigned to part of Pope's army and he participated in the second battle of Bull Run.

He was involved in many battles including South Mountain, Antietam, Fredricksburg, Chancellorville and Gettysburg. On May 3, 1864, the army crossed the Rapidan and started on Grant's campaign against Richmond. James was taken prisoner near Hanover and was confined to Andersonville Prison for about seven months.

When he was in Andersonville, all of the men in his tent turned over anything they had of value. Whenever possible, they would tie some of the articles in a handkerchief and put them under the edge of the tent. After a certain length of time they would find a small bag of potatoes. These were scraped and each man received a share. This kept them from getting scurvy. James was 6'4" tall and his usual weight was 200 pounds. He was transferred to another prison camp in Florence, South Carolina. He was weighed in there at 127 pounds and remained here for four months and was suffering from scurvy when he was taken from the prison and sent to Goldsboro, South Carolina, to be exchanged.

On the way to Golodsboro, he was dropped from the train because they thought he was dying. An old Quaker happened by and saw him. He asked him if there was anything he could do for him. James asked for some buttermilk and the Quaker left and said he would try to find some. At sundown he returned and told James there were no cows in the area, but he did bring him a bottle of vinegar water. He stayed all night and fed him a spoonful at a time and the next morning James was able to stand. When the next train came by with soldiers to be exchanged, he was picked up and taken to Goldsboro to be exchanged with the others. He always told his family he had a warm spot in his heart for the Quakers because this one saved his life.

After being exchanged, he was taken to Annapolis, Maryland, and put in the hospital there until he recovered from scurvy. When he had recuperated enough to travel he was sent to Indianapolis, Indiana, where he was mustered out on March 17, 1865 – six months over his enlistment.

His first stop was to visit his family at Homestead Farm before he left with friends from the war to drive a herd of pigs to Illinois. How he used to laugh when he told of this experience! While the details can't be remembered, it was remembered that they had twice as many pigs when they arrived as they had when they started.

After delivering the pigs they went to Quincy, Illinois, and met some fellows who had just returned from Montana with glowing reports about the Territory. They suggested that James go there for his health. He listened and decided to go.

The boat he took on the Missouri River to get to Fort Benton, Montana, was a double-decker. It was February 1866 and it was very cold. The food was not too plentiful, but it didn't take James and his friends long to find out that they could stand in line on one deck and be served and then climb to the other one and get in line again. This worked fine until they were recognized and had to stop.

They no sooner arrived in Fort Benton than they heard that a Col. Bridgewater was hiring men to drive oxen teams to Helena. James applied for a job and was shown a handsome team and told that that was the team he would be driving. He looked all of the teams over and when he had a chance, he marked the team he had been shown. He was told to report early the next morning and was given a scrawny team. Instead of taking it, he went to Col. Bridgewater and told him he had marked the team he was told he was to drive. The Colonel told him if he could show him the marks, he could have the team. The Colonel was as good as his word and James drove the finest team in the outfit to Helena.

He was 27 years old and soon found that everyone had gold fever. It wasn't too long after that he had two mines – one in Hogan and another in Radersburg where, as he put it, he was fairly successful. At this time a Digger Indian came to work in one of his mines and later stayed with him until he died of old age. At the ranch it was his responsibility to furnish meat for the table, but he always found things to do when he wasn't hunting. He taught the children how to make a needle to sew deerskin from the tendon in the deer's leg. And he taught how to skin and dress game. James told the Indian he would always have a home and not to worry because he couldn't do the things he could when he was young. When he was too old to walk he would crawl rather than give up. The Indian was missed when he died.

Four years after James arrived in Montana (1870), he was elected to the Council of the Territorial Legislature as a representative for Lewis and Clark and Jefferson Counties. In politics he was a stalwart Republican.

The formal clothes James wore when he served were preserved in a big trunk along with his Civil War cap and hat. They were taken out to air. His formal coat had satin lapels and a swallowtail. His shirt had pleats in the front and his high silk hat folded down.

He told his children and grandchildren many times that if they were ever tempted to take something to remember that he had turned down a fortune because it wasn't right. He came into the Council Room one day and each desk had $10,000 on it. Water rights for Montana were to be voted on that day, and if you voted against it the money was yours. He said he looked around and saw some of the men taking the money. He decided right then that he would never do business with any of them, but he would always remember who they were. The vote passed.

James remained in Radersburg for fifteen years. On November 17, 1880, he married the schoolteacher, Caroline Maybell. She was the daughter of Doctor and Mrs. Aaron Maybell and was born in Mineral Point, Wisconsin. She was 5' 2" tall.

Robert W. was born on December 1, 1881, in Radersburg. The following year James took some of his earnings from the mines and bought a ranch in Meagher County. They moved to the ranch in 1882 and James started raising cattle. He also tried to start a dairy but this was short-lived because the cattle ate the green onion shoots that grew along the creek where the cows were watered and all of the milk, cream and butter tasted like onions.

Montana became a state on November 8, 1889. James was named the first Postmaster in Townsend. He accepted and moved his family to live there. By this time the family had grown: Robert W., Frank C., Jessie H., and Nella C.

He resigned his post in 1892, sold half of his Meagher County property to James S. Smith and formed a partnership with him and moved to Winston. They opened three general merchandising stores – Winston, Radersburg, and Toston. These proved to be very successful, but due to James's failing health they sold the stores and James returned to the ranch and continued to raise cattle.

James's son, Robert W., liked to tell about the time he was left to watch the store in Winston while his father was away. He was twelve years old and had not been told that it was against the law to sell Indians any product containing alcohol. An Indian came into the store, found him there, and bought some vanilla. Word traveled fast and before long he had sold the entire stock of vanilla and was so happy to tell his father how many sales he had made. Another time he sold some vinegar and he had trouble turning the spigot off. When he finally did, he filled the barrel with water. When James returned, the store smelled like a vinegar barrel and that was the last time Robert stayed at the store.

A son was born to James and Caroline while they lived in Winston. His name was Wilbur W., but he died shortly after he was born. He was buried there and later moved to the family plot and his remains were put in the same grave as his mother's in Townsend. Their youngest child, Alexander (Alex) Theodore, was born on August 24, 1898.

James kept in touch with George Robinson one of the men who came west with him. One day they were riding and found themselves on top of a mountain they called Old Baldy. They looked down on two beautiful valleys. James pointed to one and said, "That is going to be mine and I'll call it Stuart's Basin." George selected another valley and that was known as the Robinson Place. Both had their wish and they each built homes and raised families. George had two sons and a daughter – George, Tom, and Bess. They remained friends all of their lives and the children all grew up at the same time and were good friends.

When the partnership between James and James S. Smith was formed they had it registered in Townsend. They had an underwritten agreement made at the same time that if anything should happen to either of them, their holdings would automatically go to the remaining partner. This proved to be a poor arrangement. Mr. Smith died shortly after James had acquired Stuart's Basin in Broadwater County.

As soon as James heard about the death of his partner, he left immediately for Townsend only to find that a man he didn't like or trust had rushed in and bought Smith's half of the partnership that included the Meagher County ranch. James went to court, hired a lawyer and had him sit at the ranch for over a year. He paid the lawyer $50.00 a day to stay there and keep the man off the property. When the case was finally settled, James bought out the man and later sold the ranch when he made Stuart's Basin his permanent home.

While this was going on he was named to run for the United States Senate. He was so involved with his lawsuit that he couldn't take time to campaign. He lost the election by four votes. A recount was unheard of in those times.

Stuart's Basin consisted of 10,000 acres with a good water supply and a forest on the south mountains. It was located twenty-two miles southeast of Townsend. In order to get there, one had to drive through a canyon. The road was narrow and followed the creek that ran through the ranch. This creek was named Dry Creek because it went underground below the ranch and reappeared in the canyon.

The first house he built in the valley had the feeling of one he probably saw many times when he was in the Civil War. The roof of both the house and the milk house had handmade shakes on them and he made all of these himself by hand. There were barns, runs, chicken coops and a bunkhouse. After the house was completed, he moved his family there from Winston.

While riding around to explore his property, he came across an Artesian spring bubbling up into a small pool under some willows. The water was ice cold and near enough to the creek to make this an ideal spot to build another house. He continued living and raising his cattle at the first location until the other house was finished.

The new house was not as attractive on the outside as the first one, but it had some unique features on the inside. When it was finished he sold the first one to a family from Townsend along with some of the land. They continued raising cattle there when James moved his herd to the new location.

Indians had inhabited this valley long before James ever saw it and they still came back to a Central Council Meeting Ground when the two houses were built and occupied by white men. They were friendly Indians. Robert W. told about going to their camp with his brothers and watching them make their arrowheads. Runners were sent to Yellowstone to bring back flint and obsidian. These stones were put in the fire and heated until they were very hot, then the Indians would fill their mouths with water from the nearby spring and insert a straw between their lips. A drop of water would then fall on the hot stone and it would flake. This was continued until they had the shape and point they desired. They also made needles and sewed their tanned deer hides into garments. They later moved on to another location.

James was the first white man in this area but it wasn't too long after that the government opened up the Territory to homesteaders. Many people from Scotland with large families came to the Territory as settlers. Because James was established, he met many of them when they arrived and housed and fed them until they built their own houses.

The ranch had the only roping corral and branding shoot in the area. This was attached to a large fenced-in area for cattle or horses. Next to this was a long covered shed and another fenced-in area. The barn for workhorses was next and it was attached to one end of the shed. The fenced-in area extended beyond the creek. The barn was divided lengthwise with one side for the horses and the other side for storing hay and grain. Attached to this barn was a smaller one with stalls for the riding horses. A gate opened up into this corral and on the east side of the gate and next to the fence was a long carriage shed. On the wall next to the fence a branding iron for each cattle raiser hung on the wall. There were the usual heavy wagons, but the carriage shed held the nice ones – from the surrey with the fringe on top to the big black carriage with fancy sidelights and leather seats. This was used for special occasions and was pulled by two black horses. Also included was the buckboard and the little buggy used to drive the children to school. A double chicken house was attached to the south end of the carriage shed. On top of the hill, the bunch house, and at the bottom was the root cellar.

On the other side of the creek James had a complete blacksmith shop with the anvil and bellows kept hot and ready to be used at any time. Neighbors brought their horses to be shod – sometimes they needed help and other times they did their own work. The granary was near the threshing machine and the steam engine. The front of the granary had a section used as a carpentry shop and tools were stored there as well.

When everyone started raising wheat as well as their cattle and sheep, James bought the treating machine and steam engine. It was too wide to come through the canyon but the neighbors all got together and widened

James Stuart Ranchhouse at Stuart's Basin. Left to Right: Jesse H. Stuart, Mollie (Maybell) Brown (Caroline Stuart's sister), Nella C. Stuart, Alex Stuart (child in front), Robert W. Stuart, James C. Stuart, Frank C. Stuart and Caroline (Maybell) Stuart – 1905.

the road a foot through the canyon. This equipment was made available to all who needed it and the men helped each other reap their crops.

Caroline decided to start a school for the children in the area. Her own children went to school in Townsend or Winston until they moved to the ranch permanently. The neighbors brought their children in the morning, Caroline taught them and fed them and sometimes kept them overnight if the weather was too severe. When a school district was formed, a schoolhouse built, and a teacher hired, Caroline's school was no longer necessary. She was instrumental in having this come about and the Wall Mountain District was a reality.

James liked people and the doormat was always out to everyone. Many a governor or important official dined at the ranch. He always insisted on having a white tablecloth on the table at dinnertime. Each place had its own napkin ring and a small cut glass salt dish was at each plate. The spoons were kept in a holder in the center of the table along with relish dishes and the vinegar cruet when lettuce was available from the garden.

Caroline made her own butter and cottage cheese. These were chilled in the springhouse at the spring that was cooled by the water running through it. The butter was made in a barrel churn and the children took turns turning the handle. If they helped they could have a glass of buttermilk – which was considered a great treat.

Caroline passed away in 1908 and was buried in Townsend, Montana. After her death, James took their youngest child, Alex, east. They visited relatives and all of the battlefields and places James had been when he was in the war. Alex brought back a box of souvenirs – something from each battlefield.

James C. Stuart died in 1914 and was buried next to his wife in Townsend, Montana.

Andrew Walter Switzer

Submitted by Madge S. Walker, Granddaughter

Andrew W. Switzer (A.W.) was born January 2, 1836, to Tavner Branham Switzer and Susanah Walter in Crawfordsville, Indiana. When Andrew was a young man, the family moved to Calumet, Indiana, where Andrew married Elizabeth Martin. On April 7, 1854, the family left Calumet for Victor, Iowa.

On April 16, 1860, Andrew and his father followed the gold rush to

Colorado. Andrew mined that summer, and in the fall of 1860 he returned to Victor. His father prospected in Colorado until 1865, and then went to Alder Gulch where another gold rush was on. He brought gold from Pike's Peak that he had made into rings for his wife and daughter-in-law, Andrew's wife, Lizzie.

Andrew returned to Montana Territory in 1865, bringing with him his wife, Elizabeth, and four children: Florence age 10; Susie age 8; Tavner (Tim) age 18 months; and May age 6 weeks. He also brought his mother; Lizzie's sister, Mary Walter; his sister, Ellen; and brother Malphus. They left Victor, May 1, and arrived in Alder Gulch on September 30, 1865. The night they arrived, the Indians came to their camp and were very much interested in Susie with her long black hair. So much interested that they offered 40 ponies in trade for her. The next day they went to the Madison Valley to the homestead established by Andrew's father, Tavner B. Switzer.

The following spring Andrew took up a homestead just north of Jeffers, and built a home for his family. The first home was a one-room cabin of hewn logs with one door. Elizabeth told of an Indian sitting down in the doorway and sharpening his knife. She was sure they would all be scalped. When the knife was sharp enough he took a turnip out of his pocket, peeled and ate it. What a relief!

With his father's help, Andrew, planted alfalfa in the spring of 1866 – the beginning of large areas of alfalfa now growing in the valley. They also had the first herd of purebred Jersey cows in the valley. From their milk, his wife made many pounds of butter and cheese for the ready market – providing money to send her girls to school in Virginia City.

Andrew was a very good carpenter, and aside from his home and ranch buildings, he built the first log schoolhouse in the valley on Cedar Creek near the present village of Jeffers. He also made the desks and benches. The Switzers were determined that their children would have an education. He also made coffins when needed, and I can remember seeing him line the inside of a baby's coffin very carefully with white cheesecloth. He also took time out to make stilts for his grandchildren.

In 1875 the IOOF Lodge was active in Virginia City, and Andrew was a charter member. He was always a staunch member of the Episcopal mission. When the Bishop of Montana visited the Trinity Mission he nearly always stayed with the Switzers. In 1902 Andrew, with the help of local craftsmen, built the Trinity Church that still stands in Jeffers.

From 1865 to 1881 the only post office in the area was in Virginia City. When anyone went for the mail they brought it back for all the people in the valley, usually in a seamless sack to Ennis, for distribution. The Switzer home was the center of the community on the east side of the river – a place to visit your friends and perhaps do a little business. In 1903 the Jeffers Post Office, named in honor of M. D. Jeffers, was set up in the M. A. Switzer store. Following other appointments, he was postmaster from 1908 to 1921. This kept him in touch with the public and was work he liked. He had sold his ranch and made his home in Jeffers until his death.

Elizabeth (Martin) Switzer died in 1921 and Andrew Switzer died in December 1926. They are both buried in the Madison Valley Cemetery in Ennis, Montana.

The community lost two wonderful people, and true pioneers. They were parents of Florence Ellen, married to Myron D. Jeffers; Susan Lois, married to J. Burton Jeffers; Tavner Branham, married to Carrie Elizabeth Pickens; Mary (May) Rebecca, married to John L. Hartman; and Nellie Claire, married to B. Judson Bailey.

Tavner B. Switzer

Submitted by Patti Switzer Gibson

Tavner Branham Switzer was born October 12, 1812, in Frankfort Kentucky. He was a farmer and a carpenter, and while quite young, moved to Indiana to make his home. On November 17, 1833, at Crawfordsville, Indiana, he married Susanah Walter. They were the parents of six children – three of whom grew to adulthood and migrated to Montana Territory with them.

On April 7, 1854, Mr. Switzer, his wife, his son Andrew (18), daughter Ellen (9), and son Malphus (6), left their home at Calumet, near Michigan City, Indiana, with two horses and a wagon. They were bound for Iowa. After a few days travel they arrived at Rock Island on the Mississippi. From there they ferried across to Davenport, Iowa. After two days travel (50 miles) from Davenport, they arrived at Iowa City, Iowa. The next day they traveled twenty miles to Marengo, Iowa, and 20 miles the following day to arrive at Victor, Iowa, in Poweshieck County. Tavner bought 160 acres of land from the government and established a home.

In the spring of 1860 gold was found in Colorado, and on April 16 Mr. Switzer and his son, Andrew, started for Pike's Peak near Denver. That fall Andrew returned home to Iowa, while his father stayed in Colorado and looked for gold. In 1863 when gold was discovered in Alder Gulch,

Montana, Tavner Switzer left for Alder Gulch via Gallatin Valley, Montana. It was here that Ray Woodworth, whom he had known in Colorado, and who had been operating a gristmill in Gallatin City, joined him. The men walked, carrying their provisions on their backs, to Madison Valley in 1863. There they were impressed by the prospects for farming. Family records do not reveal their route into the valley, but since they arrived there prior to going to Alder Gulch, it is probable they followed the Old Indian Trail into the north of the Madison Valley.

It is believed after a short stay, the two men went out to inspect the gold diggings in Alder Gulch, and remained one year before deciding their best prospects were in Madison Valley raising food for the mining camp. In 1864 they started for the valley and stayed the first night at the William Ennis cabin where the town of Ennis now stands. The men took up adjoining homesteads near what is now Madison Lake. They grew the first wheat there – threshing it by horses trampling it on the ground. They sold it then for seed wheat, and received 25 cents per pound – sand and all. That first winter the two men lived in a dugout.

In 1865 his family from Iowa joined him. He lived out his life on the original ranch that was added to additional land grants, and was surrounded by his children and their families.

Mr. Switzer was industrious and ambitious, and in addition to having one of the first crops in the Madison Valley in 1866, he made a fanning mill. Some years later he introduced alfalfa to his farmland. In 1880 he brought purebred Jersey milk cows to his ranch. In 1899 he and son Malphus strung a wire three miles long and had the first successful telephone line in the area. This home-constructed and owned phone line soon included the homes of not only their families, but also all their nearest neighbors.

Tavner B. Switzer passed away at his home at the age of 88 years, on December 21, 1900. He is buried in the Madison Valley Cemetery in Ennis, Montana.

George Thexton

Submitted by Donald Thexton, Grandson

George Thexton, son of George and Mary (Wilson) Thexton, was born April 24, 1824, in the township of Levens, Heversham Parish County of Westmoreland, England. When old enough, he served an apprenticeship of seven years to learn the trade of a blacksmith. On April 12, 1855, he married Nancy Redhead, daughter of John Redhead, Esq., and his wife Mary of Bottle-lane, Kirkdale, Liverpool. Nancy Redhead was born at Milnthorpe, Westmorland, on April 20, 1832.

The Thextons immigrated to America in 1855, and settled in Grant County, Wisconsin, at Twelve-Mile house, just north of Galena, Illinois. Mr. Thexton worked as blacksmith until 1864. Five children were born at this location: Margaret in 1856, George in 1857, John Redhead in 1859, Susannah in 1860, and Thomas in 1862. Susannah died in infancy.

George Thexton

In 1864 he heard of the wonderful richness of the placer mines of Alder Gulch, Montana Territory, and decided to go west. In his own words, he said, "I came by Bridger Route, piloted by Mr. McKnight, a French trapper from the North Platte River. We had no trouble with the Indians." He arrived at Alder Gulch July 4, 1864. He further stated, "I found living high and the place overstocked with laborers, but I bought a set of blacksmith tools at Council Bluffs which gave me a chance to start business."

After two years residence at Virginia City, he brought his family out from Wisconsin. In September 1866 he joined a group and returned to the states by boat. The following spring, George, Nancy, and their four children returned to Montana Territory by steamboat to Fort Benton, and from there to Virginia City by ox-team and wagon. The family stopped by the present site of Whitehall for a baby boy to be born. They arrived in Virginia City during the summer of 1867. The baby boy, Joseph, lived only six months.

Mr. Thexton set up a blacksmith machine shop on lower Wallace Street, and also owned and operated the Star Livery Stable that adjoined. He made the first plows ever used in southern Montana out of the spring of a carriage. The first plow was sold to Ray Woodworth of Madison Valley. George received $125.00 for it. Another plow was sold to Raymond Brothers. A third plow was sold on the Gallatin. He made a plow for Henry Buford on Beaverhead. Mr. Thexton made augers and other tools for boring the wooden water pipes for the Virginia City water system.

In 1872 he bought a 320-acre hay and stock ranch in the Madison Valley from Charles Johnson. This formed the nucleus of the ranch called "Thextondale." His cattle brand GT was recorded in 1883. Three more children had been born to George and Nancy Thexton: Annie in 1868, William Long in 1870, and Mary Ann in 1874. The latter two died of diphtheria in December 1878 and January 1879.

On March 23, 1876, Mr. Thexton became a citizen of United States. Later he was elected an Alderman of Virginia City. His eldest daughter, Margaret, became the wife of Thomas Deyarmon, founder of the *Madisonian*. In 1884 his son George Jr. married Miss Charlotte Asselstine, niece of Mrs. R. Caswell of Ruby Valley.

Soon after coming to Virginia City, Mr. Thexton became interested in mining, and discovered and developed the Alameda and Bamboo mines. He sold them in the early 1880's. He built the large stone house on upper

George Thexton residence in Virginia City, Montana – 1889.

Idaho Street, which he completed in 1884. A few weeks after moving into it, his wife Nancy died on January 22, 1885.

In 1886 Mr. Thexton returned to England where he remarried. Upon his return he brought with him his mother-less niece, Agnes Whalley, who made her home with them until her marriage to R. J. Ogden of Sheridan in 1893. About a week after their return to Virginia City, his eldest son, George Jr., died suddenly on September 7, 1886. Just seven weeks later his second son, John, also died suddenly on October 28, 1886. Mr. Thexton's second wife Catherine returned to England after approximately a year or two being unable to withstand the severity of Montana winters.

In about 1888, the family moved to the Madison Valley where he engaged in the livestock business with his son Thomas. In 1894 his daughter Annie married J. A. McAllister of McAllister, Montana. In 1899 Thomas married Mary Ann Foreman, daughter of County Assessor and Mrs. William J. Foreman.

After a long illness, George Thexton died July 5, 1904, at the age of 80. He was at the home of his son, Thomas. He was laid to rest July 7, 1904, beside his first wife, in Hillside Cemetery, Virginia City, Montana, his five children are also buried there. George was a member of the Society of Montana Pioneers.

Thomas Thexton

Submitted by Donald Thexton, Son

Thomas Thexton, son of George and Nancy (Redhead) Thexton, was born March 23, 1862, at Twelve-Mile House, Grant County, Wisconsin, where his father was a blacksmith.

In 1867 at the age of five, Thomas accompanied his parents, sister, and brothers to the Montana Territory. They traveled by steamboat up the Missouri River to Fort Benton. There his father purchased an ox-team and wagon, and the family traveled overland to Alder Gulch via Helena and Three Forks, and up the Jefferson and the Stinking Waters Rivers.

The children sometimes rode, and sometimes walked and played, along the way. They gathered buffalo chips for the fires. The family camped for a while near the present site of Whitehall, where his mother gave birth to a baby boy. They then resumed their journey, arriving in Virginia City in August of 1867, where his father set up a blacksmith shop and livery barn.

Young Tom attended the Virginia City schools and grew to manhood. He enjoyed the exciting life of being raised around an early mining camp. As a boy he did anything he could to earn spending money. He was a carrier boy for the *Madisonian*. He carried the first issue in 1873. He delivered the daily *Madisonian* to the Legislature when it was in session in Virginia City. He peddled milk and herded the city's dairy cows in the hills. On one occasion in 1874, he was thrown from his horse and suffered a broken leg from the accident.

Thomas Thexton

At the time of the Nez Percé War in 1877, when the Indians were moving through the area, families from the surrounding territory and Beaverhead County came to Virginia City for protection. Tom was issued a musket and put on guard duty in the city. His father was also on duty in the campaign that served under the leadership of Callaway.

As a young man, Tom helped his father in the blacksmith shop and livery barn, and worked in the Alameda mine that his father discovered. As well as working, he joined other young people in the activities of the day. He told of dances, church picnics, and revival meetings. He also talked of Fourth of July celebrations and horse racing. In the winter there were parties, coasting, skating, basket socials, home talent minstrel shows, and New Year's Day calling.

Mr. Thexton operated a freight line from Virginia City to Dillon, and from Dillon to Butte, before arrival of the Oregon Short Line. He hauled ore from the Alameda and other mines in the area, to the mills at

Georgia Gulch and Glendale. He also freighted brick from Bozeman, and lumber from Meadow Creek. He hauled hay for the livery barn from Sheridan, paying $20.00 per ton for it, and lumber for the large stone house his father built in 1884.

After his father purchased the ranch in the Madison Valley in 1872, the boys stayed at the ranch occasionally to care for the horses and cattle. However, at the time, the livestock required little care. They grazed on the open range where the hills and benches were covered with tall luxuriant grasses.

In 1888 Thomas, his father, and sister, moved to the ranch in the Madison Valley where they built a fine livestock business and raised Shorthorn cattle, draft and saddle horses, hay, and grain. He shipped horses to New York, New Jersey, Kansas City, and Natchez, Mississippi. The cattle were driven to the railroad at Manhattan and shipped to Chicago. For a number of years he raised horses for the United States Cavalry.

In 1890 Mr. Thexton enlisted in the National Guard of the State of Montana for three years. He was chosen in 1893, to be Marshall of the Day at the Fourth of July celebration, in Virginia City. Thomas was selected as a Republican Delegate from Madison County to the Montana State Convention in Helena, Montana, in 1896.

On December 20, 1899, at St. Paul's Episcopal Church in Virginia City, he was married to Mary Ann Foreman, daughter of the County

Thexton Ranch home built in 1912.

Assessor and Mrs. William Foreman. The young couple went to the Madison Valley where they made their home on the ranch called "Thextondale," and carried on the business started by his father. Six children were born to them: Thomas Leroy, William, Gladys, Annie, Albert, and Donald.

In 1912 the family moved to the large stone house on Thextondale Ranch that Thomas had built for them. Thomas took his family in 1915 to the World's Fair at San Francisco making the journey by train.

Mr. Thomas Thexton joined the Society of Montana Pioneers on August 5, 1917, and was an active member for many years, rarely missing an annual reunion. He was a long time member of the Virginia City Elks Lodge No. 390.

After a long illness Thomas died in Butte, November 8, 1929. He was laid to rest in the Hillside Cemetery, Virginia City, near his parents, brothers, and sister. His wife, Mary Ann, is also buried in Virginia City.

Matilda Dalton Thibadeau

Submitted by Noreen Thibadeau Swanz and Jeanne Thibadeau Biegel, Great-Granddaughters

Matilda Dalton Thibadeau was born at Holton, Maine, on August 28, 1843. Her parents were William and Clara Dalton.

About 1844 or 1845 William Dalton moved his family to Wisconsin where he took up land by Homestead and a Government Land Warrant which was received from the government for services in the war of 1812 and 1814 with England. This land was situated on the Wisconsin River about five miles from what is now Portage City.

They left Wisconsin about 1861 and moved to St. Cloud, Minnesota. William Dalton was a mining engineer and wanted to take his family to Bannack so they joined Captain Fisk's first wagon train at St. Cloud, Minnesota, in 1862.

They arrived at Fort Benton on September 26, 1862, and rested for a week. From there they went to Prickly Pear, near Helena. Prickly Pear was one of the towns, or mining camps, on the Bannack City Express Company's route that started at Great Salt Lake City. After a short time, they then moved to Bannack.

They lived at Bannack a year or so when they traveled to Virginia City where Matilda's father and mother, William and Clara Dalton, died.

They died of what at that time was called the mountain fever. Her parents had caught mountain fever while caring for the sick in the epidemic of 1863-1864. They were stricken and died within two weeks of each other. They are buried on a hill overlooking Virginia City. These two graves are set apart, distinguished and preserved, and their monument bears the inscription "William and Clara Dalton, died January, 1864." William Dalton was a Mason and his funeral was the second Masonic funeral to be held in Montana. In 1972 a new historical marker was placed by their graves in the old mining camp's original cemetery. All of the other graves near them were moved to a new cemetery by relatives but there were no relatives near to move their graves.

Matilda Dalton was one of three girls under twenty on the Fisk Expedition and they all remained friends in Bannack. Matilda Dalton and Carrie Abbot Tyler exchanged letters frequently through the years.

Literary gentlemen called Matilda Dalton "Desdemona," which was a tribute to her youth, charm and beauty. She was a fine, healthy, and active girl who was deeply devoted to her father and mother. She loved to swim and ride horseback.

Matilda (Dalton) Thibadeau. Called "Desdemona" by some of the swains of Bannack. Matilda Dalton was an important and charming figure in the town's social life.

Matilda was left alone by the death of her parents. That following spring at the age of twenty, she married Zebulon B. Thibadeau on April 24, 1864. Mr. Thibadeau was not of French Canadian descent as were so many French settlers in Montana territory. He was of aristocratic lineage, a descendant of Count Anton Claire Thibadeau who came to America with a brother and Napoleon's two brothers.

After Matilda Dalton and Zebulon Thibadeau were married they moved to Oshkosh, Wisconsin, where their three children were born, William Wallace born on February 26, 1865, Estelle (Trask) born on April 17, 1867, and Helena Frances was born on November 10, 1869. Matilda and Zebulon lived in Wisconsin about ten years.

Zebulon Thibadeau died in 1890 and is buried at Wallace, Idaho. Matilda Thibadeau was alone for forty years.

Matilda educated her three children, William Wallace Thibadeau of the Dillon Audit Company, Mrs. Estelle (Thibadeau) Trask who married a mining engineer, and Helena Frances Thibadeau.

She was a member of the Society of Montana Pioneers and attended the Pioneer's Reunion at Anaconda in 1918 for the first time. At the time she attended her last Montana Pioneer's meeting, Matilda and her daughter Helena were living in Couer d'Alene, Idaho. She attended her last meeting in Butte in August of 1931 and was one of two women living who crossed the plains with the first Fisk Expedition.

Matilda Thibadeau died December 16, 1931, at the age of 88, and is buried at Dillon, Montana.

William T. Tinney

Submitted by Rolland L. Tinney

William T. Tinney was born at Cottsmoorhead, Otterham, Launceston, Cornwall, England, on January 2, 1835. He came first to Ontario, Canada, by ship in 1856 at age 21, and then proceeded overland to Beaver Dam, Wisconsin, and on to Strong's Prairie, Adams County, Wisconsin, where his brother Steven was located.

On September 7, 1864, Mr. Tinney arrived in Virginia City, Montana. William made his living in Montana by freighting from Fort Benton to Helena, and from Corinne, Utah, after the Union Pacific Railroad was completed to that point. Part of the time he freighted for the

Walker Bank to Virginia City. The Walker Bank was a Utah concern established in 1859. He also did a little prospecting on the side. When he returned to Wisconsin in 1869, he took gold that was later made into rings for his daughters and pins for his sons.

William married Sallie Lavina Hinman on November 27, 1872, in Wisconsin. Sallie Lavina was born at LaGrange, Wallworth County, Wisconsin, on January 1, 1848. Four children were born to William and Sallie: Albert William, my father (September 12, 1873), Harry J. (Mary 23, 1877), Clara Jane (February 11, 1883), and Flossie Mary (December 17, 1887). All of their children were born at Spring Creek in Adams County, Wisconsin.

When he returned to Wisconsin, he bought a farm and also dealt in cattle that he would buy and then ship west to sell at a profit. He went to Montana, in the fall of 1892, and bought the Pioneer Hotel in Kalispell, which he rented out for $60.00 a month. In the spring of 1893, he had an auction sale in Spring Creek, Wisconsin, and sold all his livestock except three horses and a few milk cows. The remaining livestock and household goods were loaded on a freight train and shipped to Kalispell, which was

William T. and Sallie Lavina (Hinman) Tinney.

then located on the Great Northern Railroad. He sent his son, Albert, on a second-class ticket with the livestock to see that they were fed and to milk the cows.

The family settled on a farm eight miles south of Kalispell, which they rented, but soon moved to another rental closer to town. About that time, the people who rented the hotel got behind in their payments, so William's family moved in to take it over. Some of the linens and silver are still in existence today. The girls, Clara and Flossie, remembered the daughter of C.E. Conrad being driven to school each day, dressed in furs, in a buggy behind magnificent horses, and with a uniformed driver.

Left to Right: Albert William and Harry James Tinney, children of William and Sallie Lavina Tinney.

Albert had stayed on the rented farm for a year and then started venturing toward eastern Montana. In 1898 both Albert and William took up land north of Saco. In due course Sallie Lavina and the girls arrived from Kalispell where the hotel and other holdings had been sold. The oldest daughter, Clara, became a teacher in the first Saco school in 1902. William was one of the first to be buried in the Saco Cemetery.

William died on June 17, 1901, at his ranch north of Saco. His wife Sallie Lavina died on September 23, 1935, in Camas Hot Springs, Montana, and both William and Sallie are buried in the Saco Cemetery.

Following is a portion of Mr. Tinney's diary outlining his trip from Omaha, Nebraska, to Virginia City, Montana, May 10–September 7, 1864.

There are also some journal entries through November 1865. Everything is written as Mr. Tinney wrote it.

En route for Idaho 1864:

May 1864

10   We crossed the Missouri at Omaha. Cold windy weather we went 5 miles out from Omaha and camped for the night It was a cold night it rained the ice was nearly 1/2 inch thick
11   we drove about 12 miles today and Windy
12   we went about 6 miles Camped on a Stream called Elk river very fine weather
13   fine weather traveled 14 miles We laid up 3 days at Fremont weather dry and fine.
19   Traveled 15 miles Camped at north Bend
20   13 miles good day for driving dry with good breeze of wind. Camped 2 miles from Shell Creek.
21   Traveled Weather dry and fine it blew hard wind storm in the evening after we went to Bed. We had to git up and hold our tent from blowing away
22   We got our wheel set and crossed the Lute fork ferry went about one mile and camped

Saco, Montana – circa 1900.

Tinney Ranch north of Saco, Montana – 1913.

23	Traveled rather windy with light rains and hale storms Camped on the Bend of Plat Wood water and grass
24	Warm and dry traveled twenty miles
26	we went about 18 miles weather dry and very warm
27	we traveled 18 miles
28	Quite a hot day traveled about 20 miles camped across the river oposit from Fort Kerney
29	5 miles camped 200 miles from Omaha
30	fine weather Camped on Buffalo Creek
31	Cold and windy Some Bluffs sandy roads

<u>June 1864</u>

1	very cold and Windy
2	passed Low sandy Bluffs extending to the river very sandy roads. Traveled 270 miles
3	good day for driving. Crossed Skunk Creek and one good Spring rather sandy Camp on the North Platte
4	Cross black mud Creek and a small Creek fine weather
5	Sunday Laid over about one mile from the North Bluff fork We spent the day in hunting seen some antelope did not get a shot at any of them Weather fine and pleasant

6	Cross north Bluff Fork weather Cold, sandy Bluffs west foot Sandy Bluffs East foot Bluff Creek 4 feet wide 1 foot deep Bluff Creek spring
7	Crossed Goose Creek and several small Creeks road sandy weather rather cold
8	Laid over one in our Train broak a wagon wheel we took a ramble out in the Bluffs very hot day rain in the evening
9	Cross Wolf Creek and some sand Bluffs good day for driving
10	fine weather Traveled 398 miles
11	Cold and squally cross Watch Creek Ash hollow on the south side the river Castle Creek and Castle Bluffs rain in the evening
12	Sunday Cold Blustry winds Cross Crab Creek very windy and rain and our Cattle Stampead in the night and did not git them till noon Monday drove and Camped at ancient Bluffs wind and rain We Climed the bluffs and got some wood Drove our cattle on the island Laid in our tent sun songs while it rained and blowed Thus we passed the 13 day of June on the Plains
14	Cloudy in the morning good for driving
15	Weather fine roads soft and Mudy Camped oposit Chimley Rock
16	Weather fine roads mudy
17	roads a little Better fine weather
18	fine weather Traveled 506 miles
19	Sunday a very hot day Camped on rawhide Creek A very heavy hale Storm in the evening some hale fell nearly as large as hens eggs
20	very warm drove 6 miles camp 6 miles from Laramie great many wagons Camp here to night we had a dance in the evening
21	very warm I went to Laramie drerie rair in the even
22	here the road Leaves the river and goes through the Black hills pass spring at noon wagon wheel Broke left part of our Train behind Camp on the river roads very rough and hilly had to double
23	road leaves the river warm weather roads rough Camped at spring in the black hills about one hundred and twenty five wagons Camp here it Looks Like a villige to see the camp fires burning in the evening
24	We Laid over to rest our Cattle very warm day I had to go on gard the first part of the night for the first time on the trip
25	drove to the river rather winding roads good
26	Sunday good day for driving Grass has been scarce about a week

27	only at the Spring Traveled 602 miles
27	Some very rough road very hot day 69 head horses Drove off by the Indians about day Light that was camped near by us they was bound for navada
28	Some of our train Laid over as their was one of their men sick thair was another stamped about 5 miles from where we camped the Indians Came within a few rods of the camp jump off their Ponys untied some horses and droved off 27 the Emagrants followed them 3 miles in the bluffs got a fight with them and had to retreat then Was sopose to be about 25 or 30 indians and seven white men the Indians shot one horse and one ox But not hurt Bad the report came to us at noon that the party whare we camped catched up with the indians 7 miles in the Bluffs shot 2 of them the indians Wounded one man and killed one horse But did not git any of thare horses Came back got reinforcements recaptrued 28 horses and Mules killed three indians Tellagraphaed to Laramie for Soldiers to follow the indians 28 day of June in the Plains and in the Black hills
29	fine weather the roads rather sandy Pass Deer Creek soldiers Camp here on the south side of the river
30	Quite a hot day roads sandy pass the lower Platt bridge

July 1864

1	quite warm roads sandy and hilly pass the upper Bridge Camped on the river 7 miles above the Bridge
2	here we leave the river roads some hilly fine weather here we pass Briger Cutouff we had Quite a contest about which rout to take one wagon turned to go on the Cutoff Could not git any to follow him so he had to Turn Back Drove Camped at Willow Springs
3	roads some sandy Weather fine Camped at independence rock on the sweet water military Post here We spent the fourth of July at independence rock quite a pleasant day Traveled 707 miles
5	fine weather roads sandy and Level mountains on each side road runs along sweet water Creek Camped one mile from sage creek
6	Cold windy day Cold enough to were a over coat in the morning roads Levell and sandy Pass 3 Crossings here the Sweet water runs Between rocky Bluffs Camped one mile from the military Post I stand gard to night rather cold night

7	we came in sight of the Snowey range this morning the mountains was covered with Snow one of our boys killed Elk fine weather
8	Weather fine Laid over and went about 15 miles and packed in the Elk Which was a hard days work
9	fine weather roads hilly in the afternoon
10	Sunday morning frosty it has Been quite Cold and windy for some time the roads has been rough and hilly Cross 2 Branches of the Sweet water and Strawberry Creek Traveled 802 miles
11	roads good Weather quite Pleasant Past milatary Post at the Cut off one steep decent ware we strike the sweet water camp
12	on Sweet water Crossed stream 25 feet Camp on small still Creek I hard to night Camp on Big Sandy
13	Noond on Bare Creek 5 miles Camp on a small Creek
14	quite warm with Snow clad mountains on each side Camp on green river no water on the road
15	Laid over at green river a very warm day
16	noond at the 3 fork of Green river 8 miles Camped on a fork of Green river
17	I Left the train this morning and I Cross the Mountains at Sun Set I had to break ice to get a drink of water A little after dark I started a fire thinking to have some sleep the wind Blew and the fire ran and I being Cold haveing no Coat I did not sleep But got up and traveld ontill Late in the night then I started a fire and stoped till day Light
18	I traveled through the Mountains all day seeing no game But Bearies Plenty of Bare tracks and sines of other game in the evening I came in sight of a valley I made my way to that valy about dark Laid down to sleep I had no matches to start a fire it being Cold I could not sleep so I traveled most all night
19	very Cold frosty morning I traveld till about noon then I cam in sight of the road about eight miles off I traveld about three Miles at the foot of the Bluffs I Being tired and haveing nothing to Eat and scarcely any sleep for too nights I Laid down and sleep Before I went to the road to have any thing to eat I Came on the road about three oclock Tuesday afternoon I Being ahead of my Train I Walked 6 miles Back the road that evening got some supper and Camped with a train from Missouri I was in the mountain from Sunday morning Till Tuesday afternoon I saw snow six feet deep

20	I went back 15 miles to met my Train But they did not git in over the mountains till the next day about noon They did not expect to see me any more
21	We traveld they traveld 67 miles thru the mountains While I was away from them We had a heavy shower Tuesday afternoon
22	very warm Camped at the Lower end of the valley
23	a very warm roads very rough thru the hills and ravines up hill and down rain in the evening Sunday fine weather rough roads in the forenoon past numbers of Cold springs Camped 3 miles from a large marsh at a Spring
25	Cloudy some rain during the day Passed Blackfoot at the Forks of Soda Springs and salt Lake Oregon west Bannack and east Bannack and Landers cut off we take the East Bannack and Virginia road Traveled 1002 miles
26	fine weather rather Cloudy heavy shower in the evening
27	a very pleasant day
28	very hot and sultry Noond seven miles from snake river afternoon Crossed snake river ferry Camp on the west Side
29	very warm we Traveled about 8 miles up Snake river
30	Laid over weather dry and hot
31	Sunday hot 4 miles slue water for stock not fit for use 8 miles Further we got water for our out of some holes that was dug and stoped over night

<u>August 1864</u>

1	A very hot day we traveled threw a very Berran Country nothing but Sage Brush and Sand
2	very Warm roads great deal Better Came to some Poor Water about noon Camp on a Creek Traveled 1104 miles
3	quite pleasant today we traveled Through the hills Pritty good road We Crossed the deviding Ridge to day
4	Warm and Pleasant Pass the Juncion ranch here we take right hand foad for virginia Camped on Sage Creek
5	Dray and warm roads rough in the afternoon Camped on the Black Tail Deer Creek
6	Dry and warm roads rather rough
7	fine Weather Camp in sight of Navada City Traveled 1200 miles
8	We Crossed over Came Threw Virginia City Went four miles at the Island and Camped we Could not go go any farther with our

15	wagon We staid here till the 12 then we moved up at Pine Grove Commenced Work for five dollars Per day Work tooWeeks I Received Pay $60.00 Pay for Packing 4.50 I received for Crockes and Cags 1.62
29	Bought of Dodson and Cook, Claim No. 51 Below Summet Paid $300.00

September 1864

2	Down one 100
3	Received out of the Claim $20.00
10	Paid for Beef 5.28
11	Received out of the Claim 25.00
12	Heavy Snow Storm
18	Received from the Claim 15.00 Paid for frying pan .88 Money Paid out 1 shirt 2.00 for screws .23 Thread .30 W ky 3.00 key 3.12 Patees (Potatoes) 2.15 Trunk by express 3.50
24	Received from the Claim 25.00
25	Myself John a Ellis and f Rockwell left Virginia City on a Honting Expedation

October 1864

14	This Being the night of the 14 of October and I Being alone I will Set down a little about our Journey

We went on the Jefferson about 40 miles did not see much game on the 28 a mountaineer Camp with us the next morning We started back 6 miles that night f R. killed too deer Ellis did not Come to Camp that night the next day we killed one antelope and started for Bennack arrived their the 5th Ellis and Rockwell started the next day for Big hole. I started the day after on Friday the 7 went about 12 miles and Camp alone I Came to the other Boys the next night they had got one antalope Camp here day... we see some moose but did not kill any Tuesday went farther down Wednesday Ellis and f Rockwell started in persuite of game and I stopped with the teem Camp alone Thursday night Rockwell Came Back in sarch of their Ponies which had strayed from them and Started again in the morning my Cattle having strayed away that night I did not find them till noon Ellis and Rockwell having seen some moose and had shot at them while

	they was away I yoked up my Cattle started on did not find Ellis and Rockwell that night I traveled till after dark stoped build a fire Cooked some Supper and spent the evening alone
15	this morning I went about 5 miles down the Creek found the Boys They had killed one Moose But did not take care of the meat till they had found there Ponys and most of the meat was Spoiled Rockwell went to the maintains in search of game, did not git any Last night R killed a wolf at the carcass of the moose and Ellis and him is watching for them again to night I moved my wagon 3 miles down the Creek and camp alone again to night
16	This morning a wolf made his aperence close to my Camp so that I had a shot at him By the time I had him Skined Jack and red Came up with some fox an wolf which they had Caught that night we youke our cattle and started for Bennack and fred Rockwell went Back where they Camped The Night before as he said he had not got anough of them Jack and I went about 10 miles and camped for the night and started again Monday morning Jack Beeing on horseback went on ahead and saw too moose I got up about three oclock and advised him to Camp thair that night and try them later in the morning So we Camp for thie night and killed too the next day and it took us all day to dress and take Care of them in the evening fred Came up with his Prey 3 foxes an a wolf the next morning we started for Bannack again and got in on Saturday the 21 day of October it ws giting Late in the fall and we had beeing Camping out ever since the first of April on Sunday morning we started for the woods after logs to build a Cabin (about 12 miles) it being late and our wagon broke we did not git down with a load that night Came down to Bannack and went back again in the morning and Wednesday fred and I went after a load and Camped up at the mountain over night

November 1864

3	we got our house up so as to move our things in and sleeped in it it being the first time we had slept in a house since we left
25	I camed at dies mill and went after wood the next day and stoped at the mill on my way Back and got into Bannack Sunday Fred and I goes Back to the mill that night and Commenced drawing Wood with Dies Cattle on Monday the 28 day of Nov.

January 1865
4   I Left Bennack Camped at rattlesnake the 5th went to Big hole
6   went to Sayarses and stoped over night
7   got to Virginia

November 1865
27   Bought of David McKoll one yoke of Cattle and one hundred and forty dollars Johnson commenced work worked for 55 dollars a month 7 days commenced work for 3 dollars a day

Poem in Journal:

I Smoke My Last Cigar

It was off the Blue Canary Isles
One glorious summer day
I sat upon the quarterdeck
And swept my cares away.

And as the smothered smoke arose
Like incense in the air
I breathed a sigh to think in short
It was my last cigar.

I learned upon the quarter rail
And looked down in the sea
And then the wreath of purple smoke
Was curling gracefully.

Oh what had I at such a time
To do with waiting care
Alas the trembling tear proclaimed
It was my last cigar.

Martin Trepp

Submitted Thelma M. Dorris, Granddaughter

Martin Trepp was born in Nufenen, Granbunden, Switzerland, on February 22, 1843, in a typical Swiss, stone home. The home is still standing and is used to this day. It is now about 300 years old. Martin had five brothers and two sisters, Georg, born November 30, 1828; Susanna, born November 13, 1829; Christian, born November 1, 1831; Hans Martz (John M.) born January 12, 1834; Michael, born June 19, 1836; Elizabeth (Lizzie), born December 22, 1837; and David, born June 1, 1841.

All of Martin's brothers except David had immigrated to America. His older brother, Michael had settled in Council Bluffs, Iowa, where he was a baker specializing in cake decorating. In 1864 Martin left Switzerland and joined Michael in Council Bluffs. That same year, they crossed the plains together by ox team and arrived in Virginia City, Montana. Michael was the cook for the expedition.

The trip was an arduous one, but completed safely. The Indians paid the immigrants several visits, uninvited, and each time there was danger and

Martin and Anna (Fimian) Trepp.

Trepp home in Nufenen, Switzerland.

some fear. It was never known what their mission might be, peaceful or warlike. One time a brass band that was organized from the membership of the expedition charmed the Indians so that they went away without molesting the emigrant train or the expedition. A Mormon minister was one of the immigrants. On a later occasion, a band of Indians on the warpath were appeased by this minister "pow wowing" with them and inducing them to go on their way.

The two brothers landed in Confederate Gulch, Diamond City, Montana, which was reputed to have the richest gold bar in the world. Somehow, Martin and his brother obtained 100 feet of this rich bar. They sluiced and panned $30,000 in 30 days, and then the claim washed out. Despite this good fortune they never returned to mining.

With the profit from their mining venture, they were able to go into the horse and cattle business on a large scale at a ranch they bought in the Missouri River Valley near Townsend, Montana. This ranch is still known as the Trapp (Trepp) Ranch today. The Trepp brand for cattle was OTO, branded on the left hind flank. The brand for horses was a letter T on top of letter O with a bar placed underneath the brand to indicate the animal had been sold. The brothers raised horses, including racehorses, on a large scale. Their "stable" ran at fairs, annually at the territorial fair (later state fair) in Helena. They won so often that a common expression was "Trepp brothers could put a cow on the track and win."

In 1882 Martin's older brother, David, sent a photograph of his family in Switzerland to Martin. This picture was of David, his wife Margaretha Grischott Fimian Trepp, his stepdaughter Anna Fimian (1857-1919), and David's own five daughters. David was twelve years younger than Margaretha. Upon seeing the family photo, Martin declared he would go to Switzerland and marry David's stepdaughter.

After an absence of 19 years, he returned to Switzerland. When Martin met Anna, it was love at first sight. After a short courtship, they became engaged and were married in Switzerland. They made the trip across the Atlantic in an old steamboat. Accompanying Martin and Anna were David's daughter Rosina Trepp, and John, David's nephew.

They returned to Montana via New York by train and were met in Montana by Michael. The newlyweds made their home in a large two-story frame, log house at the Tolson Ranch. Four October births followed: Elisa Christina (Lizzie) in 1884, David Martin in 1885, Margaret Charlotte in 1886, and Elsbeth Anna (Elsie) in 1891.

About a year after Martin was married, Michael went to Switzerland on a like mission. The first child born to he and his wife was born in early spring 1886. A second child died when she was two years old. Michael's wife had an operation, at the ranch, for kidney trouble and did not recover.

In 1885 David and Margaretha along with daughters Margaret,

Martin Trepp and "Team."

Betty, Mary, and Nina left Switzerland and moved to Montana. After spending a considerable amount of time with his brothers Michael and Martin, they moved to the Judith Basin, Little Rock Creek, about 14 miles west from where Lewistown now stands.

David and Margaretha's daughters married as follows: Rosina married John Branger, Margaret married Peter Yegen, Anna Marie's (Mary) first husband was William A. Shaules and her second husband Jacob Weistaner, Christina (Nina) married Anton King, and Elsbeth (Betty) married Joe King.

The 1870 and 1880 censuses both show their last name spelled as Trapp. A bill of sale for cattle shows the Trapp spelling. It is uncertain when it changed to Trepp.

Although there were a large number of Indians living nearby, the brothers were on friendly terms with most of them. However, one day when Martin was alone on the ranch, lying in bed with a broken leg, he heard the approach of a large band of marauding Indians. A number of white men had been killed and scalped. A terrified Martin managed to hobble to the hayloft where he watched the braves steal all of his horses. This was a considerable loss for the Trepps. Not long after the raid, friendly Indians, including their chief, returned all the stolen horses – a demonstration of their friendship.

The hard winter of 1886-1887 resulted in the loss of about 80 percent of the Trepp range stock. Cowboy artist Charles Russell also created his first painting that memorable winter. The painting was first titled *Waiting For a Chinook* and later called *The Last of 5,000*. Russell was a

Trepp Ranch 12 miles from Lewistown, Montana.

frequent visitor to the Trepp Ranch where dances were a favorite pastime for cowboys and ranch hands for miles around. Russell rode the "Shonkin Circle," Judith Basin, along with Joe King, Martin Trepp, and their cowhands.

On March 30, 1893, Martin was visiting his ill brother, David, on the other side of Little Rock Creek. By two o'clock in the afternoon the creek had risen and became a roaring river. This pioneer of the 60s, having crossed such rivers as the Missouri and the Yellowstone, could not be dissuaded from crossing the creek. While his terrified brother, Michael, watched from shore, Martin and his horse were swept into the raging river. Martin was swept through two wire fences and disappeared around the bend of the creek. Although the horse made it out, Martin, tragically drowned. His body was recovered half an hour later.

Martin's funeral in Lewistown was the largest to that date. He was buried in the Lewistown Cemetery. Martin provided well for the family he left behind.

After Martin's death, Anna Trepp sold the ranch and cattle and moved to Lewistown to raise her children. Four years later (1897) Anna married James Corcoran. Corcoran Street is named after him. Twin

Trepp Family. Left to Right: David Martin, Anna, Elisa Christina "Lizzie", Elsbeth Anna "Elsie", picture of Martin Trepp and Margaret Charlotte.

daughters were born in 1899: Mable Lily and Myrtle Rose. James died in 1905, leaving Anna a widow once again. Anna Fimian Trepp died August 9, 1919, and was buried in Lewistown, Montana.

David Tuttle (father of Sherman "Doc" Tuttle).

Lucinda (Cornwall) Tuttle (wife of David Tuttle).

Sherman "Doc" Ferson Tuttle

Submitted by Terry Aileen (Tuttle) Maple, Great-Granddaughter

Sherman F. Tuttle was born in on July 21, 1848, in Noble County, Indiana, one of 13 children of David and Lucinda (Cornwall) Tuttle. He weighed only three pounds at birth – his bed a cigar box. The family did not dress him for several days after his birth, thinking that he would not live. It was amazing that he did survive at that weight, as it is a struggle even today for infants that small.

In 1849, the family moved to Iowa where Sherman, at an early age, received the nickname "Doc" which stuck the rest of his life and fit him well in later life. He was called upon many times to doctor or nurse the sick in Fish Creek, Montana. Once during a severe scarlet fever epidemic he had so many patients that he was swamped. Fearing that he was not doing everything he should, he traveled horseback to Butte, a distance of 30 miles, to consult with a physician. The doctor told him "you are doing fine – I would not have done anything differently."

In 1862 the Tuttle family crossed the plains to Denver and then headed North. Doc's older brother Terry went on the Oregon Trail to

Elgin, Oregon. David, Lucinda and the rest of the children (Phebe, Luther, Catherine, Harvey, Ruth, Elihu (Elec), Francis, Sherman (Doc), Hanna, Harrison, David and Miles) arrived in Virginia City in July 1864.

After a short, unproductive attempt at mining, David, Lucinda and the younger sons (Luther, Harvey, Elihu, Francis, Doc, Harrison, David and Miles) moved to the Fish Creek area to take up farming. A younger brother, Harrison (Hatch) cut and hauled logs and Doc peeled and hewed them to build a cabin for the family. Doc was considered one of the best ax men in the country.

Sherman "Doc" and Derinda (Butts) Tuttle.

After the homestead was established, Doc decided to branch out on his own. He took a small herd of cows to Butte and started a dairy in 1868. The irony of this venture was that his cattle corrals were built over what later became one of the richest zinc mines in the Butte area – the Black Rock Mine.

On January 15, 1870, Doc's father, David Tuttle, died and Doc came back to Fish Creek to help his mother run the farm. After his return home he met Derinda Butts. She had been going with his brother Harve and had laughed at his funny little brother Doc. But Doc overcame her amused indifference and they were married on March 15,1873.

Doc's financial status was not very good at the time and he borrowed $10.00 to pay the preacher. In later years when Derinda fussed about the financial status of the prospective sons-in-law, they reminded her of Doc's poor start and later fair financial success.

Doc took his bride into the family home and they leased some ground to plant grain. The crop looked promising, but grasshoppers wiped it out in one night. Financially ruined, he hired out as a day laborer, barely getting by with loans from his thrifty brother Elec.

The summer of 1874 brought another poor crop so they Doc and Derinda moved to Pipestone Creek for a placer mining venture with his brother Luther and his wife Ann (Hoblett). It was a fair success, but Luther's wife Ann was not enamored with such a forsaken place. After finding her 3-year-old child chasing a rattlesnake, she and Luther returned to Iowa. During this mining venture, Doc didn't have a horse so he walked eight or nine miles each week to Fish Creek Store – carrying supplies from the store on his back.

The crops improved and with profit from the mining venture Doc went back to the farm where, with his brother Elec, they went into the dairy and cheese business. The two men milked 40 cows – 20 apiece. If one of them happened to be gone, it meant one man had to milk 40 cows as there were no milking machines in those days. It was during this period they started a side business of keeping travelers. Mrs. Tuttle's excellent cooking soon earned a wide reputation and often cooked an extra meal for 12-14 people. Sherman was appointed postmaster for the area about this time.

Sherman "Doc" Tuttle Family home in Whitehall. Left to Right: Derinda (Butts) Tuttle with Julian Errett Tuttle, Lulu (Tuttle) Wellin, Ada (Tuttle) Moore and Earl Tuttle – 1897.

The dairy and cheese business must have proven quite successful for they gradually branched out into the cattle business and finally dropped the dairy business. Doc formed the "Tuttle Brothers Cattle Company" with brothers Elec and Hatch. It lasted many years without any squabbling. The bond between them was very close and they were fair and honest with each other. The cattle were shipped from Fish Creek every winter to the lush grasses of the Judith Basin. The cattle were wintered, fattened and then shipped to meat packing centers in Chicago or Kansas City. Doc's oldest son, Arthur, was sent to ride the range in the winter of 1886-1887 – one of Montana's harshest winters. It was said after that losses were so heavy that along drifts where the cattle died, a man could have walked for miles on the carcasses of the dead animals. Jesse Phelps, owner of the OH Ranch, received a letter from Louie Kaufman, one of the biggest cattlemen in the country. When Kaufman heard the cattle were dying, he wrote to ask how the cattle were doing. Charles Russell, the cowboy artist, was riding range for the OH Ranch at that time and drew a postcard-size sketch to send and titled it *Waiting For A Chinook*. Later the subtitle *The Last of Five Thousand* was added to the sketch. Years later, Charles Russell recreated the sketch into a larger size painting.

Sherman "Doc" Tuttle Family at Boulder, Montana. Left to Right: Back Row: Ada, Claude, Arthur, Earl, Sherman and Lulu. Front Row: Sherman "Doc", Cora, Errett and Derinda.

In 1900 Doc was elected Jefferson County Treasurer and the family moved to Boulder where they bought the Belcher Stock Ranch. This ranch provided a better cattle range and shipping center.

In 1907 the ranch was sold and Doc and Hatch bought the controlling interest in the Bank of Boulder. Doc was President and his oldest son Arthur was Assistant Cashier. The bank was a good, profitable institution but like many of the small banks credit was too free to new settlers. Hatch had moved to Pomona, California but returned to Boulder when he heard that many loans were being made that he had opposed. Doc got the bank in better shape, but a second blow hit. For political reasons, county officers withdrew their personal as well as county money and deposited it in the Whitehall Bank – supposedly to garner more votes from Whitehall. Reserves for the Boulder Bank fell below the amount required by law, and it appeared the Bank would have to default. Doc found a group of wealthy businessmen in Butte willing to take over the Bank. The new bank collected most of the outstanding debts and realized far more than they ever thought was possible. But when the bank holiday came in 1933, they chose to close entirely. Each depositor got every cent they had coming – with interest.

Ranch and residence of Tuttle brothers in Fish Creek, P.O., Montana.

Sherman F. Tuttle died October 23, 1927, at the age of 79. He and Derinda had 11 children – nine who lived to be adults. One baby died at the age of 9 months and one son, Frank, died at the age of 13 when a horse fell on him. Doc, Derinda and many of the family are buried in the Fish Creek Cemetery.

Earl Tuttle, of Whitehall, Montana, was the 5th son of Doc and Derinda and my grandfather. Ferson Earl Tuttle was my father, the eldest son of Earl.

I respectfully submit this history of my Montana pioneer ancestor with thanks to Roy Milligen of Whitehall, Montana, who recorded much of this history from my father.

Otis Crocker Whitney

Written by W.C. Jeffers, Family Friend
Submitted by Amy Orser Swoboda, Great-Granddaughter

Otis Crocker Whitney was born in Whitneyville, Maine, in 1815. Mr. Whitney came to Alder Gulch in July 1864, by way of Wisconsin, Minnesota, and Colorado. Shortly after arriving in Alder Gulch, the Whitney's and Mrs. Whitney's daughter, Miss Zelpha Parks, moved to the Madison Valley.

Whitney home location two miles east of Ennis on O'Dell Creek, built circa 1875.

The Whitneys had used cattle to draw their wagons across the plains and these cows formed the nucleus of the dairy herd that they expanded to thirty-five head of cows. Butter was selling at $1.00 a pound in the latter 1860's and it is said Mr. Whitney sold 5,000 pounds in one year.

He was the first man to raise barley in the valley. His first crop went 80 bushels to the acre and sold for 25cents per pound. He brought the first bull, a purebred Durham, into the valley. He also bought a bunch of mustang mares that were the first working stock of the valley.

Otis Crocker Whitney

Mr. and Mrs. Whitney had lost four sons, before arriving in Alder Gulch. Their family consisted of Thomas H., Emma O, and Ellen Maria, all born on the Madison Valley home place. This was about two miles east of Ennis. It is still known as "The Whitney Place" and is now owned by Paul Love.

Otis C. Whitney conducted a ferryboat business across the Madison River in the latter 60's and early 70's. In 1871 he built the first bridge to span the Madison River. It was made from huge logs. A toll to cross was charged for two years. Otis and the county were about to close a deal on the bridge when it was washed out and he lost several thousand dollars.

In the fall of 1871 Mr. Whitney was elected as representative of the territorial legislature of Montana, which convened in Virginia City, then a territorial capital. The assembly met from December 4, 1871, until January 12, 1872.

In the early eighties, Mr. and Mrs. Whitney took two small children to raise. They were Georgia and Osborn Baker Wingate, children of Thomas Wingate of Virginia City, whose wife had died.

Mrs. Whitney died in July 1892 and Mr. Whitney died on September 19, 1892. Their last resting place is the Evans Cemetery east of Jeffers.

Thomas H. Whitney

Written by Winifred Jeffers, Family Friend
Submitted by Amy Orser Swoboda, Grandneice

Thomas "Tom" was the son of Mr. and Mrs. Otis C. Whitney, who arrived in Alder Gulch, Montana Territory, in 1864. He was born on the home ranch in Madison Valley in February 1866. The place is still called "The Whitney Place" and is about two miles east of Ennis.

Tom Whitney

Tom attended local schools and helped his father with the ranch work. Otis C. Whitney bought a bunch of mustang mares in the early days. This was the first band to be brought to the valley. From this stock came the horses that provided the working stock of the valley. Here the bronc-busting careers of the riders of Madison Valley began. Tom Whitney, Joe and Jack

Spray, Harry and Will Thompson were among those bronc-busters.

Tom married Ida Thompson, daughter of Mr. and Mrs. Ben Thompson, and sister of Harry and Will. Tom and Ida were parents of four boys and two daughters, Arthur, Earl, Asa, Cecile, Audra and Carl. The family moved to Canada in 1903, and returned here in 1905. Ida died here in 1907. Tom went back to Canada and located in the Cypress Hills near Maple Creek, Saskatchewan, where he acquired extensive holdings, and where he established the family home.

Utilizing the knowledge of the cattle business he gained on the Madison, he became a "big" cattleman of that area and for years was roundup captain. His boys and their sons were known all over western Canada for their prowess as bronc riders, rodeo performers, and horse handlers.

He turned his ranch holdings over to his sons and came back to the Madison for a few years where in 1920 he and Elizabeth Jarrett were married. Tom took his wife back to Canada to live and had a family of one son, Thomas Jr., and a daughter, Betty.

The home ranch in the Madison Valley was leased until 1946 when Paul Love bought it.

In Tom's later life he became known as a teller of tales of the Old West, and of his personal contacts with both the good and the bad of early Montana days. No little detail escaped his telling and he held his listeners spellbound.

Tom's marriage to Elizabeth was dissolved and he continued to live in Maple Creek, Saskatchewan. He died on May 25, 1952, following a lengthy illness and was buried in Maple Creek, Saskatchewan, Canada. He was cheerful to the end.

Funeral services were conducted in Maple Creek, following Tom's earlier request that they sing "The Old Rugged Cross" and "Home on the Range". Thus passed one of Madison Valley's colorful characters.

Fort Benton, Montana, head of navigation on the Missouri River. Northwest Fur Company on the right with the large steamboat, the Luella, on far left and the smaller steamboat, Tom Stevens, on the right. Photographer: A. S. Addy. (Courtesy of the Schwinden Library – Montana Agricultural Center, Fort Benton.)

Freight waiting to be transported to points in Montana Territory by Coulsen Freight Company. The gentleman in the white shirt and tie is Col. Clendenen, Manager for Coulsen Steamboat Company. Col. Clendenen later had mining interests in the Neihart area. Some of the places mentioned were Gold Run, Clendenen, Hughesville and Barker Mining District. He was killed in a mining accident. (Courtesy of the Schwinden Library – Montana Agricultural Center, Fort Benton.)

Mule team with T. C. Powers & Bro. – circa 1860s. (Courtesy of the Schwinden Library – Montana Agricultural Center, Fort Benton.)

St. Mary's Mission, Stevensville, Montana. Established in 1841. (Courtesy of Rod Johnson)

Bannack, First Territorial Capital which hosted the first territorial legislative session in December, 1864. (Courtesy of Jack Weidenfeller.)

Virginia City. Territorial Capital moved to Virginia City in 1865. (Courtesy of Jack Weidenfeller.)

Garnet – circa 1880. (Courtesy of Jack Weidenfeller.)

St. Ignatius. (Courtesy of Jack Weidenfeller.)

Anaconda and Old Works. (Courtesy of Jack Weidenfeller.)

Marysville – 1889. (Courtesy of Jack Weidenfeller.)

Hoyt Store, Ovando – 1894. (Courtesy of Jack Weidenfeller.)

N.P.P.R. Depot, Arlee – 1895. (Courtesy of Jack Weidenfeller.)

Northern Pacific Roundhouse, Missoula. (Courtesy of Jack Weidenfeller.)

Sawmill at Lothrop. (Courtesy of Jack Weidenfeller.)

Bearmouth – 1900. (Courtesy of Carol Crowther.)

Montana Hotel, Anaconda – 1900. (Courtesy of Jack Weidenfeller.)

Columbia Gardens, Butte – 1905. Courtesy of Jack Weidenfeller.)

Entrance to the Bitter Root Valley – 1916. (Courtesy of Jack Weidenfeller.)

Tar Box Mine, Saltese – circa 1917. (Courtesy of Jack Weidenfeller.)

Saltese – 1919. (Courtesy of Jack Weidenfeller.)

Missoula, Montana Territory – 1870. (Courtesy of Jack Weidenfeller.)

S.N. Boys branding calves in Howard, Montana. (Courtesy of Carol Crowther.)

Pioneer. First Gold Camp in Montana – circa 1890s. (Courtesy of Martin J. Briggeman.)

Clayton O. Ingalls (gentleman on the right with camera), Ingalls Portrait Company – circa 1890. The office was located in First National Bank Building on the corner of Front Street and Higgins Avenue, Missoula. (Courtesy of Jack Weidenfeller.)

Pioneer. Kohrs & Bielenberg – circa 1880. (Courtesy of Martin J. Briggeman.)

Pioneer – circa 1895. (Courtesy of Martin J. Briggeman.)

Helmville – 1914. (Courtesy of Pat (Geary) Guay.)

Stewart Gold Dredge (the first in the Gold Creek area) – circa 1905-1906. (Courtesy of Martin J. Briggeman.)

Appendix

Index

A
Allen, George Washington 46
Allen, Zadock Montgomery 48

B
Baxter, Warren Strickland 51
Beatty, George 55
Bedard, Thedore 61
Bernier, Oliver L. 62
Bielenberg, Charles P. H. (Col.) 72
Bielenberg, Nicholas John "N. J." 76
Bien, Moritz and Johanna 82
Bruffey, George Alexander 86
Burns, Alexander F. 91
Butts, Jonas 94
Byrd, John 97

C
Carney, Patrick 103
Chaffin, Milton 107
Chouquette, Charles 110
Chowning (Ennis), Jennie W. 156
Christenot, Charles 112
Cook, Charles W. 117
Cooney, Thomas Jeremiah 120
Coughlin, Cornelius "Con" 124

D
Doggett, Moses 127
Doney, William J. 128
Dudden, Benjamin Henry 136
DuMontier, Pierre Napoleon 138

E
Ellis, Francis "Frank" R. 140
Ennis, Katherine S. 158
Ennis, William 161
Evans, Charles Alexander 163
Ewing, W. H. 166

F

Fergus, Andrew	169
Fergus, James	180
Fifer, John	190
Filson, M. R. George	192
Flaherty, John Thomas	196
Freeser, John Henry	200

G

Geary, Michael Lewis	202
Guy, John Craig	207
Guy, Robert James	212

H

Hanna, Ira Monroe	215
Hardgrove, George Hezekiah	217
Harris, Adelaide Price Berry	218
Harris, Evan J. and Amelia (Davis)	220
Harris, Howell	230
Harris I, John	222
Hayes, Edward Sherman	234
Herrin, Daniel S.	237
Hickey, William C.	238
Higgins, William Booth Sheldon	241
Hollenback, Gregory J.	252

J

Jeffers, Myron D.	257
Jones, John	259

L

LaLonde, Adam Agustus	263
Largent, John	265
Lavey, Eliza Foster Carlton Holden	245
Lepine, Aime	270
Levengood, Peter	273
Lewis, Edward A.	276
Lyons, George R.	280

M

McDonald, Catherine "Kate"	281
McKnight, Patrick and Winifred	283
McMillan, Angus	285
Merritt, Theodore Barstow	288
Miles, Thomas Odber	294

Millen, Nick L. ... 297
Moore, John Clarkson ... 300
Moran, Pat and Katherine ... 301
Moran, Will and Nellie (Hickey) ... 239

N
Noble, Daniel Bohan ... 304

P
Patterson, Thomas John Robert ... 307
Pfeifer, John Peter ... 311

Q
Quinlan, Henry, Patrick and John ... 316

S
Smith, Robert ... 321
Sparrell, George H. and Augusta ... 325
Sparrell, George T. ... 327
Staudaher, George L. and Catherine (Millen) ... 329
Stone, Manoah ... 332
Stuart, Granville ... 335
Stuart, James C. ... 348
Switzer, Andrew ... 355
Switzer, Tavner ... 357

T
Thexton, George ... 358
Thexton, Thomas ... 361
Thibadeau, Matilda Dalton ... 364
Thomas, Margaret Edwards Harris ... 228
Tinney, William T. ... 366
Trepp, Martin ... 378
Tuttle, Sherman Ferson ... 383

W
Whitney, Otis Crocker ... 388
Whitney, Thomas H. ... 390

Montana Pioneer List – 2001

(**Editor's Note**: *The following list is of those individuals officially listed as Pioneers in the State of Montana. Names marked in bold type represent those whose names also appeared in "Society of Montana Pioneers. Vol. I," published in 1899. This new listing was compiled for this publication by Shirley Herrin, Secretary-Treasurer.*)

ABSACAL, ELIZABETH
ABT, FRANK
ACCOLA, JOHN
ACCOLA, LOUISE (KETTERER)
ADAMI, MARIE (WHITE)
ADAMS, CATHERINE
ADAMS, GEORGE
ADAMS, HENRY
ADAMS, J. C.
ADAMS, JAMES C.
ADAMS, JOHN A.
ADAMS, MARY
ADAMS, MARY BELLESS
ADAMS, MARY S.
ADAMS, THOMAS
ADDOMS, HENRY
ADDOMS, CATHERINE (O'NEILL)
ADKINS, H. FRANK
AGNEW, O. P.
AIKEN, ADA RODGERS
AIKEN, EDWARD D.
AKELEY, ELIZABETH N.
AKIN, JARVIS
ALBRIGHT, FRANCES EMMA
ALDEN, ISAAC R.
ALDERSON, EDWARD C.
ALDERSON, JOHN J.
ALDERSON, MAMIE
ALDERSON, MATT W.
ALDERSON, MRS.
ALDERSON, WILLIAM W.
ALFIELDT, EDMUND
ALLBRIGHT, FRANCES E.
ALLEE, AUGUSTUS WILLIAM
ALLEN, A. T.
ALLEN, ALMIRA
ALLEN, DAVID GEORGE
ALLEN, DWIGHT M.
ALLEN, G. J.
ALLEN, GUY WASHINGTON
ALLEN, INEZ
ALLEN, J. L.
ALLEN, JIRAH ISHM
ALLEN, JOHN
ALLEN, JOHN F.
ALLEN, JOSEPH WOLF
ALLEN, LEVI
ALLEN, LUMAN W.
ALLEN, LYDIA
ALLEN, MARTHA
ALLEN, MARY (HOPPING)
ALLEN, O. L., MRS.
ALLEN, W. N.
ALLEN, WILLIAM HOMER
ALLEN, WILLIAM N.
ALLEN, WILLIAM R..
ALLEN, ZADOCK M.

ALLIN, GEORGE SPENCER
ALLIN, WILLIAM GRANT
ALLPORT, J. D.
ALLSTIN, ELLA DEASEY
ALSTON, EDWARD D.
ALWARD, ELLA FREDERIKA
AMACKER, MARIA
AMOS, JOHN
ANCENEY, CHARLES
ANDERSON, J. M.
ANDERSON, JOHN
ANDERSON, JOHN GEORGE
ANDERSON, JOHN MORGAN
ANDERSON, MARY RASMUSSIN
ANDERSON, REZIN
ANDERSON, ROBERT M.
ANDERSON, SALLIE
ANDERSON, SAMUEL
ANDERSON, THOMAS WILSON
ANDREOLI, CARLO SR.
ANDRUS, MARGARET H. ROSENBAUM
ANGUS, CHARLES
ANNIS, HORACE
ANNIS, PORTIA (NICHOLS)
ANTHONY, JAMES G.
ANTHONY, LEWIS C.
ANTONIOLI, PETER
APLIN, JAMES
ARCHER, WILLIAM

ARGYLE, JEANNETTE PARKINSON
ARGYLE, JOHN T.
ARMELL, ELLEN STUART
ARMINGTON, JERAULT TIBBETS
ARMITAGE, CHARLES HARRY B.
ARMITAGE, J. A.
ARMITAGE, JESSE
ARMITAGE, JOSHUA
ARMITAGE, MAUD NOYES
ARMITAGE, WILLIAM A.
ARMSTRONG, NOAH
ARNOLD, WALTER W.
ARNOLD, WILLIAM
ARNOLD, WILLIAM H.
ARNOUX, JAMES M.
ARRIAS, THOMAS
ASHBY, SHIRLEY CARTER
ASMELL, CECELIA B.
ASPLING, CHARLES E.
ASPLING, THOMAS
ASPLING, THOMAS, MRS.
ASTEL, MARTHA HOWARD
ASTLE, JOHN E.
ATCHISON, J. S.
ATCHISON, JOHN
ATCHISON, JOHN S.
ATKINS, T. L.

AUBRAY, SARAH, MRS
AUCHINOOLE, JAMES E.
AUDIFFRED, SEBASTIAN
AULT, T. M.
AUSTIN, C. H.
AUSTIN, DAVID
AUSTIN, ELLA DEASEY
AUSTIN, JAMES B.
AUSTIN, JAMES WARD
AUSTIN, M. H.
AUVINGER, JOHN WESTLEY
AVERY, CATHERINE
AXE, ALLEN T.
AXE, ERASMUS
AYLESWORTH, WILBUR N
BABCOCK, A. B.
BABCOCK, W. N.
BABCOCK, WILLIAM H.
BADGLEY, ALPHIUS
BAILEY, J. A.
BAILEY, J. A., MRS.
BAILEY, JAMES A.
BAILEY, JAMES M.
BAILEY, JOSEPH
BAILEY, NELLIE CLAIRE SWITZER
BAILEY, NEWTON
BAILEY, REUBEN P.
BAILEY, THEVA
BAILEY, WILLIAM G.
BAKER, ARURELIA MC TAGGART
BAKER, GEORGE A.
BAKER, J. C.
BAKER, J. W.
BAKER, J. Y.
BAKER, J. Y., MRS.
BAKER, JACOB
BAKER, JACOB H.
BAKER, JACOB HULL
BAKER, JACOB W.
BAKER, JOHN
BAKER, JONATHAN C.
BAKER, JOSEPH A.
BAKER, P. W.
BAKER, SARAH
BAKER, THOMAS
BALL, E. S.
BALL, EDWARD SMITH
BALL, EDWARD SMITH, MRS.
BALL, JAMES STERLING
BALL, JAMES. S.
BALL, ROSE A. (MC CAULEY).
BALLARD, DEWITT CLINTON
BALLARD, G. B.
BALLARD, GEORGE B.
BALLARD, JAMES MADISON
BALLARD, LENA E.
BALLARD, W. T.
BANTER, JAMES
BANTER, JOHN
BAP, WILLIAM EDWARD
BARBEAU, DELIA M. B.
BARBER, ANDREW
BARBER, ORLANDO BEECH
BARDWELL, EMILY AUGUSTA
BARDWELL, GEORGE
BARIL, ANTOINE
BARKELL, JAMES H.

BARKELL, LONEVILE S., MRS.
BARKELL, LONEVILLE S.
BARKELL, LOUVILLA B.
BARKELL, RICHARD T.
BARKER, CHARLES
BARKER, GEORGE M.
BARKER, JAMES
BARNES, HANSON HARVEY
BARNES, JOHN
BARNES, JOHN S.
BARNES, MARTHA E. WUNDERLIN
BARNES, ROBERT
BARNES, ROBERT C.
BARNES, WILLIAM RIDGEWAY
BARRETT, ALICE E.
BARRETT, ANTHONY H.
BARRETT, LAURA B.
BARRETT, M. C.
BARRETT, MARTIN
BARRETT, W. S.
BARRETT, WALTER S.
BARRON, W. N.
BARRY, JAMES FRANCIS
BARTLETT, W
BARTLETT, WILLIAM FRANKLIN
BARTON, E. A.
BARTRUFF, CARROLL HENRY
BARTRUFF, JOHN S.
BARWELL, IRENE
BASS, DUDLEY CHASE
BASS, VIRGINIA GIBBS
BASS, WILLIAM EDWARD
BASSFORD, ISAAC F.
BATCHELDER, GEORGE
BATCHELDER, SAMUEL
BATEMAN, CORNELIA JURGENS
BATEMAN, DORA
BATEMAN, ELLEN A. CRAWFOOT
BATEMAN, HELEN
BATEMAN, R. P.
BATEMAN, ROBERT M.
BATEMEN, JAMES C., MRS.
BAUER, JACOB
BAUER, JOHANNA D. MYER
BAWDEN, SETH
BAXTER, EDSON C.
BAXTER, ELIJAH S.
BAXTER, ELIZAR
BAXTER, ELSON C.
BAXTER, JAMES
BAXTER, WARREN S.
BAY, WILLIAM C.
BEABER, JACOB
BEACH, ALICE VIVIAN GRAY
BEACH, CALVIN
BEACH, DANIEL W.
BEACH, ELIZUR
BEAL, GEORGE W. DR.
BEAL, MRS G. W. (S.J. TOWNSEND)
BEAL, PERRY H.
BEALL, ALEXANDER D.
BEALL, BENJAMIN M.
BEALL, JOHN A.
BEALL, JOHN M.
BEALL, JOHN NELSON
BEALL, MARY M.
BEALL, ROSA V.

BEALL, W. J.
BEALL, W. J., MRS.
BEALL, WILLIAM HENRY
BEALL, WILLIAM JOHNSTON
BEATTY, GEORGE
BEAUFIE, JOSEPH
BEAUFIE, MARGARET FELLEL
BEAUMONT, EMMA
BECK, AGNES
BECK, D. R.
BECK, JOSIAH F.
BECK, OLIVER CROMWELL
BECKER, CONRAD
BECKER, J. Y.
BECKER, J. Y. MRS.
BECKHORN, GEORGE W.
BECKWITH, JIM
BEDARD, THEODORE
BEEDING, ROSETTA
BEEHRER, C. A.
BEEHRER, FRANK G.
BEEHRER, GEORGE WILLIAM
BEHRINGER, GEORGE
BEIDLER, G. A.
BEIDLER, JOHN X.
BELANGER, LOUIS
BELANGER, NATHALIE GIRARD
BELCHER, A.
BELCHER, BARTLETT BYRON
BELCHER, CLARA M.
BELCHER, ELLA E.
BELLESS, WILLIAM DANIAL
BEMBRICK, BENJAMIN. F.
BENEDICT, GILBERT
BENJAMIN, GEORGE
BENNETT, ALDEN
BENOIRS, XAVIER
BENSON, ANNIE
BENSON, BENJAMIN
BERKIN, JANE HALL
BERKIN, JOHN
BERKIN, WILLIAM
BERKINS, FANNY LaPOINTE
BERNIER, OLIVER L.
BERRY, ALDIE (ADELAIDE) (HARRIS)
BERRY, CHARLES
BERRY, CHARLES WILLIAM
BERRY, CHASE
BERRY, DANIEL
BERRY, WILLIAM
BERUBE, STEPHEN
BESS, GEORGE B.
BESS, GEORGE BAIRD
BESSETTE, AMEDE
BEVERIDGE, ANNIE JANE SIDAL
BEVERIDGE, LENNY
BICKETT, ANNA E. THOROUGHMAN
BICKETT, ELIZA (WELLS)
BICKETT, H G.
BICKETT, WILLIAM J. W. DR.
BICKFORD, S. E.
BIELENBERG, CHARLES PETER HENRY
BIELENBERG, JOHN
BIELENBERG, NICHOLAS JOHN
BIEN, MORITZ
BIGGS, MARIANA
BIGNELL, SAMUEL

BILL, FRANCIS R.
BILL, J. R.
BILLEDEAUX, XAVIER
BILLINGSLEY, DAVID
BILLMAN, ANDREW
BILLMAN, SARAH E.
BINGA, JORDAN
BIRD, JESSE J.
BIRD, THOMAS J.
BIRDSEYE, CHARLES GRANDISON
BIRDSEYE, MATTIE
BIRMINGHAM, ANNIE CALEY
BIRMINGHAM, PATRICK
BISEL, B. F.
BISEL, B. F. MRS.
BISHOP, CHARLES LLOYD
BISHOP, JEROME A.
BISHOP, JOHN FERNANDO
BISHOP, WILLIAM MARCY
BLACK, CHARLES W.
BLACK, ROSA GRACE (FRIDLEY)
BLACK, SAMUEL
BLACKBURN, CHARLES A.
BLACKBURN, FLETCHER A.
BLACKER, DAVID
BLACKMAN, AUGUSTA (STEWART)
BLACKMAN, AUGUSTA C.
BLACKMAN, GEORGE C. B.
BLACKMAN, GEORGE W.
BLACKWELL, JOSEPH E.
BLAINE, O. L.
BLAIR, EMMA FEISTER
BLAIR, EMMA J.
BLAIR, JOHN W.
BLAIR, WILLIAM A.
BLAIR, WILLIAM G.
BLAISDELL, HIRAM M.
BLAISDELL, SARAH F.
BLAKE, ABRAHAM S.
BLAKE, HENRY NICHOLS
BLAKE, JOHN E.
BLAKE, STERNE
BLAKELY, C. F.
BLAKELY, CHARLES P.
BLAKELY, ELIZABETH DOWNING
BLAKEMAN, HENRY
BLEVINS, DANIEL O'NEAL
BLIVENS, CHARLES
BLOCK, J. D.
BLODGET, JOSEPH S.
BLODGETT, LYMAN JOHNSON
BLOSSOM, HENRY DWIGHT
BOARDMAN, ANNIE KOHRS
BOARDMAN, M. D.
BOATMAN, GEORGE THOMAS
BOATMAN, MARY I. TOWNSEND
BOATMAN, ROBERT THORNTON
BOCK, J. DANIEL
BODERSTON, GEORGE W.
BODINE, CHARLES CORNELIUS
BODURTHA, GEORGE W.
BOEHL, JOHANNA
BOHLER, AUGUSTA
BOHLER, JOSEPH
BOHM, FERDINAND
BOKEN, AMELIA McTAGGART
BOLES, JEROME W.

BOLON, JOSEPHINE BOWERS
BOLT, JOHN
BOMAR, OLIVER C.
BOND, FRED G.
BONEPART, MARIE
BONER, JAMES
BONNER, E. I.
BOOKER, GEORGE
BOOKER, MATTIE E. WALTON
BOONE, DIDAMA
BOOTH, H. P.
BOOTH, MARY E.
BORIN, LOUIS
BOSE, HENRY
BOSE, HENRY J.
BOSTWICK, MARY L.
BOSTWICK, SAMUEL ALFRED
BOTTCHER, FREDERICK
BOTTCHER, GERTRUDE K.
BOULET, JOSEPH
BOWDEN, SETH
BOWE, PATRICK
BOWER, ALEXANDER MARSAILLES
BOWER, JOHN
BOWERS, SAMUEL
BOWMAN, SARILEE JOSEPHINE
BOY, WILLIAM C.
BOYCE, J. E.
BOYCE, JAMES RICHARD, JR.
BOYCE, JAMES RICHARD, SR.
BOYD, LOCKHART
BOYER, JOSEPH J.
BOYER, MARY LYNCH
BOYER, WILLIAM J.
BOYLE, CATHARYN C. WATERMAN
BOYLE, PATRICK
BRADLEY, CATHERINE MALLOY
BRADLEY, JAMES M.
BRADWAY, WILLARD
BRADY, JOHN
BRANAGAN, JOHN
BRANDEN, SARAH J. PEIRSTORFF
BRANDER, A. G. JUDGE
BRANDT, CHARLES WILLIAM
BRANNAN, JOHN
BRASSEY, EDWARD
BRATTON, ELIZA VINCENT CAIN
BRATTON, HUGH
BRATTON, IDA B. MC GILLVRAY
BRAUN, WILLIAM
BRAWNER, DAVID G.
BRAY, CORNELIUS
BRAY, PATRICK
BRECK, EDWARD WALLACE
BRECK, MOLLIE MORTON
BRECKBILL, ELLEN SILVERTHORNE
BRECKENRIDGE, GEORGE E.
BREMER, J. H.
BRENNAN, ROSE A.
BRENNEMAN, DAVID I.
BREWDAGE, HIRAM
BREWER, JAMES SCOTT
BREWINGTON, A. P.
BREWINGTON, W. H.
BREWINGTON, WILLIAM
BREWSTER, AGNESS HOLLAND
BRICE, ELIAS

BRIGGS, ANDREW J.
BRIGHT, A. F.
BRINKMAN, HERMAN
BRISTOL, JOHN F.
BRITTAIN, MARGARET WAKEFIELD
BROADWATER, CHARLES ARTHUR
BROCK, J. W.
BRODERICK, JOHN
BROGAN, PATRICK
BROOKE, BENJAMIN CODINGTON
BROOKE, CHARLES WALTER
BROOKE, EDWARD GANTT
BROOKE, LULU I. STANLEY
BROOKE, MARY (R. W. NOBLE)
BROOKE, MARY A. TINSLEY
BROOKE, SARAH A.
BROOKS, J N., MRS.
BROOKS, JAMES NEWELL
BROOKS, JOHN
BROOKS, SANDERS, MRS.
BROOKS, W. R.
BROTHERTON, LOUISA
BROWN, ALEXANDER
BROWN, ASA A.
BROWN, CHARLES
BROWN, ELIZA HOULE
BROWN, EZEKEL M.
BROWN, FRANK D.
BROWN, FRANK G
BROWN, GEORGE M.
BROWN, JAMES D.
BROWN, JAMES JACKSON
BROWN, JOHN
BROWN, JOHN D.
BROWN, JOSEPH
BROWN, MILES WRIGHT
BROWN, MYRON S.
BROWN, ROMULUS
BROWN, SADIE J.
BROWN, WILLIAM
BROWNE, JOSEPH ALOYSIUS
BROWNLEE, BELLE (FORBIS)
BROWNLEE, ELIZA LAVINA
BRUBAKER, ALBERT
BRUCKERT, ALBERT
BRUCKERT, ALBERT JR.
BRUCKERT, ALBERT SR.
BRUCKERT, GEORGE EDWARD
BRUCKERT, JOHN
BRUCKERT, RACHEL (WHITMAN)
BRUCKNER, ADOLPH
BRUFFEY, GEORGE ALEXANDER
BRUFFEY, JANICE F.
BRUFFEY, REBECCA B. (HARGROVE)
BRUNDAGE, E. H.
BRUNDAGE, HIRAM
BRUNDAGE, MARGUERITE
BRUNDY, HENRY
BRUNEAU, PIERRE
BRYSON, NATHANIEL GREEN
BUCHANAN, JOHN
BUCHANEN, THOMAS WILLIAM
BUCHETT, MAHLON WILSON
BUCK, AMOS
BUCK, DANIEL W.
BUCK, HENRY
BUCK, ISAAC N.

BUCK, JOHN D. JR.
BUCK, JOHN D. SR.
BUCKER, SOLITUDE TEABEAU
BUCKHOUSE, ELIZABETH
BUCKHOUSE, HENRY
BUCKHOUSE, JOHN
BUDD, NEWTON
BUFORD, SIMEON ROBERT
BUHRER, GEORGE W.
BUKER, JOHN B., DR.
BULFINCH, GEORGE W.
BULFINCH, M. L.
BULL, EDWARD WILKINSON
BULL, FRANK
BULLARD, M. W.
BULLARD, MASSENA
BULLARD, WILLIAM F.
BULLARD, WILLIAM L.
BULLOCK, SETH
BURCH, CLAVIN
BURCH, ELLA S.
BURCH, JOHN
BURCH, V.
BURCH, VINCENT SR.
BURCHER, W. P.
BURCHETT, B. B.
BURD, JULIAN F.
BURD, MYRON HAWLEY
BURD, SAMUEL
BURD, SAMUEL CONRAD
BURDEN, THOMAS
BURDISS, ROBERT S.
BURFIEND, HENRY
BURFIEND, HENRY
BURKE, EDWARD
BURMASTER, ELLEN THOMPSON
BURNS, ALEXANDER
BURNS, EDWARD BRECK
BURNS, MICHEAL
BURNS, MIKE
BURNS, T. C.
BURNS, WILLIAM K.
BURR, FREDERICK H.
BURRIS, MARY HERMAN
BURT, NATHANIEL
BURTON, FELIX
BURTON, ISAAC
BURTT, LUCIUS D.
BUSICK, MARY ANN
BUSKETT, JOHN W.
BUSSIER, FREDERICK
BUTLER, DARWIN C.
BUTLER, HARWOOD
BUTLER, JAMES H.
BUTLER, SARAH C.
BUTLER, WILLIAM
BUTT, WILLIAM
BUTT, WILSON
BUTTS, DERINDA J. TUTTLE
BUTTS, JONAS
BUXTON, JOHN H.
BYAM, DON L. MRS.
BYERS, BENJAMIN
BYONE, JOHN
BYRD, JOHN
BYRD, THOMAS J.
BYRNS, MICHAEL

BYWATER, FLETCHER (ANTHONY)
BYWATER, MARY (READ)
CADIGAN, JAMES
CAGLE, DAVID H.
CAGLE, LAURA A.
CAHALIN, PATRICK
CAHILL, HENRY T
CAHILL, INARRA A.
CAHILL, MARIE AGNES COONEY
CAHILL, STEPHEN
CAIRNS, MARY
CALDWELL, EDWARD JAMES
CALLAN, THOMAS J.
CALLAWAY, JONES HOY
CALVERT, MARGERT (STRICKLAND)
CALVIN, AMOS
CAMERON, ANGUS
CAMERON, ANNIA KINSLEY
CAMERON, J. B.
CAMERON, J. D.
CAMERON, JOHN
CAMERON, WILLIAM D.
CAMP, JENNIE CURTIS FLY
CAMPBELL, ALEXANDER
CAMPBELL, ALLEN G.
CAMPBELL, ANNA DUNBAR
CAMPION, JULIA BRENNAN
CANNON, CHARLES WESLEY
CANNON, HENRY
CANTNER, MONTANA MRS.
CAPLICE, JOHN
CAPP, HANNAN POPE
CARDWELL, EDWARD
CAREY, MARY EMERSON
CAREY, NICKOLAS
CARHARTT, WILLIAM
CARLETON, GEORGE W.
CARLINE, MARGARET SHINNICK
CARLS, A. J.
CARLS, ELIZABETH ANN CORDILIA DUKE
CARNES, JOHN
CARNEY, ANNETTE
CARNEY, PATRICK
CARPENTER, B F.
CARPENTER, BENJAMIN F.
CARPENTER, DANIEL DEWITT
CARPENTER, E. W.
CARPENTER, EMMA E.
CARPENTER, GEORGE E.
CARPENTER, MARY
CARR, BENJAMIN
CARR, F. M .
CARR, MARTIN, MRS.
CARR, MICHEAL
CARROLL, J. A.
CARROLL, MATTHEW
CARROLL, MIKE
CARROW, EDWARD
CARRUTHERS, JOHN B.
CARTEN, JOHN
CARTER, A. P.
CARTER, ANNA SELWAY
CARTER, ARTHUR P.
CARTER, WILLIAM B.
CARTER, WILLIAM JR.
CARTER, WILLIAM M.
CARTWRIGHT, MILO

CARVER, CHARLES H.
CARYL, HENRY
CARYL, NETTIE
CASSIDY, MARGARET SMITH
CASTNER, JOHN K.
CASWELL, RICHARD
CATLEN, BENJAMIN
CATLIN, JOHN
CAVANAUGH, MILES J.
CAVANAUGH, MILES MRS.
CAVE, WILLIAM
CHABOTT, JOHN B.
CHAFFIN, ALEXANDER M.
CHAFFIN, ANTHONY
CHAFFIN, BAALAN SIEGEL
CHAFFIN, ELIJAH
CHAFFIN, ELIZA (MITCHELL)
CHAFFIN, JOHN S.
CHAFFIN, MILTON
CHAFFIN, MILTON P.
CHAFFIN, MOSES L. B.
CHAFFIN, NANCY (SIMMONS)
CHAFFIN, NEWTON J.
CHAFFIN, PENELOPE (WILLIAMS)
CHAFFIN, SAMUEL O.
CHAFFIN, THOMAS A.
CHAMBERS, HENRY
CHARLES, THOMAS
CHARNEWSKY, (SILVERMAN)
CHATFIELD, JOHN
CHEMEDLIN, NICHOLAS T.
CHEMEDLIN, NICHOLAS T., MRS.
CHERWAY, JAMES S.
CHESSMAN, WILLIAM ALLEN
CHILDS, CHARLES NELSON
CHOUQUETTE, CHARLES
CHOWNING, JENNIE ENNIS
CHRISMAN, JOHN
CHRISTENOT, MARTHEY CRAIG
CHRISTENSON, CATHERN (LONGLEY)
CHRISTIANSEN, CAROLINE A. CRANE
CHRISTIANSEN, MARY
CHRISTIANSEN, NIELS P.
CHRISTIANSON, CARRIE
CHUMASERO, WILLIAM
CISLER, ALFRED
CISLER, ANNIE (NICHOL)
CISLER, JOSEPH E.
CLAESSENS, WILLIAM
CLAIRMONT, LOUIS
CLARK, A.M, MRS.
CLARK, ALBERT GALLATIN SR.
CLARK, AMELIA (BAKER).
CLARK, BRIDGER (McCAULEY)
CLARK, CARRIE SENNETT
CLARK, CATHERINE E.
CLARK, ELIZABETH (DAUGHERTY)
CLARK, EMILY R.
CLARK, GEORGE H.
CLARK, HARRIS JOHNSON
CLARK, HENRY HARMON
CLARK, HENRY S.
CLARK, JAMES O.
CLARK, JOSEPH
CLARK, JOSEPH K.
CLARK, LAURA (ROBERTS)
CLARK, MONTE
CLARK, MRS P. B. (TOOTIE BROWN)
CLARK, OSCAR
CLARK, P. B.
CLARK, P. H. DR.
CLARK, R. A.
CLARK, TOM
CLARK, WILLIAM A.
CLARK, WILLIAM ANDREWS
CLARKE, HELEN PIOTOPOWAKA.
CLARKE, MALCOLM
CLARKE, RICHARD WATSON
CLARY, THOMAS
CLEM, BYRON I.
CLEM, ISRAEL
CLEM, SAMUEL
CLEMENS, MOSES
CLEVELAND, GEORGE W.
CLEVELAND, MARY (ANNIS)
CLEWELL, TILGHMAN H.
CLINE, ANNIE PICKERING
CLINE, J. A.
CLINE, V. E.
CLINE, VICTOR E.
CLOSTEN, HATTIE S.
CLOWES, MILES T.
CLOWES, T.
CLOWES, WILLIAM EDWARD
COBERLY, MARY ESTHER ASTLE
COBURN, ROBERT
COBURN, WALTER M.
COBURN, WILLIAM M.
COCHRAN, JOSEPH M. V.
COCHRAN, WILLIAM DOUGLAS
COCHRANE, JAMES
COCKERILL, VARDAMAN ALLAN
COCKRELL, DAVID A.
COCKRELL, GEORGE
CODY, THOMAS
COHEN, DAVID SR.
COHEN, ESTER (COPINUS)
COHEN, HATTIE SILVERMAN
COHEN, RACHEAL (STRASBURGER)
COHEN, REGINA
COHEN, SAMUEL
COLBERT, CHARLES E.
COLE, ANNIE
COLE, ISAAC
COLE, NELSON
COLE, W. G.
COLE, WILLIAM G.
COLEMAN, CYNTHIA J.
COLEMAN, LEWIS
COLEMAN, LUCY HAMMOND
COLEMAN, MATTHIAS
COLEMAN, MIKE
COLEMAN, THOMAS
COLEMAN, WILLIAM
COLLET, ABRAHAM
COLLET, MARTHA
COLLIER, IRVIN
COLLINS, BERNARD
COLLINS, DENNIS
COLLINS, ELIZABETH (SMITH)
COLLINS, HENRY C.
COLLINS, JAMES L., MRS.
COLLINS, MARION
COLLINS, TIMOTHY E.

COLLINS, VIOLET
COLLINS, VIOLO
COLON, JAMES
COLON, MARGARETE WHITE
COLSON, J. M.
COMEGYR, JOHN MYERS
COMER, JOHN Z.
COMER, PHILEMON
COMFORT, JOHN R.
COMMONS, GEORGE W.
CONINE, FLETCHER WILLIAMS
CONLEY, JAMES HENRY
CONLON, JAMES
CONLON, MARGARET WHITE
CONLON, PATRICK
CONLON, R. A.
CONNER, JOHN THOMAS
CONNOLLY, NICHOLAS
CONRAD, GEORGE EDWARD
CONRAD, JOSEPH D.
CONRAD, JOSEPH D., MRS.
CONRAD, RAYMOND(ALLEN) MRS.
CONRAD, WILLIAM G.
CONREY. WILLIAM W.
CONROW, JOHN M.
CONROY, PHILIP
CONSTANS, PHILIP
CONTOIS, DAVID
CONWAY, ANNA LOWMAN
CONWAY, FRANK THOMAS
CONWAY, JAMES R.
CONWAY, JOHN M.
CONWAY, MARGARET BANNEN STERLING
CONWAY, MARGARET J. HOWELL
CONWAY, ROBERT
COOK, CHARLES W.
COOK, CHRISTOPHER
COOK, EMMA I (SWEET)
COOK, FRANK, L.
COOK, GEORGE
COOK, HELEN A. MOFFETT
COOK, RICHARD T.
COOK, SAMUEL SMITH
COOK, SUSAN (HARRIS)
COOLEY, WILLIAM A.
COOMBES, EDWARD H.
COON, EMLEY E. MC CLAIN
COONEY, CRAIG
COONEY, MARIA A.
COONEY, THOMAS
COOPER, B. G.
COOPER, CHARLES
COOPER, DWIGHT
COOPER, MARGARET J. WILLIAMS
COOPER, MARION D.
COOPER, MILTON D.
COOPER, MILTON H.
COOPER, THOMAS E.
COOPER, W. L. D. MRS.
COOPER, WALTER
COPALL, JOSEPH
COPE, GEORGE FREDERICK
COPINUS, ALBERT
COPINUS, ERNISTINO
COPINUS, ESTHER
COPINUS, WILLIAM
COPPOCK, HENRY

COPR, GEORGE F.
CORBALLY, WILLIAM
CORBLY, ANDREW L.
CORBLY, JACOB I.
CORBLY, WILLIAM L.
CORKWELL, JAMES
CORNELL, CRAIG
CORNFORTH, ALMA E. DICKEY
CORNFORTH, ASA
CORRY, ANDREW VAN
CORY, CHARLES
COSENS, CORCAS ALLEN
COSENS, LUCULLUS
COSGROVE, GEORGE
COSGROVE, ROSE
COSHOW, ALICE FERGUSON
COTTER, CHARLES
COTTER, MARY ANN COUGHLIN
COUGHLIN, CORNELIUS
COUGHLIN, DAVID J.
COUGHLIN, DELLIA MULLIN
COUGHLIN, MARGARET (PALLY)
COUGHLIN, MARY A.
COUGHLIN, MARY ANN MC CORMICK
COUGHLIN, MAURICE F.
COUNTRYMAN, SARAH ELIZABETH (WOODY)
COURTS, JOHN
COURTWRIGHT, MILO
COURVILLE, LOUIS
COVERT, IRA S.
COVERT, TOM
COWAN, ANDREW
COWAN, DAVID
COWAN, EMMA J
COWAN, GEORGE F.
COWAN, JOHN
COWAN, JOSEPH H.
COWDEN, HENRY
COWER, ANNIE (THOMAS)
COWER, CHARLES H.
COWLEY, ALICE (KELLY)
COX, ALICE M. (BACEN)
COX, GENEVIEVE
COX, GEORGE L.
COYLE, PETER
COYNE, WILLIAM
CRABS, JOHN
CRAFTON, JOHN W.
CRAIG, WARREN
CRAIL, AUGUSTUS F.
CRAIN, C. R..
CRANE, FRANCIS
CRANE, GEORGE W.
CRANE, JULIA EONE PAYNE
CRANE, PHILLIPA
CRANE, S. MRS.
CRAVEN, JOSEPH WOOD
CRAWFORD, ROBERT H.
CREIGHTON, MARY SAMPLE
CREWS, WILLIS SAMUEL
CRISP, WILLIAM M.
CRISPIN, MARIE OWENS
CROCKETT, SOPHRONIUS
CROFF, GEORGE A.
CROFF, LOUISE (LIVERMORE)
CROSS, JERUSHA, MRS.
CROSSMAN, ADAM

CROSSWHITE, BENJAMIN F.
CROTHERS, WILLIAM
CROUCH, CHARLES L.
CROUNSE, SILAS HILTON
CROUSE, HENRY
CROW, J. B.
CROWELL, ALBERT G.
CROWLEY, IDA MARIE SEARS
CRUMP, JAMES WESLEY
CRUSE, THOMAS
CUFF, MARGARET GALLAGHER
CULBERTSON, JOSEPH W.
CULBERTSON, ROBERT SIMPSON
CULLISON, GEORGE W.
CULVER, J. A.
CULVER, KATE VIRGINIA (CAVEN)
CUMMINGS, THOMAS A.
CUNNINGHAM, DENNIS
CURRAH, JOSEPH
CURRAN, WILLIAM
CURTIN, ARTHUR P.
CURTIN, JOHN C.
CURTIS, CHARLES DAVID
CURTIS, ELLEN (MELTEN)
CURTIS, EMMA (WHITCOMB)
CURTIS, FRANCIS EGBERT
CURTIS, JOHN H.
CURTIS, OTHO
CURTIS, WILLIAM. W.
CURTIS, WOLCOTT R.
CURTISS, DANIEL W
CUTCLIFF, AGNESS E. (REED)
CUTLER, CLARK LEWIS
CYR, ELOI
DADDOW, JOSEPH
DADDOW, JOSEPH S.
DAEMS LEVINUS S.
DAEMS, HENRY B. (HARRY)
DAEMS, LEVINUS D. DR.
DAEMS, MARIE LOUIS (WALTZIN)
DAGGETT, L. J., MRS.
DAHLER, CHARLES L.
DAILEY, ANDY
DAILEY, EBENEEZER
DAILEY, EBERNEEZER, MRS
DAILEY, FRANK
DAILEY, JANE
DAILEY, MARY
DAILEY, NEWT
DAILEY, SAMUEL
DALTON, MATHILDA
DALY, CECELIA
DALY, HUGH
DALY, JOHN
DALY, JOHN MITCHELL
DALY, PETER
DANA, EDWIN L.
DANCE, WALTER B.
DANIELS, JAMES B.
DANIELS, WILLIAM C.
DANIELS, WILLIAM CHARLES
DARBY, MARGARET (O'BRIEN)
DARBY, MOLLIE
DARBY, PATRICK
DARLINGTON, CAREY A.
DARLINGTON, MARY FRANCES
DARRELL, MARGARET BANNON

DARRELL, THOMAS JOSEPH
DART, GEORGE W.
DASHIELL, ESNA D.
DAVENPORT, DONNELL
DAVENPORT, RACHEL (MELONE)
DAVENPORT, WILLIAM
DAVID, ABRAHAM F.
DAVIDSON, AURORA (RAY)
DAVIDSON, AUSALEM J.
DAVIDSON, E. M.
DAVIDSON, JAMES
DAVIES, HARPIN
DAVIES, WILLIAM JOHN
DAVIS, ADRIEL B.
DAVIS, ANDREW JACKSON
DAVIS, AQUILLA
DAVIS, DAVID
DAVIS, DONALD WATSON
DAVIS, E. A.
DAVIS, GEORGE E.
DAVIS, GEORGE MONTANA
DAVIS, HARRIET B. KEENE
DAVIS, HENRY
DAVIS, HENRY TUNLEY
DAVIS, HOWELL C.
DAVIS, HOWELL COBB
DAVIS, J. J.
DAVIS, JAMES B.
DAVIS, JAMES L.
DAVIS, JANET URGUHART LOVELL
DAVIS, JOSEPH
DAVIS, JOSEPH D.
DAVIS, MARGARET
DAVIS, MARGARET JANE JENKINS
DAVIS, MARY HARRIS
DAVIS, MARY HITHENS
DAVIS, NATHANIEL JOHN
DAVIS, THOMAS M.
DAVIS, W. D.
DAVIS, WILEY
DAVIS, WILLIAM HENRY
DAVIS, WILLIAM JOHN
DAVIS, WILLIAM A.
DAVIS, WILLIAM F.
DAVIS, WILLIAM G.
DAVISON, MARY OLIVE RAYMOND
DAWES, BENJAMIN M.
DAWSON, ANDREW
DAWSON, ISABEL (CLARKE)
DAWSON, JOHN W.
DAY FRANK
DAY, JAMES
DAY, WILLIAM
DE MERS, DELLA
DE MERS, LOUIS
DE MERS, T. J.
DE MOSS, W. L.
DE RIAR, WILLIAM H.
DE SMET, PETER JOHN
DEACON, JAMES
DEAN, E. R.
DEAN, ISAAC
DEAN, JOHN R.
DEAN, MARY M
DEASCY, WILLIAM
DEASON, JAMES
DECKER, CATHERINE

DECKER, CLARA
DECKER, GEORGE L.
DECKER, HARRISON
DECKER, JOHN
DECKER, MARETTA
DECKER, MATTIE
DECKER, PERRY
DECKER, WILLIAM
DEDWICK JACOB
DEEGAN, WINIFRED CARROLL
DEGENHART, BENJAMIN
DEGENHART, LEE
DEHORT, W. L.
DELACY, WALTER WASHINGTON
DELEHANTY, KATE
DELETRAZ, GASPARD F.
DELMA, A
DEMONTIER, NAPOLEON
DEMPSEY, MARY CLINE
DEMPSEY, PATRICK H.
DEMPSEY, ROBERT M.
DEMPSEY, ROBERT W.
DENBLE, JOHN J.
DENNING, ELIZABETH FERRELL
DENNIS, EDWARD
DENO, DELIA FORREST
DENO, MARY A.
DENOILLE, ROBERT W.
DESBORNBRS, HENRY L
DesCOMBES, HENRY L.
DESKINS, MARGARET P. ROE
DETWEILER, GEORGE
DEWEY, DAVID SCOTT
DEXTER, BENJAMIN MAIDEN
DEXTER, WHEELER O.
DEYARMON, THOMAS
DeZOURDI, ELIE
DICKEY, JAMES EDGAR
DICKEY, JAMES R.
DICKEY, WILLIAM
DICKINSON, WM. HENRY HARRISON
DICKSON, EMMA STREET
DICKSON, GEORGE W.
DICKSON, MARY FRANCES FRANCISCO
DIDAWICK, JOSEPH
DIETRICH, JOSEPH MARION
DILLET, LUELLA F.
DILLIE, HENRY
DINGEE, WILLIAM A.
DINGWALL, DUNCAN
DINGWALL, WILLIAM
DITTIS, HENRY
DIXON, JAMES A.
DIXON, WILLIAM WIRT
DOBBINS, GEORGE W.
DOBBINS, JAMES K.
DOBBINS, JEFFERSON LEE
DOBBINS, LOUIS
DODGE, MINNIE ERNESTINE RICKER
DOGGETT, CHARLES B.
DOGGETT, JEFFERSON
DOGGETT, MOSES
DOGGETT, SUSAN (ROSE)
DONALDSON, F. H.(JENNIE)
DONALDSON, W. M.
DONALDSON, WILLIAM M.
DONEGAN, JOHN

DONEY, WILLIAM J.
DONLON, JOHN
DONOVAN, PAT
DORR, CHARLES O.
DOTSON, OLIVER
DOTSON, SARAH FLEMMING
DOUGHERTY, ELIZABETH CLARK
DOUGHERTY, MARY HILGER GERTRUDE
DOUGHTY, ALFRED H.
DOUGLAS, CALISTA (ALLEN)
DOUGLAS, ELMER A.
DOUGLAS, ELMER A. B.
DOUGLAS, GEORGE AUGUSTUS
DOUGLAS, MARY E. COOK
DOUGLAS, MARY SLOAN
DOW, GEORGE
DOWDEN, ELLEANOR
DOWLING, BERNARD
DOWNHOUR, JOHN JACOB
DOWNS, SAM E. HAYWARD
DOYLE, FRANCES ARELLA
DOYLE, MARGARET WICKHAM
DRINKWATER, J. C.
DRISCOLL, DENNIS
DUANE, PATRICK
DUEDEN, BENJAMIN HENRY
DUER, CHARLES E
DUER, CHAT E
DUER, OLIVIA ORE
DUFF, ALEXANDER T.
DUFF, SHELTON
DUFF, TABATHA HUNTER
DUFFY, JOHN
DUFRESNE, CHARLES
DUKE, CATHERINE (DEERING)
DUKE, ELIZABETH
DUKE, FLORENCE
DUKE, GEORGE
DUKE, GEORGE L
DUKE, VIRGINIA
DUKES, JOSEPHINE (MEININGER-WHITE)
DULANEY, ADAM L.
DUMONCHEL, NARCISSE (DUMONCHEL)?
DUMONT, STANFORD
DuMONTIER, NAPOLEON
DUNBAR, FRANK
DUNBAR, FRANK J
DUNBAR, JAMES FRANK
DUNCAN, CAROLINE VANDORN
DUNCAN, CHRISTIANA (YOUNG)
DUNCAN, HARRY
DUNCAN, HUGH
DUNCAN, HUGH JR.
DUNCAN, INFANT DAUGHTER
DUNCAN, JAMES
DUNCAN, JEANNETTE (GAMMEL)
DUNCAN, LEANDER
DUNCAN, THOMAS
DUNCAN, TYSON D.
DUNHAM, JOHN W.
DUNKELBERG, DAVID M.
DUNKS, MUNROE
DUNN, BRIDGET FENTON
DUNN, RICHARD
DUNNAVAN, SILAS L.
DUNNIGAN, FRANCES
DUNNIVIN, JOHN A.

DUNPHY, ELIJAH M.
DUNPHY, ELIJAH M. JR.
DUNPHY, EMMA FRAZIER
DUNPHY, MARY A. (SMALL)
DUPUIS, E. S.
DuPUIS, ELISE HENAULT
DUREY, ELLEN MARIE KIRBY
DURFEE, FRANCIS MARION
DUTRO, DANIEL
DUVAL, JOHN C,
EARHART, SAMUEL A.
EARLE, ANNA N. JOHNSON
EARLY, HUGH
EASTERLY, ALLAN M.
ECCLESTON, LUCY
ECHOLS, ABRAHAM TURNER
EDDY, JOHN W.
EDGAR, CLARA A.
EDGAR, HENRY FINNIS
EDGAR, JOHN
EDGERTON, MARTHA ROLFE
EDGERTON, PAULINE
EDGERTON, SIDNEY
EDGERTON, SIDNEY CARTER
EDMUNDS, FREDERICK
EDMUNDS, STEPHEN
EDSALL, ANDREW J.
EDWARDS, CALDWELL
EDWARDS, CHARLES WILLIAM
EDWARDS, FRANK J.
EDWARDS, HORACE
EDWARDS, HUGH HUMPHREY
EDWARDS, JESSE F.
EDWARDS, O. H., MRS.
EDWARDS, WILLIAM R. H.
EGGERS. FREDERICK
EGLERLY, HENRY
EHERT, ISADERE
EHRICK, ANDREW
EHRICK, JULIUS HERMAN
EHRICK, MARY S.
EICKEY, WILLIAM
EKLUND, EMILY C. SHEPHERD
EKLUND, PETER A.
ELIASON, AUGUSTA TRASK
ELIASON, JOHN E.
ELLEDGE, JULIA R.
ELLEDGE, NATHAN
ELLING, HENRY
ELLIOT, D. C.
ELLIOTT, CLARA E.
ELLIOTT, D. C., MRS.
ELLIOTT, DAVID C.
ELLIOTT, EMILY MARGARET
ELLIOTT, LEANDER C.
ELLIOTT, WIILLIAM T.
ELLIOTT, WILLIAM L
ELLIOTT, WILLIAM THOMAS
ELLIS, CHARLES A.
ELLIS, CHARLES F.
ELLIS, FRANCIS (FRANK)
ELLIS, IDA SYKER
ELLIS, JOHN J.
ELLIS, P. B.
ELLIS, T. H.
ELLIS, THOMAS H.
ELLS, R. S.

EMBRY, BILLY
EMERICH, GEORGE WILLIAM
EMERSEN, JAMES C.
EMERSON, EMMA J.
EMERSON, JAMES C.
EMERSON, JOHN
EMERSON, KATE McDONALD
EMERSON, MARY
EMERSON, ROBERT G.
EMERSON, WILLIAM HENRY
EMERY, WESLEY P.
ENGLAND, ABNER GRIER
ENGLAND, JOHN
ENGLISH, HARVEY W.
ENNIS, CATHERINE (SHRIVER)
ENNIS, FANNIE D.
ENNIS, FANNIE L. (DAVIS)
ENNIS, JENNIE W.
ENNIS, WILLIAM
ENNIS, WILLIAM J.
ENSCH, MATHIAS
EPPEL, HENRY
EPPERSON, ANNA HACKSHAW
EPPERSON, JOHN
EREAUX, LAZAIRE
ERWIN, DAVE
ERWIN, SIDNEY H.
ERWIN, WILLIAM LEROY
ESLER, ALFRED M.
ESLER, ALFRED M., MRS.
ESSLER, OPHELIA JOHNSTON
ESTES, MELIA ELLA
ESTES, SIMEON
ESTILL, JAMES WALLACE
ETHERINGTON, C.
EVANS, ANN (EVANS)
EVANS, ANNA MURPHY
EVANS, CARRIE MILLEGAN
EVANS, CHARLES
EVANS, CHRISTIAN G.
EVANS, GWENLIAN (EVANS)
EVANS, HANEY D.
EVANS, HENRY W.
EVANS, HENRY W. B.
EVANS, JOHN MORGAN
EVANS, JOSEPH
EVANS, L. F.
EVANS, LEMAN F
EVANS, LUTIE LEE LISTER
EVANS, MARY B.
EVANS, MARY B.(POWELL)
EVANS, MORGAN
EVANS, MYTILENE MILLEGAN
EVANS, NATHANIEL P.
EVANS, PHILIP E. MANUEL
EVANS, PHILLIP
EVANS, RACHEL
EVANS, ROBERT
EVANS, ROBERT HENRY
EVANS, SUSAN WILLIAMS
EVANS, WARREN EUGENE
EVANS, WILLIAM
EVANS, WILLIAM J.
EVEAUX, LEGRE
EVERETTT, CHARLES D.
EWING, REBECCA HILL
EWING, REBECCA (TAYLOR)

EWING, WILLIAM H.
EZEKIEL, BENJAMIN
FADDEN, AMELIA (MONROE)
FAIRFIELD, OLIVE ANN EDWARDS
FAIRWEATHER, BILL
FALEN, CHARLES ANTHONY
FALK, BENHARD
FALK, BENJAMIN
FALK, LIZZIE DAVIS
FALKINBURG, JAMES
FALLAN, PATRICK
FALLIS, SAMUEL MARTIN
FANNING, MARGARET HANNA HARRIS
FANT, JOHN JOSEPH
FARLIN, WILLIAM L.
FARMER, CHARLES C.
FARRELL, ROSE A. BRENNAN
FARRELL, THOMAS JOSEPH
FARRON, CAROLINE SURPRENANT
FARROW, JOSEPH D.
FARWELL, EDNA ROZELLA GROGAN
FARWELL, IVEN W.
FARWELL, J. W.
FAULKNER, JAMES HIGHLAND
FAULKNER, JOSEPH
FAULKNER, MARTHA E. HIGHLAND
FEATHERLY, EUNICE DAILEY
FEATHERMAN, JAMES A.
FEBES, JAMES HENRY
FEHRING, JOHN BERNARD
FELDBERG, JACOB
FELDBERT, EMMA HYMAN
FENN, MARGARET ANN
FENN, WILLIAM
FENNER, LAWRENCE A.
FENNER, ROBERT
FERGUS, ANDREW
FERGUS, JAMES
FERGUS, LILLIE MAURY
FERGUS, PAMELIA (DILLIN)
FERGUSON, BENJAMIN
FERGUSON, CLARRISA ANN WARD
FERGUSON, JOHN
FERGUSON, JOHN YOUNG
FERGUSON, LUELLA
FERGUSON, ROBERT M.
FERM, WILLIAM
FERRELL, BROWN
FERRELL, ELIZA DEMING
FERRELL, JOSEPH
FERRIS, CHARLES H.
FERRIS, CHARLES W.
FERRON, CAROLINE SUPREVANT
FERSTER, JAMES S.
FERSTER, RUFUS A.
FEVIN, WILLIAM
FIELD, R. B
FIFER, ALVINA
FIFER, JOHN
FIFER, M. S. MRS.
FIFER, MEREDITH S.
FIFER, MOLLIE J. MOORE
FIFER, ZELDA JANE
FILES, JAMES H.
FILSON, A.
FILSON, D. B.
FILSON, GEORGE M.
FILSON, MARY FRANCIS CARPENTER
FILSON, MAXWELL ROBERT GEORGE
FILSON, W.
FINK, ADAM
FINLEY, RICHARD
FINLEY, WILLIAM N.
FINLEY, WILLIAM P.
FINN, LUKE R.
FISE, JAMES M.
FISHEL, SAMUEL K.
FISHER, A. J.
FISHER, ALBERT
FISHER, JOHN S.
FISHER, ROBERT
FISHER, THOMAS W.
FISK, ADAH C. TRAIN
FISK, ADAM
FISK, ALICE (REED)
FISK, ANDREW J.
FISK, CLARA A. WILCOX
FISK, DANIEL W.
FISK, JAMES L.
FISK, MIRNA JOHNSON
FISK, VAN H.
FITCH, HENRY
FITSCHEN, GEORGE C.
FITSCHEN, GUS
FITSCHEN, LOUISE PFEIFER
FITZPATRICK, MABEL
FLAHERTY, INO
FLAHERTY, JOHN
FLANAGAN, MERRITT
FLANAGAN, MICHAEL ALBERT
FLANAGIN, CHARLES HENRY
FLANAGIN, CHARLOTTE
FLANAGIN, DELIA M.
FLANAGIN, ELLA GENEVA BURCH
FLANAGIN, HENRY W.
FLANAGIN, MARTHA ELLEN
FLANAGIN, SARAH
FLANDERS, GEORGE W.
FLANNAGAN, SARAH SANDERS
FLANNERY, ELLEN OPP
FLANNERY, WILLIAM
FLARARTY, MARION
FLARARTY, MARTHA
FLEGHER, HARRY
FLEMING, WILLIAM
FLETCHER, BLANCHE MONTANA THOMPSON
FLETCHER, J. P.
FLETCHER, WILLLIAM A.
FLETHCHER, HENRIETTA M. JACKSON
FLICK, JOSEPH P.
FLOWEREE, DANIEL A. G.
FLOWEREE, WILLIAM K.
FLOWERS, WILLIAM D.
FOLEY, PETER
FOLEY, THOMAS
FOLSOM, DAVID EDWIN
FONCANNON, HARESON
FOOTE, EFFIE (REED)
FOOTE, GEORGE B.
FORBES, FANNIE IRVINE
FORBIS, AMERICA A., MRS. (PERRIN)
FORBIS, JAMES WADE
FORBIS, JOHN FRANKLIN
FORBIS, WILLIAM P.

FORD, AARON T.
FORD, AARON TOLMAN
FORD, DELPHIA ANN PATTERSON
FORD, HENRY B.
FORD, J.P.
FORD, JOSEPH
FORD, MARY LOUISE CHOQUETH
FORD, ROBERT LEWIS
FORD, ROBERT SIMPSON
FORD, SAMUEL
FORD, THOMAS
FORD, WILLIAM H.
FOREMAN, MARY ISABELL HALSE
FORREST, MARY A. DENO
FORREST, ROBERT
FORREST, WILLIAM
FORT, ANDREW JACKSON
FORT, FRANCES C.
FOSTER, ALONZO H.
FOSTER, E., MRS.
FOSTER, EMILY YOUNG
FOSTER, FRANK
FOSTER, LEE WASHINGTON
FOSTER, MARY E. BEARD
FOSTER, ZENUS D
FOUTS, THOMAS HART BENTON
FOWLER, KATE
FOWLER, PETER HILL
FOX, A. W.
FOY, JOHN M.
FOY, PATRICK
FRAKES, ELIZABETH HENDRICKS
FRANCISCO, CHARLES
FRANCISCO, DAVID A.
FRANCISCO, DAVID ANDREW
FRANK, ALBERT B.
FRANK, EDWARD
FRANK, EMMA
FRANK, HENRY
FRASER, JOHN A.
FRATT, DAVID
FRAZER, MAY JANE FISHER
FRAZIER, ANNA BEACH
FRAZIER, ELIZABETH HEARD
FRAZIER, ELMIRAH HEARD
FRAZIER, G. W. A.
FRAZIER, GEORGE W.
FRAZIER, GEORGE W. A.
FRAZIER, JAMES ANDREW
FRAZIER, W. A.
FREDERICK, ANNA (RAY)
FREDERICK, WALTER E.
FREELER, CASPER
FREELER, DOMINIC
FREELER, HERMAN
FREEMAN, JACOB
FREEMAN, JEANNETTE PORTER (MRS)
FREESER, JOHN H.
FREGEAU, NAZAIRE
FRENCH, ANTHONY M
FRENCH, E. M.
FRENCH, GEORGE D.
FRENCH, GEORGE W.
FRENCH, MILO
FRENCH, OLIVER D.
FRENCH, ZERCH
FRETZ, NICHOLAS

FREWEN, THOMAS
FREYLER, CHARLES
FREYLER, HUGO
FRIDLEY, EDWIN LIBERTY
FRIDLEY, FREDRICK FRANKLIN
FRIDLEY, J.
FRIEDMAN, PAULINE SOBOLSKY
FRIELDS, GEORGE W.
FRIELDS, KATHERINE MORROW
FRIELER, ANTONE
FRIELER, VALENTINE (WEHELL)
FRIEND, FRANKLIN
FRITH, JOHN
FRITZ, B NICHOLAS
FRITZ, WILLIAM
FROST, FRED R.
FRUSER, JOHN W.
FRYLER, CHARLES
FULKERSON, LUCINDA
FULLER, KATHERINE REISS
FULLER, THOMAS PEAK
FULTON, HENRY
FURLONG, GEORGE
FURLONG, JAMES
FURLONG, MARGARET MAHER
FURNELL, M.
GAINAN, STEPHEN J.
GALAHAN, WILLIAM J.
GALEN, HUGH F.
GALLAGHER, ALONSO HUGH
GALLAGHER, FRANK
GALLAGHER, MARY LEU
GALLAGHER, THOMAS
GALLOP, JAMES H.
GALUSHA, JANUS L.
GALUSHA, SARAH (DUNCAN)
GAMER, FRED
GAMMELL, JENNETTE
GAMMON, FANNIE
GANNON, MICHAEL
GANS, JOSEPH
GANS, LOUIS
GARDINER, CHARLES
GARDINER, SUE
GARDNER, THOMAS BROWNELL
GARLAND, WILLIAM HENRY
GARNET, BRIDGET F.
GARNET, ELLEN (DOOLING)
GARNET, MICHAEL
GARNET, PATRICK
GARRETT, LeROY PATRICK
GARRETT, PAUL A.
GARRITY, VIRGINIA GEMMELL
GARWOOD, A. J.
GASS, PATRICK McLENE, SGT.
GAUGLER, FRANKLIN J.
GAUNT, JAMES MITCHELL D.
GEARY, ANNA McLAUGHLIN
GEARY, KATHERINE LAHERTY
GEARY, MICHAEL
GEARY, MICHAEL LEWIS
GEARY, WILLIAM
GEDIS, GEORGE
GEE, NOAH
GEEHRDTS, CASPER
GEEHRDTS, MARGARET (SLOKOTORER)
GEMMELL, CHARLES HARRISON

GEMMELL, JAMES
GEMMELL, JOSEPHINE IRWIN
GEMMELL, MARIA BROWN
GEORGE, JAMES (YANKEE JIM)
GERDTS, MARGARET BRANSER
GETCHELL, CHARLES H.
GETCHELL, F. S., MRS.
GETCHELL, FRANK S.
GETTS, SAMUEL V.
GIBBONS, ANNA STOREY
GIBBONS, BENJAMIN F.
GIBBS, ISRAEL
GIBBS, LaFAYETTE
GIBSON, ALEXANDER
GIBSON, EDWARD
GIBSON, JAMES
GIBSON, JAMES C.
GIBSON, NATHAN
GILBERT, FRANCES EMMA
GILBERT, HENRY SPANG
GILBERT, J. P.
GILBERT, JOHN R.
GILBERT, MARGARET McMUNN
GILBERT, MARY J. (RUSS)
GILBERT, WILLIAM H.
GILDERSLEEVE, CHARLES L.
GILG, FRANK
GILLESPIE, DAVID
GILLESPIE, L. R., MRS.
GILLESPIE, ROBERT
GILLETTE, WARREN C.
GILLICK, ANN BRADY
GILLIE, NETTIE EMERSON
GILLOGLY, MATILDA GALEN
GILMAN, A. L.
GILMAN, ELLA PAGE
GILMAN, HARVEY
GILMAN, ISAAC H.
GILMORE, MICHAEL CHARLES
GILPATRICK, L. F. MRS.
GILPATRICK, LUELLA (FERGUS)
GILPATRICK, STEPHEN
GIRARD, F. X.
GIRARD, NATHLIE
GITTHENS, LUELLA ROBERTSON
GLASGOW, MATTHEW
GLAUDE, NAPOLEON
GLENN, CLAUDE
GLENN, HUGH L.
GLENN, JAMES CLAUDE
GLENN, MARTHA GILSON
GOFF, CORTEZ
GOFF, SARAH JANE STRANGE
GOHN, ANNA (ZWEIFELL)
GOHN, GEORGE
GOHN, GEORGE EDWARD
GOHN, GEORGE H.
GOHN, KATE MacDONALD
GOODELL, CLARENCE M.
GOODELL, DWIGHT T.
GOODELL, PHOBE P. (TRAIN)
GOODMAN, MARY SABOLSKY
GOODMAN, MAURICE
GOODWIN, JAMES
GOODWIN, JAMES L.
GOODWIN, MRS. R. A.
GORDEN, JAMES
GORDON, GEORGE LESLIE
GORDON, HANNAH M.
GORDON, JAMES
GORDON, SARAH E. LATTA
GORDON, WILLIAM
GORE, MOLLIE
GORHAM, CATHERINE WILMOTH GAUNT
GORHAM, RICHARD T.
GORHAM. THOMAS L.
GORMLEY, AUSTIN CARLOS
GORMLEY, JULIA GOOD
GORMLEY, THOMAS JEFFERSON
GOSS, F. S.
GOURLEY, JAMES
GOWIN, THOMAS J.
GRAETER, AUGUSTUS F..
GRAETER, MARGARET A.
GRAHAM, ARTHUR
GRAHAM, HENRY
GRATTAN, HATTIE E.
GRATTAN, MARTHA M. ROBERTS
GRATTAN, MARY (WELLS)
GRATTAN, STEPHEN A.
GRATTAN, WILLARD
GRAVES, FIELDING L.
GRAVES, HENRY CLAY
GRAVES, J. H.
GRAVES, LEOTIE NAYE
GRAY, MARY A. HICKEY
GRAY, ROBERT N.
GRAYDON, WILLIAM
GRAYSON, GEORGE
GREDEL, NICHOLAS
GREEN, ANDREW
GREEN, BENJAMIN F.
GREEN, CHARLES HENRY
GREEN, ELIZA
GREEN, FRANCES F. SULLIVAN
GREEN, HATTIE N LINDNER
GREEN, ISABELLE
GREEN, JAMES
GREEN, JAMES A.
GREEN, JOHN H.
GREEN, JOSEPH
GREEN, JOSEPH A.
GREEN, KATHERINE LLOYD
GREEN, MARGARET (WILLWOOD)
GREEN, MARTIN VAN BUREN
GREEN, MARY JANE
GREEN, MELISSA
GREEN, WILLIAM
GREGSON, ELI
GREGSON, GEORGE W.
GRENON, ODILE MARCOTTE
GREY, IDA
GREY, LELIA
GRIDLEY, LEONARD A.
GRIERSEN, ROBERT
GRIFFITH, JOHN
GRIFFITH, JOSEPH MILTON
GRIFFITH, T. H.
GRIFFITH, THOMAS
GRIFFITHS, AGNES THOMAS
GRIFFITHS, JOHN F.
GRIM, MARY
GRIM, MARY M. (ZIEGLER)
GRIM, SIMON PETER

GRIMES, WILLIAM
GRINSELL, EDWARD
GRISWOLD, CORNELIUS
GROGAN, DARIUS F.
GRUBBE, A. J.
GRUWELL, C. OSCAR
GRUWELL, C. OSCAR MRS.
GUM, ELLEN E. MURRAY
GUM, JACOB
GUNEAU, ANTHONY A
GUNN, JACOB H.
GURNETT, MICHAEL
GUTHRIE, WILLIAM HUBBARD
GUTRAS, OLIVER
GUY, JOHN CRAIG
GUY, ROBERT JAMES
GUYAZ, JULES
HACKNEY, JOHN S.
HACKNEY, W. H.
HACKSHAW, AGNES
HACKSHAW, CORNELIUS
HACKSHAW, ENOCH
HACKSHAW, JOHN A.
HACKSHAW, JOHN C
HACKSHAW, SOPHIA JANE HUETT
HADZAR, GEORGE F
HAHN, WILLIAM H.
HAIN, JENNIE HAINES
HAINDS, JOSEPH
HAINE, JACOB
HAINES, WILLIAM
HAISLOP, ROBERT E.
HALE, GEORGE E.
HALE, N. B MRS. (FRENCH)
HALE, N. B.
HALE, QUINCY H.
HALE, R. S.
HALE, ROBERT S.
HALE, WILLARD HARLOW
HALFORD ELLEN McKNIGHT
HALFORD, DODLEY
HALFORD, DON M.
HALFORD, JAMES B.
HALFORD, JAMES HUSTON
HALL, AMOS C.
HALL, AMOS CROSS
HALL, CHARLES SAMUEL
HALL, JOHN
HALL, JOHN S.
HALL, JOHN JAY
HALL, JOHN JOE
HALL, JOHN S.
HALL, JOHN W.
HALL, JOSEPH EDGAR
HALL, LEVI
HALL, NANCY (HARTER)
HALL, NANNIE (MOORE)
HALL, SAMUEL
HALL, SARGEANT
HALLAWAY, JOHN
HALPIN, BRIDGET
HALSE, MARY ISABELLA FOREMAN
HALZ, CHARLES SAMUEL
HAMILTON, ALFRED B.
HAMILTON, BEN S.
HAMILTON, G. B.
HAMILTON, LAURA BRANDT
HAMILTON, MARY AGNES (FERGUS)
HAMILTON, MARY J. (STANCHFIELD)
HAMILTON, ROBERT STAVELY
HAMILTON, THOMAS C.
HAMILTON, THOMAS H.
HAMILTON, WILLIAM
HAMILTON, WILLIAMTHOMAS
HAMMOND, GEORGE L.
HAMMOND, WILLIAM
HAMPER, WILLIAM
HANCHILD, ALBERT O.
HANCHILD, GEORGE WILLIAM
HANLEY, SAMUEL AQUILLA
HANNA, IRA MONROE
HANSEL, JACOB
HANSEN, ANN (PETERSEN)
HANSEN, ANNA
HANSEN, JOSEPH
HANSEN, L. C.
HANSEN, MARY (JENSEN)
HANSEN, MATT
HANSEN, NILES
HANSEN, WILLIS
HANSON, ANNIE C.
HANSON, HORATIO
HANSON, J. B.
HANSON, JANE McCARTY
HANSON, JENNIE E. WARREN
HANSON, RANDALL W.
HARBY, JAMES
HARCUM, CHRISTOPHER C.
HARD, CHARLES A.
HARD, CHARLES D.
HARDENBROOK, A.
HARDENBROOK, ALLEN DR.
HARDENBROOK, ANNA TOOLE
HARDENBROOK, ELIZA (WALKER)
HARDGROVE, AMANDA (GEARY)
HARDGROVE, HEZIKIAH
HARDGROVE, JOHN WILLIAM
HARDING, ANNA LOUISE
HARDING, DWIGHT
HARDING, MARY KENEALY
HARDING, STEPHEN J.
HARDWICK, T. W.
HARGROVE, WILLIAM
HARKINS, MICHAEL
HARLAN, W. B.
HARLOW, WILSON B.
HARNOIS, FRANCIS XAVIER LUKEN
HARPER, THOMAS B.
HARRINGTON, FAYETTE
HARRINGTON, H. M. MRS. (BOWER)
HARRINGTON, ISAAC
HARRINGTON, JEREMIAH
HARRINGTON, JERRY
HARRINGTON, JOHN
HARRINGTON, KATE KELLEY
HARRIS, ADDIE F.
HARRIS, B. N.
HARRIS, BARNABY
HARRIS, BATHESDELEU MRS.
HARRIS, D. L.
HARRIS, E. J.
HARRIS, FRANK B.
HARRIS, FRANKLYN BENJAMIN SR.
HARRIS, HENRY S.

HARRIS, HOWELL
HARRIS, ISAAC
HARRIS, JOHN
HARRIS, JOHN DAVID
HARRIS, MARGARET HANNA FANNING
HARRIS, MARY
HARRIS, ROBERT THOMAS
HARRIS, THOMAS
HARRIS, THOMAS W.
HARRIS, THOMAS WOODSON
HARRISON, ALMARETTA E. (DEAR)
HARRISON, ELTON KLEINSCHMIDT
HARRISON, HENRY CLAY
HARRISON, JOSEPH
HARRISON, PATRICK
HART, A. MRS.
HART, ALBERT MARSHALL
HART, EMMA
HART, JACOB
HARTCORN, M. C.
HARTER, H. S.
HARTLEY, MINNIE L. JONES
HARTLEY, SARAH JANE SHERRILL
HARTMAN, MARY REBECCA SWITZER
HARTS, CORA D.
HARTWELL, CHARLES ALBERT
HARTWELL, JOSEPH W.
HARTWIG, JACOB
HARTWIG, PAULINE PFIEFER
HARTWIG, PETER
HARTZ. PETER
HARTZELL, FRANK B.
HARVEY, HUGH K.
HARWOOD, JOHN J.
HARWOOD, ROBERT H.
HARWOOD, THOMAS B.
HASH, AHART
HASKELL, MARY JANE (SMITH)
HASKELL, WILLIAM S.
HASKINS, CEPHAS W.
HASTINGS, SARAH MYERS
HATCH, LUKE D.
HATFIELD, JOHN EDWARD B.
HATFIELD, MICHAEL ASEAL (ACILE)
HATHAWAY, I. W.
HATHAWAY, JAMES W.
HATHORNE, JOHN RIPLEY
HATTON, LOUISA
HAUKE, JOHN K.
HAUKE, JOS.
HAUSE, JAMES
HAUSER, JOSEPH
HAUSER, MARY E.
HAUSER, SAMUEL THOMAS
HAUSWORTH, JOHN
HAUSWORTH, SIMON
HAWLEY, CHARLES R.
HAWLEY, CYRUS B.
HAY, HENRY JR.
HAY, HENRY SR.
HAYDEN, CAROLINE (HUME)
HAYDEN, ELIZABETH OSWALD
HAYDEN, JOHN F.
HAYDEN, SAMUEL
HAYES, EDWARD S.
HAYES, MARVIN
HAYES, SOPHIA McHUGH

HAYS, WILLIAM ORMAN PARK
HEALEY, CHARLES HENRY
HEALY, JAMES
HEARS, ELMYRA McCOY
HEARTZ, PETER
HEATH, ARCHIBALD
HEATZELL, ALICE KUNKEL
HEDGE, ROBERT
HEDGES, CORNELIUS
HEDGES, DeFOREST
HEDGES, EDNA LaFAYETTE
HEDGES, HENRY F.
HEDGES, ROBERT
HEDGES, WYLLIS ANDERSON
HEEB, H.
HEEB, H., MRS.
HELAY, JOHN JEROME
HELDT, F. GEORGE
HELDT, JOHN N.
HELLINGER, H., MRS.
HELLINGER, MARY E.
HELMS, HENRY JOHN
HELMS, J. H.
HEMPSTEAD, JOHN
HEMPSTEAD, MARY INGLE
HENAULT, ELSIE DUPUIS
HENAULT, MAXIUM FRANCIS
HENDERSON, JOSEPH
HENNEBERRY, JOHN
HENNEBERRY, MARGARET B. (BARY)
HENNEBERRY, MICHAEL A.
HENNEBERRY, MICHAEL B.
HENNESSY, MARY FURLONG
HENNESSY, DAVID W.
HENRY, DANIEL BRADLEY
HENRY, MARIE E. DUFF
HENSLEY, W. A. MRS.
HENSLEY, WILLIAM ALLEN
HERBERT, GEORGE
HERENDEEN, EDWARD G.
HERHOLD, MARY (McKAY)
HERMAN, JACOB
HERMAN, JOHN
HERNDON, JAMES M.
HERNDON, SARAH RAYMOND
HERR, MINERVA WINTERS
HERRIN, DANIEL. S.
HERRMAN, JAKE
HERRMANN, ANNA
HERSHFIELD, AARON
HERSHFIELD, LEWIS H
HEWINS, HOMER DEWOLF
HEYBURN, HENRY J.
HEZEKIAH, JOHN
HIBBARD, EDWARD
HICKEY, EDWARD
HICKEY, JAMES J.
HICKEY, JANE O'NEILL
HICKEY, MARY A.
HICKEY, WILLIAM C.
HICKMAN, RICHARD OWEN
HICKS, SARAH J. B.
HIEGER, MARY GERTRUDE
HIGGINS, CHRISTOPHER POWERS
HIGGINS, FRANK G.
HIGGINS, L. B.
HIGGINS, WILLIAM B. S.

HIGGINS, WILLIAM W.
HIGHBEE, ERWIN
HIGHBEE, JESSIE B.
HILGER, DAVID
HILGER, LOUISA E. G.
HILGER, MATTHEW
HILGER, NICHOLAS
HILGER, SUSANA
HILL, HENRY M.
HILL, JOSEPH S.
HILL, SARAH JANE (BERKIN)
HINCH, CHARTY C. (TAYLOR)
HINCH, WILLIAM
HINCHCLIFF, S.
HINES, JOHN
HIRSHBURG, JOSEPH
HIRST, EMMA
HOBACK, RICHARD
HOBBINS, JOHN
HOBSON, NATHAN
HODGE, TRUMAN L.
HODSON, ALVIN
HODSON, ENOCH
HODSON, L. A., MRS.
HOEPFNER, ADOLPH
HOEPFNER, CHARLES
HOFFELT, MARGHERETTA (JOHNS)
HOFFMAN, CHARLES WHEELER
HOGAN, CATHERINE EMPIRE
HOGAN, DION J.
HOGAN, MATTHEW
HOGLE, JAMES
HOLBROOK, GEORGE S.
HOLDEN, REUBEN JOHN SR.
HOLEHAN, PATRICK
HOLLAND, BENJAMIIN B.
HOLLAND, JOHN
HOLLENBECK, G. J.
HOLM, ANDREW
HOLM, ANDY H.
HOLMEAD, JOHN
HOLMES, LEVI EDWIN
HOLT, J. P.
HOLT, JAMES R.
HOLTER, ANTON B.
HOLTER, ANTON M.
HOLTER, MARTIN M.
HOLTER, MARY PAULINE
HOLTER, NORMAN BERNARD
HOOBAN, TOM
HOOPES, WILLIAM PIERIE
HOOVER, A. BENTON
HOOVER, ALFRED BENTON
HOOVER, DAVID
HOPKINS, JOHN W.
HOPKINS, TRUMAN
HOPPE, ALBERT G.
HOPPE, H. J.
HOPPE, H. J., MRS.
HOPPE, WALTER MONROE
HOPPING, JACOB OSBORN
HOPPING, MARY E. ALLEN
HOPS, JOHN
HORN, BANK
HORNE, JAMES E..
HORNE, REBECCA (OSBORNE)
HORSKY, JOHN

HORSKY, JOSEPH
HORTON, H. S.
HORTON, SARAH
HOUKES, JOHN K.
HOULE, JOSEPH
HOUSE, JAMES
HOUSEL, JACOB
HOUSER, MARY E.
HOUSTON, ELIZABETH LINA
HOUSTON, HARRY
HOWARD, GEORGE C.
HOWARD, H. H. MRS.
HOWARD, JOSEPH
HOWARD, KATHERINE E.
HOWE, EDWARD
HOWE, GEORGE W.
HOWE, MARY J. (WYRONCK)
HOWELL, HORATION S.
HOWELL, L. M.
HOWELL, THOMAS W.
HOYT, DEBORAH M. (RUSSELL)
HOYT, EDWARD M.
HOYT, JAMES
HOYT, SARAH
HUDSON, ANNIE
HUDSON, MARY ELIZABETH (POWERS)
HUFF, JACOB
HUFF, MARTHA PRICE
HUFFEL, MARGHERETA (JOHNS)
HUFFER, ELIZABETH
HUFFMAN, GEORGE
HUFFMAN, MARTIN V.
HUGHES, AGNES
HUGHES, BARNARD
HUGHES, RICHARD
HUGHES, SAMUEL
HUGHES, SILVAN
HULBERT, CHARLES R.
HULL, JOHN J.
HULLER, ISABELLA
HULLER, ISABELLA MARY
HUMBERT, EUGENE
HUME, W. H.
HUMPHREY, G. O.
HUNDLEY, ALEXANDER
HUNT, BETHUEL HOWARD
HUNT, THOMAS R.
HUNT, TRYPHENE, MRS.
HUNTER, ANDREW JACKSON
HUNTER, HATTIE (BOWLER)
HUNTER, MARY ELIZABETH (HARRINGTON)
HUNTER, SILAS A.
HUNTER, SUSAN CELESTA (MURRAY)
HUNTER, TABITHA (DUFF)
HURDLE, JOSEPH
HUSON, ELIJAH T.
HUSSEY, ANNA L.
HUSTON, ROBERT G.
HUTCHINSON, HECTOR
HUTCHISON, HECTOR W.
HUUSBERGER, JOHN
HYDE, JOSEPH A.
HYDE, JOSEPH E.
HYDE, WILLIAM
HYNES, PETER
IMKAMP, HENRY
IMMEL, AMELIA NORRIS

IMODA, CAMILLUS (S. J.)
INGERSOLL, CYRUS STONE
INGLIS, JAMES
INGRAM, GEORGE FELIX
INGRAM, JOHN T.
INNES, JOHN C.
IRA, PHYLLIS ALLIS
IRVIN, GEORGE W. II
IRVINE, ANNA ELIZA FORBIS
IRVINE, AVIS JOSEPHINE
IRVINE, C. E., MRS.
IRVINE, CALEB E.
IRVINE, DAVID C.
IRVINE, DAVID L.
IRVINE, EDWIN HART
IRVINE, ELLA
IRVINE, FANNIE L. RUSSELL
IRVINE, FORBIS
IRVINE, GELLE BOYD BRYAN
IRVINE, MOLLIE ELLEN MITCHELL
IRVINE, THOMAS C.
IRVINE, THOMAS CORWIN
IRVINE, THOMAS H.
IRVINE, WILLIAM
ISDELL, NELSON J.
JACK, ALEXANDER
JACK, PRESTON
JACKSON, EDWARD
JACKSON, GEORGE
JACKSON, JACOB H.
JACKSON, JOSEPH
JACKSON, PETER V.
JACKSON, R. G.
JACKSON, THOMPSON COLLINS
JACKSON, WILLIAM DOWMAN
JACOB, JOHN
JACOBS, ADELE
JACOBS, EMMA AUSTIN
JACOBS, HENRY
JACOBS, JULIUS
JACQUEMUN, CHARLES B.
JACQUES, GEORGE
JAMES, CHARLOTTE THOMAS
JAMES, ESAU
JAMES, MELINDA E.
JAMES, PHILIP H.
JAMES, THOMAS JEFFERSON
JAMES, WILLIAM M.
JAMES, WILLIAM M. MRS
JAMES, WILLIAM R..
JAY, O.W.
JEFFERS, FLORENCE SWITZER
JEFFERS, MYRON D.
JEFFERS, SUSAN LOIS SWITZER
JEFFRIES, MARY L.
JELM, JAMES
JENKINS, ROSSER PRICE
JENNINGS, JOSHUA
JENSEN, MARY JERGENSEN
JENSEN, MATTIE HANSEN
JERGENSEN, CHRIS
JERGENSEN, LARS
JERGENSEN, MARY JENSEN
JESSEE, DAVID H.
JESSEN, PETER
JEWELL, ISSACHER WESLEY
JEWELL, WILLIAM E.

JOHNS, ENOCH
JOHNS, T. JEFFERSON
JOHNS, WILLIAM
JOHNSON, ADAH H. KELLY
JOHNSON, ALFRED
JOHNSON, BENJAMIN FRANKLIN
JOHNSON, C. MAC
JOHNSON, CHARLES L.
JOHNSON, CHARLES P.
JOHNSON, DAVID A.
JOHNSON, EBENEZER
JOHNSON, ELMER F.
JOHNSON, ISABELLE GILLS
JOHNSON, JOHN
JOHNSON, JOHN A
JOHNSON, JOSEPH R.
JOHNSON, LAURA A. CAGLE
JOHNSON, LIZZIE (KELLEY)
JOHNSON, LUCINDA
JOHNSON, N. D.
JOHNSON, NELSON
JOHNSON, NEWMAN
JOHNSON, PERRY
JOHNSON, REUBEN A.
JOHNSON, ROBERT
JOHNSON, RUFUS
JOHNSON, SPENCER
JOHNSTON, JOHN A.
JONES, ANNA
JONES, CHARLES B.
JONES, EDWARD W.
JONES, EUGENE
JONES, JACOB HARDESTY
JONES, JAMES G.
JONES, JANE (BURCH)
JONES, JOHN
JONES, JOHN C.
JONES, JOHN S.
JONES, JOHN WESLEY
JONES, LEWIS
JONES, MINNIE (HARTLEY)
JONES, MORRIS
JONES, R. S.
JONES, REBECCA F. (HARDESTY)
JONES, THOMAS B.
JONES, WESLEY W.
JONES, WILLIAM WILLIAMS
JORDAN, CELESTE GRACE
JORDAN, WALTER M. B.
JOSLYN, NANNIE B. (KELLEY)
JUMP, C.
JURGENS, JOHN HENRY
KAISER, EDWARD
KAISER, LOUISA
KAISER, MICHAEL
KAMP, JENNIE (CURTIS)
KANE, JOHN
KARNES, SARAH
KARTNER, JAMES M.
KAY, JAMES
KAY, JOHN M.
KAY, MARY HOPE
KEASTER, EDWARD
KEATING, JOHN A.
KEATON, LIZZIE FRANCES
KEELER, ELEANORA (BRANNIN)
KEENE, FLAVIUS J.

KEENE, HARRIET BYRON (DAVIS)
KEENE, HARVEY LANE
KEENE, THOMAS
KEILEY, MICHAEL
KEIM, LEVI FULLMER
KELLEY, FRANCIS M.
KELLEY, GEORGE W.
KELLEY, J.
KELLEY, JOHN EMMETT
KELLEY, KATE R. (NAPTON)
KELLEY, MARY L. (FORMAN)
KELLEY, NANCY
KELLEY, OWEN
KELLEY, RICHARD H.
KELLEY, ROBERT LEE
KELLEY, ROBERT S.
KELLOGG, CLARK WESLEY
KELLOGG, L.
KELLOGG, LUCIUS
KELLY, ADAH H.
KELLY, EDWARD
KELLY, F. M. MRS.(JOHNSON)
KELLY, FRANCIS M.
KELLY, JOHN E.
KELLY, JOHN S.
KELLY, NANCY (WARNER)
KEMNA, ANNA MARGARET
KEMPER, HENRY
KENCH, THERESA (ODENWALD)
KENCK, CHRISTIAN
KENCK, JACOB
KENCK, JOSEPH M.
KENEALY, DANIEL
KENNEDY, CLARISSA
KENNEDY, ELIZABETH (SWEENEY)
KENNEDY, J. J.
KENNEDY, JAMES F.
KENNEDY, JAMES H.
KENNEDY, JOHN J.
KENNEDY, STEPHEN
KENNEDY, T. H.
KENNEDY, WILLIAM
KENNERLY, HENRY ATKINSON
KENNETT, FERDINAND
KENNEY, CATHERINE ADELIA (KEIME)
KENNICOTT, JENNIE ALLEN (LEWIS)
KENNON, FANNIE
KENNON, R. T., MRS.
KENNON, RICHARD T.
KENT, GRESS
KENT, JAMES
KENT, THOMAS
KENYON, CHARLES D.
KEPPLER, J. G.
KEPPLER, JOSEPH C.
KERNAN, ELLEN
KESSINGER, CAROLINE M.
KESSLER, NICKOLAS
KESSLER, PETER N.
KEUNER, METTIE M.
KILLIAN, HENRY
KIMBERLEY, ALLAN
KING, CARLYLE WARREN
KING, GEORGE T.
KING, HUGH
KING, JAMES
KING, JAMES MELVIN

KING, MINNIE NOBLE (BROOKE)
KING, SILAS F.
KING, WALTER J.
KINGREY, HENRY
KINGREY, ISAAC M.
KINGSBURY, ADKIN WALLACE
KINGSBURY, BENJAMIN C.
KINNA, JANET (MC GOVERN)
KINNA, JOHN
KINNASON, ANNIE
KINNEY, GEORGE PARKE
KINNEY, KATHERINE
KINYON PELICK DALY
KIPP, JAMES
KIPP, JOSEPH
KIRBY, ARALEN (ARRIE) (WALTON)
KIRCHER, PETER
KIRKALDIE, FRANKLIN LUTHER
KIRKENDALL, HUGH
KIRKENDALL, ISABELLA
KIRKENDALL, NETTIE E.
KIRKPATRICK, CLARA (KEPPLER)
KIRKPATRICK, JAMES
KIRKPATRICK, ROBERT
KIRKWOOD, WILLIAM F.
KLAUE, CHRISTIAN
KLAUS, CHARLES
KLEIN, BEN
KLEIN, HENRY
KLEINSCHMIDT, ALBERT
KLEINSCHMIDT, REINHOLD H.
KLEINSCHMIDT, THEODORE H.
KLINE, BEN
KLINE, MARY J.
KLINE, MOLLIE J.(FIFER)
KLINE, PETER J.
KLING, HERMAN I.
KLOEDEN, WILLIAM
KLUND, PETER E.
KNADLER, E. M.
KNIGHT JULIAN M.
KNIGHT, AGNES (LOBB)
KNOWLES, FREEMAN H.
KNOWLES, HIRAM
KNOX, R. C.
KOCH, AUGUST B.
KOCH, CHARLES
KOHLS, VIRGINIA BELLE (KELLOGG)
KOHRS, AUGUSTA
KOHRS, AUGUSTA
KOHRS, CONRAD CARSTON
KOLKSCHNEIDER, HENRIETTA (SCHNEPLE)
KOLTZ, AUGUST
KONANCE, HIGEN
KRAEMER, FREDERICK
KRANICH, WILLIAM
KRANICK, CHARLES
KRANICK, CHARLES W.
KRATTECER, GEORGE WASHINGTON
KRAUS, HENRY
KRENZBERGER, MICKEL
KREUGER, LAVIS A. E.
KROHN, JOHN
KROPF, VALENTINE (KROPP)
KROSSMAN, ADAM
KRUG, CHARLES
KUNTZ, LOUISE ANNA

LABEAU, JOHN B.
LABONCHERE, JOSEPH
LACAFF, JOSEPH
LACBLIN, LOUIS B.
LACEY, ELLEN (RYAN)
LaCROIX, LUCIAN FRANCIS
LaDOUX, NARCISSE
LaFLUER, MARY (MILOT)
LaFOUNTAIN, J. M.
LaFOUNTAIN, PETER M.
LAFTON, FRANK
LAFVERSON, OLAF
LAHERTY, CATHERINE MAHER (COUGHLIN)
LAHERTY, WILLIAM
LAHMIRE, HENRY H.
LaLONDE, ADAM A.
LAMASTER, LIZZIE
LAMBERT, GENEVIEVE (COX)
LAMBRECHT, ALPHONSE
LAMOTT, JOHN
LANCASTER, BENJAMIN
LANCASTER, JOHN WESLEY
LANCASTER, NANCY JANE
LANCASTER, SARAH S.
LANGFORD, NATHANIEL PITT
LANGHORNE, SAMUEL W.
LANNAN, BRIDGET
LANNAN, EDWARD
LANSING, ANDREW J.
LANSING, PETER
LAPIER, FRANK
LaPOINTE, GEORGE
LARABIE, JULIA WOOLFORK
LARABIE, SAMUEL EDWARD
LaREAU, FRANK
LAREAU, WILLIAM E.
LARENCE, CECILE VENNE
LARGENT, JOHN
LARGENT, JOSEPH LEWIS
LARGEY, PATRICK A.
LARKIN, MICHAEL C.
LARKIN, PETER
LARREN, HANAH
LARSEN, ANNA MARY (GRIFFITH)
LARSEN, JOSEPH
LARSEN, LARS CHRISTIAN
LARSEN, MARY D.
LARSEN, MASSI
LARSEN, MIELS
LARSON, JOHN
LaSALLE, ADOLPH
LATIMER, JOHN R.
LATTA, JAMES C.
LATTA, JAMES LOUIS
LATTA, SARAH E.
LAUGHLIN, DAVID N.
LAURIN, JEAN BATISTE
LAVADDIE, THOMAS
LAVEY, ELIZA HOLDEN (CARLTON)
LAW, JOHN
LAWRENCE, AQUILLA (QUILL)
LEARY, JOHN
LEAVITT, ERASMUS DARWIN
LeBEAU, JEAN BAPTISTE
LeBEAU, PETER
LEDBEATER, MARK D.
LEE, SAM F.

LEE, W. H.
LEEDY, FRANK
LEEDY, JEANETTE (MORROW)
LeFEFRE, JESSE
LEFFLER, J. H.
LEGGAT, CATHERINE
LEGGAT, RODERICK D.
LEGGAT, RODERICK D. MRS.
LEHMAN, CAROLINE (BACH)
LEHMAN, CHARLES
LEHMAN, FREDERICK
LEHMAN, JOHN C.
LEINDECKER, CHARLES
LEISER, J. S. MRS.
LEISER, JACOB S.
LEITH, CHARLES B.
LELAND, JOHN W.
LELAND, JOHN WILKINSON
LEMON, JAMES H.
LENIHAN, MAURICE
LEONARD, HUGH
LEONARD, W. W.
LEPINE, AIME
LEPPER, FRANK J.
LESSARD, AGNES H.
LESSARD, JOSEPH
LESTER, ANNIE (O'KEEFE)
LETTICE, HENRY
LETTICE, MARIA ANN (BOGALY)
LETTICE, MARY ANN (TRAYNOR)
LEUPOINT, GEORGE, MRS.
LEVENGOOD, ELIZABETH (McFERSON)
LEVENGOOD, PETER ANDREW
LEWIS, ANNE
LEWIS, EDWARD A.
LEWIS, EDWARD W.
LEWIS, GEORGE LEONARD
LEWIS, GEORGE S.
LEWIS, GEORGE TAYLOR
LEWIS, ISABELL TABER B.
LEWIS, J. R.
LEWIS, JENNIE KENNICOTT
LEWIS, JENNIE X.
LEWIS, JOHN T.
LEWIS, SOPHIA GARDNER
LEWIS, THOMAS
LIDDLE, ANN JANE
LIFFRING, SARAH A.
LILLERY, LeROY
LINCOLN, ALVIN RIPLEY
LIND, ELLA MURRAY
LINDER, WILLIAM JASPER
LINDLEY, JOSEPH MILLER
LINEBARGER, DAVID H.
LINK, MARY BARKER
LINN, JOHN
LINSLEY, J. REXFCRD
LISCOM, GEORGE W.
LISSNER, MARCUS
LISTER, LUTIE LEE (EVANS)
LIVINGSTON, W. J., MRS.
LIVSE, CLARA (MARKS)
LLOYD, CATHERINE (GREEN)
LLOYD, GEORGE HENRY B.
LLOYD, HANNAH MARIA
LLOYD, JOHN
LLOYD, WILLIAM R.

LOBB, MORTIMER. H.
LOCKE, JOHN F.
LOCKER, ANDREW J.
LOCKEY, RICHARD
LOCKWOOD, AMANDA
LOCKWOOD, FRANK M.
LOCKWOOD, MYRON M.
LOEB, BERNARD
LOEB, JACOB
LOFTON, FRANK
LOGAN, WILLIAM COLUMBUS
LOHMIRE, CAPT
LOMBARD, C. W.
LONG, ELLEN B.
LONG, JOHN
LONGLEY, JOHN I.
LONGTIN, STEPHEN
LOONEY, MARY JANE
LORENZ, JOSEPHINE
LORENZ, WILLIAM
LOTT, JOHN S.
LOTT, MELVINA J., MRS.
LOTT, MORTIMER HEWLETT
LOVELL, GEORGE W.
LOVELL, PHILIP
LOVEY, LAWRENCE
LOWDERS, WILLIAM M.
LOWE, WILLIAM
LOWERY, MICHEAL
LOWMAN, JACOB BANICH
LOWMAN, JACOB BARRACK
LOWRY, THOMAS JEFFERSON
LUCE, GEORGE E.
LUCE, TIMOTHY L.
LULL, PHIINEAS F.
LUND, ANNA REED
LUNDWALL, O. A.
LUNN, KATE POINDEXTER
LUPPOLD, WILLIAM
LYING, H. O.
LYMAN, LORENZO BRANCH
LYNCH, CHARLES ALEXANDER
LYNCH, EDWARD
LYNCH, ELIZABETH (ALEXANDER)
LYNCH, JOHN
LYNCH, NEPTUNE
LYNCH, THOMAS
LYNG, HALVOR O.
LYNN, ROSETTA BARNES
LYON, E. S.
LYON, ELIZA (HAYDEN)
LYON, GEORGE
LYON, GEORGE D.
LYON, GEORGE H.
MACARTNEY, FREDERICK C.
MacGOWAN, ANN MEIKLEJOHN
MACHEAU, JOSEPH
MacKENZIE, JOHN P.
MACLAY, EDGAR GLEIM
MACOMBER, ARCHER
MACOMBER, MARTHA (BORTON)
MAGGARD, FIDELIA ANN (STARK)
MAGILL, MARY (THOROUGHMAN)
MAGINNIS, MARTIN
MAHAN, IDA
MAILEY, JOHN
MAILEY, ROSE ROMEY

MAILLET, LOUIS R.
MAJORS, GREEN
MALBEN, BENJAMIN
MALLORY, CHARLES GEO. MASTERSON
MALLORY, PHILIP
MALONEY, JOHN
MALONEY, MICHAEL
MALOY, PATRICK A.
MANDEVILLE, H. M.
MANLEY, MARGARET (MODESTO)
MANLEY, MATTHEW
MANLOVE, JOHNATHAN H.
MANN, JAMES M.
MANNING, MABEL (ELLEDGE)
MANOR, JEANNETTE (WHITEHEAD)
MANSFIELD, JAMES
MANWARRING, FLORA
MAQUIRE, H. N.
MARATTA, JAMES
MARBLE, ETTA LOUISA
MARCHESSEAU, SOPHRONIUS
MARCOTTE, LEWIS
MARCOTTE, ODILE
MARCUM, J. E. MRS.
MARCUM, KATE (BIGNELL)
MARDEN, MARY H.
MARDIS, ADDIE H.
MARDIS, HARRIET ADELAIDE (NOE)
MARDIS, J. W.
MARDIS, JOHN HENRY
MARION, ALPHONSE
MARION, JOHN
MARION, JOSEPH EDWARD
MARKET, JULIA STAUBACK
MARKS, CLARA
MARKS, CLARY LERY
MARKS, DAVID
MARKS, JAMES RUFUS
MARKS, LEOPOLD
MARKS, MOSES H.
MARSDEN, JAMES WILLIAM
MARSHALL, JIM J.
MARSHALL, JOHN JOSEPH
MARSHALL, JOSEPH
MARSHALL, SARAH E.
MARSHALL, THOMAS
MARSTEN, SIM (SAM)
MARSTON, ELIZA (VALTZIN)
MARSTON, LEANDER FITZALLEN
MARTENS, JOHN B.
MARTIN, ELIZABETH
MARTIN, HENRY
MARTIN, JAMES E.
MARTIN, MARTHA F.
MARTIN, R. W.
MARTIN, WILLIAM
MASON, ABBIE LOUISE (SPARRELL)
MASON, ALBERT
MASON, BENJAMIN PARKER
MASON, FRANK
MASON, JAMES
MASON, ROBY ADELAIDE (WALKER)
MASON, THERESA (LINSLEY)
MASTETTNE, BENGLEN FRANKLIN
MATHIAS, C.
MATT, LOUIS
MAULDIN, JAMES

MAULDIN, WILLIAM T.
MAURER, HERMAN
MAURY, FRANK
MAXEY, DANIEL
MAXEY, MARGARET
MAXON, JAMES H.
MAXON, JOHN H.
MAXWELL,NELLIE K.
MAY, MARTIN V.
MAY, RICHARD F.
MAYFIELD, A. A.
MAYGER, WILLIAM
MAYNARD, ETHEL A.
McADAMS, JAMES
McADOW, PERRY W.
McADOW, WILLIAM B.
McALLISTER, H. A.
McALLISTER, JAMES
McANDRES, JAMES S.
McANDREWS, WILLIAM
McBREEN, MARY A. (RIES)
McCAFFREY, JOHN
McCALL, ANNNETTE (FOSTER)
McCALL, WILLIAM WESLEY
McCAMMON, JAMES D.
McCANN, EDWARD
McCARTHY, ANTHONY J.
McCARTHY, ARTHUR
McCARTHY, J. W.
McCARTNEY, JAMES C.
McCARTY, ALICE
McCARTY, CHARLES FRANCIS
McCARTY, FRANCIS MARION
McCARTY, JOHN W.
McCARTY, MABEL
McCAULEY, BRIDGET G. (CLARK)
McCAULEY, CASS H. (BEABER)
McCAULEY, HENRY
McCAULEY, JEFFERSON
McCAULEY, MICHAEL
McCAULEY, MICHAEL M.
McCAULEY, NATHANIEL MITCHELL
McCAULEY, THOMAS HENRY
McCLAIN, JACOB P.
McCLAIN, JOHN PERRY
McCLAIN, JOHN S.
McCLEERY KATE (ADAMS)
McCLEERY, FRANK
McCLOUD, JENNIE L.
McCLURE, ALEXANDER KELLY
McCLURG, JOHN E.
McCOMAS, WILLIAM R.
McCORMICK, JOHN
McCORMICK, KATHERINE (HIGGINS)
McCORMICK, LUVINIA OATMEN (WELLS)
McCORMICK, MATTIE
McCORMICK, PAUL
McCORMICK, ROBERT
McCORMICK, WASHINGTON J.
McCOY, E. J.
McCOY, JESSE
McCRANOR, DAVID
McCUNE, JOHN
McDANIEL, CALVIN MORGAN
McDANIEL, CHILNESSA JANE (YOUNG)
McDANIEL, L. A.
McDERMOTT, CHARLES

McDERMOTT, DELIA
McDERMOTT, JEFFERSON
McDERMOTT, JOHN
McDEVITT, JAMES
McDONALD, ANGUS
McDONALD, CATHERINE (EMERSON)
McDONALD, CHARLES HICKLEN
McDONALD, HARRIET ELIZA (DAVIS)
McDONALD, J. H.
McDONALD, JOHN
McDONALD, JOHN H.
McDONALD, KATE
McDONALD, M. P
McDONALD, RICHARD
McDONALD, RONALD
McDONALD, W. F.
McDONEL, JAMES
McDONNELL, JOHN
McDONNELL, JOHN, MRS.
McDONNELL, MICHAEL
McDOWELL, ROBERT
McEVILY, JAMES P.
McFADDEN, ROSE C. (COSGROVE)
McFARLAND, EUGENE A.
McFARLAND, J. H.
McFARLAND, WILLIAM T.
McGARVEY, MARY (OWENS)
McGOVERN, JAMES
McGOVERN, JANET (KINNA)
McGOVERN, MARY
McGOVERN, PHILIP
McGREGOR, ARCHIBALD
McGUIRK, MATTHEW
McHUGH, CORNELIUS
McHUGH, SOPHIA (HAYES)
McINTIRE, M. D.
McINTOSH, ALEXANDER W.
McINTOSH, CHARLES MONROE
McINTOSH, DANIEL JOHN
McINTOSH, HENRY A.
McINTOSH, JOHN CHARLES
McINTOSH, SARAH HUDSON (RANDALL)
McINTOSH, WILLIAM L.
McINTOSH, WILLIAM R.
McIRWIN, JOHN
McKABE, ANNA MARY (McPHAIL)
McKAY, A. J.
McKAY, ALEXANDER
McKAY, CAROLINE
McKAY, ZAIDEE MABEL (BROWN)
McKEE, JOSEPH L.
McKENZIE, J. PATTERSON
McKENZIE, W. S.
McKEOWN, WILLIAM E.
McKIMENS, WILLIAM
McKINNEY, W. L.
McKINNEY, WILLIAM
MCKINSEY, GEORGE E.
MCKINSTRY, THOMAS B.
MCKINZIE, SARAH
McKNIGHT, JOSEPH HEMPSTEAD
McKNIGHT, MARY (PEABODY)
McKNIGHT, PATRICK
McKNIGHT, WILLIAM H.
McKNIGHT, WILLIAM HENRY
McKOIN, MARANDA (CULLISON)
McLAUGHLIN, JOHN S.

McLEOD, JOHN
McLURE, CHARLES D.
MCMAHON, PETER
McMAHONE, KATHERINE (DARBY)
McMASTER, JAMES B.
McMASTERS, JAMES
McMILLAN, ANGUS
McMINN, RACHEL (THOMAS)
McMINN, MARGARET S. (GILBERT)
McNALLY, HENRY CLINTON
McNAMARA, WILLIAM J.
McNAMARA. THOMAS J.
McNEAL, ELI W.
McNIEL, RICHARD
MCNULTY, FLORA (MCKAY)
McPHAIL, ALLEN A.
McPHAIL, ARCHIE A.
McPHAIL, MARY A. (MCCABE)
McPHERSON, ELIZABETH (LEVENGOOD)
McQUAID, HUGH
McTAGUE, TOM
McUIRE, JOHN
McVAY, MARGARET ANN
McWILLIAMS, THOMAS JAMES
MEAGHER, GENERAL THOMAS FRANCIS
MEAGHER, MARGARET (LEARY)
MEIER, HENRY
MEIKELJOHN, DAVID
MEIKLEJOHN, ALICE (ROACH)
MELLEN, WILLIAM F.
MELO, HENRY
MELONE, RACHEL (DAVENPORT)
MELTON, ALBERT
MELTON, AMOS .
MELTON, CEALIA A. (STUART)
MELTON, CORNELIUS
MELTON, ELLEN (CURTIS)
MELTON, HARRIETT
MENARD, MOISE
MENDENHALL, JOHN F.
MENEFEE, ROBERT PHILIP
MENTEREY, J.
MERIDITH, MARGARET (O'NEILL)
MERK, FREDERICK ROBERT
MERK, GEORGE WILLIAM
MERK, MARY ELIZABETH
MERK, WILLIAM WALLACE
MERRILL, JOSIAH M.
MERRILL, THOMAS GALE
MERRIMAN, ELIAS
MERRIMAN, JENNIE (VERGE) B.
MERRIMAN, NATHANIEL
MERRITT, ANNIE M.
MERRITT, DAVID
MERRITT, ELLEN (WHITE)
MERRITT, THEODORE B.
MERRY, JOHN
METCALF, HENRY
METLEN, DAVID E.
METLEN, E. A. MRS. (KENNISON)
METZEL, ALEXANDER
METZEL, ANNIE E. (SPICER)
METZEL, FRANK S.
METZGER, PETER
MEYERSICK, FREDERICK WILLIAM
MICHEAN, AMELIA
MICHEAN, JOSEPH
MICHEM, JOSEPH
MICHEM, JULIA
MICHNER, LEWIS
MICKELJOHN, ELMIRA (NOYES)
MIFFLIN, E. M.
MILER, ANNA (YATES)
MILES, DANIEL L.
MILES, NELSON A.
MILES, ORISON H.
MILES, THEODORUS CLOWE
MILES, THOMAS OBER
MILKS, DANIEL
MILKS, RUTH A. BURTON
MILLEGAN, MARTHA A.
MILLEGAN, R.
MILLEGAN, WALLACE L.
MILLEGAN, WILLARD. L.
MILLEGAN, WILLIAM L. JR.
MILLEN, GEORGE
MILLEN, NICK
MILLER, ANNIE (JENSEN)
MILLER, ANTON E.
MILLER, CHARLES E.
MILLER, CHARLES EDWIN
MILLER, FINIS BARNET
MILLER, GEORGE
MILLER, GEORGE S.
MILLER, GEORGE SLOAN
MILLER, HENRY
MILLER, IGNACE
MILLER, JAMES E.
MILLER, JAMES KNOX POLK
MILLER, JAMES NATHAN
MILLER, JESSE
MILLER, JESSE N.
MILLER, JOHN H.
MILLER, JOSEPHINE
MILLER, KATHERINE
MILLER, LOREN R.
MILLER, LUCRETIA (WORDEN)
MILLER, MARY (HUFF)
MILLER, PHILIP
MILLER, SAMUEL
MILLER, SARAH J. (RICHMOND)
MILLER, SARAH JANE
MILLER, SOLOMON
MILLING, WILLIAM
MILLS, PETER B.
MILOT, HENRY
MILOT, HUBERT ALPHONSE
MILOT, IDA SHANNON B.
MING, JAMES
MING, JOHN HOLLINS
MINNETTE, JOHN
MINNETTE, PETER
MISHEAU, ENCELIA
MISHEAU, THOMAS
MITCHELL, ALEXANDRE. J.
MITCHELL, ARMASTAD H.
MITCHELL, HENRY B.
MITCHELL, JAMES B.
MITCHELL, MARGARET (CHAFFIN)
MITCHELL, MARY E.
MITCHELL, MRS MARY ELLEN (IRVINE)
MITCHELL, SIDNEY
MITCHELL, SUSAN JANE
MITCHELL, W. L. C.

MITCHELL, WILLIAM
MOFFITT, JOHN
MONFORTON, HENRY
MONROE, GEORGE C.
MONROE, HENRY
MONTEVILLE, ELI
MONTGOMERY, LEE
MOOD, HENRY H.
MOODY, THOMAS D.
MOOG, ALBERT
MOOG, FREDERICK
MOORE, CATHERINE (THOMAS)
MOORE, IRENE MRS (LEWIS)
MOORE, JAMES
MOORE, JAMES CLAYBORN
MOORE, JAMES L.
MOORE, JAMES M.
MOORE, JAMES MELTON
MOORE, JOHN CLARKSON
MOORE, JOHN M.
MOORE, JOHN T.
MOORE, MARK A. JUDGE
MOORE, NAOMI HALL
MOORE, OLIVER PERRY
MOORE, PERRY J.
MOORE, SANFORD
MOORE, TERRY
MOORE, THOMAS R.
MORAN WILLIAM HENRY
MORAN, ANN McCORMICK
MORAN, EDWARD VALENTINE
MORAN, JOHN
MORAN, KATHERINE (MULLIGAN)
MORAN, PATRICK
MORAN, THOMAS
MORAN, THOMAS F. B.
MORAN, THOMAS T.
MORAN, WILLIAM
MORGAN, ABRAM M.
MORGAN, HARRY B.
MORGAN, HARRY NORTON
MORGAN, WICKFORD
MORGAN, WILLIAM B.
MORIER, ELIZA
MORIER, HENRY
MORLEY, JAMES H.
MORLEY, JULIUS F.
MORRIS, DAVID
MORRIS, JOHN L.
MORRIS, MOSES
MORRIS, REGINA A. (DENBLE)
MORRIS, THOMAS L.
MORRIS, WILLIAM W.
MORRIS, WILLIAM WARDER
MORROW, DAVE M.
MORROW, DAVID
MORROW, ISABELLE (GREEN)
MORROW, JEANNETTE (MATHESEN)
MORROW, KATHARINE (FRIELDS)
MORROW, MALCOLM
MORROW, MALCOLM, JR.
MORROW, WILLIAM T.
MORSE, EBENEZER
MORSE, GEORGE W.
MORSE, MARY ELIZABETH (COX)
MORTEY, JULIUS F.
MORTON, GEORGE

MOSS, GEORGE
MOSS, JOEL A.
MOULTEN, AMOS, H.
MOUNT, E. B.
MOUNTS, FRANK M.
MOUNTS, MATTHIAS
MOUNTS, RAULANA OSTEN
MOXLEY, I. C.
MTICHELL, JAMES
MUDOON, ANNA (MURRAY)
MUFFLY, CHARLES SIDNEY
MUFFLY, MARGARET J. (BYAM)
MUFFLY, THEOPHILUS
MULLAN, JOHN
MULLER, J. J.
MULLER, MARTIN
MULLINIX, STEPHEN D.
MULVANEY, THOMAS B.
MUMFORD, SARAH A. (McCLURG)
MUNCKMEIER, HENRY
MUNGER, LYMAN PAIGE
MUNROE, HENRY
MUNSON, L. E.
MUNTES, MARTIN
MURPHY, ADDIE LEE (SMITH)
MURPHY, AUGUSTUS C.
MURPHY, BERNARD WILSEN
MURPHY, DANIEL
MURPHY, JOHN
MURPHY, JOHN THOMAS
MURPHY, MARY
MURPHY, THOMAS W.
MURRAY, BERNARD WILSON
MURRAY, C. P.
MURRAY, ELZY
MURRAY, ETTA R.
MURRAY, J. E.
MURRAY, JOHN
MURRAY, PETE
MURRAY, THOMAS B
MURRAY, W. H.
MUSSIGBROD, CHARLES FREDERICK DR,
MYERS, ALFRED
MYERS, ELLA (WOOD)
MYERS, H. C.
MYERS, IRA
MYERS, W. B.
MYERS, WILLIAM F.
MYERS, WILLIAM VANCE
NAFUS, CORNELIA (WOODS)
NAFUS, W. H.
NAPTON, KATE R.
NAPTON, WELLING JUDGE
NASH, HERBERT OLIVER
NAUGHTON, THOMAS
NAVE, ERONDAL FRANKLIN
NAVE, JACOB
NAY, BYRON
NAY, HELEN M. (GLEASON)
NAY, MARTIN V.
NEAL, HENRY S.
NEAL, MARY (POCUETTE)
NEELY, JAMES H.
NEILL, THOMAS
NELSON, ARVIE J. (SMITH)
NELSON, AUGUST
NELSON, CHRISTIAN

NELSON, E. J.
NELSON, GEORGE
NELSON, JOHN
NELSON, JOHN W.
NELSON, JOSEPH
NELSON, JULIE (ANDERSON)
NELSON, LAVINA ANN (CLARK)
NELSON, LUCY
NELSON, MARGARET (SHORTLY)
NELSON, MARSHALL T.
NELSON, MONROE
NELSON, PETER S.
NELSON, RASTUS
NELSON, ROBERT
NELSON, ROBERT SMITH
NELSON, SARAH ANN (EVANS)
NELSON, WILLIAM
NEUBERT, JOHN
NEWBURG, ABEL T.
NEWELL, E. L.
NEWELL, J. H.
NEWELL, LUCY J.
NEWKIRK, ANNIE
NEWKIRK, ELLA
NEWKIRK, GEORGE W.
NEWMAN, ASA D.
NEWMAN, CHARLES H.
NEWMAN, EDWIN MARTIN
NEWMAN, NATHANIEL
NEWMAN, ORSON NICKISON
NEWMAN, THOMAS
NICHOLS, ALFRED F.
NICHOLS, CASSIUS CLAY
NICHOLS, CASSIUS M.
NICHOLS, CYRUS SALVEYRUS
NICHOLS, PONTIUS PROCRASTUS CYREATUS
NICHOLS, STEPHENS FITZLAND
NICHOLS, WILLIAM CYREATUR
NICHOLSON, CELIA MARION
NICOL, ROBERT W.
NIEDENHOFEN, CATHERINE
NIEDENHOFEN, WILLIAM
NIELD, THOMAS
NIELSON, C.
NILAN, MARGARET (OWENS)
NILSIN, ELSIE (MARSTON)
NISSLER, CHRISTINA
NIXON, J. H.
NOAH, ADDIS (MARDIS)
NOBLE, AMY
NOBLE, CYNTHIA
NOBLE, DANIEL BOHAN
NOBLE, DANIEL H.
NOBLE, FLORA A.
NOBLE, MARY
NOBLE, MILLICENT
NOBLE, MINERVA J. (PEET)
NOBLE, ROBERT W.
NOLEM, JOHN H.
NOOG, ALBERT
NORMANDIE, FRANK
NORMANDIE, FRANK MRS.
NORMANDIE, PETER
NORMANDIN, PETER
NORRIS, ALEXANDER
NORRIS, FRANK B.
NORRIS, GILMAN R.
NORRIS, JAMES EPHRIAM
NORRIS, JEROME
NORRIS, MILTON
NORRIS, WILLIAM EDWARD
NORRIS, WILLIAM H.
NORWOOD, WILLIAM J.
NOTESTINE, B. H. (BENJAMIN)
NOYES, ALVA JOSIAH
NOYES, G. R.
NOYES, JOHN
NURSE, GEORGE
NYE, JOHN A.
NYHART, GEORGE WASHINGTON
NYHART, JOHN
NYHART, JOHN A.
NYHART, JORDAN
O'BANNON, FANNIE (IRVINE)
O'BANNON, ORVILLE B.
O'BRIEN, DAVID
O'COMER, WINIFRED
O'CONNELL, ANDREW
O'CONNELL, ELIZABETH (LOGAN)
O'CONNOR, THOMAS
O'DAY, BRIDGET (PRICE)
O'DELL, A. H.
O'DONNELL, JAMES
O'DONNELL, TERRENCE
O'KEEFE, ANNA (LESTER)
O'KEEFE, CORNELIUS C.
O'KEEFE, DAVID C.
O'KEEFE, MARY E. (ROSS)
O'KEEFE, REMY
O'LEARY, DENNIS
O'NEIL, ELLEN MARY (DAGENHART)
O'NEIL, HUGH
O'NEIL, HUGH O.
O'NEIL, JANE (HICKEY)
O'NEIL, MARGARET
O'NEILL, ELIZA P. (THOMPSON)
O'NEILL, JOHN
O'NEILL, JOHN P.
O'NEILL, JOSEPH
O'NEILL, WILLIAM
O'ROURKE, JOHN
O'ROURKE, MARY (HOWARD)
O'ROURKE, MARY ELIZABETH (NASON)
O'ROURKE, RICHARD NASON
OAKS, JOHN
OLDHAM, GABRIEL HOUSTON
OLDHAM, JAMES ALBERT
OLDS, LOREN B.
OLDS, ROHECIA
OLIVER, WILLIAM C.
OLIVER, WILLIAM H.
OLLER, MARY (MORROW)
OLLINGER, JOHN W.
OLSEN, AMELIA
OLSEN, CHARLES
OLSEN, LARS
OLSON, ANNA (BOYLE)
OLSON, CHRISTINE (PETERSON)
OLSON, HENRY
ORANCE, R., MRS.
ORANCE, RICHARD
OREM, JOSEPH C.
ORR, CAROLINE M.
ORR, EMELINE

ORR, GEORGE
ORR, JAMES B.
ORR, OLIVIA (DUER)
ORR, SAMPLE
ORR, WILLIAM C.
ORTON, ALFRED WALLACE
ORTON, FRED L.
ORTON, JAMES C.
ORTON, JAMES J.
ORTON, L. VAN
ORTON, PAULONA (MOUNTS)
ORTON, W. C.
OSBORN, ALMYRO
OSBORN, H. S.
OSBORNE, JENNIE E.
OSTAN, JAMES M.
OSTRANDER, ALONZO
OSWALD, CORALIN (HUMES)
OSWALD, ELIZABETH
OSWALD, GEORGE
OTTEN, HERMAN C.
OWENS, JAMES
OWENS, JOHN
OWENS, MARGARET (NILAN)
OWENS, MARY (McGARVEY)
OWENS, OWEN
OWSLEY, WILLIAM
OYLER, GEORGE ENOS
PADDEN, ANNA
PAGE, JAMES MADISON
PAGE, MARY C.
PAGE, S. B. MRS.
PAGE, SAMUEL B.
PALLAGEN, E. M.
PALMER, D. A.
PALMER, THOMAS JEFFERSON
PAMBRUM, ALEXANDER
PANENT, JOSEPH
PARBERRY, WILLIAM DR.
PARCHEN, HENRY MARTIN
PARDEE, JAMES R.
PARK, ALICE ELLEN (PATTERSON)
PARK, EDWIN W.
PARK, LUCIA A. (EDGERTON) (DARLING)
PARK, PERRY H.
PARKENSON, W. L
PARKER, JANE (STEPHENS)
PARKER, MARY ALICE (MALONEY)
PARKER, NAHUM
PARKHURST, ROSWELL
PARKINS, WILLIAM J.
PARKINSON, JOHN T.
PARKINSON, WILLIAM H.
PARRISH, OREN ENOCH
PARROT, ROBERT
PARROTT, GEORGE
PASCHALL, W. S.
PATCH, JAMES B.
PATRICK, JOHN WALKER
PATTEE, DAVID D.
PATTEE, JOSEPH B.
PATTEN, F. E. W.
PATTEN, WILLIAM H.
PATTERSON, DANIEL
PATTERSON, DAVID
PATTERSON, FRED SUMMIT
PATTERSON, JESSE

PATTERSON, JOSEPH L.
PATTERSON, MARTHA ELLEN
PATTERSON, THOMAS JOHN ROBERT
PATTERSON, WILLIAM H.
PATTON, HUGH
PAUL, JOHN E.
PAUL, MARGARET
PAULEN, HARRISON
PAYNE, CHRISTOPHER L.
PAYNE, EDWARD WARREN
PAYNE, RUFUS
PAYNTER, WOODMAN S.
PEABODY, MARY
PEASE, FELLOWS D.
PEASE, H. A.
PEASE, J. A.
PECOTT, WILLIAM
PEEL, ELLEN (SELLEY)
PEEL, MARTIN
PEELER, MARY JANE
PEERY, HIRAM
PELKY, ROBERT A.
PELKY, ROBERT ANTHONY, JR
PELLETIER, JOSEPHINE (WHITE)
PELLETIER, PAUL ONIZON
PEMBERTON, WILLIAM YOUNG
PENDARVIS, CHARLES W.
PENDARVIS, I. S.
PENNINGTON, JOSEPH
PENWELL, LEWIS
PENWELL, MARY
PENWELL, MERRITT W.
PENWELL, OSCAR ELIJAH
PERKINS, JAMES
PERKINS, JENNISON L.
PERKINS, JOHN
PERKINS, MAY
PERKINS, WILLIAM
PERRIMAN (PERIMAN) MARGARET ELLA
PERRIMAN (PERIMAN) WILLIAM GREEN
PERSELL, REBECCA T.
PERSELL, THOMAS BENTON
PERSELL, WILLIAM EDGAR
PETERS, R. W.
PETERSON, ANNA
PETERSON, ANNA C. (HANSON)
PETERSON, GEORGE
PETERSON, LORAN
PETERSON, MARY (HEMPSTEAD)
PETERSON, NELS
PETERSON, OTTO
PETERSON, SOREN
PETTIE, DAVID
PETTIT, B.
PFEIFER, BARBARA
PFEIFER, JOHN P.
PFOHL, GEORGE
PFOUTS, WILLIAM G.
PHELPS, GEORGE H
PHELPS, JAMES
PHILLIPS, ANN HARRIET (EVANS)
PHILLIPS, BENJAMIN DAVID
PHILLIPS, EDWARD
PHILLIPS, HARRIET W.
PHILLIPS, JOHN F.
PHILLIPS, JOHN YOUNG
PHILFOTT, JULIS (McCOY)

PICHLER, A. S.
PICHTER, GEORGE E.
PICKENS, JOHN
PICKENS, WILLIAM
PICKERING, JOHN GEE
PICKLER, A. L.
PIERCE, CATHERINE
PIERCE, JAMES HARRISON
PIERCE, JOSEPH H.
PIERCE, JOSEPH H. MRS.
PIERCE, MARY
PIERCE, PETER.
PIERSTORFF, ANDREW
PIERSTORFF, SARAH
PILKIE, JOSEPHINE (WHITE)
PILLSBURY, A. W.
PINCKNEY, SIMEON D.
PINNEY, FANNIE E. (WOOD)
PITCHER, THOMAS B.
PLACY, JOSEPHTE
PLASSMAN, MARTHA A. (EDGERTON)
PLATNER, MARSHAL D.
PLUMB, JOSEPH
PLUMMER, ASBURY
POAD, ELISHA
POINDEXTER, PHILIP HENRY
POIRIER, ALEXANDER A.
POLLEY, MARGARET (COUGHLIN)
POLLINGER, ELIJAH MILLER
POND, HENRY S.
POND, MONTANA PEARL
POOL, ALICE M. (SCHAAF)
POOL, MELISSA (WILLIAMS)
POORE, JAMES
POPE, FRANCIS
POPE, G. W.
POPE, HANNAH (COPP)
POPHAM, J. W.
PORTER, ALICE
PORTER, H. H.
PORTER, HENRY
PORTER, L. D.
PORTER, THOMAS C.
PORTER, WILLIAM
POST, ABRAHAM
POST, MARTIN
POTTER, JOHN
POTTER, W. H.
POWELL, CLARISSA JANE (CRUMP)
POWELL, JOHN H.
POWELL, JOHN W.
POWELL, MARY B. (EVANS)
POWELL, SAM
POWER, MARY E.
POWER, THOMAS C.
POWERS, FRANCIS
POWERS, FRANK
POWERS, HENRY C.
POWERS, JACOB M.
POWERS, JOHN W.
POWERS, MARY JANE (NOLEN)
POWERS, MAURICE
POZNESKY, ALFRED J.
PRATT, WALTER ROLLINS
PRENEVEAN, WILLLIAM
PRENTICE, S. C.
PREUITT, WILLIAM GREEN

PRICE, BENNETT
PRICE, CHARLES WEBSTER
PRICE, ELIAS
PRICE, EVAN J.
PRICE, HENRY JOB
PRICE, JOHN M.
PRICE, JOSEPH BERT
PRICE, MARY JOSEPHINE
PRICE, ROBERT
PRICER, BENNETT L.
PROFFITT, ALEXANDER
PTOMEY, NELSON
PURDY, JAMES
PUTNAM, FRANKLIN STANLEY
QUAINTANCE, ABLE CARY
QUESNELLE, JULIS (MICHEAU)
QUIGLEY, JOHN R.
QUINLAN, HENRY
QUINLAN, JOHN
QUINLAN, MARGARET GRACE
QUINLAN, MARY GRACE
QUINLAN, PATRICK
QUINN, BERNARD
QUINN, WILLIAM
QUIRK, JAMES
QUIRK, JOHN AMBROSE
QUIVEREAUX, FRANCIS
RADER, CHARLES THOMPSON
RAHN, JOHN
RAILSBACK, EDMUND O.
RAINSFORD, JOHN C.
RALSTON, JAMES NELSON
RALSTON, LOUISA L. (WALTERS)
RALSTON, MARY FRANCES
RALSTON, SAMUEL F.
RALSTON, SAMUEL F. JR.
RALSTON, WILLIAM ALEXANDER
RALSTON, WILLIAM R.
RAMSAY, GEORGE E.
RAMSAY, GEORGE E., MRS.
RAMSDELL, CLARA (WILLIAMS)
RAMSDELL, CLATON
RAMSDELL, JOSEPH
RAMSEY, G. E., MRS.
RAMSEY, JOHN MARSHALL
RANDALL, ELLEN R.
RANDALL, OSCAR E.
RANDALL, ROSALTHA
RASMUSSEN, RASMUS
RAUSCH, ELIZA F.
RAUSH, GEORGE
RAVALLI, ANTHONY
RAY, EMMA L.
RAY, SOPHIA (BYARS)
RAY, THOMAS A.
RAY, VERENA L.
RAYMOND, ELBRIDGE G.
RAYMOND, ELLEN (BATEMAN)
RAYMOND, HENRY
RAYMOND, OLIVER
RAYMOND, SARAH (HERNDON)
RAYMOND, WILLIAM HILLHOUSE
RAYMOND, WINTHROP
REA, JAMES A.
REA, MARY K.
REA, MARY M. (VALITON)
REA, SARAH (HUDSON)

REA, WILLIAM
REA, WILLIAM, JR
REACH, ALICE J.
READ, ALEXANDER PERRIN
READ, FRANCIS S.
READ, LAURA T. MRS
REAHM, CHARLES
REARDON, DENNIS
REBBE, ELIZABETH
REDDING, EMANUAL O.
REDDING, NICHOLAS ALFRED
REDDING, SARAH (FUENISH)
REDDING, WILSON
REDFERN, FRANCIS
REDFERN, JAMES
REDFERN, JOHN
REDFERN, WILLIAM JOHN
REDHEAD, NANCY
REDING, HENRY C.
REDING, JACOB
REED, AGNES E.
REED, GEORGE W.
REED, HART FRANCIS
REED, HENRY J.
REED, JOHN
REED, MINNIE
REED, RANDELL
REED, TAL
REED, W. H.
REED, WILLIAM
REED, WILLIAM R.
REEL, WILLIAM R.
REESE, EVAN
REESE, FREDERICK
REESE, GOMER
REESE, JOHN E.
REESE, JOHN J.
REESE, MARY E.
REESE, THOMAS
REESE, THOMAS MRS.
REEVES, BIDDLE
REEVES, GEORGE P.
REEVES, JOSEPH J.
REEVES, MOISE
REID, MARGARET (GILBERT)
REID, RACHEL (EVANS)
REIF, FANNIE ELLEN (STRONG)
REILLY, THOMAS D.
REINHARD, JAMES P.
REINHARDT, DAVID F.
REINIG, M.
REINIG, MATILDA (MRS HEGLEY)
REINIG, MICHAEL
REINS, JOHN POWELL
REIS, HENRY P.
REISS, CONRAD F.
REISS, KATHERINE MRS (FOLLER)
RENNERT, CHARLES
RENOIS, XAVIER
RENSHAW, ANNA
RENSHAW, ROBERT McADAMS
REW, FRANCES MRS (GOHN)
REYNOLDS, J. B.
REYNOLDS, MARY J. (MICHEAN)
REYNOLDS, RICHARD A.
REYNOLDS, WELLINGTON HENRY
RIALE, C. K.

RICE, ELIZABETH (PORTER)
RICHARDS, GEORGE
RICHARDS, HENRY
RICHARDS, JOHN D.
RICHARDS, R. K.
RICHARDSON, SAMUEL E.
RICHES, JAMES
RICHMOND, CLINTON M.
RICHMOND, JOSEPH ORRIN
RICHMOND, REUBIN
RICHMOND, SARAH JUNE (MILLER)
RICHTER, CHARLES
RICHTER, WILHEMINA CAROLINA
RICKER, JOSHUA CLARENCE
RICKER, MARTHA PERMEALIA (HATCH)
RIDDLE, WILLIAM CHILES
RIDNOUR, C. W.
RIES, JOHN H.
RIGGIN, IDA L. (JORDAN)
RIIS, MARY (CADIGAN)
RILEY, PATRICK
RINDA, VENZLE CHARLES
RINGWOLD, GEORGE I. MRS (SPITZLEY)
RITCHEY, SAMUEL I.
RIVERS, CHARLES
ROACH, JEREMIAH
ROACH, JOHN M.
ROBBINS, LUCY JANE
ROBBINS, THOMAS M.
ROBBINS, WILLIAM L.
ROBERTS, BENJAMIN R.
ROBERTS, HORACE V.
ROBERTS, JENNIE (MORTON)
ROBERTS, JOSEPH S.
ROBERTS, LELA V.
ROBERTS, MARY J.
ROBERTS, MATHEW
ROBERTS, ROBERT MORGAN
ROBERTS, W. KEMP
ROBERTSON, EVA J. (PRICE)
ROBERTSON, JOHN S.
ROBERTSON, OSCAR A.
ROBINSON, ALMON C.
ROBINSON, EDWARD
ROBINSON, ELIZABETH
ROBINSON, FLORENCE (GRAVES)
ROBINSON, J. P.
ROBINSON, JAMES D.
ROBINSON, JOHN MARION
ROBINSON, MARGARET (FRENCH)
ROBINSON, WILLIAM
ROCKERFELLER, MARTHA (MILLEGAN)
RODDA, JAMES
RODGERS, A. T.
RODGERS, WILLIAM
RODGERS, WILLIAM H.
ROE, MARGARET P
ROE, WILLIAM
ROGERS, IKE
ROGERS, MAMI (ROGERS)
ROGERS, TED
ROGERS, TOM
ROHRBAREGH, JOHN J.
ROLFE, HERBERT P
ROMAINE, CORDELIA
ROMEY, ADELE
ROMEY, AUGUST L.

ROMEY, LOUIS L.
ROMEY, LUCIEN
ROMEY, MARY (BRION)
ROMEY, MARY ANN
ROMEY, ROSA (MAILEY)
RONAN, MARY C. (SHEEHAN)
RONAN, PETER
ROOT, DELIA M.
ROOT, FREDERICK
ROSEBOROUGH, WILLIAM L.
ROSENCRANS, HENRY J.
ROSENSTEIN, HARRIS
ROSENSTEIN, SOLOMON
ROSENTHAL, JOSEPH
ROSS, GEORGE P.
ROSS, JAMES
ROSS, MARY (O"KEEFE)
ROSS, MRS.
ROSSBACK, LILLIE (WHITE)
ROSSITER, H. D.
ROTE, O. W. W.
ROTWITT, LOUIS
ROTZ, AZARIAH L.
ROUSE, DANIEL E.
ROWE, CHARLES
ROWE, MOLLIE D.
ROWE, WEARN
ROWE, WILLIAM
ROWLEY, DAVID LEWIS
ROWLEY, LYMAN
RUDD, A. F. MRS
RUFFNER, SANFORD
RUMLEY, CHARLES
RUMSEY, LOTTIE M.
RUMSEY, WILLIAM ASHLEY
RUNDELL, HENRY M.
RUSSELL, FANNIE L. (FORBIS)
RUSSELL, J. S.
RUSSELL, JOHN W.
RYAN, EDWARD
RYAN, JAMES M.
RYAN, WILLIAM V.
SABOLSKY, JENNIE (LISSNER)
SABOLSKY, PAULINE F.
SABOLSKY, REUBEN
SABOLSKY, SAMUEL
SACKET, THEOPHILUS BUSH
SAILE, RAIMUND
SALLY, SUSAN (THOMPSON)
SANDER, LOUIS
SANDERS, BENJAMIN F.
SANDERS, GEORGE F.
SANDERS, HARRIET PECK (FENN)
SANDERS, JAMES UPSON
SANDERS, JUNIUS GALUSHA
SANDERS, WILBUR EDGERTON
SANDERS, WILBUR FISKE
SANDFORD, JOHN B.
SANDIAGE, NELIA (FAULKNER)
SANDIDGE, LUKE D
SANFORD, EVA
SANFORD, JOHN R
SANGUEIN, SAMUEL JOHN
SAPPINGTON, H. H., MRS.
SARGENT, CHARLES C.
SARISH, JOSEPH
SATTERWHITE, JACK

SAUNDERS, JAMES W.
SAUNDERS, PHILIP
SAVAGE, J. A. JUDGE
SAVERY, MONTANA (NOAG)
SAWYER, EDMUND F.
SCANLON, JOHN H.
SCHAAF, ALICE M. (POOL)
SCHEMMELS, ANNA
SCHEMMELS, CAROLINE M. (ORR)
SCHEMMELS, CHRISTIAN
SCHEMMELS, PETEE
SCHEMRICK, HENRY
SCHEUER, FREDERICK V.
SCHMIDT, CHARLES
SCHNEIDER, ELIZABETH (MILLER)
SCHNEPLE, HENRY
SCHNETZ, STEPHEN
SCHOTT, CAROLINE (LEHMAN)
SCHRAMMECK, HENERY
SCHROEDER, EMILY (WILLIAMS)
SCHULZ, ANNA MARGARET (KEMMA)
SCHULZ, FREDERIDO J.
SCHULZ, JULIE NA. (PHILPOT)
SCHWAB, BENJAMIN
SCHWAB, SAMUEL
SCIDENSTICKER, FREDERICK
SCIDENSTICKER, JOHN C.
SCOLLAND, CATHERINE (SMITH)
SCOTT, ALEXANDER
SCOTT, JAMES W.
SCOTT, LAFAYETTE
SCOTT, LUCY M.
SCOTT, MARY (NOKES)
SCOTT, SAMUEL
SCOTT, WILLIAM
SCRIBNER, H.
SEADORE, ANNIE (MARTIN)
SEARLES, DANIEL
SEARLES, JESSE D.
SEDMAN, OSCAR ALFRED
SEE, BENJAMIN FRANKLIN
SEE, FRANK JR
SEE, MARGARET JONES
SEE, SAMUEL C.
SELBY, ELLEN PEEL
SELWAY, JAMES
SELWAY, JOHN R.
SELWAY, ROBERT H.
SELWAY, THOMAS M.
SENNETT, ARTHUR H.
SEVERANS, DANIELS
SEWARD, NEWTON
SHAFER, DAVID LAURENCE
SHAFFER, AMY EVA (PLUMMER)
SHANNON, JOHN E.
SHANNON, ROBERT
SHARP, MARY
SHARP, WILLIAM J.
SHAW, CLARA T.
SHAW, LOREN LORENZO
SHAW, THOMAS MELVIN
SHEARON, JOHN E.
SHEDD, MARY ISABELLE (WILLIAMS)
SHEEHAN, JAMES
SHEEHAN, JOHN
SHEEHY, JOHN F.
SHEEHY, THOMAS JAMES

SHELDEN, ENOS
SHELLEY, MARK
SHELLEY, MARK H.
SHELLEY, MRS MARK (SAMPSON)
SHELTON, WILLIAM
SHEPHERD, EMMA CHARLOTTE (EKLUND)
SHEPHERD, NEWTON
SHERIFF, COURT
SHERMAN, B. R.
SHERMAN, C. I.
SHERMAN, HERBERT
SHERMAN, IRA
SHERMAN, SOPHIA B. (WRIGHT)
SHERRILL, JACOB TAYLOR
SHERRILL, THOMAS C.
SHERWOOD, JAMES KILBOURNE ODGEN
SHINEBERGER, JOSEPH
SHINGLETON, SANFORD CHANCELLOR
SHINNICK, THOMAS
SHIRLEY, W. S.
SHOATE, ABIGAIL (ZEIGLER)
SHOBER, JOHN H.
SHOEMAKER, GEORGE W.
SHORTHILL, JOHN R.
SHOWERS, HARVEY
SHOWERS, HENRY S.
SHOWERS, MARY ANN (THOMAS)
SHRINER, KATHERINE
SHULTZ, STEPHEN
SILVERMAN, HATTIE
SILVERMAN, JULIUS
SILVERMAN, MORRIS
SIMONTON, WILLIAM Y.
SIMPSON, ELLEN KATHELEEN (HARDGROVE)
SIMPSON, JOHN
SINCOX, EDWARD
SINGER, J. C.
SITES, JAMES EZEKIEL
SKELLEY, WILLIAM
SKELTON, STANFORD W. SR.
SKELTON, WILLIAM
SKINNER, OLIVE C. MERRIMAN
SKLOWER, BETTIE (SILVERMAN)
SLACK, JOHN A.
SLACK, MARY (CHAFFIN)
SLATER, J. W.
SLAVENS, LOU ELLA (CARPENTER)
SLOAN, ASA H.
SLOAN, SEYMOUR
SLOAN, THOMAS DOUGLAS
SLOAN, WASHINGTON F.
SLOAN, WILLIAM K.
SLOSS, JOHN C.
SMART, JAMES S.
SMILEY, ELLA ELIZABETH
SMITH, A. W.
SMITH, ADDIE L.
SMITH, ANDREW JACKSON
SMITH, ANNA (STEWART)
SMITH, ARVIE J. NELSON
SMITH, CHARLES PLATT
SMITH, CON
SMITH, E. L.
SMITH, EDWARD G.
SMITH, EDWARD LYON
SMITH, GEORGE W.
SMITH, H. P. A.
SMITH, ISABELLE FRANCES (REID)
SMITH, JACOB
SMITH, JAMES ALFRED
SMITH, JAMES M.
SMITH, JAMES MARTIN
SMITH, JARAD
SMITH, JERRY G.
SMITH, JOHN
SMITH, JOHN A.
SMITH, JOHN T.
SMITH, JOSEPH
SMITH, LEWIS WILLIAM
SMITH, LOU P.
SMITH, MANILLA RAYMOND
SMITH, MARGARET (SHORTLEY)
SMITH, MARTHA CATHERINE
SMITH, REGINA A.
SMITH, ROBERT
SMITH, ROBERT W.
SMITH, THOMAS SLOANE
SMITH, W. B.
SMITH, WILLIAM M.
SMITH, WILLIAM N.
SMOOT, SARILLA EVALINE (SMITH)
SNAPP, J. B.
SNELL, CHARLES H.
SNYDER, HENRY
SCET, CORNELIA (VAN GUNDY)
SOMERVILLE, J C.
SONNEFIELD, HENRY F.
SOUTHMAYD, W. C.
SPAFFORD, CHARLES
SPALDING, DON O.
SPARRELL, GEORGE H.
SPENCER, ALMON
SPENCER, JOHN
SPENCER, JOSEPH
SPERLING, LEWIS
SPICER, ANNA (METZILL)
SPIER, ERNEST
SPIETH, JACOB
SPRAGUE, HOWARD
SPRAGUE, WILLIAM M.
SPRINGER, HENRIETTA
ST. ATMOURE, THEOPHILE CHRISTEN
STACDEN, MARTHA J. (VANCAMP)
STACKPOLE, EDWARD S.
STAFFORD, GEORGE
STAFFORD, ISAAC SAMUEL
STAFFORD, J. N.
STAFFORD, JAMES JEFFERSON
STAFFORD, JOSEPH V.
STANDAHER, GEORGE L.
STANHAN, MAY L. (BOSTWICK)
STANLEY, REGINALD
STANLEY, WILLIS OGDEN
STANTON, ASA KIMBAL
STAPLETON, GEORGE W.
STAR, BESIER
STARK, CHARLES THOMAS
STARK, EUGENE
STATELER, L. B., MRS.
STATELER, LEARNER BLACKMAN
STAUBACH, KATHERINE
STAUBACH, VAL
STAUDAHER, CATHERINE (MILLEN)
STAUDAHER, GEORGE L.

STEEL, M. L.
STEELE, AGNES (FORBIS)
STEELE, JAMES A.
STEELE, JAMES OSCEOLA
STEELE, JOSEPH GUYTON
STEELE, WILLIAM L. DR.
STEELE,, GEORGE
STEELL, GEORGE
STEFFANIC, JULIA
STEGER, JOHN C.
STEPHENS, ALBERT JOSEPH
STEPHENS, ALFRED
STEPHENS, FRANK
STEPHENS, JANE P.
STEPHENSON, EMMA I.
STEVENS, ALBERT J.
STEVENS, DAVID C.
STEVENS, HENRY
STEWARD, JOHN MARSHALL
STEWART, JOHN
STILES, EDWIN R.
STITT, MARGARET ANN (SPENCER)
STOCK, JULIA MAY
STOLTE, WILLIAM
STONE, FRANK
STONE, HIRAM HAYWARD
STONE, HOWARD
STONE, MANOOK
STONE, SALENA (TINSLEY)
STONING, EDWARD
STOREY, EDWARD
STOREY, GEORGE W.
STORY, ELLEN (TRENT)
STORY, NELSON
STRANGE, WILLIAM ALLEN
STRASBURGER, ISIDOR
STRAUB, CHARLES F.
STREET, THEODORE L.
STREET, THOMAS P.
STRICKLAND, BENJAMIN
STRICKLAND, MONEY
STRONG, FANNIE ELLEN
STRONG, JANE
STRONG, JOHN
STRONG, JOHN ALDER
STUART, GRANVILLE
STUART, J. S.
STUART, JAMES
STUART, JAMES S.
STUART, KATE
STUART, THOMAS
STUBBLEFIED, ALBERT
STUCKEY, JACOB
STUCKY, GOTLEIB
SUET, MONTANA J. (KANTNER)
SULLIVAN ARTHUR
SULLIVAN, ANNIE
SULLIVAN, HARRY G.
SULLIVAN, HARVEY
SULLIVAN, J. T.
SULLIVAN, JEREMIAH
SULLIVAN, JOHN J.
SUMNER, W. F.
SURPREVANT, JOSEPH V.
SUTHERLAND, JOHN
SUTHERLIN, R. H.
SUTHERLIN, WILL H.
SUTTON, CHARLES W.
SWANEY, LIZZIE (KENNEDY)
SWEAT, LORETTA M. (WARD)
SWEENEY, JOHN L.
SWEENEY, JOHN M.
SWEET, HENRY J.
SWEET, WILLIAM T.
SWIFT, JOSEPH
SWIFT, JULIA A. (LETHLEAN)
SWING, JOHN
SWITZER, ANDREW WALTER
SWITZER, FLORENCE E. (JEFFERS)
SWITZER, MALPHUS A.
SWITZER, SUSIE (JEFFERS)
SWITZER, TAVNER BRANHAM
SYKES, HARRY NATHANIEL
TABER, MARCUS WILLIAM, CAPT.
TAFT, WELLINGTON LAFAYETTE
TALBOT, J. A. , MRS. (RAMSDELL)
TALBOT, JAMES A.
TAMBOR, LOTTA (KOCH)
TANNER, A. W.
TANNER, CYNTHIA E. (STANLEY)
TASH, SUSAN
TATE, CAREY M.
TAYLOR, A. B.
TAYLOR, CHARITY (HINCH)
TAYLOR, D. M.
TAYLOR, ELONAR
TAYLOR, FRED J.
TAYLOR, HORACE
TAYLOR, J. B.
TAYLOR, J. M. D.
TAYLOR, JONATHAN C.
TAYLOR, MARY E. (WILSON)
TAYLOR, REBECCA TAYLOR
TAYLOR, WILLIAM
TAZE, JOHN
TEICHMAN, JUDITH (HAY)
TEMPELTON, HEZEKIAH L.
TENDERHILL, HANNAH (SRIETTE)
THALE, HARRY H.
THEXTON, GEORGE.
THEXTON, GEORGE. F.
THEXTON, THOMAS SR.
THEY, PHOEBE (DOWNHONS)
THIBADEAU, MATILDA (DALTON)
THIBADEAU, Z. B.
THOMAS, AMOS J.
THOMAS, CHARLES
THOMAS, CHARLES PETER
THOMAS, DANIEL
THOMAS, EVAN PRICE
THOMAS, GEORGE D.
THOMAS, GEORGE EDGAR
THOMAS, GEORGE L.
THOMAS, H. W.
THOMAS, HYRUM M.
THOMAS, J. D.
THOMAS, JOHN
THOMAS, JOHN J.
THOMAS, JOHN P.
THOMAS, JOSEPH
THOMAS, JOSEPH HENRY
THOMAS, JULIA (PHILPOT)
THOMAS, LUCY A. (ALEXANDER)
THOMAS, MARGARET (EVANS)

THOMAS, MARGARET JANE
THOMAS, MARY ANN (SHOWERS)
THOMAS, OLIVER
THOMAS, SAMUEL HOMER
THOMAS, SOPHIA
THOMAS, WILLIAM PRICE
THOMAS, Z. EDWIN
THOMPSON, C. L.
THOMPSON, C. S.
THOMPSON, CHARLES WESLEY
THOMPSON, CORA B. (FILSON)
THOMPSON, JOB
THOMPSON, JOHN Q.
THOMPSON, M. B.
THOMPSON, MARTHA C.
THOMPSON, MARY A.
THOMPSON, NATHAN
THOMPSON, PRUDENCE M. (WRIGHT)
THOMPSON, RUFUS
THOMPSON, WILLIAM
THOMPSON, ZACHARIAN N.
THORBURN, JOHN
THORNE, WALTER W.
THOROUGHMAN, LAURA (READ)
THOROUGHMAN, OLIVER HAZARD PERRY
THOROUGHMAN, ROBERT PERRY
THORPE, PHILLIP
THRAIKILL, ANNIE E. (ASTLE)
THRAILKILL, CARROLL W.
THRAILKILL, CHARLES W.
THRELKELD, FRANK
TICHNOR, GEORGE E.
TIERNAN, ELLEN
TIERNEY, ANN
TIERNEY, JOHN
TIETJAN, JACOB
TILLMAN, EVA LENA (MISER)
TILLMAN, JULIA W. (WHALEY)
TILTON, DANIEL WEBSTER
TILTON, HELEN E. (BARBER)
TILTON, J. W.
TIMBERLAKE, OBED. M.
TINGLEY, H. S.
TINGLEY, OLIVER C.
TINGLEY, R. S.
TINGLEY, ROBERT S.
TINNEY, WILLIAM
TINSLEY, JOSEPH HAMILTON
TINSLEY, MARTHA E.
TINSLEY, RACHEL VIRGINIA (TATE)
TIPTON, RICHARD
TOM, SAM
TOMKINS, JAMES
TOMLINSON, JOHN J.
TOMLINSON, MARGARET E. (HAUSE)
TOOLE, CLAIDIUS BRUCE
TOOLE, EDWIN WARREN
TORD, SAMUEL
TORREY, ERNEST R.
TOSTON, THOMAS
TOWER, EDGAR MELTON
TOWNSEND, HETTIE (FOSTER)
TOWNSEND, KITTIE
TOWNSEND, TAYLOR D.
TOWNSLEY, BENJAMIN
TRACY, WILLIAM H.
TRAHANT, ELLEN

TRAHANT, HILAIRE
TRAIN, EDGAR H.
TRASK, AUGUSTA
TRASK, ERNEST MELVIN
TRASK, M. W.
TRAUTMAN, FREDERICK
TRAVIS, GEORGE
TRAVIS, PHILEMON
TREPP, MARTIN
TREPP, MICHAEL
TRESCH, JOHN
TROPLETT, CHARLES
TROTIER, JOSEPH
TRUCHOTT, FRANCIOS
TRUDEAU, A.
TUDOR, B. F.
TUFTS, JAMES
TULLOCK, M. A.
TUTTLE, DAVID W.
TUTTLE, HANNAH M. (GORDON)
TUTTLE, MILES L.
TUTTLE, S. F.
TWEEDY, THOMAS
TWOHY, MARGARET (COLEMAN)
TYLER, GEORGE BURT
UPSON, JAMES EDWARD
URLIN, ALFRED J.
UST, MARY
VALITON, HENRY G.
VALITON, MARY (MCREA)
VALSIN, ELSIE (MARSTEN)
VALSTEN, ELISE
VAN CAMP, UEPHOMIA (SAPPINGTON)
VAN DE WERKEN, HENRY
VAN DORN, FRANK
VAN DORN, HEZEKIAH
VAN GUNDY, JACOB E.
VANDERBILT, JOHN
VANHOOSE, J. M.
VANN, PETE
VANWART, SARAH JANE (SIMONTON)
VARNEY, O. B.
VAUGHN, JOHN
VAUGHN, MARY (GRAHAM)
VAUGHN, ROBERT
VENABALE, JOSEPH M.
VENE, MICHEL
VETTER, JOHN G.
VICKERS, ROBERT
VINCENT, ADDISON
VINCENT, ELIZA
VINCENT, H.
VINCENT, JOHN
VINEYARD, GORDON C.
VIVION, JAMES M.
VOGT, A. W.
WACKERLIN, J. H.
WADAMS, WILSON
WADE, GEORGE W.
WAGENER, JOHN
WAGNER, JOHN
WAKEFIELD, GEORGE W.
WALKER, ALEXANDER MILTON
WALKER, CHARLES
WALKER, DAVID DAVIS
WALKER, FRANK
WALKER, JOSEPH C.

WALKER, JOSEPH CULTON
WALKER, MAMIE (CONREY)
WALKER, NANCY (PIERCE)
WALKER, THULA
WALKER, WILLIAM
WALLACE, WILLIAM
WALTER, E. J.
WALTER, EDMUND J.
WALTERS, LOUISA (RALSTON)
WALTERS, MARY JANE (KINYON)
WALTON, DANIEL
WALTON, M. E.
WALTON, ODA B.
WALTON, WILLIAM
WALTON, WILLIAM II
WARD, JOHN T.
WARD, RETTA (SWEAT)
WARMINGTON, HENRY
WARN, JOHN S.
WARNER, HENRY
WARNER, ORIN C.
WARNER, WILLIS O.
WARREN, CHARLES S.
WARREN, T. B.
WARREN. THOMAS C.
WASHINGTON, MARGARET
WASWEILER, CAROLINE (WARREL)
WASWEILER, F. J.
WATERBURY, EDWIN B.
WATERHOUSE, THOMAS
WATERMAN, C. H.
WATERMAN, C.C., MRS.
WATKINS, FRANCES (FORT)
WATKINS, GEORGE SPENCER
WATSON, ALEXANDER H.
WATSON, JOHN RANDOLPH
WATSON, THOMAS
WATTERMAN, CHARLES
WEAVER, ALEXANDER
WEAVER, E. D., MRS.
WEBER, D. W.
WEBSTER, NEWELL HARLAND
WEEDEN, HENRY G. DR
WEGGENMAN, JOSEPH NICKOLAS
WEGNER, FRANK
WEGNER, JOHN F.
WEIDMAN, RACHEL
WEINGARD, ALFRED
WEINGART, ALFRED M.
WEINGART, BENEDICT
WEISENHORN, AUGUST.
WEISNER, CATHERINE (OWENS)
WELLER, SIMEON G.
WELLHOUSER, HENRY F.
WELLS, CHARLES KELLOGG
WELLS, FRANK
WELLS, HARVEY
WELLS, JANE (REESE)
WELLS, JOHN K.
WELLS, ROSE (HAMMOND0
WELSH, WILLIAM
WENTWORTH, WILLIAM F.
WESSEL, GEORGE
WESTFALL, PERRY
WESTON, DANIEL H.
WESTON, J. R.
WEYDERT, ANNA M. (WIEDEMAN)

WEYDERT, PETER C,
WHALEY, DAVID
WHALEY, HANNAH E.
WHALEY, HENRY
WHALEY, JOHN C.
WHALEY, JULIA
WHALEY, JULIE W. (TILLMAN)
WHALEY, MARY (FAY)
WHALEY, P. C.
WHALEY, PETER
WHALEY, PHILLIP H.
WHALEY, WILLIAM C.
WHEAT, GILBERT B.
WHETSTONE, FRED C.
WHITCHER, WARREN
WHITCOMB, E., MRS.
WHITCOMB, EDMUND
WHITCOMB, ELIZABETH (GILBERT)
WHITE , FRED
WHITE, ANDREW J.
WHITE, ANDREW J.
WHITE, GEORGE P.
WHITE, JAMES
WHITE, JOHN
WHITE, THOMAS H.
WHITEHEAD, JOHN
WHITELEY, A. J.
WHITESIDES, ANDREW J.
WHITESIDES, ANDREW MRS. (ERRICK)
WHITFORD, O'DILLON B.
WHITLATCH, JAMES
WHITLOCK, J. W.
WHITNEY, ELLEN (HILL)
WHITNEY, OTIS CROCKER
WHITNEY, THOMAS H.
WHITSON, J. B.
WHITTEMORE, JAMES MADISON
WHITWORTH, ISABEL (WARD)
WICK, SARAH B.
WICKHAM, BYRON OSCAR
WICKHAM, G. J.
WICKHAM, GEORGE J.
WICKHAM, GEORGE JEROME
WICKHAM, JOHN T.
WICKHAM, PATRICK
WILBUR, A. E.
WILCOX, ALVIN H.
WILCOX, TIMOTHY
WILCOX, WILLIAM
WILD, LEVI S.
WILDMAN, JOHN H.
WILDMAN, MRS J. H.
WILHART, JOHN
WILKINSON, EZEKIEL S.
WILKINSON, RALEIGH F.
WILKISON, MARGREATE
WILLIAMS THOMAS
WILLIAMS, ALICE MELISSA (SCHAAF POOL)
WILLIAMS, BENJAMIN C.
WILLIAMS, CHARLES FRANCIS
WILLIAMS, CLINTON
WILLIAMS, ELIAS HARDIN
WILLIAMS, ELIZABETH (LEDFORD)
WILLIAMS, EMILY (SCHRODER)
WILLIAMS, JACOB W.
WILLIAMS, JAMES
WILLIAMS, JOHN BARRETT

WILLIAMS, JOHN HART
WILLIAMS, JOHN M.
WILLIAMS, JOHN W.
WILLIAMS, LEWIS
WILLIAMS, MARGARET
WILLIAMS, MARTHA
WILLIAMS, MRS M. T. (HOPPE)
WILLIAMS, WILLIAM
WILLS, ROBERT
WILLSON, LESTER Z.
WILSON, ANDREW J.
WILSON, ENOCH
WILSON, GEORGE R.
WILSON, JOHN BARNES
WILSON, JOHN F.
WILSON, JOHN FRANCIS
WILSON, JOHN RUSSELL
WILSON, JOSEPH SEDGWICK
WILSON, LIZZIE
WILSON, PETER
WILSON, T. H.
WILSON, T. M.
WILSON, WILLIAM
WILSTON, MARTIN P.
WING, ROBERT T.
WINGATE, T. B.
WINSLOW, CORNELIUS C.
WINSLOW, ELLEN CHRISTINE
WINSLOW, JAMES J.
WINSTON, MARY J.
WINTER, CHARLES
WITHERS, ELIZABETH (FLOWEREE)
WOHLSCHLARGER, JOHN
WOLF, EDWARD A,
WOLF, GUSTAVUS A
WOLFE, ADDISON
WONDERLY, CHARLES PETER
WOOD, JAMES L.
WOOD, JOHN M.
WOOD, NATHANIEL H.
WOOD, W. F.
WOOD, WELLINGTON E.
WOODMANCY, S. D., MRS.
WOODMANCY, VAN R.
WOODS, ALLEN W.
WOODS, ANN F.
WOODS, EDWIN PRICE
WOODS, GEORGE M
WOODS, JAMES W.
WOODS, JOHN J.
WOODS, LIZZIE F. (KEATON)
WOODS, MONTIE WELTON
WOODS, PATRICK
WOODWARD, MARGARET S. (THOMAS)
WOODWARD, SOPHIE (THOMAS)
WOODWORTH, GEORGE
WOODWORTH, JURNISHA (McKENZIE)
WOODWORTH, MARY (EVENSA)
WOODY, FRANK H.
WOOLMAN, JOSEPH PEDRICK
WORD, R. I.
WORD, SAMUEL
WORDEN, FRANCIS (FRANK) LYMAN
WORDEN, LUCRECIA
WORDEN, LUNINA LAURS (STERLING)
WORK, JOHN F.
WORLEY, JOHN M.

WREN, JOHN
WRIGHT, A. S.
WRIGHT, A. S., MRS.
WRIGHT, ALPHA (KIRBY)
WRIGHT, ATHOL F.
WRIGHT, GEORGE EDWARD
WRIGHT, HENRY J.
WRIGHT, MARY
WRIGHT, WILLIAM BEVERLY
WRIGHT, WILLIAM M.
WUNDERLIN, JOSEPH
WYCOFF, CHARLES D.
WYNNE, JOHN ELLIS
WYROUCK, JACOB
WYROUCK, M. J. (HOWE)
YATES, GEORGE L.
YATES, MARY
YATES, MARY (WELLS)
YATES, SARAH E. (MARSHALL)
YATES, SUSANNA (ACCOLA)
YEARIAN, THOMAS
YOUNG, JOE I
YOUNG, MERRET M.
YOUNG, P. R.
YOUNG, W. H.
YOUNG, W. H MRS. (MCDONALD)
YOUNG, WILLIAM HENRY
ZEIGLER, FRANK
ZEIGLER, JOHN A.
ZEIGLER, URIAH F.
ZEPINE, AIME (LEPINE)
ZIMMERMAN, EDWARD I.
ZINN, DANIEL

Society of Montana Pioneers Presidents

1884 – James Fergus
1885 – Walter W. DeLacy
1886 – Granville Stuart
1887 – Frank Woody
1888 – Wilbur F. Sanders
1889 – Anton M. Holter
1890 – William A. Clark
1891 – Samuel Word
1892 – Walter Cooper
1893 – Walter Cooper
1894 – John T. Conner
1895 – Conrad Kohrs
1896 – William L. Steele
1897 – Nickolas Kessler
1898 – Henry Elling
1899 – William W. Alderson
1900 – Henry F. Edgar
1901 – Ausustus F. Graeter
1902 – Timothy E. Collins
1903 – O' Dillon Whitford
1904 – Cornelius Hedges
1905 – John P. Thomas
1906 – Paul Mc Cormick
1907 – Charles S. Warren
1908 – Andrew J. Fisk
1909 – Warren C. Gillette
1910 – William Y. Pemberton
1911 – Rod D. Leggat
1912 – Mortimer H. Lott
1913 – Martin Maginnis
1914 – James M. Page
1915 – John W. Blair
1916 – George W. Morse
1917 – Frank D. Brown
1918 – Charles W. Hoffman
1919 – William A. Clark
1920 – John F. Bishop
1921 – Charles W. Cook
1922 – William A. Coleman

1923 – Richard Lockey
1924 – Thomas R. Moore
1925 – Mary Valiton
1926 – Alfred W. Orton
1927 – Patrick Carney
1927 – Mrs. M. F. Trask
1928 – Wyllys A. Hedges
1929 – Molly Kline
1930 – David Heilgn
1931 – W. C. Certon
1932 – Miles Cavanaugh
1933 – Merling Held
1934 – Henry Evans
1935 – Augusta Trask
1936 – Andrew Erickson
1937 – John H. Miller
1938 – Will Cave
1940 – Jennie Ennis Chownig
1941 – Mary Evans
1942 – Joseph Larson
1943 – Joseph Larson
1944 – Augusta Trask
1945 – William L. Milligan
1946 – Harry N. Morgan
1947 – William K. Burns
1948 – Julia R. Elledge
1949 – Mary Doane
1950 – Byron Wickham
1951 – Luman W. Allen
1952 – Tom H. Mc Cauley
1953 – Fannie Davis Ennis
1954 – Fannie Davis Ennis
1955 – Helen Allen Conrad
1956 – Henry R. Daems
1957 – Julia Mae Stock
1958 – Julia Mae Stock
1959 – Josephine Gilg
1960 – Luman Allen
1961 – Luman Allen

Source: Sons and Daughters of MT Pioneers Records – 2000

Sons And Daughters of Montana Pioneers Past Presidents And Secretaries

YEAR ELECTED	PRESIDENT	SECRETARY
1892	ALBERT I. LOEB	MARIE L. KLEINSCHMIDT
1893	NO CONVENTION	
1894	EDWARD HORSKY	GERTRUDE HICKMAN
1895	FRANCIS A. JURGENS	CORNELIUS HEDGES, JR.
1896	FLORENCE RYAN	W. B. THOMPSON

Year	Name	Name
1897	W. B. THOMPSON	MAE L. CURTIS
1898	CHARLES N. KESSLER	MAE L. CURTIS
1899	GEN CHAS. F. ENGLISH	C. S. MUFFLY
1900	JUSTICE R. L. WORD	FRANK B. NORRIS
1901	HON. FRANK G. HIGGINS	FRANK B. NORRIS
1902	HON. FRANK G. HIGGINS (HOLDOVERS)	FRANK B. NORRIS
1903	CHARLES F. WORD	FRANK B. NORRIS
1904	NO CONVENTION	
1905	DR. CHAS. REINIG	MATIE T. HIBBARD
1906	BARRY FALK	MAY MC HUGH
1907	NO CONVENTION	
1908	NO CONVENTION	
1909	BESSIE WHITCOMBE	LOTTIE M. RUMSEY
1910	ALLAN P. BOWIE	LOTTIE M. RUMSEY
1911	ALLAN P. BOWIE	LOTTIE M. RUMSEY
1912	DR. H. A. MAILLET	LOTTIE M. RUMSEY
1913	W. A. CLARK, JR.	LOTTIE M. RUMSEY
1914	J. HENRY MAILEY	LOTTIE M. RUMSEY
1915	J. HENRY MAILEY	LOTTIE M. RUMSEY
1916	RUTH BURTON	LOTTIE M. RUMSEY
1917	W. B. OREM	LOTTIE M. RUMSEY
1918	FRED W. SCHEUER	LOTTIE M. RUMSEY
1919	WASHINGTON J. MC CORMICK	LOTTIE M. RUMSEY
1920	GEORGE P. PORTER	LOTTIE M. RUMSEY
1921	NYE H. BLACK	LOTTIE M. RUMSEY
1922	CHARLES WATERMAN	LOTTIE M. RUMSEY
1923	RONALD HIGGINS	LOTTIE M. RUMSEY
1924	RONALD HIGGINS	LOTTIE M. RUMSEY
1925	W. A. CLARK III	LOTTIE M. RUMSEY
1926	W. A. CLARK III	LOTTIE M. RUMSEY
1927	JAMES BROWN	LOTTIE M. RUMSEY
1928	JAMES BROWN	LOTTIE R. WILLETT
1929	GEORGE P. PORTER	LOTTIE R. WILLETT
1930	NORMAN HOLTER	LOTTIE R. WILLETT
1931	FRED W. SCHEURER	LOTTIE R. WILLETT
1932	MRS. GEORGE K. DICK	LOTTIE R. WILLETT
1933	NO CONVENTION	
1934	MRS. GEORGE K. DICK	LOTTIE R. WILLETT
1935	MRS. HENRY W. EVANS	LOTTIE R. WILLETT
1936	WILLIAM C. ORTON JR.	LOTTIE R. WILLETT
1937	E. W. TOWNSEND	LOTTIE R. WILLETT
1938	ROY M. CRISMAS	LOTTIE R. WILLETT
1939	ROY M. CRISMAS	LOTTIE R. WILLETT
1940	LESTER H. LOBLE SR.	CECELIA M. DICK
1941	LESTER H. LOBLE SR.	CECELIA M. DICK
1942	PHIL G. GREENAN	CECELIA M. DICK
1943	LESTER H. LOBLE SR.	CECELIA M. DICK
1944	JOHN L. EVANS	CECELIA M. DICK
1945	LENA BISSONETTE	EDITH R. MAXWELL
1946	ARTHUR M. WOODS	EDITH R. MAXWELL
1947	HERBERT G. DUNBAR	EDITH R. MAXWELL
1948	EDITH R. MAXWELL	JULIA POIRIER
1949	JEAN BISHOP	IONE PIERRE

Year		
1950	WM. BYRON KANTNER	IONE PIERRE
1951	ROBERT COONEY	IONE PIERRE
1952	MONCURE COCKRELL	KATHLEEN M. LINDQUIST
1953	MONCURE COCKRELL	KATHLEEN M. LINDQUIST
1954	THELMA DUNBAR KEYSER	KATHLEEN M. LINDQUIST
1955	LOUISE ENNIS MC LEOD	KATHLEEN M. LINGQUIST
1956	RALPH STARR	BETTY M. MC KEAN
1957	WESLEY W. DAVIS	BETTY M. MC KEAN
1958	ARTHUR COX	VIRGINIA B. ANDERSON
1959	ARTHUR COX	VIRGINIA B. ANDERSON
1960	TED MANNIX	VIRGINIA B. ANDERSON
1961	TED MANNIX	VIRGINIA B. ANDERSON
1962	HOWARD TOM	VIRGINIA B. ANDERSON
1963	BERNIECE PALMER	VIRGINIA B. ANDERSON
1964	BERNIECE PALMER	VIRGINIA B. ANDERSON
1965	MARGUERITE ENGEBRETSON	VIRGINIA B. ANDERSON
1966	LEO A. KILROY	BERNIECE PALMER
1967	LEO A. KILROY	BERNIECE PALMER
1968	CHARLES CROUSE	BERNIECE PALMER
1969	CHARLES CROUSE	BERNIECE PALMER
1970	ARALEN HARDIN	BERNIECE PALMER
1971	ARALEN HARDIN	BERNIECE PALMER
1972	ELLEN TOWNSEND	BERNIECE PALMER
1973	E. WALLIS TOWNSEND	DARLENE FASSLER
1974	E. WALLIS TOWNSEND	DARLENE FASSLER
1975	JOHN H. BIELENBERG	DARLENE FASSLER
1976	GEORGE HARBISON SR.	DARLENE FASSLER
1977	GEORGE HARBISON SR.	DARLENE FASSLER
1978	JUNE WESTON	DARLENE FASSLER
1979	HELEN KAMBO	DARLENE FASSLER
1980	VIRGINIA ANDERSON	DARLENE FASSLER
1981	VIRGINIA ANDERSON	DARLENE FASSLER
1982	STEPHEN GILPATRICK	DARLENE FASSLER
1983	STEPHEN GILPATRICK	DARLENE FASSLER
1984	BRUCE LOBLE	DARLENE FASSLER
1985	BRUCE LOBLE	DARLENE FASSLER
1986	GEORGE MUELLER	DARLENE FASSLER
1987	GEORGE MUELLER	DARLENE FASSLER
1988	HAROLD SCHNEIDER	DARLENE FASSLER
1989	HAROLD SCHNEIDER	DARLENE FASSLER
1990	DICK THOROUGHMAN	DARLENE FASSLER
1991	DICK THOROUGHMAN	DARLENE FASSLER
1992	PATRICK TROSTLE	DARLENE FASSLER
1993	PATRICK TROSTLE	DARLENE FASSLER
1994	DOROTHEA NEATH	DARLENE FASSLER
1995	DOROTHEA NEATH	DARLENE FASSLER
1996	M. EARLENE NEVINS	SHIRLEY HERRIN
1997	M. EARLENE NEVINS	SHIRLEY HERRIN
1998	SHIRLEY A. GROFF	SHIRLEY HERRIN
1999	SHIRLEY A. GROFF	SHIRLEY HERRIN
2000	DALE A. CLARK	SHIRLEY HERRIN

Source: Sons and Daughters of Montana Pioneer Records – 2000

Sons And Daughters of Montana Pioneers
Convention Sites

1892 - HELENA
1893 - NO CONVENTION
1894 - HELENA
1895 - HELENA
1896 - HELENA
1897 - HELENA
1898 - HELENA
1899 - HELENA
1900 - HELENA
1901 - MISSOULA
1902 - HELENA
1903 - HELENA/GT. FALLS
1904 - NO CONVENTION
1905 - HELENA
1906 - ANACONDA
1907 - NO CONVENTION
1908 - NO CONVENTION
1909 - HELENA
1910 - DEER LODGE
1911 - BUTTE
1912 - DEER LODGE
1913 - MISSOULA
1914 - BOZEMAN
1915 - GREAT FALLS
1916 - HELENA
1917 - LIVINGSTON
1918 - ANACONDA
1919 - BUTTE
1920 - GREAT FALLS
1921 - LEWISTOWN
1922 - MISSOULA
1923 - DEER LODGE
1924 - BUTTE
1925 - BOZEMAN
1926 - FORT BENTON
1927 - MISSOULA
1928 - BUTTE

1929 - GREAT FALLS
1930 - BILLINGS
1931 - BUTTE
1932 - MISSOULA
1933 - NO CONVENTION
1934 - GREAT FALLS
1935 - ANACONDA
1936 - DEER LODGE
1937 - GREAT FALLS
1938 - HELENA
1939 - BUTTE
1940 - LEWISTOWN
1941 - MISSOULA
1942 - HELENA
1943 - DEER LODGE
1944 - DEER LODGE
1945 - ANACONDA
1946 - FORT BENTON
1947 - VIRGINIA CITY
1948 - BOZEMAN
1949 - BUTTE
1950 - MISSOULA
1951 - HELENA
1952 - DEER LODGE
1953 - VIRGINIA CITY
1954 - DILLON
1955 - BUTTE
1956 - BOZEMAN
1957 - MISSOULA
1958 - ANACONDA
1959 - DEER LODGE
1960 - HELENA
1961 - VIRGINIA CITY
1962 - BUTTE
1963 - DILLON
1964 - BOZEMAN
1965 - BILLINGS

1966 - MISSOULA
1967 - LEWISTOWN
1968 - GREAT FALLS
1969 - BUTTE
1970 - DEER LODGE
1971 - ANACONDA
1972 - HELENA
1973 - LEWISTOWN
1974 - MISSOULA
1975 - BOZEMAN
1976 - GREAT FALLS
1977 - BUTTE
1978 - VIRGINIA CITY
1979 - HELENA
1980 - KALISPELL
1981 - LEWISTOWN
1982 - MISSOULA
1983 - FAIRMONT HOT SPRINGS
1984 - GREAT FALLS
1985 - BOZEMAN
1986 - VIRGINIA CITY
1987 - DEER LODGE
1988 - BUTTE
1989 - HELENA
1990 - WHITEFISH
1991 - DILLON
1992 - GREAT FALLS
1993 - MISSOULA
1994 - POLSON
1995 - BUTTE
1996 - HELENA
1997 - VIRGINIA CITY
1998 - FORT BENTON
1999 - BOZEMAN
2000 - MISSOULA
2001 – GREAT FALLS

Headstone of Margaret (Edwards) Harris Thomas. (Please see story on Page 228)